Princeton Theological Monograph Series

Dikran Y. Hadidian

General Editor

34

ON THIS ROCK

A COMMENTARY ON FIRST PETER

DONALD G. MILLER

ON THIS ROCK

A COMMENTARY ON FIRST PETER

☙PICKWICK *Publications* • Eugene, Oregon

Pickwick Publications
An imprint of Wipf and Stock Publishers
199 W 8th Ave, Suite 3
Eugene, OR 97401

On This Rock
A Commentary on First Peter
By Miller, Donald G.
Copyright©1993 by Miller, Donald G.
ISBN 13: 978-1-55635-020-7
Publication date 1/1/1993
Previously published by Pickwick, 1993

To

the memory of

MY MOTHER

Who brought me into this world,

Who nurtured me in early childhood,

Who suffered over me in early adolescence,

Who embodied a quality of Christian character

seldom achieved,

And who died before I could show her the profundity

of her influence over my life in my mature years.

CONTENTS

Preface   xi

PART ONE

INTRODUCTION

Chapters

    I. IS 1 PETER A TRUSTWORTHY RELIGIOUS
       DOCUMENT?   3

   II. WHAT IS THE LITERARY NATURE OF 1 PETER   11
      Is 1 Peter a Paschal Baptismal Liturgy?   11
      Is 1 Peter a Baptismal Homily?   15
      Does 1 Peter Embody a Collection of Hymns?   18
      Is 1 Peter a Unified or a Composite Document?   21
      What Are the Sources and Literary Affinities of
         1 Peter?   25
      Conclusion as to the Literary Nature of 1 Peter   31

  III. WHEN WAS 1 PETER WRITTEN?   33
      When Did Peter Die?   33
      What Type of Suffering Does 1 Peter Reflect?   35
      What Conclusion Does the Internal Evidence
         Suggest?   40
      Does the Attitude toward the Jews Reflect a
         Later Date?   41

IV. WHERE WAS 1 PETER WRITTEN?	43
Where Was Babylon?	43
Was Peter Ever in Rome?	45
V. WHAT IS THE THEOLOGICAL VIEWPOINT OF 1 PETER?	47
What Is the Teaching about God?	48
What Is the Teaching about Jesus?	49
What Is the Teaching about the Holy Spirit?	50
What Is the Teaching about Redemption?	50
What Is the Teaching about the Church?	51
What is the Doctrine of the Ministry?	53
What Is the Relation of 1 Peter's Theology to Peter's Speeches in the Acts?	54
VI. WHO WROTE 1 PETER?	57
Who Did the Early Church Think Wrote 1 Peter?	57
Could Peter Have Written Greek?	60
Would Peter Have Included More Personal References to Jesus?	65
Would Peter Have Written so Pauline a Letter?	67
Would Peter Have Written to Christians in Asia Minor?	69
Was Peter a Witness of the Sufferings of Christ?	70
Would Peter Have Called Himself an Elder?	70
How Did Peter's Name Get Attached to This Document?	71
Conclusion on Authorship	73
VII. TO WHOM WAS 1 PETER WRITTEN?	77
Where Were the First Readers Located?	77
Were the First Readers Jewish or Gentile?	79
Who Evangelized the First Readers of 1 Peter?	82
Were the First Readers of 1 Peter First Generation Christians?	83

VIII. WHY WAS 1 PETER WRITTEN?	85
What Is 1 Peter's Stated Purpose?	85
What Is the Implicit Broader Purpose of 1 Peter?	87

PART TWO

THE COMMENTARY — 95

OUTLINE — 97

BIBLIOGRAPHY — 375

PREFACE

The Bible is a difficult book. Although Luther and Calvin favored translating the Bible into the mother tongue of the people, thus making it available for them to read on their own, neither of them approved turning them loose with the Bible without guidance as to its meaning. They both preached and lectured incessantly from the Bible and wrote commentaries with a view to aiding readers in understanding it.

Commentaries are intended as teaching devices, designed to aid others in their efforts to come to terms with Scripture. The Bible is centuries old, originally written in languages no longer current, embodying historic backgrounds, social customs, and ways of thinking often strange to modern folk. An intelligent friend, a university professor trained in the scientific disciplines and with a lifelong interest in the humanities surpassing that of many scientists, when told that I was working on a commentary on 1 Peter, wrote: "When I got home I read 1 Peter, and was surprised to find it so . . . *bewildering*" (emphasis added). A commentary is an attempt to help overcome such bewilderment.

But how to do this? Some of the best commentaries tend to increase, rather than to dispel, bewilderment for nonspecialists. They are filled with scholarly names with which the reader may not be conversant, with references to books and periodicals to which the reader has little access, and written in a lingo designed for fellow scholars which can only confuse those outside the guild. When scientists write for fellow scientists, they presuppose a familiarity with outstanding scholars, scientific issues, and terminology that merely befuddle those not abreast of the field. Scholarly biblical commentaries can likewise confuse rather than enlighten those without sufficient prior knowledge to grasp them. The "massive erudition" of these scholarly "monuments" is read by specialists only. Thereby scholars communicate with one another, not the public. On the other hand, in an effort to overcome this difficulty, popular commentaries often seek to be inspirational rather than intellectual, and allow the reader to bypass any serious wrestling with problems or any engagement with profound theological issues. They tend to "short circuit the determination of the meaning for the benefit of an immediate 'relevance' or 'spirituality.'"

It is the aim of this commentary to avoid either of these approaches. Without cluttering the text with the names of authorities, nor overloading the pages with footnotes indicating the sources on which the work is based, nor printing either the Greek text nor English transliterations of the Greek, nor burdening the reader with technical terminology unfamiliar save to the specialist, it is the hope that it will be apparent that the author has carefully consulted the literature on 1 Peter, both in periodicals and in commentaries, and has laid out the issues in such a way that the reasons for and against any viewpoint are clear enough for the reader to follow the course of thought and to make his own reasoned judgment.

The bibliography appended to the commentary will indicate the range of literature I have consulted. I have tried to keep the mechanics of my use of the works of others as inconspicuous as possible for the sake of the nonspecialist in the field, but quotation marks indicate where authorities have been cited verbatim. Translations from French and German works, where quoted, are my own.

The plethora of modern translations made it difficult to decide which text to follow as a basis for comment. It seemed wise, however, to choose the *Revised Standard Version*, in the light of the fact that perhaps more American readers of the Bible use it than any other at present. Although there was a revision of that work in 1990, called the *New Revised Standard Version*, it is likely that the majority of those who use the *Revised Standard Version* have the prerevision text. The difference between the two versions is not sufficient likely to annoy one who might be following the new version. In any case, the commentary is based on the original Greek rather than the English text, so that the particular English version followed would have no bearing on the interpretation. I have pointed out a few places where I feel that the translators of the *Revised Standard Version* have followed an understanding different from my own.

In the commentary section of the book, where the English text of the *Revised Standard Version* is quoted, it is set in bold face type to aid the reader in seeing what specific words are being discussed.

1 Peter is brief, but bristles with interpretative problems. Introductory questions—such as the type of literature, authorship, readers, place of origin, date, etc.—are particularly thorny. One passage (3:18-22), along with a companion passage (4:6), is perhaps the most difficult in the New Testament to interpret and to coordinate with other New Testament teaching. The epistle as a whole, however, is a gem of early Christian writing, reflecting many of the issues faced hy the nascent Christian group living out its destiny in a hostile pagan environment, and how they sought to solve them in loyalty to Him who was the source of their faith and the living companion of their journey. In many instances, light is thrown on current difficulties faced by the church in the modern world. The epistle is so valuable, in fact, that one current scholar has said that if he were cast up alone on an uninhabited island and could have but one of the New Testament letters, the case could be made that "1 Peter would be the ideal choice, so rich is its teaching, so warm its spirit, and so comforting its message in a hostile environment."

It is hoped that anyone who will study 1 Peter under the guidance of this commentary will discover for himself the spiritual riches which gained for this document a firm and unquestioned place in the canon of the early church, and have continued to be a source of strength and guidance in the long generations since. I have sought throughout to relate Peter's thought to its deep roots in the Old Testament, as the early Christians understood that body of truth, and also to the thought of the Gospels and other letters of the New Testament. In this way I have endeavored to point out the interweaving of Peter's insights with some of the major theological emphases of the emerging early Christian community.

1 Peter has held my interest for a long time. Over some years I conducted a seminar on it with Senior seminary students both at Union Theological Seminary in Richmond, Virginia and at Pittsburgh Theological Seminary in Pittsburgh, Pennsylvania. Thereafter, other demands claimed my time and attention. It has been a real joy to undertake work on this document once more, and to put into writing what I have learned from my own study and from my students through the years. 1 Peter is gradually coming into its own as a focal point of interest in New Testament studies. Theories about its composition and meaning and significance are legion, and often irreconcilably contradictory. I am well aware of what one writer has called "the danger which

confronts every exegete of turning his chosen solution into a Procrustean bed where all unfavourable evidence is either stretched or trimmed to suit an *a priori* idea." No one can wholly escape his own predilections and prejudices. I have tried, however, to distinguish between "opinions" and "evidence," and have sought to face issues as impartially as possible. Wherein I have differed from the conclusions of those whose claims to scholarship are greater than mine, I trust I have given adequate and courteous consideration to their viewpoints. Where the truth ultimately lies must be left to the judgment of the readers, and to the refining fires of subsequent scholarship and time.

I should like to express my appreciation to Professor Dikran Y. Hadidian, editor and publisher of the Pickwick Publications, who encouraged me to write the commentary and brought it into print. Gratitude is due also to Dr. Daniel W. Hardy, Director of the Center of Theological Inquiry at Princeton, New Jersey, and his staff, who gracioualy shepherded me through several months of study in that delightful place. Professor James F. Armstrong, Librarian of Princeton Theological Seminary and his staff, especially William O. Harris, Librarian for Archives and Special Collections, and Kate Skrebutenas of the reference staff, went beyond all reasonable expectation in furthering my research, for which I am profoundly grateful. In the friendship and assistance of fellow workers one experiences new dimensions of "the communion of saints." Finally, deepest gratitude goes to my wife of more than fifty-five years, who has been a sounding board for my ideas, a helpful critic of my literary style, a spiritual anchor for my soul, and a secure haven of love in the midst of a turbulent world.

Donald G. Miller

PART ONE

INTRODUCTION

1

IS 1 PETER A TRUSTWORTHY RELIGIOUS DOCUMENT?

The *New Yorker* is sometimes the source of good theology. A remarkable article on the Bible and modern thought suggests that modernism in Western culture could almost be defined by the erosion of biblical terms and concepts from the "common currency of recognition." For secular scholarship the Bible has long lain like an "unplayed Stradivarius" in an "air-conditioned glass case of dispassionate regard." The "natural echo chamber of our consciousness," which once reverberated with the resonant tones of Scripture vocabulary and thought in Milton, Lincoln, Carlyle, Ruskin, Emerson, Hardy, Thomas Mann, Gide and Proust, and in much of classical music and drama, has for a long time been silent. The "shared legacy" of the Bible in political and social concerns has been almost extinct, robbing us of "the primary images of justice, of communal destiny, of responsibility in observing the covenant of caring which are instinct to democracy."

Recently, however, the Bible has become the subject of interest by secular literary critics. In a strange way, the flow between the Bible and modern culture has been reversed. The Church Fathers, the Talmudists, the Schoolmen of the Middle Ages, the Reformers and their heirs, established methods and standards of literary criticism of which our modern methodologies were the heirs. The methodologies of faith were absorbed by the secular world. Now, by contrast, what Matthew Arnold saw coming a century ago has happened. In our time the presuppositions of faith have been widely abandoned. The Bible has been "stripped, for most educated and agnostic sensibilities, of its numinous, divinely inspired aura and its revealed-truth function," and is itself being approached as an aesthetic object of beauty rather than a dynamo of faith.

Attempts are now being made to apply the latest "modern literary criticism and analysis" to a literary understanding of features peculiar to the Bible which, from a purely secular standpoint, reverse, and are an improvement upon, many of the results of the higher critical study of the Bible made from within the faith. For example, some literary critics see "the brusque changes of intonation, of narrative point of view, and stylistic form in Genesis and in certain parts of Exodus or Matthew" not as signs of "multiple authorship nor of textual corruption but of the subtle literary skills and complex intentions of the ancient masters of storytelling and portraiture." In this way, secular scholars preserve the "unity and coherence" of the Bible better than earlier generations of religious scholars.

However valuable this effort may be, it ends in a blind alley by failing to come to grips with the unique quality of the biblical literature as *religious* documents. It never occurred to the writers of the Bible that they were producing works of art. They were not consciously creating "literature." They were writing documents of *faith*. They were dealing with the transcendent realities which overwhelmed them in the presence of the living God, realities which gave to a modern translator of the Bible a feeling as though he were grasping live electric wires. They were describing the soul's terror and transformation in its confrontation with the divine and eternal. The cry of Job's heart, "Oh, that I knew where I might find him," and the natural response to his contemplation of God's dealing with him, "I am terrified at his presence," were not penned for literary effect. Paul's falling to the ground and his three-day blindness were not fictitious literary creations designed to evoke responses on the part of the reader. The record that the women at the empty tomb on Easter morning were seized with "trembling and astonishment . . . for they were afraid," can hardly be classed as breathtaking fiction writing, aspiring to a Pulitzer prize. These are descriptions of the life-shattering experiences of those upon whom the ends of the ages had broken in, the visceral response of humans whose drab pathway had been intersected by the eternal world and who had had dealings with the eternal God. As the writer of the *New Yorker* article put it: "I can—just—come to imagine for myself that a man of more or less my own biological and social composition could have written 'Hamlet' or 'Lear' and gone home to lunch and found a normal answer to the question 'How did it go today?' I cannot conceive of the author of the Speech Out of the Whirlwind in Job writing or dictating that text and dwelling within common existence and parlance . . . ." In other words, the current rationalistic separation between "theological-religious experiencing of Biblical texts and a literary one is radically factitious." That which the latter omits is what, to the Bible writers, "is the essential."

To rhapsodize over the Bible while giving a "polite dismissal" to those aspects of it "whose source and levels of meaning" are wholly other than mere literary considerations is to miss the point. The Scriptures, however fascinating they are as literary achievements, are documents of faith. Taken as a whole, they move inexorably toward Christ, who has "brought us God and destroyed our guilt." Those who "have been his patients" and owe him their lives find in the records which speak of him far more than literary fascination.

The literary quality of 1 Peter is debatable. Some think it too elegant for a Galilean fisherman. Others find it stylistically primitive and plain. But of one thing we may be sure: Whoever wrote it was not engaged in a mere literary exercise, and those who preserved it and bound it in with the other documents in the Bible were not motivated by mere aesthetic concerns. They read it, and preserved it for future generations, because they found in it a channel of communication between them and their God which gave them hope and courage as they threaded their way through the perplexities and challenges and fears and joys of their pilgrimage toward that city "whose spires lie beyond the rim of the sky." It was the word of a wise theologian who said, "Where you stand determines what you see." It is the aim of this volume to stand, insofar as it is possible, where the writer and first readers of 1 Peter stood, to see if in so doing we can see what they saw—the light of eternity on the pathways of time.

1 Peter raises a quandary for some who dare to believe that the Scriptures contain a unique and authoritative quality as permanent guides to the faith and life of the church, and to the meaning and destiny of human life. It has been called "the storm centre of New Testament study." It involves "a number of traps." How can it be that such a brief writing—less than nine small pages of Greek text and four pages of English translation—can call forth such a variety of judgments on the part of the church's interpreters? Why is it so difficult to find a consensus on such questions as the authorship, first readers, date, place of origin, background, structure, nature, purpose, sources and message of this little work? In the light of this quandary, may we maintain a sure and settled confidence in the message of this document? Did the church

do well to include it in its canon of sacred writings?

In answer, it might be well to recall Mark Twain's remark that what concerned him about the Bible was not what he did not understand about it, but what he did! In spite of the many seemingly unanswerable problems with 1 Peter, there is a great deal about which there is a general consensus—enough to make the work an extremely valuable introduction to the early Christian faith and its significance for life.

Then, too, the process of struggling to answer elusive questions about the literature of the faith may serve to remind us that the faith is a *living* thing which, like any living organism, confronts us with issues about which pat answers are difficult to come by. A prominent surgeon once remarked: "In spite of the amazing advances in the study of modern medicine, the truly remarkable thing is how much we do *not* know about the human body." So it is with the Bible—the more it is studied, the more it yields up its riches, the more its mysteries as an ancient document obtrude themselves. The wider the circle of light becomes, the greater is the circle of darkness around it.

Furthermore, it is well to be reminded that our faith rests not on answers to the problems of the literature of the faith, but rather on the trustworthiness of him to whom that literature bears witness. At long last, our spiritual destiny rests not on the answer to every question that can be raised about the sacred writings, but on the adequacy of the God about whom they were written. Faith in God preceded the sacred writings, and God outlasts the sacred writers. It was because of this faith and this God that the writings came into being. "There is a knowledge by faith as sound of its kind as the knowledge . . . by science."

When Isaiah or Jeremiah addressed their hearers, no sacred Scriptures were available to attend their word. When the church first announced the "good news" about Jesus, there was no New Testament to affirm or deny its validity. Hearers had either to believe or disbelieve as their response to the self-authenticating quality of what they heard. The Bible is simply the written record of that spoken word which was unaided by any external authority. The modern reader must make his decision of faith as the first hearers did, without the corroboration of theories of inspiration or the authority of the church. The truth addresses us directly, and we must take the terrible risk of responding Yes or No. Even if we try to shift our trust to an authority outside the truth itself, it is *we* who must make that decision. When Cardinal Newman sought, by accepting the authority of mother church, to escape "th' encircling gloom" of his soul when the night was "dark" and he felt "far from home," it was *he* who made the decision to do so. At long last, he could not shift the responsibility for his own destiny. As Luther once remarked: "It is thy neck that is at stake." We are always confronted as persons by a personal God, a God who far antedates the Bible and will survive its dissolution. We cannot wait to believe until all the problems of the literature concerning him are solved. A Harvard professor, who said that he was waiting until all the evidence is in before making the decision of faith, was once reminded that if he took all the courses offered at Harvard, it would take 120 years! It is impossible to wait until *all* the evidence is in. Faith rests on God, and God alone—not on a book nor a church nor on the final critical judgments of the scholars.

Some questions about 1 Peter can be answered only with intelligent conjecture, similar to an erstwhile popular television program called "To Tell the Truth." In it four characters appeared before a panel of expert inquisitors. Their task was, by the question and answer method, to determine which of the four was the person described by the moderator, when all four claimed to be that one. The true candidate did not have to tell the truth, but the impostors were bound to answer with unfeigned honesty. After the experts had made their choice, the moderator would say: "Will the real Mr. _____ please stand up," whereupon the wisdom of the panel was either confirmed or contradicted. The panel was frequently wrong. In facing many questions posed by 1 Peter, the available evidence is often conflicting and confusing. We must, therefore, be aware that our judgments, like those of the panelists', could be wrong.

The opening words of 1 Peter declare the Apostle Peter to have been the author. The document concludes with a statement of the author's special relationship to Mark not unlike that which tradition assigns to Peter (5:13). Throughout most of Christian history, these indications of Petrine authorship were taken at face value. In our time, however, Peter's authorship is widely doubted. One scholar has dismissed the issue curtly by saying: "We may assert without hesitation that if the first word, Peter, of our epistle were absent, no one would have imagined that it had been composed by him." On the surface of things, it seems strange that Peter's name should have been attached to a writing so un-Petrine! If it was a forgery, why make the forgery so patently discoverable?

But even if Peter were not the author, can the attachment of his name to the document be something other than blatant forgery? We are faced with three possibilities: either 1) Peter wrote it; or 2) someone thought he wrote it and put his name to it; or 3) someone, or some group, knew that he did not write it, but attached his name to it anyway.

If the first were true, there is no problem.

The second possibility would raise no difficulty with regard to the quality of the document. For example, Christian Hymnals up to the 1930s listed Luther as the author of the lovely children's carol, "Away in a Manger," the carol often called "Luther's Cradle Hymn." By the 1940s the musicologists had decided that the attribution to Luther was false. Since then the author is listed as Anonymous. When the author was believed to have been Luther, the hymn furnished a delightful foil for Luther's rugged bluntness when, for example, he referred to "his most hellish Highness Pope Paul III." How good it was to ponder contradictory elements in Luther's genius, when such a combative nature as his could at the same time embody the gentleness and grace of this carol. This dual feature in Luther, although real, must now be illustrated in other ways. This historic error, however, by no means detracts from the beauty and winsomeness of the carol. Its intrinsic worth remains the same. Likewise, if the attribution of 1 Peter to the Apostle Peter should prove to be a historic error, it would have no bearing on the theological and religious value of the document.

The third possibility, if true, would be more difficult to surmount. If, however, it could be proved that whoever first offered 1 Peter to the public in the name of Peter knew that he was not the author, that would not necessarily brand it as a fraud. Before doing that, we would have to know more than we know at present about ancient attributions of works to authors before copyright laws and modern rules of plagiarism were established. And we would have to know the motivation that prompted the use of a substitute name. Why, for example, did Mary Ann Evans write under the name of George Eliot, or Dean Swift under the name of Lemuel Gulliver, or Samuel Clemens under the name of Mark Twain? What was the motivation which prompted attaching a name to a document which was authored by someone else? Was this always nefarious?

Those who have delved deeply into such matters have proposed various motivations for the use of pen names, especially those of well-known past figures.

One is *financial gain*. The kings of Egypt and Pergamum who amassed the great libraries of antiquity offered monetary rewards for copies of ancient author's books, thus prompting spurious works to be passed off as authentic. Obviously, whoever put Peter's name on 1 Peter had no such motivation.

Malice was another motivation. Paul's enemies apparently circulated letters under his name falsely, to involve him in theological difficulties (2 Thess 2:2). The simple statement of early church theology in 1 Peter rules out any attempt here to embarrass or undercut any other church leader.

A third motivation was *dramatic enhancement*, such as the speech Shakespeare put into the mouth of Mark Antony in his play *Julius Caesar*, giving his own literary flare to what he conceived were the thoughts of Antony on that occasion. That this procedure was not calculated to deceive is plain from the fact that Josephus put two different speeches on the lips of Herod in two accounts of the same occasion. Even so, the nature of the content and style and circumstances of 1 Peter rule out any such motivation.

Another reason why false names might have been attached to ancient documents was the *teaching device* of assigning students of oratory the task of producing addresses in the style of well-known ancient orators. Conceivably those which were well done might, in the vagaries of history, became falsely attriibuted to the authors being imitated. Such a historic circumstance can hardly be conceived in connection with 1 Peter.

The *accidents of copying* account for some false attributions of authorship, where there were two authors of the same or similar names. Many account for the attribution of the Fourth Gospel to John the son of Zebedee as a false identification of him with the presbyter John. Certainly no historian has come up with another Peter in the early church with whom the apostle could have been mistakenly identified.

Although the motivations so far surveyed do not support the rejection of apostolic authorship, another might possibly be relevant: namely, *love and respect* for a teacher whose thought a disciple, or group of disciples, wanted to perpetuate. In the case of 1 Peter, this would mean that one or more of his admirers felt that they knew the apostle Peter's mind well enough to produce a work which expressed what he would have said had he been writing it. If 1 Peter must be dated later than Peter's death, this could well account for the attachment of his name to the document. Although one modern scholar, in defense of Petrine authorship, says: "Frauds are still fraudulent, even when perpetrated from noble motives," it might be pointed out that there are indications in the early church that such a process would not have been considered fraudulent. 2 Peter, for example, claims to have been written by the Apostle Peter, but for reasons which cannot be elaborated here, it is almost universally now acknowledged as coming from someone other than the Apostle. In spite of that, it finally worked its way into the New Testament canon, indicating that the church was willing to accept as authoritative apostolic teaching that which likely did not come directly from the pen of an apostle.

If, then, the evidence should conclusively prove that 1 Peter, bearing Peter's name, was not written by the apostle, we need not reject it as Holy Writ, nor reflect on its contents with hesitation. As a Christian writer of the 5th century said about another document: "we ought to be more concerned about the intrinsic value of its contents than about the name of the author." In seeking a solution to the quandary posed by conflicting evidence, we can only do what a jury has to do in reaching a verdict in a court of law—thoughtfully examine the evidence and make a decision.

The task is complex, for the final judgment about authorship rests on the answer to many related questions, such as, What is the *literary* nature of the document? Who were the *first readers*, and what were their *circumstances*? *When* was 1 Peter written? From *where* was it written? What is the *purpose* of 1 Peter? The weighing of the evidence is a difficult and sometimes confusing task. At certain points, the evidence is scanty and highly debatable. Conclusions, therefore, must be somewhat tentative.

We shall now seek to lay out the evidence for and against the various views, and state our own conclusions, leaving the reader to form his own judgment in the light of the discussion. Let it be understood, however, that in our judgment, the document is priceless, whatever be our views of the debated issues. 1 Peter is veritably "a microcosm of Christian faith and duty."

2

WHAT IS THE LITERARY NATURE OF 1 PETER?

Efforts to answer this question have been complicated and ingenious. The document itself purports to be a letter similar to other New Testament letters. It opens with a salutation to specific readers in a specific area (1:1-2). It concludes with affectionate greetings sent from a specific place (5:12-14). Between the salutation and conclusion a writer, who refers to himself as "I," claims that he desires to "declare" once more what the Christian faith is, and to "exhort" his readers to remain loyal to that faith, especially by their virtuous behavior under pressure of misunderstanding and malevolence.

Within the past century, however, many scholars have abandoned this simple and seemingly natural view. Having decided that the document postdates Peter's lifetime, they have looked for clues in terminology, literary structure and the theology and liturgical practice of the church at the time of the alleged later date, to devise explanations of how it came into being.

Is 1 Peter A Paschal Baptismal Liturgy?

One of the most elaborate and carefully worked out hypotheses is that 1 Peter is based on a liturgy containing "various prayers and homilies spoken by a bishop at various stages of an Easter baptism service." The theory divides the document into five parts:

Opening Prayer (1:3-12)
Charge to Baptismal candidates (1:13-21),
   followed by baptism
Welcome to the Newly Baptized (1:22-25)
Homily on the Sacraments (2:1-10),

followed by the sacrament
Homily on Duties of the Christian Disciple (2:11-4:11)
1. Moral Code (2:11-3:12)
2. Vocation to Suffering (3:13-4:6)
3. Concluding Admonition and
Doxology (4:7-11)

The first reaction to such a theory is that it trenches upon one's common sense. If one wanted to send to others a baptismal liturgy for use on Easter Sunday, would he do it this way? Would he disguise it in the form of a letter, and omit the rubrics which indicate the various parts in the service as they arise? Or, on the other hand, if one wanted to write a letter, would he copy out a liturgy, add a salutation and closing greeting, and send it off? Or, if neither, how did a liturgy finally get circulated in the similitude of a letter? Ingenious as the theory is, it raises more questions than it answers. It would seem to reflect the working of the modern scholarly mind more than the design of early Christian evangelists.

A second questionable feature of this is that it does not account for the entire document. No place is to be found here for the opening (1:1-2) nor the closing verses (5:12-14), nor is any account taken of the final section (4:12-5:11). (An earlier champion of a liturgical setting did suggest that 4:12-5:11 is a closing service for the entire congregation following the baptisms). Were the theory not dubious on other grounds, to leave these parts of the document unexplained, and to furnish no clues as to how they may have become attached to the liturgy, makes it suspect.

But what of the effort to make of 1 Peter a paschal, or Easter, document? The evidence offered for this, at some points, strains credulity. It is, for example, suggested that there is a play on words relating the Greek word for Easter, *paskha*, to the Greek word for suffering, *paskho*. The Greek word which the Christians used for Easter is the same as that used for the Passover. It is clear that what the Passover meant to the Jew, Easter came to mean for the Christian. This finds clear expression in a hymn of John of Damascus:

> The day of resurrection!
> Earth, tell it out abroad;

> The Passover of gladness,
> The Passover of God.

Since some early Christian writers related the Passover to the sufferings of Christ, and elaborated their meaning in terms of the symbolism of the escape from Egypt, the miraculous deliverance through the Red Sea, and the wilderness wanderings, it is alleged that 1 Peter's frequent mention of Christ's sufferings must be interpreted in the same way; ergo, 1 Peter is a paschal, or Easter document. What can be said of this?

For one thing, interpreting Christ's sufferings with relation to the Passover is a type of interpretation which postdates 1 Peter. The writings where this connection is emphasized are from the latter part of the second century. 1 Peter can hardly, on any reckoning, be dated that late. Although it is alleged that this type of interpretation is "in line with a long tradition," the evidence would seem to suggest otherwise. Paul does say that "Christ, our paschal lamb, has been sacrificed" (1 Cor 5:7), but it is in an ethical context where, rather than expanding on the relation of Christ's sufferings to elements of the Exodus Passover record, he is stressing that the readers' lives should embody "the unleavened bread of sincerity and truth." Philo, in one passage, has the word for "Passover" and the word for "suffering" within four lines of one another, but it is in a context where he is using the word for "suffer" in its neutral sense of "to experience," whether good or bad. It is doubtful, therefore, whether the alleged connection between "Passover" and "suffering" in 1 Peter can turn this document into a Paschal work, especially in the light of the fact that the author never once mentions the Passover, nor the leaving of Egypt nor the crossing of the Red Sea. Why would this theme be so subtly worked into the document if its major meaning were Paschal?

Furthermore, even though a tradition may have developed later of baptizing new converts on Easter Sunday, can we be sure that such a custom had developed as early as 1 Peter may be dated? Since every Sunday was Easter Sunday for the early Christians, it would seem more likely that making certain festival occasions special was a later development. Historians indicate that the mention of Easter as an especially appropriate time for baptism can be found no earlier than Tertullian, around the beginning of the third century. As one of them remarked: "There are dangers in arguing from Tertullian to first century practice."

Other details pointing to 1 Peter as a Paschal document are unconvincing. "Gird up your minds" (1:13) is said to reflect the Passover instruction in Exodus to eat with "your loins girded" (12:11). But this expression is found frequently elsewhere in the New Testament where it most certainly cannot be related to the Passover (see Acts 12:8; Luke 12:35, 37; Eph 6:14). 1 Peter's reference to Christ as "a lamb without blemish" (1:19) is also said to be a reference to the Passover lamb. But the expression "without blemish" is used in the Old Testament of lambs other than the Passouer lamb (Lev 14:10 et al), and is frequently used of animals other than lambs (Lev 4:3, 23; 9:2, et al).

Many other details too numerous to review here go into the argument for making 1 Peter a Paschal Liturgy. But individually and cumulatively, they are not, in my judgment, convincing. One feels as though the process whereby they are brought together is somewhat like lying on one's back and looking at the clouds. In so doing, one may see elephants, or tigers, or chimpanzees or peacocks. These figures exist only in the mind of the viewer, with no relation to reality. Some years ago a jointly authored psychobiography of Woodrow Wilson was published, where many traits of his character and personality were explained on psychological grounds. One of Wilson's biographers, who has been for years editing the Wilson papers, made an address thereafter in which he pointed out indisputably that most of the book's conclusions were stuff and nonsense, subjectively created in the minds of the interpreters but with no basis in reality. For example, the book claimed that, although Wilson had a middle name, he refused to use it because of some association with a girl friend who had jilted him. The historian granted that Wilson had a middle name which he did not use, but that he had dropped its use quite before he had ever met the girl in question! So it seems with the Paschal Baptismal Liturgy theory of 1 Peter. One writer said of the scholar who had worked it out in most detail, he seems to be "discovering pieces of evidence that might fit in with his hypothesis if it were true, rather than finding any evidence to show that it is in fact true."

Do we need any explanation of 1 Peter's frequent mention of suffering other than that it is "so clearly linked up with current facts"? The readers had been, or were about to be suffering for their faith. The writer wanted to encourage them, in the light of their Lord's suffering for them and the opportunity their suffering gave, to demonstrate to a pagan world what their faith meant to them under these circumstances.

Is 1 Peter a Baptismal Homily?

If 1 Peter is not a Paschal Baptismal Liturgy, is it possibly a Baptismal Homily—a sermon developed around the baptismal theme? Is it centered in baptism at all?

Some who believe that the document is to be dated later than the lifetime of Peter (see discussion of date, pp. 33ff.), and therefore falsely bears his name, have seen in it "a sermon to a group of baptized persons" (1:13-4:11), to which has been added a "letter of encouragement in time of persecution" (4:12-5:11). But why is it necessary to interpret 1 Peter in terms of baptism?

The word "baptism" is used only once. Is it not strange that, in the light of the fact that other concepts of the document appear frequently, the alleged central concept around which the entire writing is organized should escape further mention? What further witness is needed to make the theory suspect? And is it not merely another theory necessitated by insisting on a late date for 1 Peter which would not be necessary if a date during his lifetime were granted?

Again, the frequency of the word "now" (two different words are used for this in the Greek) is alleged to refer to a baptism *now taking place*, as though the service were currently in progress. An examination of the setting of these words, however, makes this highly improbable. The "now" in verses 6 and 8 of chapter 1 are contrasting the suffering of the present experience of the readers with the coming "salvation ready to be revealed in the last time"—a contrast between the present state of Christian existence and that of the glorious state which awaits them when the kingdom fully comes. It is a contrast between *history* and the *end of history*, between *time* and *eternity*. It applies to all Christians, not just to those *now being baptized*.

The "now" in 1:12 is contrasting the *prophetic age* of the Old Testament with the *present age* of the gospel. The prophets were perplexed by that which was stirring in their spirits which went beyond anything they had experienced, but *now*, through those who have "preached the good news . . . through the Holy Spirit sent from heaven," the mystery "into which angels long to look" is made known. This is not made known only to current baptizees but to all.

The three "nows" in 2:10 and 2:25 are open to a like explanation. The setting is a declaration that the pagan converts to Christianity have now entered "the Israel of God" (Gal 6:16). *Formerly* they were nobody; *now*, they are the people of God, heir to all the Old Testament promises. *Before*, they lived in "darkness" (2:9), their "futile ways inherited from [their] fathers" (1:18) consisting of "licentiousness, passions, drunkenness, revels, carousing, and lawless idolatry" (4:3). *Now*, they exist to "declare the wonderful deeds of him who called [them] out of darkness into his marvelous light" (2:9). This was true of them all, not just the newly baptized.

The "now" of 3:21, where we are told that "baptism . . . now saves" does not refer to an event now taking place, but is rather a contrast between "the days of Noah" and the Christian era—then, the flood and the ark, now, baptism and the resurrection of Jesus Christ.

In my judgment, the conclusion of a competent scholar is valid: that the repeated "nows" of 1 Peter do not indicate the changed status that obtains immediately following baptism, but "the new situation that obtains when Gentiles, with Jews, are being together formed into Israel and the tide of the universal Gospel is felt to be in full flood."

A further argument in behalf of 1 Peter as a baptismal document is to make of the expression "born anew" in 1:3 and 1:23 references to a baptismal rite. To a sacramentarian who believes in the inherent efficacy of the sacraments, as though birth into the kingdom were effected by the outward rite, this theological connection could he made. The context in each case, however, suggests that the writer of 1 Peter is not thinking so much of the efficacy of a rite as he is of "the resurrection of Jesus Christ from the dead" as the "efficient cause" of the new birth. This efficient cause functions in us as the "good news" is *preached* to us, through which preaching it becomes "the imperishable seed" of "the living and abiding word of God." It is the "resurrection" and the "living word" which effect regeneration. The author is thereby saying a word similar to that of James: "Of his own will he brought us forth by the word of truth . . . " (1:18). Had the emphasis been on the rite of baptism the author certainly bungled his opportunity to make his meaning clear.

A further alleged reference to the rite of baptism is the passage in 2:2: "Like newborn babes, long for the pure spiritual milk, that by it you may grow up to salvation." Stress is put on "*new*born," as though it were "*now*born," implying that "baptism took place a moment ago." But if one were not trying to bolster a theory that this is a baptismal document would the expression mean anything more than "long for spiritual nourishment as eagerly as newly born babies do for physical nourishment?" Both Paul (1 Cor 3:2) and the writer to the Hebrews (5:12ff.) addressed themselves to immature or static Christians who needed milk, not meat, and it is likely that through the long generations more Christians than not have needed a similar admonition. Milk is needed not only by the newly baptized but by Christians of arrested development. Furthermore, is it not stretching credulity to suggest, as has been done, that the word "milk" here reflects a custom of the later church of offering to the newly baptized a cup of milk and honey, symbolizing their bonds to the ancient community of faith who dwelt in a "land flowing with milk and honey"? There is no honey here, and the custom involved is hardly as early as the first century. The mention of milk here seems purely illustrative and metaphorical, not liturgical.

One other alleged parallel between 1 Peter and the baptismal customs of the second century church is the reference in 3:3ff. about the "braiding of hair, decoration of gold, and wearing of robes." In preparing for baptism the regulations were for the women to let down their hair, and remove their jewelry and their outer garments. Does the exhortation in 1 Peter reflect this? Hardly, for at least two reasons. The motivation in 1 Peter is to imitate the "holy women of old," not a second century baptismal custom. Secondly, the baptized women would replace their customary garments and ornaments following the rite, which would hardly be carrying out the exhortation to humility and modesty given here.

When the evidence for making 1 Peter a baptismal homily is considered, the hypothesis seems highly questionable at best. If the document were a homiletical offering to a group of people just entering the Christian family by the rite of baptism, and the writer were trying to instruct them in the rite they were undergoing, would he have used the word "baptism" but once? And would he have buried his meaning so deeply that only a clever bit of scholarly legerdemain could unearth it? The hypothesis sounds more as though the writer were addressing twentieth century scholars rather than his audience of first century humble folk who had abandoned their paganism for membership in the Christian community.

Baptism certainly lies in the background of the document as it does in the whole of the New Testament, since baptism was the outward rite by which the decision to become Christian was ratified. But 1 Peter is less interested in instructing his readers in the meaning of the rite than in exhorting them to the type of life which they should embody in loyalty to Him to whom they had sworn allegiance in baptism. One who has made a careful study of the question seems to me to have reached the right conclusion: the baptismal undertone of the letter "is most satisfactorily accounted for by acknowledging the importance of baptism as the outward mark of the Christian's transition from a pagan way of life to a new way of life marked by obedience, righteousness, suffering and joy . . . which is, in the view of the author of 1 Peter, the real meaning of baptism. To say that the letter, or most of it, is a baptismal homily or liturgy is to treat as explicit, direct and prominent what is only implicit, presupposed and subsidiary. 1 Peter is paraenetical, not catechetical and its main theme is the conduct of Christians in a situation of testing and adversity." Most theories that go beyond this seem to have been, as one scholar put it, "formulated with a lively imagination indeed!"

Does 1 Peter Embody a Collection of Hymns?

It is plain that hymns were sung in Christian worship from the very first. In this, Jewish Christians were merely continuing the tradition which came out of Judaism. Mark tells us that on the last night of Jesus' life, "when they had sung a hymn, they went out to the Mount of Olives" (14:26). That Gentile Christians continued this tradition is confirmed by the counsel to the church at Ephesus to address one another "in psalms and hymns and spiritual songs" (Eph 5:19), and the description of the Christians at Corinth and Colossae doing likewise (1 Cor. 14:26, Col 3:16)—all Gentile churches. We know, too, that Paul and Silas "were . . . singing hymns" in the Philippian jail (Acts 16:25). Traces of this custom are here and there apparent in the New Testament writings elsewhere. Just as modern writers who are familiar with Christian hymnody will quote lines or stanzas of hymns which give effective expression to what they are saying, those who wrote the Scriptures on occasion did likewise.

How are these stanzas or fragments of hymns in the New Testament writings to be identified? One clear indication would be for the writer to indicate that he is quoting. In a few instances, the New Testament writers do this. Ephesians 5:14 introduces a quotation with the phrase: "Therefore it is said." Likewise 2 Timothy 2:11 indicates the same with the statement: "The saying is sure." There can be little doubt here that the writer is quoting. 1 Timothy 3:16 is introduced by the statement "we confess," as though the following words were a part of a hymnic "confession." Revelation 15:3 prefaces a song with the title: "the song of Moses, the servant of God, and the song of the Lamb." Since the ensuing stanza says nothing either about Moses or the Lamb, it could well be that it was from a hymn or a collection of hymns which bore some such title.

A second indication of hymn quoting would be the recognition of hymns known from elsewhere. If one is familiar with a passage in Shakespeare and finds it included in another's writing, one can immediately identify it, whether the writer does or not. Obviously, this method of identification cannot be used with the New Testament, for there is no available record of Christian hymns by which to check. We know they sang hymns, but we do not know what those hymns were.

A third means of identifying hymns, or parts of hymns, would be from internal evidence—their "rhythmical structure." The rhythmic patterns of Old Testament psalms can serve well here. Most scholars take the Magnificat (Lk 1:46ff.), the Benedictus (Lk 1:68ff.) and the Nunc Dimittus (Lk 2:29ff.) as liturgical hymns of the early church. They are made up largely of the historical, prophetic and liturgical parts of the Old Testament. They also resemble the Psalms in form so much that it is difficult not to think of them as hymns. The great passage on the humiliation and exaltation of Christ in Philippians 2:6-11 is considered by many scholars, though not all, to have been a hymn written in praise of Christ, which Paul found it convenient to quote. The songs in the Revelation (e.g. 11:17ff.; 15 3ff.; 19:1f., 5, 6ff.) are also rhythmic in form and widely considered to reflect early Christian hymnody.

Beyond these, however, can other hymns, or fragments of hymns, be unmistakably identified in the epistolary literature of the New Testament? The only method by which this could be done is a highly subjective procedure based on stylistic or vocabulary differences between the alleged hymn and that of the writer, or on content quite different from the author's customary way of thinking, or on an alleged "rhythmic structure" which seems clearly to brand it as a hymn. As early as 1925, a French scholar remarked that "the epistles of Paul have preserved some poetic fragments of patently lyric tenor which could have been types of expression taken from apostolic worship forms." He added, however: "this no one has any means of proving." In other words, the effort is guess work.

In spite of this, however, the guessing game has been applied to 1 Peter. A French writer has produced a book in which he professed to have discovered four hymns in 1 Peter, and the search has been pursued by other writers. There are times when literary sensitivity can detect certain aspects of a work, especially if they are of a psychological nature. When Charles Dickens read George Eliot's *Silas Marner*, he said that he had no idea who wrote it, but of one thing he was sure—it was written by a woman! This he detected by the depiction of the child in the story, which Dickens said no man could have written. There are, however, no such psychological clues to determine the inclusion of hymns in 1 Peter.

The difficulty of establishing authorship by vocabulary, style and content seems almost insurmountable. If, two thousand years from now, one were to find a copy of the late Archhishop Temple's Gifford lectures, *Nature, Man and God*, and at the same time discover a copy of his lectures to young people, *Basic Convictions*, and the title page of both were missing, it would be difficult indeed to conclude that both came from the same author. But they did. How difficult it is to determine, on the basis of internal evidence alone, what any writer may or may not have written!

A British writer, taking issue with the attempt, wrote an article entitled: "Fashionable Sports: Hymn-Hunting in 1 Peter." He demonstrated the precariousness of using "tests of vocabulary and style" to "produce convincing evidence" that any given passage in a work "was not written by the same hand as that which wrote the rest of the text." He referred, for example, to a passage from a creditable scholar arguing that a document could not possibly have been written by a Greek writer because of the lack of a certain particle commonly used by Greeks. He examined another work, twice the length of the passage in question, which is indisputably known to have been written by a Greek writer, and found no use of that particular particle! After studying the vocabulary and style of the so-called hymn fragments in 1 Peter and comparing them with the surrounding text, he concluded that one cannot say: "Here is a sentence, a phrase, which could not have been written by the author of the Epistle."

The hymns allegedly buried in the Pauline literature are "reasonably coherent blocks of material," whereas those proposed for 1 Peter "are scarcely more than isolated words and phrases" which must be collected from various parts of the document. The process whereby these fragments of alleged hymns are identified, modified, retouched and interpreted is too intricate to be discussed in detail. Suffice it to say, the whole process baffles ordinary responses to the canons of evidence, and leaves the impression of an effort to bolster a subjectively created theory more than to clarify the message of the document. If there should be some fragments of hymnody which, familiar to the author, well up here and there out of the unconscious to affect his mode of writing, it is too precarious a process to try to "unscramble the eggs" without undue subjectivity and without doing violence to the text as it now stands. Is it not possible that the "rhythmic structures" which suggest to hymn-hunters the presence of hymn fragments may be merely the reflections of the author's own literary gifts and style? At least, the burden of proof would seem to lie with those who propose the hymn theory.

Is 1 Peter a Unified or a Composite Document?

It has been widely held that 1 Peter falls into two disparate parts. The first includes 1:3-4:11 which, as we have seen, is thought by some to be a baptismal liturgy, a sermon, or a concatenation of hymns, but not a letter, and is rounded off with a closing doxology—"To him belong glory and dominion for ever and ever." The second (4:12-5:11) is considered to be a letter, to which the opening address (1:1-2) and the closing greetings (5:12-14) properly belong.

This view is based largely on the claim that the tone of the two parts concerning suffering demands two different settings. In 1:3-4:11 suffering is allegedly dealt with in the optative mood—that is, suffering is a "vague possibility" but not a present reality. The writing is said to manifest "deliberate care and slow elaboration," with a "calm and measured tone" and a pervading mood of tranquillity, . . . while the peace of the churches was as yet undisturbed by the sudden outbreak of terror" reflected in the latter part of the writing. The fact that 4:11 concludes with a doxology is also used as evidence that the earlier section originally ended there.

Some who hold this view believe the two sections to have come from different writers; others see "no need to postulate two different authors." The stylistic differences may be accounted for, they claim, by the change of setting to which the two parts were addressed. It was as though the author, called upon to comfort and strengthen his disciples in a great crisis of suffering, stuffed into the envelope in which he sent his letter a copy of one of his earlier sermons which was prepared in a calmer time.

A highly respected British scholar has devised a theory to account for the shift from the optative to the indicative mood in the latter part of the letter by proposing that the same author prepared two versions: "one for those not yet under actual duress" (1:1-4:11, 5:12-14), "and the other—terser and swifter—for those who were in the refining fire" (1:1-2:10, 4:12-5:14). The appropriate version was then read "to each community according to the situation." One can see how, if this were the case, the two versions "were copied continuously, one after the other, within the common framework of salutation and farewell," when the New Testament writings were being collected. Another Britisher has proposed that the difference in tone with regard to suffering between the earlier and later part of the writing may be accounted for by the fact that "fresh news [about the addressees' suffering] had arrived while the letter was actually being written." This is a typical British common sense conjecture, and who can gainsay it?

But do we need such conjectures? Are the two parts of the document really that different?

For one thing, there is no evidence in any of the early manuscripts of 1 Peter that 1:3-4:11 ever existed apart from the letter form as it now stands. It is possible, of course, that, as the originator of one of the proposals has suggested, when the sacred writings were collected two separate letters from the same hand were put together as one. But we do not know that, and if the letter as it now stands manifests a unity, why do we need to make such conjectures?

Secondly, Ephesians 3:20f. is a doxological outburst in the middle of a letter. The same is true of Romans 11:33-36. Why, then, does the doxology in 1 Peter 4:11 necessarily signal the end of a writing?

Thirdly, is the tone and mood with regard to suffering so much different in the two parts of the letter? Does the judgment of one who champions this view, that in the section 1:3-4:11 there is "not a line to suggest that the people to whom it is addressed are undergoing persecution," hold up under scrutiny? Does not 1:6, "though *now* for a little while you may have to suffer various trials," suggest that the suffering of which the writer speaks is current? The translators of the *Revised New English Bible* have rendered this: "even though for a little while *you may have had to suffer* trials of many kinds" (emphasis added). Or, as another translation has it: "at present, if it need be, *you have been made sorrowful* by various trials" (emphasis added). To speak of this as a "calm and measured tone," written in the "mood of tranquillity," to remind the readers that although "the sky is not entirely clear" yet "no storm has broken over their heads," would seem like writing to Anne Frank in her Dutch attic in unruffled and leisurely terms and a "pervading mood of tranquillity" which philosophized about her situation and quietly suggested that nothing *real* had taken place in her experience because the Nazis had not yet gotten her to the gas chamber!

The terminology of 1:6f. is strangely like that of the second part of the document. Suffering is called a "trial," a "testing," whereas the "ordeal" of 4:12 is denoted by exactly the same word—a "proof" or a "test." It also speaks of being tested by "fire," whereas 4:12 speaks of the "fiery" ordeal. Both passages also lay stress on the "resultant glory" which is the outcome of faithful endurance of the test—"praise and glory and honor at the revelation of Jesus Christ" in 1:7, "when his glory is revealed" in 4:13.

As to the shift from the optative to the indicative mood in the two parts of the document, I would agree with a writer who said that it is "a misunderstanding to say that in 3:14,17 ["if you do suffer," "if that should be God's will"] suffering is regarded as a mere possibility, not a pressing reality." The force of the optative is not that "suffering is merely possible." It expresses rather "the delicate and affectionate attitude of the writer, who wishes to spare the feelings of his readers rather than frighten them with too blunt a reference to the painful trial of persecution. Like a good shepherd "only when he has spoken of the "nobiliity and value of Christian suffering" in "general principles" does he "face directly and powerfully the severe ordeal which hangs over the Christian communities and which in fact has already begun." Furthermore, "the 'general principles' which are supposed to be a characteristic of the first section of the epistle are found, in equal measure, in the second, not merely in the repetition of persecution maxims (4:13-16) found earlier in the epistle, but even more obviously in the general exhortations of 5:1-11."

Other passages in 1:3-4:11 reflect the fact that the addressees were undergoing perils while the document was being penned. There is the possibility of suffering "for righteousness' sake" (3:14). There must have been sufficient examples of this having happened to make this reminder relevant. They were not to "fear" nor be "troubled" by their tormenters (3:14). They were likely to be called "to account for the hope" that was in them (3:15). They would he "abused" by those who reviled their "good behavior in Christ" (3:16). They were to keep before them the example of Christ who demonstrated in his death that "it is better to suffer for doing right . . . than for doing wrong" (3:17). They were to remember that "Christ suffered in the flesh" by doing "the will of God" even though it was costly (4:1f.). They were "abused" by the pagans because they did not join in the "wild profligacy" in which they indulged (4:4). Can all of these words have had only a theoretic relevance to the readers? Was the writer raising problems that were unreal to their experience? Or, on the contrary, was he not speaking to their condition in every day life? The frequency of such references makes it difficult to believe that the readers were living in the relatively safe protection of an indifferent society such as that under which we live here in America. They must have been facing something more like what Paul experienced when he first evangelized parts of the same area (Acts 13, 14) or minorities of Christians do today in some pagan lands. Otherwise, why talk so much about something that was alien to their experience?

Fourthly, a careful scholar has pointed out that there are striking unstudied similarities between the two sections of the document which reflect a unity of authorship and occasion. For example, the word "to entertain" or "get entertained" or "lodged" is used seven times in the New Testament with that connotation. It can mean, however, "to surprise" or "be surprised." It is used only three times in the New Testament with this meaning, and two of those are in 1 Peter. (The other is in Acts 17:20, where the Athenian philosophers speak of Paul's teaching as a "strange" or "surprising" thing.) This unusual use of the word is found in both parts of 1 Peter (4:4, 4:12), which relates them in a marked way. Also, the word "wrongdoer" is used nowhere else in the New Testament, but is used three times in 1 Peter, twice in the early part (2:12, 14), and once in the latter part (4:15). Likewise, the word "brotherhood" is unique to 1 Peter, but is used in both parts (2:17, 5:9). Then, too, the word "rejoice," although used in the Gospels, the Acts and the Revelation, is used nowhere in the epistolary literature of the New Testament save in 1 Peter, and there it is found in both sections (1:6, 8; 4:13).

Again, similar themes are found in both parts of the document: Christian suffering as an imitation of Christ's sufferings (2:21, 4:13); unmerited suffering (3:17; 4:15f.); subjection to others as a virtue (2:13, 18; 3:1; 5:5); the nearness of judgment (4:7, 17); the expression "a little while" with relation to suffering (1:6, 5:10). Although, as we have seen earlier (p. 20), stylistic *differences* are precarious guides in assigning authorship, since one writer may have more than one style, this concentration of stylistic and thematic *likenesses* in the short space represented by the two parts of this document would seem to point not only to one author for both parts but to bind them together into a literary unity.

What Are the Sources and Literary Affinities of 1 Peter?

One of the major sources on which 1 Peter depends is the *Old Testament*. It is generally agreed that the author "makes more extensive use of the Old Testament in proportion to the size of his letter than any other book in the New Testament except Revelation." The text abounds in direct citations and in indirect allusions. References are made to all three divisions of the Old Testament—the Law, the Prophets and the Writings, although the Law appears only three times, two of which are allusions rather than citations. Among the Writings, the Psalms appear seven times, and the Proverbs five. Reference is made to the prophets sixteen times, of which thirteen are to Isaiah and one each to Jeremiah and Hosea.

It is evident that the author makes a "Christological" use of the Old Testament in that he sees it as pointing throughout to the Christ. Early in his presentation (1:10ff.) he tells his readers that the prophets "prophesied of the grace that was to be *yours*" (emphasis added). In other words, what the prophets said had a significance quite beyond what they and their hearers were experiencing at the time they spoke. Just as certain things in a play are obscure when first presented in the early scenes, but are clarified when the climax is reached, so God, as the author of the play, had meanings in what the prophets said which come clear only as now seen in the light of Christ. Now that the climax of the divine drama has been reached, we can look back and see that the prophets spoke more than they knew—they were dealing with "the things which have now been announced to [us] by those who preached the good news" (1:12).

It is a quality of all works of inspiration to "transcend the conscious horizon of the artist;" to embody realities of which the artist was not aware. The effort to capture this transcendent element, of course, must be controlled by reasonable procedures. To use the dimensions of Noah's ark as a divinely inspired guide to boat building, as I have heard done, is to shift from biblical to technical concerns alien to the purpose for which the story was told. Deeper meanings which are seen in biblical passages must be controlled by their original intention. They must carry the passage further "on its own road," arriving at destinations determined by the direction given by the original passage itself. The New Testament writers, therefore, were doing no violence to the meaning of the Old Testament passages they "Christianized." They were simply going further down the road to which the Old Testament writers pointed, and finding at the end of that road not something other than the writers meant but something consonant with what they were saying, yet fuller, grander, more glorious. As a French scholar has put it: but more than all other authors of the New Testament, "Peter would likely have been in accord with Origen," who, commenting on one of the Psalms, affirmed: "The Old Testament proclaims Christ crucified." Origen did not mean that the Old Testament writers could have written one of our Gospels, nor that they had seen all the theological meaning of the crucifixion of Christ without that event having taken place. He rather meant that the patterns of meaning in the Old Testament, when carried far enough down the road which they traveled, finally land us at Christ.

A current scholar has written: "I have become convinced . . . that historical 'understanding' of a biblical text cannot stop with the elucidation of its prehistory . . . with its focus on the intention of the author. Understanding must take into account the text's posthistory, i.e., as the way in which the text itself as a source of human self-interpretation in a variety of contexts, and thus through its historical interpretations, is participating in the shaping of life." It is important to know, therefore, not only what the Old Testament meant to the ancient

Jews, but what it *came to mean* to the early Christians in the formation of their own thought and life and faith, as they traveled down the road further than was possible for pre-Christian believers.

The tension between the Old and New Testaments, along with that between Judaism and Christianity, has been a problem from the earliest days of the Christian church. The kinship between the two is undeniable. *There is no Christianity without Judaism.* Said our Lord: "salvation is from the Jews" (John 4:22). For the Christian, that is where it all began! And any Christianity which cuts its roots from Judaism is spurious Christianity. The earliest form of deviation from the classic Christian faith was that of Marcion who discarded the Old Testament and all of the New Testament save Paul and Luke, whom he considered cleansed of Old Testament influences. The church decisively pronounced this heresy. The early Christian missionaries who took the gospel to the Gentiles did not merely proclaim to them Jesus—they proclaimed Jesus *Christ,* the Jewish Messiah. Peter, in the first sermon preached to Gentiles, called the gospel the word which God "sent to Israel, . . . good news of peace by Jesus Christ" *(Jesus Messiah—the Jewish Messiah!)* (Acts 10:36). Paul described the gospel as "what God promised to the fathers" (the Jewish fathers) (Acts 13:32). To him, the Jews were "the natural branches" of the tree of faith into which the Gentiles, "wild olive" branches, were grafted (Rom 11:17, 21). The New Testament insists that there is a continuity between Judaism and Christianity.

And yet—*and yet, they are not one and the same thing.* There is a radical discontinuity. There is a uniqueness about Christianity which Judaism does not share. The same Paul who thought of the Christian gospel as the fulfilment of Judaism insisted that the man Jesus, who stemmed from Judaism, has wrought a "forgiveness of sins" and freed all men from everything from which they "could not be freed by the law of Moses" (Acts 13:38f.). One of my mentors used to insist that one can speak correctly of "the Jewish-Christian tradition" but not of "the Jewish-Christian religion." Any devout Jewish believer will confirm this. If asked whether Christianity is the same as his religion, he will respond with a resounding No! We Christians are at home with Abraham, Isaac, Jacob, Moses, David, and the prophets. A devout Jew, however, is not at home with Jesus Christ. It is an ongoing problem which, however difficult to solve, the church must never forget—the amazing kinship of Christianity to Judaism, yet its amazing difference. Salvation is "from the Jews," but Judaism is not Christianity. For this reason, the Christian must read the Old Testament differently from the Jew—he must read it in some sense "Christologically," listening for its witness to Jesus Christ.

The purpose for which the author introduces his Old Testament citations and allusions does not seem to be to confirm an argument by founding it on the authority of the Old Testament, "to prove the truth of the gospel by Scripture"; nor does he intend to "give an explanation of Scripture, " to elaborate on what the Old Testament writer meant. He rather uses Scripture for "edification" and "encouragement." For example, one writer has demonstrated that the various allusions to Isaiah may be divided into three groups: 1) those which relate to the advance of the Assyrians against Judah; 2) those which relate to the return from captivity after the Assyrians had deported the people; and 3) those which are drawn from the last of the four Servant songs. These references to Isaiah are not to prove anything, nor is the emphasis on interpreting the passages involved. The first, relating to the Assyrian threat, is used to exhort his readers to keep their "confidence in Jahweh" in the face of pagan threats, even as the ancient Jews were encouraged to do in face of the Assyrian threat. The second, dealing with the return from captivity, "accentuates the power of Jahweh who destroys human powers and leads his people back home," thus encouraging the readers to trust that same power. The third, which refers to the Suffering Servant, "serves as a model for the sufferings which the Christians had to endure." 1 Peter is pastoral throughout. He is using the Old Testament to motivate his readers, not to argue or prove or to instruct.

The author is consistent in his use of the Septuagint (the Greek translation of the Old Testament) rather than the Hebrew. He is often quite free in changing certain expressions of the Greek text, whether exercising his own freedom in so doing, or following a pattern which had been developed in the early church to "Christianize" the Old Testament and adapt it to its own needs. In any case, he is seeking to make the Old Testament relevant to the actual situation which his readers faced.

Some have concluded from the absence of the author's use of the Hebrew text of the Old Testament that he could not have been of "Jewish Palestinian origin." This seems farfetched, however. There were Greek-speaking Jews living in Jerusalem (Acts 6:1, 9) who must have used the Greek version of the Old Testament. How can we be sure that even a Palestinian-born Jew may not have been familiar with the Greek version? Furthermore, the readers to which 1 Peter is addressed were Greek-speaking, and any familiarity with the Old Testament they may have had would have been through the Greek version. Why, then, should they not have been addressed with that version? To exclude Petrine authorship on the basis of the document's use of the Greek Old Testament would seem to be resting the argument on a weak reed at this point.

Another possible source on which 1 Peter may have depended is *other New Testament writings*. There are parallel expressions to be found in I and II Thessalonians, Romans, Ephesians, James, Hebrews, Titus and the Acts of the Apostles. Totally opposite conclusions have been drawn from this. Some have argued that 1 Peter is dependent on all these, therefore later than them all, thus could not have been written by Peter, who died before these had been circulated. Others have drawn the exact opposite conclusion, that all of these were dependent on 1 Peter, therefore it was written earlier than them all and was authored by Peter. Efforts to prove priority either way involve more technical literary detective work than can he gone into here.

Suffice it to say, however, that methodologically "literary *affinity* must be distinguished from literary *dependence*" (italics added). The weight of current scholarship seems to be in the direction of attributing the common literary expressions among the various New Testament writings to the use of a "broadly varied (liturgical, parenetic, and catechetical) tradition" rather than to direct literary dependence. In our own time one can often, by hearing a person speak, identify the speaker with a certain religious group by his use of terminology unmistakably characteristic of that group. So, the early Christian group, which was in the first century a definite closely knit minority, developed terminological patterns of speech through their preaching, worship, and catechetical instruction which became the property of all and found their way naturally into their writing without conscious dependence one upon another. Furthermore, if the author were Peter himself, he, as the leading Jerusalem apostle, would have had a part in forming the early Christian tradition, so that alluding to that tradition would be tantamount in many cases to using his own words.

Another source on which 1 Peter rests is the *sayings of Jesus* and references to *incidents in the Gospel accounts* in which Peter was a central participant. For example, 1 Peter 1:4 speaks of "an inheritance which is imperishable, undefiled, and unfading, kept in heaven for you." This is suggestively similar to Luke's recording of Jesus' words in 12:33, where he speaks of "a treasure in the heavens that does not fail, where no thief approaches and no moth destroys." 1 Peter 1:13, "gird up your minds, be sober, set your hope fully upon the grace that is coming to you at the revelation of Jesus Christ" sounds suspiciously like our Lord's saying recorded in Luke 12:35: "Let your loins be girded and your lamps burning, and be like men who are waiting for their master to come home . . . , so that they may open to him at once when he comes and knocks." 1 Peter 3:14 speaks of suffering "for righteousness' sake," which reflects our Lord's own words recorded in Matthew 5:10: "Blessed are those who are persecuted for righteousness' sake." Several of these striking parallels have been noted by scholars for a long time, one of whom nearly fifty years ago remarked that the alleged words of Christ in 1 Peter was "a wide field" lying open to study.

A careful and detailed study of such allusions has been made by one scholar, which has occasioned a great deal of debate. The writer identified nearly two dozen passages which he felt were definite allusions to the words of Jesus, or to the actions of Jesus, as represented in the Gospels. But even more striking is the fact that these "refer to contexts in the gospels which are specially associated with the Apostle Peter or treat topics that would especially interest the Apostle Peter according to the gospel tradition concerning him." This scholar thought he had discovered a "Petrine pattern" in the words of Christ in the relation of Peter to the historic Jesus reflected in the document. One example of this would be Peter's elaborate dealing with the stone-motif in 1 Peter 2:4-8 in the light of Jesus having named him Peter, or Rock. This is strengthened by Peter's reference in one of his early sermons (Acts 4:11) to Jesus as the rejected cornerstone. Another would be 1 Peter's frequent reference to Jesus' suffering,"as if the scene of the crucifixion had left an indelible impression on the author's mind." For example, his counsel to suffering readers to "entrust their souls to a faithful creator" (4:19) seems reminiscent of Jesus' last word from the Cross:"Father, into thy hands I commit my spirit!' (Luke 23:46; "entrust" and "commit" are the same word in the Greek). From the rather astounding array of correspondences between 1 Peter and the words and events of the Gospel story where Peter is a chief participant, the author concludes: "It is easier to believe in Petrine authorship for 1 Peter than to believe that this phenomenon is due either to chance . . . or to the subtlety and ingenuity of a pious forger."

Needless to say, this conclusion has been challenged, and one highly technical and scholarly article by a very creditable author was devoted to a detailed examination of the above article in an effort to discredit it. The writer of the original article replied to this, and I can only say that he demonstrated so many weaknesses in the response to his earlier article that, in my judgment, the evidence seems to point to a rather solid case for Petrine authorship on the basis of the consonance of 1 Peter with the sayings of Jesus and the Gospel record of the man Peter.

Although absolute certainty is not possible, there would seem to be no reason why an examination of the literary sources and affinities of 1 Peter does not make a good case for Petrine authorship of the document.

Conclusion as to the Literary Nature of 1 Peter

After examining the different theories proposed to account for the composition of 1 Peter, the evidence seems to suggest that it is not a Paschal Baptismal Liturgy, nor a Baptismal Homily, nor a highly skilled working together of a group of early Christian hymns. It appears to be a unified literary document based on a Christian understanding of the Old Testament; a body of ideas which had become a common Christian tradition growing out of the early church's worship, preaching, catechetical instruction and defense of the faith, to which the author of the document had likely contributed a great part; and the author's own reminiscences of the words and actions of the historic Jesus.

Although these conclusions cannot be indisputably established, there is as much ground, if not more, for believing than denying that 1 Peter is just what it claims to be, a "piece of genuine correspondence" between an Apostle and a group of churches in Asia Minor who needed both instruction in the faith and encouragement to hold on to it in spite of persecution and hardship.

3

WHEN WAS 1 PETER WRITTEN?

If 1 Peter were written by the Apostle Peter, it would be relatively easy to date it. Since, by almost universal agreement, Peter died under Nero in 65 A.D., or shortly thereafter, that would have been the latest possible date for his writing. Inasmuch as that was but thirty-five years after the death of Jesus, and it would have taken some time for the gospel to have spread throughout Asia Minor, where the churches he addressed were located, it may be assumed that the document came from relatively late in his life. A date somewhere near 65 A.D. would fit the circumstances well.

When Did Peter Die?

We know relatively little of the facts concerning the death of Peter. A fairly clear reconstruction of the situation, however, may he pieced together from tradition. An early Christian wriiter, Clement of Rome, writing in 95 or 96 A. D., spoke of Peter who, "when he had at length suffered martyrdom [along with "a great multitude of the elect"], departed to the place of glory due to him." This was undoubtedly under Nero who, to clear suspicion as an arsonist from his own name, turned his fury on the Christians. The Roman historian, Tacitus, indicates that after the burning of Rome, relief operations and efforts at temporary housing for the burned out inhabitants were followed by careful plans for the rebuilding of the city, with "precautions . . . suggested by human prudence" against such a disaster in the future. But, he added, "neither human help, nor imperial munificence . . . could stifle scandal or dispel the belief that the fire had taken place by order." Nero, therefore, "to scotch the rumor . . . substituted as culprits, and punished with the utmost refinements of cruelty, a class of men, loathed for their vices whom the crowd styled Christians." He indicated that "vast numbers were convicted, not so much on the count of arson as for hatred of the human race." Some were dressed in beasts skins and thrown to the dogs, some were crucified, some served as lighted torches in Nero's gardens. The terror was so intense that among the populace "there arose a sentiment of pity, due to the impression that they were being sacrificed not for the welfare of the state but to the ferocity of a single man."

The fact that the persecution did not break out until relief measures had been implemented and plans for the rebuilding of the City had been drawn, suggests that it must have been some months after the fire, at least, that it took place. Since the fire was in 64, the persecution could hardly have been under way until at least 65.

Was Peter martyred in the first stages of terror, or was his end somewhat deferred? We can only conjecture, but there is some basis for the hypothesis that he survived for a time. One of the beautiful legends about him may serve as a clue. Legends are not always untrue. They are stories coming from the past "popularly taken as historical though not verifiable." A British scholar of sufficient depth to have given one of the famous Bampton lectures at Oxford has argued that the famous *Quo Vadis* legend "may possibly have an historical foundation." It contains a story, he insists, that "is not improbable," based on "events that really occurred." The legend is that Peter's friends encouraged him to escape from Rome to avoid Nero's fury. He finally succumbed to their wishes. As he came to the limits of the city, however, he received a vision of Jesus. "Lord, whither goest Thou?" asked Peter. Christ replied: "I am coming to Rome to be again crucified." Peter said to him, "Lord, wilt Thou again be crucified?" to which the Lord answered "Even so, I will again be crucified." Peter replied, "Lord, I will return and will follow Thee," whereupon he went back to face his martyrdom.

"The Peter described here," says the Bampton lecturer, "is the Peter of the Gospels—brave, loving, but in critical moments irresolute." As he succumbed to his friends' persuasion to escape, he could well have recalled that not long before he had written to his friends in Asia Minor,"if one suffers as a Christian, let him not be ashamed, but under that name let him glorify God." His thoughts, too, could have leaped back to an upper room when he had said to Jesus, "Lord, where are you going? [Quo Vadis!] . . . . Lord, why cannot I follow you now? I will lay down my life for you" (John 13:36f.), after which he had denied him three times. In the light of this, determined not to repeat it, he returned to face his martyrdom. The legend may be a true depiction of what went on in Peter's mind, and give a clear picture of why he chose to die rather than try to escape. How long thereafter it was before he was executed is not known, but Nero left Rome for Greece in the year 66, so it is likely that Peter's death took place before the end of the year 65. If he were the author of this document, that is the latest possible date for its composition, and it seems to have been written some months before, in the light of its cordial attitude toward the Roman government (1 Pet. 3:13f.).

What Type of Suffering Does 1 Peter Reflect?

What of the internal evidence in the document itself? Laying aside the question of Petrine authorship for the moment, if his name were not attached to it, what lines of inquiry would be appropriate in seeking to establish the date? What can be drawn from the circumstances of the readers to which it is addressed that may help to determine when it was written? Does the type of suffering it describes necessarily reflect an official government persecution such as that under Nero in 65 A. D.? Or Domitian in 95? Or Trajan in 112? Although scholars have argued for each of these, the evidence seems to suggest that none of them qualifies. No official state persecution is intimated in the writing itself, but rather a sort of unofficial pogrom, the personal and social ostracism of an alien, misunderstood minority group in a pagan society, which "can he more nerve-racking and hardly less difficult than open official persecution."

Those who favor a date for the document after the death of Peter rest their case largely on the correspondence of Pliny, the governor of Bithynia-Pontus—one of the provinces to which 1 Peter is addressed—with the emperor, Trajan. Pliny is inquiring about those who have been accused "as Christians." Should punishment be for "the mere name apart from secret crimes," or only for "the secret crimes connected with the name?" 1 Peter's expression in 4:14, "reproached for the name of Christ," and his reference in 4:16 to suffering "as a Christian," are alleged to reflect Pliny's expression about "the mere name," suggesting therefore that 1 Peter was written at a time when it had become a crime against the State just to bear the name of "Christian." Also, those who favor a late date propose that the counsel against suffering "as a murderer" in the same setting as suffering "for the name of Christ" (4:14f.), makes the latter a legally "indictable offense" against the government as the former would be. Furthermore the description of suffering as a "strange" thing in 4:12 is held to imply that the suffering was different from that heretofore experienced, hence must have been of a governmental nature. Also, reference to suffering as a "fiery ordeal" (4:12) is alleged to describe persecution of a vicious and intensive nature compatible only with that instituted by the authorities. Then, too, the description of the devil prowling around "like a roaring lion, seeking whom he may devour" (5:8) is interpreted as a fit symbol of official state fury. All of these, taken together, are used to demonstrate that a "fixed policy of the Empire towards the Christians" had by now been officially adopted. What of these arguments?

    To suffer "for the name of Christ" in no way means to run afoul of official imperial policy. As early as the first persecution of the Apostles in Jerusalem not long after Pentecost, we read that they rejoiced "that they were counted worthy to suffer dishonor *for the name*" (Acts 5:41). After Paul had met his Lord on the Damascus road, he was told "how much he must suffer for the sake of [*Christ's*] *name*" (Acts 9:16). In Acts 21:13, before 1 Peter was written, Paul declared himself ready "to die at Jerusalem for the *name of the Lord Jesus.*" Suffering "for the name" in 1 Peter reflects circumstances very similar to those spoken of by Jesus in Matthew 5:11, "Bessed are you when men revile you and persecute you and utter all kinds of evil against you falsely *on my account.*" It is also consonant with the foresight of our Lord recorded in Mark 13:13: "you will he hated by all *for my name's sake*" (emphasis added in all these). It is plain that suffering "for the name" in no way implies imperial persecution. It has been pointed out, too, that 1 Peter says "for the name" and not "for the name *only.* " Every form of Christian suffering was understood by the Christians as borne "for the name" of their Lord.

    It is "extremely questionable" whether it is "a fair inference" that the parallel between suffering "for the name of Christ" and suffering as "a murderer" makes the former a legal crime. The list of which "murderer" is a part also includes "wrongdoer" and "mischief maker." Were these also crimes punishable by death? The charge of "murderer" is "typical of the taunts of popular spite, that Christians are murderers, cannibals, fornicators and atheists" which were frequently hurled against them by the pagans The writer was not exhorting his readers to avoid murder lest the cops get you! What he meant was: If you are taunted as a murderer, be sure not to be one! Christians "must give no handle whatever for calumnies of this sort: they must be beyond reproach in conduct; their only offence must be their allegiance to Christ." There is, therefore, nothing here that suggests official government action against the Christians. The situation is quite like that which is reflected in the Book of Acts: "Jewish agitation leading to general unpopularity and suspicion, and then to mob violence . . . ."

The description of suffering as a "strange" thing does not mean that a form of persecution is beginning which is different from anything they had heretofore experienced. The context suggests that the writer is answering the question in their minds why it was that they had to suffer at all if they were the special objects of God's love and care. His answer is: "the ordeal is not a foreign experience, not something . . . . abnormal, but in the direct line of Christ," and that they should rejoice to be counted worthy of suffering "dishonor for the name" (Acts 5:41). That which they thought of as "strange" was not a new form of suffering, shifted from public obloquy to state oppression, but the age-old problem, as ancient as the Book of Job, who, sitting with his loathsome sores on his heap of ashes, had to ask why "a blameless and upright man," who fears God and turns away from "evil" and "holds fast his integrity" must suffer. It is as long standing as the perplexity of the Psalmist who saw the wicked "band together against the life of the righteous, and condemn the innocent to death" (Ps 94: 21). It is as inveterate as the outcry of the prophet Habakkuk: "Thou who art of purer eyes than to behold evil and canst not look on wrong, why dost thou look on faithless men, and art silent when the wicked swallows up the man more righteous then he" (1:13)? It is not a reflection of a change in Roman government policy, but a perpetual problem of people of faith.

Likewise, neither the expression "the fiery ordeal" (4:12) nor the picture of the devil as a "roaring lion" (5:8) point to a new spasm of wrath on the part of the imperial government. The "fiery ordeal" does not refer so much to "the fierceness of the heat" as to "the refining power of fire. 'Trial by fire' would perhaps be a better translation than 'fiery trial'." The *Didache*, a Christian document coming from the early second century, uses a similar expression in connection with the coming of the Anti-Christ, in which it refers not so much to the intensity of the suffering as to its testing nature. Paul uses a similar metaphor when he speaks of the Judgment Day as a "fire" which will "test what sort of work each one has done" (1 Cor 3:13). The "fiery ordeal," then, is hardly a reference to government persecution. The context in which the devil is described is as a "roaring lion" is exhorting to watchfulness rather than describing the intensity of his fury. Furthermore, the very next verse counsels the readers to "Resist him" (5:9), which could hardly be the case if the reference were to the Roman government, inasmuch as earlier the writer insisted that the readers be "subject . . . to the emperor as supreme, or to governors as sent by him to punish those who do wrong and to praise those who do right" (2:13f.). This admonition would have been unthinkable if the emperor had already openly become the archenemy of the church.

Some who feel that the internal evidence of the letter does not square with either the time of Trajan or Domitian or Nero, still think that it reflects official government persecution of the church—some imperial outbreak against the Christians of which we do not know. The argument rests largely on the passage in 3:15, where the readers are exhorted: "Always be prepared to make a defense to any one who calls you to account for the hope that is in you, yet do it with gentleness and reverence." The key word is "defense." It is alleged that this is a statutory term, referring to a formal defense in a legal court, thus implying official persecution. What of this? The Greek word is that from which our English word "apology" comes—apology not in the sense of regret for some hapless word or act, such as saying "I'm sorry" when we inadvertently bump into someone or fail to recall his name; but an apology with a view to defending or justifying something which others may disapprove. The word in classical Greek means simply "to speak in defence" of something or "to defend what one has done," without reference to a magistrate or a court of law. The defense could, of course, be made in a legal setting, but it could just as well be made before an angry mob of ruffians or as a personal explanation to an inquiring individual. The word is used in regard to Paul in both senses. Twice it refers to an official defense before constituted Roman authorities (Acts 25:16; 2 Tim 4:16), but it is also used with regard to his speaking to a mob in Jerusalem (Acts 22:1), in relation to the Corinthian Christians defending their action to Paul (2 Cor 7:11) and Paul's defense of his action to them (1 Cor 9:3), and twice in a general way to refer to the "defense of the gospel" (Phil 1:7, 16). It is clear, then, that the word itself does not imply a court setting, and more often than not its use in the New Testament does not relate to legal matters. Unless other evidence can be mounted to show that 1 Peter involves an official government persecution, the argument resting on the use of the word "apology" is discredited.

One other expression in 1 Peter 5:9 has been used to suggest that the persecutions reflected in the document are government imposed: namely, "the same experience of suffering is required of your brotherhood throughout the world"(5:9). This last expression, "throughout the world," it is argued, suggests a universal clamp down on the activities of the church which could not have been imposed by any other than the imperial government. The phrase in question is a difficult one. It means literally "in the world." Does this mean your brothers who "are yet in the world," meaning they have not yet died? They are "in the world" rather than "gone from the world"? Or does it mean "the whole world," as the Revised Standard translation seems to imply? A currently well-known British scholar, resting his case on the omission of the article "the" in some manuscripts, thus making it read merely "in world," has proposed that it might have been a "stock phrase . . . to mean the opposite of "in town." Just as Londoners speak of London as "the City" in contradistinction to the rest of England, so it may have been in Rome with regard to the provinces. Rome was "the City," all else was on another level! Although the author confesses that he has "made no progress in tracing this phrase back to the first century," the suggestion is clever. It poses at least two questions, however. First, is it valid? Even if it were the Roman custom thus to differentiate their city from the rest of the country bumpkins in the world outside the city, this would hardly have had significance to the dwellers in Asia Minor to whom the letter was addressed. Secondly, is it necessary? When Peter speaks of the brotherhood "in the world," is he interested in describing how widespread the persecution of Christians has become, or is he not rather merely saying to his readers that the same situation they faced is faced by their brothers elsewhere—this is a common experience. If he were interested in picturing the widespread nature of the persecution against the Christians, he could have done what Paul did when he told the Romans that their faith was known "in all the world." Paul was stressing how widespread was the knowledge of them, so he used the word "whole" to make his point (Rom 1:8). When 1 Peter uses "in the world," however, the intent is not to define the extent of the persecution but rather to comfort the sufferers to whom he is writing by reminding them that they are not alone in their difficulty but have many brothers elsewhere who are suffering likewise. Wherever there were Christians, they were misunderstood by the pagans, and had to endure much suspicion, slander and hatred. There is no reason, therefore, to conclude that the expression "in the world" requires a universal government persecution to give it meaning.

What Conclusion Does the Internal Evidence Suggest?

The internal evidence in the document itself, therefore, does not seem to point to any particular official government persecution which can be tied either to the days of Trajan, or Domitian, or Nero, or to any unknown government attack on the church. The conclusion of one who made a most thorough study of the question seems sound: "Not a word is found in the Epistle about men shedding their blood or laying down their lives for the gospel. None of the passages . . . contain any reference to, or hint of, an organized persecution. But it needs only a little reflexion in the light of actual history to convince us how much of the keenest suffering the confession of Christ must have cost these Asiatic Christians, though the State had not as yet become their enemy. They were called upon to face violence, slander, the severance of social and family ties, worldly ruin. In the earliest days of their missionary activity St. Paul and Barnabas frankly told their converts—'through many tribulations we must enter the kingdom of God.' (Acts 14:22). Such tribulations were not confined to the Churches of Asia Minor. It was well that St. Peter, out of his wider experience at Rome and elsewhere, should remind them that these sufferings were the lot of the Christian brotherhood everywhere (5:9)."

The cordial attitude toward the Roman government expressed in the document must certainly have predated Nero's persecution, although it depicts the sort of pressure against the Christians which finally resulted in that outburst. Sufficient time must have elapsed to allow the gospel to have found its way from Palestine to the provinces of Asia Minor. Hence, from the document itself, apart from the question of authorship, a fitting time for its appearance would have been some time not too long before the Neronian holocaust of 65 A.D. From the standpoint of dating the document by internal evidence, therefore, there is no reason to deny the possibility of Petrine authorship, for it could well have been written before Peter's death.

Does the Attitude Toward the Jews Reflect a Late Date?

It has been proposed that the lack of a polemic against "Israel according to the flesh," such as is apparent in some of Paul's epistles, shows that 1 Peter postdates the fall of Jerusalem in A.D. 70, after which this battle became irrelevant. This has the customary weakness of the argument from silence, but particularly so in this case. Paul, as the apostle to the Gentiles, was battling the Judaizers, and of necessity was drawn into this debate. 1 Peter, on the other hand, is not dealing with this problem but rather with the church's need for strength and endurance under persecution. (Can we justly criticize a writer for not wandering in his thought nor getting off the subject?) This, and the solid conviction of the author of 1 Peter that the "church is the true Israel of God," which, given the circumstances of his readers was not a subject of concern at that time, sufficiently accounts for the silence on this subject. It is seldom that writers can be fixed in their chronological niche in history by what they do not say!

A Swiss New Testament scholar made the point in a lecture that at least in one case, we may be thankful for sin! Had the Corinthian Christians not sinned in connection with the Lord's Supper, Paul would never have mentioned it in his writings. This silence would have led the scholars to argue that since Paul did not mention it, the Lord's Supper obviously was a development in the church later than his lifetime! This indicates the inherent weakness of the argument from silence with regard to any particular bit of writing.

On the other hand, was Peter entirely silent about the Judaizing controversy? Does not the letter deal with it implicitly, without any specifically explicit mention of it? Does not Peter's strong conviction that the church "is the true Israel of God" indicate where he stands on this question. He insists that salvation is an "inheritance" into which the new people of God were born, which transcends the old "inheritance" of Judaism (1:3ff.). He affirms that this "inheritance" was that of which the prophets were speaking (1:10ff.)—Christians are the new temple of God, the new priesthood of God, the new people of God (2:4ff.). His apologetic here is more fitting to counter Jewish claims while the structure of Judaism was still standing, prior to A.D. 70, than after history had eloquently shattered those claims by the destruction of the Temple and the priesthood and the city of Jerusalem. The general tone of the letter concerning "Israel after the flesh," therefore, seems to reflect an earlier rather than a late date for the epistle.

Furthermore, Peter did not have reason, as did Paul, to hit this subject head-on. The Judaizers' strategy with Paul was to try to undercut the authority of his position against them by challenging his apostleship. He was not one of the Twelve, they argued; therefore, he was not an apostle, and his word carried no official weight. The question was thus forced on Paul in a fashion that necessitated a direct dealing with it. There was no question that Peter was one of the Twelve. In fact, he was the leader around whom the Twelve rallied following Jesus' death. His apostleship was never challenged, and his major ministry was to "the circumcised," so that he had no occasion to man the battlefront on this question as Paul did.

His indirect dealing with the subject in his letter, however, indicates to the readers that if the question of the difference Paul had with him were in their minds, (see Gal 2:11ff.) that difference was temporary, and involved not a permanent break in principle between them. It was rather a temporary strategic rather than a theological difference, the reason for which we do not have sufficient information to fathom. The Book of the Acts indicates that Peter was the first one to take the gospel to the Gentiles (chap. 10). He amply justified this to his cohorts in Jerusalem later (Acts 11:1ff.). Then, at the Council of Jerusalem, he spoke the decisive word which swung the judgment over to Paul's view (Acts 15:7ff.). Now, by writing to Pauline churches, he is boldly indicating that he and Paul stood shoulder to shoulder on the matter in question. All of this suggests that those who use the epistle's dealing with this question as an indication of a date later than the Fall of Jerusalem are on disputable ground.

4

WHERE WAS 1 PETER WRITTEN?

In its closing verses 1 Peter addresses the readers: "She who is at Babylon, who is likewise chosen, sends you greetings" (5:13). Who is this who offers her cordial remembrances, and from where are they sent? Some have ingeniously proposed that this was a reference to Peter's wife! Did not Paul say: do I not "have the right to be accompanied by a wife, as [does] Cephas" (1 Cor 9:5)? It seems hardly likely, however, that the author of 1 Peter was conveying family social courtesy in this way. It is much more probable that he was following a common pattern, echoed in 2 John 1:1, where "the elect lady and her children" most certainly refers to the congregation from which he is writing.

Where was Babylon?

But where was Babylon? Some have proposed that since the document is addressed to "exiles" (1:1), the reference is a metaphorical allusion not to any particular geographical place but to the fact that the Christians from where the letter comes are "exiles" in the world, living as "sojourners" among the pagans as ancient Israel did in Babylon. Since, however, Silvanus is mentioned, along with Mark (5:12ff.), neither of whom can be "metaphorized" out of concrete existence, it is hardly possible to turn "Babylon" into a geographical nonentity. If Babylon is so interpreted, then those to whom the document is addressed would likewise be living in "Babylon," and there would be no distinction between the place of origin and the destination of the writing

There would seem to be but three places to which "Babylon" could refer. One was a military camp named Babylon, located near old Cairo in Egypt. This identification can hardly he taken seriously. There is no documentary or traditional hint that Peter was ever in Egypt. Furthermore, since Mark was with him, who is traditionally connected with Rome and not with Egypt, the latter place of origin is almost indisputably ruled out.

The second possible reference would be to the old city of Babylon in Mesopotamia, to which the Jews were carried into captivity in the year 587 B.C. This is highly questionable. There had been an uprising against the Jews there near the middle of the first century which had driven most of them out. Peter, even as the apostle to the circumcision, would therefore have had little reason to go there. Furthermore, Mark was with him when he wrote, and Mark seems to have been in Rome at the time of the writing of Colossians (61-63 A.D.; Col 4:10), quite near to the likely date of 1 Peter, and would hardly have been journeying to distant Mesopotamia at that time. There is not a shred of tradition connecting Peter with ancient Babylon, although there is traditional evidence that Thomas had been there. It is quite likely, therefore, that the Babylon mentioned here is not the ancient Mesopotamian City.

Eusebius, the historian of the early church, writing around 325 A.D., speaks of Peter's first epistle "which they say he wrote in Rome itself, as is indicated by him, when he calls the City, by a figure, Babylon." The Book of Revelation indicates without possible contradiction that the early Christians used "Babylon" as a cryptic name for Rome (14:8, 16:19, et al). It has been argued that the Jews did this likewise, but not until after the Fall of Jerusalem in A.D. 70 There is no reason, however, to deduce from this that the Christians did not use this cryptic term prior to that. The destruction of Jerusalem gave the Jews *historic* reason for referring to Rome as Babylon. The Christians, however, prior to that had *theological* reasons for so doing. Even though the state, during the first decades of Christian experience, had not officially turned against them, Rome had nonetheless become for them the embodiment of what ancient Babylon represented—raw human power, pride, sensuality, and moral decay. "It is entirely unwarrranted," therefore, writes one scholar, "to claim that a usage which occurs in the New Testament has to be later than its earliest Jewish/Rabbinical occurrence." In fact, he claims that there are even instances of "secular Roman authors using 'Babylon' symbolically or metaphorically for Rome before Peter and at his time." He cites a poem by one Publius who indicts the Roman culture for having tastes clothed in Babylonish golden peacock feathers! This poem is dated at the latest in 61 A.D. and may be even earlier.

It has been suggested, too, that the "name 'Babylon' conjures up the idea of the dispersion," which would well accompany, in the writer's mind, his idea of Christians as now living in "exile" (1:1, 17) or as "aliens and exiles" (2:11). Rome, then, is the church's "place of exile." The proposal that the code name may have been used, as in the Revelation, "to scatter dust in the eyes of police censors" is hardly acceptable, in the light of the writer's view that if they behave well, the government will not bother them.

There is also internal evidence linking the document with Rome. The "manifold connections" between 1 Peter and 1 Clement, which originated at Rome, are striking. A German scholar who has made a careful study of these, demonstrates almost beyond the possibility of doubt that the two writings came from the same theological milieu. They begin with "the same liturgical introductory greeting"; they both characterize "the church as an alien company in the world"; both refer to the sufferings of Christ "not by pointing to the passion narrative but with an explicit quotation from Isaiah 53"; in both "the patriarchs are seen as fathers even of the Gentile Christians"; in both "the prophets prophesied in the Holy Spirit"; both put "God" instead of "Lord" in quoting the same passage from the Greek Old Testament. The author also adduces "a whole series of expressions [well over a dozen] that in the rest of the literature of primitive Christianity are used rarely or not at all but are employed in 1 Peter as well as in 1 Clement." Even though I Clement came some years later than 1 Peter, the evidence still suggests a common pattern of thought and language linking both documents with Rome.

There is little ground for doubting that 1 Peter originated in Rome.

Was Peter Ever in Rome?

Ths history of attempts to answer the question whether Peter ever resided in Rome is so freighted with polemic motivations that it is difficult to reach a final conclusion. A highly competent Swiss New Testament scholar, in a whole volume dealing with Peter, has traced the history of the debate—and an interesting and volatile history it is. A careful examination of the literary, liturgical and archeological sources of information led him to this conclusion: "at a time which cannot be more closely determined but probably occurred at the end of his life,

[Peter] came to Rome and there, after a very short work, died as a martyr under Nero."

The Roman Catholics, of course, have always contended that Peter was the first bishop of Rome, which necessitated a longer or shorter time of residence there. The earliest challenge to this came from the Waldensians in the 12th century. They were a group of reformers before the Reformation who, with the Bible as their sole guide, interpreted its silence about this question as final. In the 14th century, Marsilius of Padua, a lay political philosopher, opposing the Pope's insistence that "secular rulers must be subject to the papacy even in 'temporal' affairs," raised the question whether it could be proved that Peter had been bishop at Rome. At the time of the Reformation, Luther had a doubt about the question and Calvin called it an "error" that Peter had been at Rome, but neither of them made much of this in their opposition to the Pope. Since the Reformation, the question has gone back and forth among scholars almost like a tennis ball. In 1897, the leading liberal church historian in Germany would seem to have settled the question, who, criticizing Protestant scholarship for its "tendentious" prejudices, wrote that the denial of a Roman stay of Peter is "an error which today is clear to every scholar who is not blind." In spite of that, the debate goes on. I believe, however, that the bulk of present scholarship would concur with the judgment of a current German writer, who after a careful examination of the arguments, both pro and con, concluded: ". . . as a matter of method what remains but to accept the martyr death of Peter in Rome as a fact?. . . In my view, this is the result which one must reach when one uses the methods and viewpoints which are valid for historical-critical study of the first and second Christian centuries."

We conclude, therefore, that we may rest easily with the view that Peter ended his days in Rome, and that 1 Peter was written in Rome. Here, again, the place of origin does not stand in the way of Petrine authorship for 1 Peter.

5

WHAT IS THE THEOLOGICAL VIEWPOINT OF 1 PETER?

The tone of 1 Peter has been described as "mainly practical." We should, therefore, "not look to it for theology in the strict sense." The scholar who expressed this judgment, however, added that it is "packed with theology, but theology which is for the most part taken for granted rather than consciously expounded." Although the theology "is not developed in any systematic form, it is indeed substantial." The writer of 1 Peter sets out to strengthen the faith of those who were relatively new converts, and to keep them from abandoning their faith under the pressure of persecution. He therefore sticks pretty closely to what the author of Hebrews called "the elementary doctrines of Christ" (6:1) and stresses the foundation truths on which the superstructure of faith rests.

Unlike Paul, who was frequently defending the faith against the errors springing either from Jewish or Gentile misunderstandings which were tending to change the gospel into a "different gospel" (Gal 1:6), 1 Peter was designed to keep his readers from abandoning the gospel entirely. For Paul, the issue was frequently *one gospel versus another gospel*. For 1 Peter is was *gospel versus no gospel*.

The differences from Paul, therefore, are marked. Not that Peter was in irreconcilable conflict with Paul. He would not "dissent from the general strain of St. Paul's teaching, much less stand in any sort of antagonism to him." In fact, 1 Peter has so many likenesses to the theology of Paul that many have argued that it is dependent on Paul's letters. That view is now pretty widely discarded, the likenesses being explained on the ground of the common fund of Christian tradition out of which they both came. In spite of these likenesses, the differences are marked.

In 1 Peter there is no discussion of justification by faith; no mention of the tension between faith and works, such as is prominent in Paul and James; there is no explicit discussion of the problem of the law; the word "church" is never used; the idea of the church as "the body of Christ" does not occur; sin is related more to sinful acts than to the principle of inner rebellion which overpowers and alienates us from God; the words "cross" and "crucify" are entirely absent; the word "flesh" describes physical existence rather than the "willing instrument of sin," as in Paul; and there is prominent stress on Christ's sufferings as an example which is lacking in Paul. These features seem to suggest a simpler, less sophisticated theological outlook than that of Paul, and are appropriate to the situation faced in 1 Peter, where the a, b, c's of belief and behavior were presented to Christians young in the faith who were tempted, under pressure of ostracism and suffering, to abandon it.

What Is the Teaching about God?

The teaching about God in 1 Peter relies heavily on the Old Testament and reflects a Jewish rather than a Greek background. God is a God of mercy, who by His own initiative has brought us into being as Christians (1:3), whose power guards us through the vicissitudes of life (1:5), and gives us hope through Christ whom He has raised from the dead (1:21). He is a holy God, who expects His followers to emulate His holiness (1:14-16). Though merciful, He is the final judge, because of which Christians should live their lives in reverential fear (1:17, 2:12). He who called ancient Israel into being has now fulfilled His ultimate intention by bringing the Christian community into being, to offer spiritual sacrifices unto Him through Jesus Christ (2:4-10). Obedience to God's will is the standard by which Christian behavior is to be measured (2:15, 3:17, 4:2, 19). God is absolutely a trustworthy Being who cares for His people in this life and assures them of a share in His glory in the life to come (5:1, 4, 7, 10).

Although no doctrine of the Trinity is developed in 1 Peter, and Jesus is never explicitly called God's Son, the trinitarian view is implicit in the description of God as "the Father of our Lord Jesus Christ" (1:3), in the implied pre-existence of Christ who was "destined before the foundation of the world" (1:20), and the mention of God, the Spirit, and Christ in close juxtaposition in 1:2.

What Is the Teaching about Jesus?

The picture of Jesus begins in eternity, as the expression "made manifest" in 1:20 suggests. The basic meaning of this expression is "to make visible what is invisible," implying that what is "made manifest" does not come into being at that moment, but rather that something already existing in the invisible realm is now made visible. Although one cannot know with absolute certainty, the judgment of a very learned and careful scholar would seem to be valid: "Taken by itself, the word suggests a previous hidden existence, and it was not likely to be chosen except in this implied sense." Jesus, therefore, existed before he was born!

His coming was foreseen by the prophets (1:10-12), so that His entrance from eternity into time was the climax of God's action through the whole history of Israel. He was not a mere detached portent, an inexplicable prodigy or freakish eruption into history, but was the fulfillment of a definite divine intention nurtured in the heart of God from all eternity, and historically prepared for by the partial and metaphorical self-revelation of God throughout the Old Testament. He came out of a background which gave His coming meaning. He was the cornerstone of a spiritual temple built up of those who believe in and worship Him (2:4ff), who become the new people of God (2:10), whose function in the world is to "declare the wonderful deeds of him who called [them] out of darkness into his marvelous light" (2:9) so that all mankind may no longer "walk in darkness, but . . . have the light of life" (John 8:12). This One who came from eternity into time was "manifested" in a wholly human life. In His life, as the "suffering servant" of Isaiah 53, He manifested what obedience of a human life to the will of God entails, as an example to His people (2:21-23). In His sacrificial death "like a lamb without blemish or spot" (1:19), He redeemed humanity from sin and became "the Shepherd and Guardian" of their souls (2:24f.; 3:18). He was raised from the dead by God, through which those who believe in Him are "born anew to a living hope (1:3f.). Following His resurrection, He ascended to "the right hand of God" where He reigns as hidden ruler over the universe (3:22). He will again be "manifested" at the end of the age, when those who have owned Him as Lord will share in His final glory (1:13; 4:13; 5:1, 4, 10).

What Is the Teaching about the Holy Spirit?

1 Peter has no developed doctrine of the Holy Spirit. Some have used this as evidence that it comes from a late date, for, they say a lack of emphasis on the Holy Spirit was not characteristic of the early church. One scholar has argued that "the sense of the active presence of the Spirit has fallen into eclipse," and adds that it is "utterly inconceivable that to Peter . . . the doctrine of the indwelling Spirit was wholly unknown, or was not of the first importance for the moral life of the Christian." He concludes from this that the document is "the product of a later generation." An examination of the document, however, leaves this argument with little force. As a matter of fact, the writer does mention, in the second verse of his writing, that the Holy Spirit is "of the first importance for the moral life of the Christian"—it is the Holy Spirit who is the source of "sanctification" in the life of the believer (1:2). But beyond that, it must he kept in mind that the author was not setting forth his theology, but sending a practical message of instruction, encouragement and warning. We have no idea of what his complete doctrine of the Holy Spirit was, but his failure to elucidate it in no way denies that he had one. The letter to the Colossians never once mentions the Holy Spirit. Does that mean that Paul, or whoever of Paul's followers may have written Colossians, had no doctrine of the Holy Spirit? The author is content to mention the work of the Spirit in enabling believers to embody the gospel in their lives (1:2), in conjoining the preaching of the prophets in the Old Testament with the preaching of the gospel in the New (1:12), and in enabling believers to "glorify God through suffering" (4:14).

What Is the Teaching about Redemption?

The redemptive work of Christ lies at the heart of the message of 1 Peter. The author introduces the death of Christ in his initial greeting in the opening salutation (1:2). He sees in the Old Testament foregleams of the glory which was to arise out of the "sufferings of Christ" (1:10ff.). He presents Christ as the sacrificial lamb who "ransomed" men from futility (1:18f.). He affirms that Christ "bore our sins in his body on the tree, that we might die to sin and live to righteousness" (2:24). He insists that Christ "died for sins once for all, the righteous for the unrighteous, that he might bring us to God" (3:18).

The death of Jesus is always seen in the light of the resurrection which follows. The dynamic power of Jesus' death functions in the believer through "the resurrection of Jesus Christ from the dead" (1:3). The saving efficacy of Jesus "ransom" is appropriated through "confidence in God, who raised him from the dead and gave him glory" (1:21). The One who "died for sins once for all" was subsequently "made alive in the spirit" (3:18). The author, who witnessed "the sufferings of Christ;" is also "a partaker of the glory that is to be revealed" through the resurrection (5:1).

The atoning work of Christ through His death and resurrection is the work of pure grace. We can only "bless" God who has done all this not by our merit but "by his great mercy" (1:3). As children have nothing to do with their birth, but exist by grace of the decision of their parents, we had nothing to do with being "born anew." The "resurrection of Jesus" (1:3), and "the living and abiding word" of the gospel by which we "have been born anew" (1:23), were the outcome of a decision of God made "before the foundation of the world" (1:20). This is all a gift from God, nothing that we have earned or deserved. And yet, 1 Peter is perhaps unique in the New Testament in his juxtaposing the "sufferings of Christ" for our redemption with His examplariness—"because Christ also suffered for you, leaving you an example, that you should follow in his steps" (2:21). Grace is a gift, but also a demand. As a French writer has put it: 1 Peter insists "on the connection between grace and union with the sufferings of Christ." The gift of grace becomes the task of life.

What Is the Teaching about the Church?

Another marked feature of the theology of 1 Peter is its view of the relation of the church to ancient Israel. There is a widespread concurrence among the writers of the New Testament that the church is the goal toward which ancient Israel was pointing. Paul actually transferred the name "Israel" to the church when he called it "the Israel of God (Gal 6:16). Without using that language, 1 Peter stresses the idea perhaps more than any other writer in the New Testament, save the author of Hebrews. He describes the Christians as having "an inheritance" (1:4). This immediately brings to mind such Old Testament passages as

Psalm 105:11: "To you I will give the land of Canaan as your portion for an inheritance." Abraham waited a lifetime for this, but received only a burial place for Sarah. Several centuries went by before his descendants entered into this land. It was a precarious inheritance, however. They were challenged for it continuously by surrounding peoples. David temporarily secured it, but under Solomon it began to disintegrate. Two centuries later the northern part of the inheritance was permanently wrested from them. A century and a half after that the southern part fell. A half century later, part of the inheritance was restored, but it existed precariously under the Persians, the Greeks and the Romans until it was finally lost in 70 A.D.

The Christians, beginning with Stephen, detached Israel's inheritance from the Holy Land as such, spiritualizing it into a "sanctioned and settled possession" in the heart of God. They saw the inheritance of Palestine as a temporary and symbolic preparation for a far greater and more permanent *spiritual* inheritance in the gift of unbroken communion with God. The ancient people of God were freed from Egypt that they might "sacrifice to the Lord [their] God" (Exod 8:27) and "serve" Him (Exod 9:1), and that the Egyptians might know that God was "Lord in the midst of the earth" (Exod 8:22). They were brought into the land of Canaan "to serve the Lord [their] God, to walk in all his ways, to love him, to serve the Lord [their] God with all [their] heart and with all [their] soul" (Deut 10:12). To the Christian, this all became an object lesson pointing forward to a greater, an "eternal inheritance" (Heb 9:15), which is not of material things but is "imperishable, undefiled, and unfading," kept in heaven for those who wait for it in faith (1 Pet 1:4). The Old Testament inheritance was a temporary, visible pattern of spiritual realities which transcend time and space. The geographical Jerusalem was transformed into "the Jerusalem above," the "heavenly Jerusalem" (Gal 4:26, Heb 12:22).

What the prophets spoke about Israel's inheritance was, therefore, now fulfilled in the church. To the writer of 1 Peter, to be "exiled" was no longer to be away from the Holy Land; but away from God (1:1, 17). The ancient Temple was transformed into "a spiritual house" of worship, built out of "living stones" gathered around Christ, the "chosen and precious" cornerstone. The old priesthood was now replaced by the "holy priesthood" of those who had faith in Christ, who offered "spiritual sacrifices" instead of the "blood of bulls and goats" (2:4-10). Even the Gentiles, who had heretofore been "alienated from the commonwealth of Israel, and strangers to the covenants of promise, having no hope and without God in the world" (Eph 2:12), were now a part of the "one new man" in Christ. Those who were once "no people" now are a part of the "chosen race, a royal priesthood, a holy nation, God's own people" (2:9).

For 1 Peter, it was not a question of a new "sect " seeking "to establish its superiority" over its rival, but rather "the expression of a very profound sense of continuity" between the Old and the New Israel. The church was what God had in mind all the time, from the days when He called Abraham in whom "all the nations" of the earth would be blessed (Gen 12:3. Gal 3:8). God had finally achieved in the church what He promised from the beginning. The church, therefore, unfolded by a natural progression out of Israel. The church was at one and the same time very old and very new. The promise to Abraham was now fulfilled in all those, Jews and Gentiles alike, who are "one new man," both reconciled to God through Jesus Christ (Eph 2:15). 1 Peter does not use Paul's words, but it is in hearty agreement with him when he said: "it is men of faith who are the sons of Abraham. . . . There is neither Jew nor Greek, . . . for you are all one in Christ Jesus" (Gal 3:7, 28).

What Is the Doctrine of the Ministry?

There is no highly developed doctrine of the ministry in 1 Peter. The one reference to it indicates that the ministers were "elders," not "bishops," pastor overseers rather than "bishops" in the ecclesiastical sense. Their function was purely pastoral, to "tend the flock of God" under the leadership of Jesus, "the chief Shepherd" (5:1ff.). This suggests an early date for the document. By the end of the first century, a highly developed doctrine of the ministry was evolving. "Bishops" rather than "elders" began to emerge as authorities in the church and as the officers around whom the church functioned. Ignatius of Antioch, who died no later than the second decade of the second century A.D, but whose views of the ministry must have been fixed prior to that, insisted on a far more highly developed church organization than is apparent in 1 Peter. Although his ecclesiastical order "was enforced almost solely as a security for doctrinal purity," nonetheless he insisted on a threefold ministry of bishops, presbyters (elders) and deacons as essential to the being of the Church. The simplicity of church order reflected in 1 Peter long antedates the end of the first century.

What Is the Relation of 1 Peter's Theology to Peter's Speeches in the Acts?

The theological affirmations of 1 Peter are strangely reminiscent of Peter's speeches recorded in the early chapters of the Acts. It cannot be proved that Luke's recording of Peter's speeches in Acts contains the very wording used by Peter on those occasions. Luke was not present and did not hear him speak. As an historian he was dependent on either oral or fragmentary written sources for his information. But whatever his source, he must have had reason for depicting Peter as he did, seeking to make the speeches representative of what he knew about Peter. There are many suggestive parallels between Peter's addresses and the content and wording of 1 Peter. This is not the place to argue the case in multiform detail. It will suffice to give but a few illustrations which stem from the work of scholars who have done so.

Peter opens his address at Pentecost in Acts by citing the event as the fulfillment of the prophecy of Joel—the "outpouring of the Spirit of Prophecy on the Church" (Acts 2:14ff.). How much like this is 1 Peter's word about "the Spirit of Christ" speaking in the prophets concerning "the things which have now been announced . . by those who preached the good news to you through the Holy Spirit sent from heaven, . . ." (1:10ff.). In Acts Christ's death is "according to the definite plan and foreknowledge of God" (2:23). In 1 Peter the lamb whose blood was shed was "destined before the foundation of the world" (1:19f.). In Acts it is declared that when Jesus died, His flesh did not "see corruption" (2:31). 1 Peter insists that although Jesus was "put to death in the flesh" yet He was "made alive in the spirit" (3:18), implying that his flesh did not see corruption. In Acts Christ's resurrection and exaltation "at the right hand of God" are closely linked (2:33). In 1 Peter we read that God "raised him from the dead and gave him glory" (1:21), and that the resurrected One "has gone into heaven and is at the right hand of God" (3:22f.). In Acts the healings are done "in the name of Jesus Christ" (3:6, 16; 4:30), and the sufferings of the Christian were for the "name" of Christ (Acts 4:17, 18; 5:28, 40; 9:16), and in 1 Peter the sufferings of the Christians are described as being "reproached for the name of Christ" (4:14). In Peter's speech recorded in Acts 4:11 he speaks of "the stone which was rejected by you builders, but which has become the head of the corner." Although this figure is found in the Gospels, 1 Peter is the only New Testament epistle which takes it up; and not only takes it up but develops it at length (2:4ff.). Twice in Peter's speeches in the Acts he speaks of the cross as the "tree" (5:30; 10:39), which expression is found also in 1 Peter (2:24). There is one instance where Paul used this expression (Acts 13:29), but it was done very early in his career in addressing Jews in a Synagogue, indicating that the expression was a Semitic one used early in the church's experience, but not later. In making his first speech to Gentiles at the home of Cornelius, Peter is recorded as saying, "Truly I perceive that God shows no partiality" (Acts 10:34). 1 Peter 1:17 speaks of God "who judges each one impartially." Parallel instances of this type could be multiplied, while more subtle affinities of thought yield themselves to careful search. These are sufficient, however, to warrant the conclusion of one careful scholar, that the close parallels between Peter's speeches in the Acts and 1 Peter "are what might be expected if both alike are utterances of the same mind . . . the common ground lies in the mind of St. Peter who gave, and was known to have given, teaching along these lines and to a great extent in these terms."

The theological and ecclesiastical outlook of 1 Peter, then, "betrays many signs of great antiquity," and reflects "an early period of the Christian Church's existence." The "theology, the ethics and the 'tone' of the writing is all in keeping with an early period of the Christian Church's existence." 1 Peter "agrees with the position of St. Peter as represented in the Acts, and that representation is consistent with all known evidence and probability, and may safely be trusted." These judgments of three eminent scholars lead us to the conclusion that there is little reason to believe that the theological substance and terminology of 1 Peter could not have come from Peter himself.

6

WHO WROTE 1 PETER?

Thus far we have been content to refer to the literary originator of 1 Peter as "the author," or "the writer," leaving his specific identity an open question. It is time now to take a hard look at the one to whom the cumulative evidence has been pointing, and face squarely the problem of who it was who wrote 1 Peter.

It is rather surprising that this should be such a debated question. Its first words are: "Peter, an apostle of Jesus Christ." Can this not be taken at face value? We have seen that when the evidence is closely examined, from the literary nature of the document itself, or from the elements in the document which suggest its date, or from the standpoint of the theology of its contents, there is little reason to believe that Peter could not have written it. Why, then, not accept Petrine authorship?

The fact is, however, that many do not accept it, and are firmly persuaded that it came from some other source. It is necessary, therefore, to take their views seriously and to face the questions they raise openly and, I hope, without prejudice.

Who Did the Early Church Think Wrote 1 Peter?

It may be well to begin with a look at the evidence on which the early church based their judgment as to the authorship of 1 Peter. We have already noted the remarkable likeness of vocabulary between Clement of Rome, one of the church fathers who wrote around 95 A. D., and 1 Peter (see p. 45). He is silent about Petrine authorship but reflects the vocabulary and thought of 1 Peter so strikingly that it is not stretching credulity to think that he was familiar with it. Could it be that his silence about authorship reflects the fact that it was not a problem at that time?

Similar echoes of 1 Peter are found in several second century church fathers, the most decisive of which is in Polycarp, who was martyred in 155 A.D. and who, not long before his death, wrote an epistle to the Christians in Philippi. He makes unmistakable quotations from 1 Peter, such as: "in whom, though now ye see Him not, ye believe, and believing rejoice with joy unspeakable and full of glory" (1:8); or "Him who raised up our Lord Jesus Christ from the dead, and gave Him glory" (1:21), or "who bore our sins in His body on the tree" (2:24); or "who did no sin, neither was guile found in His mouth" (2:22). These indicate an undoubted acquaintance with the epistle, although he does not name Peter as the author. Polycarp does mention Paul, which has been used as evidence that he did not know who wrote 1 Peter, or he would likewise have named him. There was special reason to mention Paul, however, for he too had written to the Philippians, and Polycarp was reminding them of that. He freely quotes other authors whom he does not name.

Another church father, Irenaeus, writing in the early years of the third century, quotes several times from 1 Peter, and introduces his quotations with statements such as: "Peter says in his Epistle." Thereafter, the "chain . . . of evidence" for Petrine authorship is strong, with the exception of its omission from the Muratorian Canon, which is the earliest listing of the books of the New Testament, from somewhere near the end of the second century. This work, however, is mutilated, and no final judgment may be drawn from that.

The church historian Eusebius, writing sometime around 323-325 A.D., clearly distinguishes between "disputed" works and those which were "universally accepted, . . . genuine and acknowledged by the ancient elders." He rejects the genuineness of all the works ascribed to Peter, of which there were several, with the one exception: "One epistle of Peter, that called the first, is acknowledged as genuine."

When the available evidence from the early church is carefully examined, the conclusion of an English scholar seems to be justified: "There is no book in the New Testament which has earlier, better, or stronger attestation" than 1 Peter. Its authenticity was unanimously accepted until the latter part of the eighteenth century, when a German scholar first questioned it. Since that time this issue has been the subject of vigorous debate.

Since the external evidence for Petrine authorship is so solid, those who deny it must rely on internal evidence alone. In so doing, they often too easily pass over the problem of how formidable a hurdle the external evidence is. Can it be so summarily dismissed? Eusebuis' words quoted above, distinguishing between "disputed" and "universally accepted" works, indicate that the early church fathers were neither ignorant of critical problems, nor possessed of a bent to attribute apostolic authorship where it was doubtful. Serapion, the bishop of Antioch, writing near the end of the second century, said: "For our part . . . we receive both Peter and the other apostles as Christ; but we reject intelligently the writings falsely ascribed to them, knowing that such were not handed down to us." This shows that the early church fathers were not "willingly deceived" about such matters, but also displays a certain degree of sophistication in determining them. Such a secure place in the canon as 1 Peter enjoyed was not lightly nor easily attained.

Much questioning of traditional authorship of New Testament books seems to be based on sheer assumption rather than solid argument. A British scholar has recently argued that there is "an appetite for pseudonymity [works bearing fictitious or assumed names] that grows by what it feeds on." He quotes writers who refer to the "very common . . . practice" of pseudonymity; or who assert that "possibly two-thirds of the New Testament writings are pseudonymous"; or who affirm that pseudonymity "is almost a way of life in the world of the New Testament and also in the New Testament itself." He comments: "Certainly it is among New Testament scholars!" One writer he refers to concludes: "This, alone, shows the influence of pseudepigraphy in the early church." The British scholar then adds: "If you believe it is everywhere, you cease to have to argue for it anywhere." But, he insists, although assumed authorship may have been rife among *heretical* writings at the time of the early church, "if we ask what is the evidence for orthodox epistles being composed in the name of apostles within a generation or two of their lifetime, and for this being an acceptable literary convention within the church, the answer is nil ."

Heretics did try to pass off their works under the names of apostles, but "these were never accepted as such by the church." Paul certanly took a dim view of letters purporting to have been written by him which he did not write. He tells his readers "not to be quickly shaken in mind or excited, either by spirit or by word, or by letter purporting to be from us" (2 Thess 2:2). To forestall such a practice, he resorted to signing letters dictated to others with his "own hand," saying: "This is the mark in every letter of mine; it is the way I write" (2 Thess 3:17). Paul, at least, knew of "no harmless literary convention" of this sort. Another scholar cites an instance of a writer near the end of the second century being deposed from his ministry for falsely issuing works under the name of Paul. "The author," he says, "was orthodox; he . . . made strenuous efforts after verisimilitude. He was, furthermore, inflamed with the noblest *pietas*, love of Paul, and it was with the best of intentions that he wrote. Yet he was deposed—for forgery." False attribution of authorship was "not merely not tolerated but emphatically condemned."

Although some scholars make much of the lack of external evidence for the authorship of New Testament books, they seem unaware that "it is surely much more significant that at no point is there the slightest external testimony to the collusion in innocent falsification to which appeal is so constantly made. . . ." One writer sums up the matter thus: those who hold to non-Petrine authorship of 1 Peter are "forced to suggest a pseudo-authorship which succeeded in getting the epistle through the mesh of early Christian suspicion and facilitated its emergence without challenge in an incredibly short time to take its place among the genuine epistles."

Could Peter Have Written Greek?

One of the favorite, and more formidable, arguments to deny Petrine authorship to 1 Peter is that the Apostle Peter could not have known and written Greek, or at least would not have had a command of Greek embodied in the epistle which bears his name. Was he not a fisherman of limited education, described in the Acts as an "uneducated, common" man (Acts 4:13). What of this?

In the first place, those who branded Peter as "uneducated" were a group of "supercilious Sanhedrists, preoccupied with Hebrew purism and contemptuous of Aramaic spoken with a broad Galilean accent." It was the sort of remark that a group of Harvard professors might have made about the longshoreman immigrant, Eric Hofer, who became a practical philosopher and newspaper columnist. One can imagine them disagreeing with one of his columns by saying: "What does an uneducated laborer know about these things?" The word in itself may mean simply "untutored" or "unschooled," without academic credentials, without the imprimatur of the learned authorities. It does not necessarily have anything to do with one's native intellectual ability. It could mean only that Peter had no credentials as a religious leader from the rabbinic college of Jerusalem! Also, as has been pointed out, "what struck the authorities [about the apostles] was what they were capable of *despite*" their lack of training.

Furthermore, Peter's social standing may not have been as modest as we are sometimes led to think. We know, at least, that Zebedee, the father of James and John, was a businessman with hired employees (Mark 1:20), whose business may have furnished him with a fair degree of financial and social status in the community. As friends of his, Andrew and Peter may have enjoyed a relatively secure social position. The fisherfolk of Galilee have been described as "a prosperous and intelligent body of men, engaged in the busiest industry of the region." But social position or not, who can say what Peter's native intellectual gifts were? As reported in the Acts, he certainly had gifts of leadership and of speech, which made him stand out in his group as pre-eminent.

Peter's boyhood and early manhood were spent in Bethsaida, not far from where the Jordan river joins the Sea of Galilee (John 1:44). Greek influences had spread into this area ever since the days of Alexander the Great. Later, under the Seleucids, when Antiochus Epiphanes tried to remake Palestine into a Greek area, against which the Maccabees rebelled, there were many Jews who went along with the mood. Bethsaida was a bilingual community, near the Decapolis region, where the majority of the population were Gentile and Greek-speaking. A herd of swine at one of them, Gadara, numbering "about two thousand" (Mark 5:13), certainly indicates a large non-Jewish population. It has been estimated that the Greek inhabitants of the area may have been as many as a million. Peter's brother, Andrew, and his friend Philip, both had Greek names, showing how widespread were Hellenistic influences even among the Jews. Anyone who grew up in Bethsaida, therefore, "understood Greek and was familiar with Hellenistic culture." It has been said: "To suggest that a Jewish boy growing up in Galilee would not know Greek would be rather like suggesting that a Welsh boy brought up in Cardiff would not know English."

There is evidence that Greek was spoken even in the Jerusalem area of Palestine. Stone coffins, dating from the first century A.D. or earlier, have been unearthed in the vicinity. Of one group of them, 97 carried Hebrew or Aramaic inscriptions, 64 were in Greek, and 14 were bilingual, indicating how much Greek was in use at that time in and near Jerusalem. Although the plaque unearthed by archaeologists from the Temple entrance in Jerusalem, warning Gentiles to stay out on pain of death, was written in Greek so that the Gentiles could read it, it suggests that "Greek was assumed to be the language which . . . every Gentile in Jerusalem could read and understand. Therefore, if the Jews in Jerusalem spoke with Gentiles at all . . . they probably would have spoken in Greek." There is also an inscription written in Greek from the wall of a synagogue built on the hill south of the Temple area, indicating that its builder was a ruler of the synagogue and the son and grandson of synagogue rulers.

The name "Sanhedrin," which described "the highest governing body in Judea," composed of high priests, elders, and scholars, and meeting under the presiding of the ruling high priest, is a Greek word, showing how much Greek influence had crept into official Jewish cicles in Jerusalem. It is significant, too, that when Pilate had Jesus crucified, he placarded the accusation against Him: "Jesus of Nazareth, the King of the Jews," in three languages, "in Hebrew, in Latin, and in Greek" (John 19:20).

A scholar of unimpeachable credentials has concluded: "that the most commonly used language of Palestine in the first century A.D. was Aramaic, but that many Palestinian Jews, not only those in Hellenistic towns, but farmers and craftsmen of less obviously Hellenized areas used Greek, at least as a second language . . . in fact, there is indication . . . that some Palestinians spoke only Greek."

Much has been made by some of the fact that an early church father, Papias, described Mark as an "interpreter" of Peter, deducing from this that Peter could not speak Greek, and needed his Aramaic translated into Greek by Mark. Such use of this passage is ruled out for the following reasons:

1. The word "interpreter" is used by others to mean "amanuensis," or one who writes for another—a secretary, rather than a translator from one language into another. This is the natural meaning in Papias' statement, when taken in its setting. He says: "Mark, having become the interpreter of Peter, wrote down accurately . . . whatsoever he remembered of the things said or done by Christ." He adds later that "Mark committed no error while he thus wrote some things as he remembered them." The role of interpreter here was not to translate Peter's language into another language, but to record what he remembered having heard him say. Papias also said: Mark "was careful of one thing,

not to omit any of the things which he had heard, and not to state any of them falsely." The purpose of Papias' statement, therefore, is to authenticate the Gospel by Mark through stressing "Mark's closeness to Peter, not to provide information about Peter's linguistic abilities."

2. Another church father, Clement of Alexandria, relates a similar tradition about Mark's relationship to Peter. He writes: "Mark, the follower of Peter, while Peter was preaching publicly the gospel at Rome in the presence of certain of Caesar's knights . . . being requested by them that they might he able to commit to memory the things which were being spoken, wrote, from the things which were being spoken by Peter, the Gospel which is called according to Mark." Here Peter is preaching publicly in Rome with no mention of an interpreter, and Mark's function is to remember and write down what Peter had said.

Further evidence that Peter must certainly have known Greek lies in the necessities of carrying on his missionary work. To be the apostle "of the circumcision" even in Jerusalem would have required a knowledge of Greek, for there were many Greek-speaking Jews living in Jerusalem (Acts 6:1ff.). Peter worked also in Caesarea (Acts 10), a Hellenistic city; in Antioch (Gal 2:11); likely in Corinth (1 Cor 9:5); and in Rome. It is "inconceivable," remarks one scholar, that Peter "can have exercised any kind of leading ministry in Antioch or even Jerusalem, let alone in Rome, without the use of Greek."

Many have sought to justify the quality of Greek in 1 Peter by suggesting that Silvanus was his amanuensis—the ideas are Peter's but the language is that of Silvanus. 1 Peter concludes: "By Silvanus, a faithful brother as I regard him, I have written briefly to you" (5:12). The problem here is whether the preposition "by" suggests a secretary or rather the "bearer" of the letter. Silvanus is likely the Latinized form of the name of Paul's friend, Silas (Acts 15:40). The arguments as to whether Silvanus was the "scribe" or the "bearer" of the letter seem to be somewhat indecisive. Although I once thought otherwise, the evidence for him as "bearer" seems more compelling.

Tertius, the scribe of Paul's letter to the Romans, appended a personal greeting in his own name (Rom 16:22), which we might have expected from Silvanus if he were the writer, but this is lacking in 1 Peter. The commendation "a faithful brother" would have been somewhat embarrassing to Silvanus if he were the penman, although it is possible that Peter may have dictated such an expression for him to write. The style of the letter, too, seems to be more direct than would be likely for an amanuensis to have developed were he writing another man's thoughts. The experience of Silas after the Council of Jerusalem would be an exact parallel if he were the "bearer" rather than the "writer" of the letter. The Acts tells us that he and one other, "leading men among the brethren," were "sent" with the letter to the church at Antioch (Acts 15:22). Furthermore, after the letter was read, they were to "tell . . . the same things by word of mouth" which the apostles had written (Acts 15:27). It would seem that Peter likewise chose Silvanus to be the "bearer" of his letter to the churches in Asia Minor. He mentions the fact that he has written "briefly," suggesting that there is much more to be said than he has written. He also accredits Silvanus as "a faithful brother," indicating that he expects him to elaborate the letter's contents by word of mouth, with his full approval.

The Silvanus theory to account for the Greek of the letter, therefore, seems unnecessary. His role as "bearer" of the letter is more in accord with what we would expect, and fits the facts well.

Who can know what Peter's linguistic gifts were? The novelist, Joseph Conrad, spoke Polish as his mother tongue. At the age of 17 he joined the French navy, and learned French. It was not until the age of 23, when he became an officer in the British merchant marine, that English became his third language. Yet he produced what is considered to be some of the finest English writing known. He wrote to a friend: "My first English reading was the . . . newspaper, and my first acquaintance by the ear with it was in the speech of fishermen, shipwrights and sailors. But in 1880 I had 'mastered' the language sufficiently to pass the first examination for officers . . . . But 'mastered' is not the right word; I should have said 'acquired.' I've never opened an English grammar in my life."

To give an instance from my own experience, a French student some years ago arrived in America in September to do graduate theological study, without ever having had any instruction in English. About seven months later he read a paper in a Greek seminar I was conducting on 1 Peter in flawless English! Also, I once had a guide on a trip to Morocco who spoke quite good English. When I asked him where he had learned English, he replied: "In talking to people like you."

Knowing how much Greek was spoken in Peter's environment as a youth, and how much time he spent as an adult in Greek-speaking surroundings, to deny him the possibility of writing the sort of Greek found in 1 Peter is to make a vacuous assumption for which little evidence can be amassed. As one scholar has expressed it: "There may be many valid arguments against the assumption of apostolic authorship to 1 Peter . . . but the linguistic argument can no longer be used with confidence among them."

Would Peter Have Included More Personal References to Jesus?

It has been argued that if 1 Peter were written by Peter, it would have contained more personal recollections of Jesus' life and words. We have already dealt with this to some extent, showing that there were many subtle reflections of the words of Jesus in the epistle (see pp. 29ff.); but it may be well to pursue the matter a bit further. Scholars who give this argument force, seem to me to be in danger of arguing in a circle. On the one hand, they insist that if Peter wrote the letter, it would have contained more personal memories. On the other hand, when such are pointed out in the letter, it is denied that they are personal recollections. Given this situation, it is difficult to reach a conclusion.

To demand that the letter should contain more direct memories of Jesus is a purely subjective requisition. It is in effect saying: This is not the way I would have done it had I been Peter! Who can get inside the mind of a writer and insist that if he were the one he is claimed to be, he would of necessity have done it the way I would? In all fairness, can we not allow the writer the freedom to write what he wanted to write rather than what we think he should have written? And had the letter been full of references to personal experiences of Peter with Jesus, these would have been discredited as the marks of a forged document. It is precisely on such grounds that many reject 2 Peter as nonapostolic. And the apocryphal writings are rejected precisely because, to give them credence, they were filled with "pretended recollections." As one has remarked: "Certainly the fact that any claims or allusions are so indirect argues more strongly against pseudonymity than authenticity."

But beyond the echoing of the words of Jesus, there are reflections of Peter's personal experiences with Jesus, sometimes subtle but eloquent to the sensitive reader. Could anyone but one who knew Jesus have written: "Without having seen him you love him; though you do not now see him you believe in him and rejoice with unutterable and exalted joy (1:8)? Someone observed: "Paul could never have said this." The clear implication here is that although *you* have never seen Him, *I have!* It has been well remarked: "Those who have not seen and yet have believed are what they are because there once were men who believed because they did actually see." And who but an eyewitness of Jesus in His demeanor with the mob in the Garden and at His trial could have written: "He committed no sin; no guile was found on his lips. When he was reviled, he did not revile in return; when he suffered, he did not threaten" (2:22f.)? "Does it not burst upon one's vision," asks a German writer, "that here Jesus' way of suffering appears as a vivid pictorial contrast to Peter, exactly as his counter portrait? In his mouth was guile, as he denied Christ; he threatened with the sword, as Jesus was arrested." Also Peter describes himself as "a witness of the sufferings of Christ as well as a partaker in the glory that is to be revealed" (5:1). He here surely means something other than his statement that his readers "share Christ's sufferings" and "may also rejoice and be glad when his glory is revealed" (4:13). In the latter expression he is speaking of his readers' *future* experience of sharing Christ's glory, whereas in the former expression he speaks as though he had *already been* a partaker in that glory. What can his claim to be "a witness of the sufferings of Christ" mean other than that he was present during Jesus's passion? And what can his claim to have been "a partaker in the glory of Christ" mean other than that he was present at the Transfiguration, which has a proleptic experience of Jesus' resurrection and final glorification, and had also participated in the postresurrection appearances of His Lord (see pp. 333ff.)?

Other references could be cited, but these are sufficient to indicate that 1 Peter *does* contain recollections of Peter's experience of Jesus; but since they are not the subject of his writing, they find their way into the document in natural, subtle ways, which is just what one would expect under the circumstances. He did not need unnaturally to load his text with personal recollections of Jesus, which were not the subject on which he was writing. And since he didn't, are we to conclude that he had not been with Jesus? My grandfather, at about 14 years of age, lied about his years and entered the Union army during the Civil War. For some reason, he never discussed his war experiences with his grandchildren. Does that mean he had not had them?

Would Peter Have Written so Pauline a Letter?

Another argument against Petrine authorship is that the theology of 1 Peter is too close to that of Paul to have come from the pen of his rival, Peter. The answer to this objection seems clear. First, as we have already noted (see pp. 47f.), although 1 Peter embodies theological likenesses to Paul's writings, yet the major distinctive Pauline accents do not appear. It is plain from this that Peter was drawing on a common source of Christian tradition which he and Paul shared rather than repeating Paul's *distinctive* views. A differentiation is to be made between *affinity* and *dependence*. Furthermore, Peter, being in Rome from where he wrote 1 Peter, most likely would have read Paul's letter to the Roman Church. He had also conversed with Paul at length on more than one occasion (Gal 1:18, 2:9; Acts 15; Gal 2:11), and knew his theology well enough to reflect some of it in a general way in his own writing.

Second, why should he not have had a broad likeness to Paul's theology in his own writing? The so-called rivalry, or major theological disagreement, between Peter and Paul has been greatly exaggerated. In fact, it may be totally a mythology. There is a wide difference between diverse *emphases* and *disagreement*. With one exception, everything that the New Testament tells us about the relationship of Peter and Paul indicates a warm and cordial personal feeling between them, and a hearty agreement in theology. It is true that "Peter had been entrusted with the gospel to the circumcised" and Paul "had been entrusted with the gospel to the uncircumcised" (Gal 2:7), but *different tasks* and *different methods* and *different emphases* do not mean *disagreement* or rivalry. The missionary to India is not a rival of the missionary to Africa, any more than the orthopedist is an enemy of the internist in medicine. In fact, on the very occasion when the division of labor between Paul and Peter was determined, Paul says that "James and Cephas and John . . . . gave to me and Barnabas the right hand of fellowship, that we should go to the Gentiles and they to the circumcised" (Gal 2:9).

Peter was the first to preach to and baptize a Gentile (Acts 10). When he was criticized for so doing, he defended his behavior vigorously (Acts 11:4). When Paul's ministry to the Gentiles was put on trial at the Council of Jerusalem, it was Peter who settled the issue by a strong defense of Paul's work. In so doing, he took a theological position very similar to that of Paul by calling the law "a yoke . . . which neither our fathers nor we have been able to bear," and concluding with Paul's distinctive doctrine of justification by faith: "But we believe that we shall be saved through the grace of the Lord Jesus, just as they will" (Acts 15:7ff.). Unquestionably, Peter and Paul were essentially at one in their theology.

It was not bad theology but *bad behavior* for which Paul withstood Peter on the one occasion when they differed (Gal 2:11)."You are not embodying your theology in your behavior," Paul was saying. The whole matter involved missionary strategy rather than theology. Peter's theology had allowed him to eat with Gentiles. When representatives from James, the head of the Jerusalem church, arrived in Antioch, under pressure from them Peter withdrew from eating with the Gentiles. It was all a matter of church politics. Paul was not beholden to James and the Jerusalem church. He worked totally independently of them. Peter, on the other hand, was their representative. He was dependent on the Jerusalem church for support in his mission work. And the pressure the Jerusalemites put on Peter was so strong that even Barnabas, Paul's trusted helper and missionary colleague who first brought him into his work (Acts 11:25), was "carried away" and at least temporarily succumbed to their position (Gal. 2:13). Peter's behavior on this one occasion when he broke with Paul was a matter not of theology but of a strategic retreat from his own theological position for purposes of quieting an extremist party in the church in the matter of mission support.

One further consideration is the fact that the church father, Clement of Rome, writing near the end of the first century, places Peter and Paul together at Rome at the end of their lives, celebrating them "in the same breath without a trace of rivalry," suggesting a warm personal relationship between them, with seemingly no awareness that there had ever been any antagonism between them. To Clement, they were close partners in one cause—devotion to their Lord, which led to their martyr deaths.

To deny Petrine authorship to 1 Peter because of its affinity to the theology of Paul's letters, therefore, seems wholly unnecessary.

Would Peter Have Written to Christians in Asia Minor?

Another argument against the authenticity of 1 Peter is that he did not know the Christians in Asia Minor, therefore would not have written to them. For one thing, we have no way of knowing whether he would have written to them, even if he had not known them. Reports of their suffering could have come to him in Rome through travelers from Asia Minor to the capital City, prompting him to write a letter of encouragement, even though they had never met.

Secondly, we do not know whether Peter ever visited Asia Minor or not. There are wide gaps in our knowledge of his career. Luke's purpose in writing Acts is as least partially to trace the progress of the gospel from Jerusalem, where it began, to Rome, the capital of the world, thus depicting its expansion from a small Jewish sect to a worldwide religion. Since Luke was a Gentile, and his purpose focused his interest on that part of the story, he followed the work of Paul, the apostle to the Gentiles, who had been the instrument of it. He allowed Peter, the apostle to the Jews, to disappear into the background. We simply do not know, therefore, whether Peter ever visited Asia Minor. There is no reason, however, to deny him the possibility of writing a letter there.

Thirdly, simply because Peter was the apostle to the Jews does not mean that he would have had no interest in the Gentile churches. After all, it was he who brought the first Gentiles into the church (Acts 10), and he must have maintained an interest in the progress of the church in all facets of its life.

Furthermore, he may have had an interest in writing to the Gentile churches in Asia Minor, some of which Paul had founded, as a means of promoting the unity of the church. The stresses that developed between the Jewish and Gentile branches of the church were a deep concern of Paul, who risked his life in taking a Gentile offering to the Jewish church in Jerusalem as a sign of their oneness in Christ (see Acts 20:22, 24; 21:4, 10ff.). Could not Peter have been likewise motivated? What could have better symbolized the oneness of the Jewish and Gentile churches than this warm and encouraging letter to Gentile Christians from the leader of the Jewish group?

Was Peter a Witness of the Sufferings of Christ?

It has been argued that Peter could not have been the author of 1 Peter, since, when Jesus suffered, Peter forsook Him and fled (Mark 14:50; Luke 22:62), and was therefore not a witness to His sufferings, as 1 Peter claims (5:1). Even if Peter had not seen Jesus actually crucified, he certainly was with Him during His agony in the Garden, and saw Him mocked during His trial. Certainly, this experience with Jesus during His last hours, whether he witnessed the crucifixion or not, would justify the claim to have been a witness of His sufferings.

But who can produce evidence that Peter did not see His Lord's suffering on the cross? We know that when Jesus refused to allow Peter to defend Him with the sword in the Garden (John 18:10f.), Peter forsook Him and fled. Yet after that he followed Him into the court of the High Priest quarters to watch the trial (John 18:15ff., 25ff.). We know that when Jesus turned and looked at Peter as the cock crowed following his denial, Peter "went out and wept bitterly" (Luke 22:62). But what he did thereafter, who knows? Who knows where he was during Jesus' agony on the cross? He may have been on the edge of the crowd, watching. A remark of Luke certainly makes this a possibility. Luke writes that "all [Jesus'] acquaintances and the women who had followed him from Galilee stood at a distance and saw these things" (23:49). But even without that statement, our knowledge of the fact that Peter followed Him from the Garden into the trial hall—confused, heartbroken, fearful, in despair, but too attached to Jesus to leave the scene—almost compels us to believe that his attachment to Jesus was such that he stood somewhere on the edge of the crowd, watching to the end.

Would Peter Have Called Himself an Elder?

One other objection to Peter's having written 1 Peter is that, as an Apostle, he would not have called himself "a fellow elder" in exhorting the church leaders in Asia Minor (5:1). Peter was an "apostle," more than an "elder," and would he not have used his apostolic authority in admonishing the lesser leaders of the church? This hardly seems significant enough to discuss, but since it has been raised, it must claim brief attention (see pp. 330ff.).

For one thing, Peter began his letter by declaring himself "an apostle of Jesus Christ" (1:1). Why should he repeat it, when no one was questioning his apostleship and it seems to have no bearing on anything he was saying other than to identify him and lend the weight of apostolic authority to what he writes? For another thing, could not an apostle be modest? One scholar has suggested that this fits "with the modesty" of his whole approach in the letter. Though chosen by God as an apostle, who had been on the scene "during all the time that the Lord Jesus went in and out among [them], beginning from the baptism of John until the day when he was taken up from us," and who was a "witness to his resurrection" (Acts 1:21f.), yet Peter, as a minister of Christ, stood on the same level as his brothers who had been set aside for special service in the church. By identifying himself with them as a humble believer, he was embodying what he was commending to them— "Tend the flock of God . . . not as domineering over those in your charge but being examples to the flock" (5:3). Needless to say, had the letter been written by a forger, he most certainly would have stressed his apostleship *ad nauseum* to give it credence.

Some insist that Peter would have called himself a "fellow shepherd" rather than a "fellow elder." To this an effective reply has been made: "If the author speaks of himself as a fellow elder and then speaks of the work of elders as shepherding, he implies that his own work as an elder is shepherding. And he has just addressed the leaders as 'elders'—it would have been clumsy to address them initially with the figurative term 'shepherds'—so it naturally follows that he would write of himself as a 'fellow elder' and then move on to their common ministry under figurative language borrowed from Jesus' commission to him, 'Shepherd my sheep'." There is little reason to believe that the author's description of himself as a "fellow elder" disqualifies Peter as being the author.

How Did Peter's Name Get Attached to This Document?

As one goes over the evidence for and against Petrine authorship, one question keeps coming to mind again and again. If Peter did not write this document, and someone wanted to make it authoritative by placing an apostle's name on it, why would he have chosen Peter if all the objections to his authorship have any validity? If it is true, as one scholar insists, "that if the name 'Peter' did not stand at the head of the Epistle, it would never have occurred to anyone to suggest him as the author," how did it *ever* occur to anyone to do just that? If Peter could not have written Greek, why did anyone ever put his name on a Greek document? If there are no references in the letter to personal experiences with Jesus, why attach the name of one whom everybody knew was with Him from the beginning? If Peter's theology differed so from Paul's, why attach his name to such a Pauline document? If Peter had never visited Asia Minor, nor had any interest in Gentile Christianity, why attribute a work to him which for those reasons could easily be detected as not his? Surely, if someone were wanting to pass off a document under an assumed name, he could have been more clever in covering his tracks. I repeat: The above statement raises a most significant question. If "it would never have occurred to anyone" to put Peter's name on this document, why did it occur to someone to do it? One wonders whether our "chronological snobbery," which tends to brand those who lived before the modern age as naive and lacking in critical judgment, does not sometimes interfere with *our* critical judgment. It would seem to be an unanswerable question: If the arguments against Petrine authorship are valid, how did Peter's name ever get attached to it?

A solid British scholar has stated the issue clearly: "A close study of the document itself reveals no motive, theological, controversial, or historical, which explains it as a forgery. It denounces no heresy. It supports no special system of doctrine. It contains no rules as to Church life or organization. Its references to the words and the life of Christ are unobtrusive. It presents no picture of any scene in St. Peter's earlier life, and does not connect itself with any of the stories current in the early Church about his later years. Why, moreover, should a forger . . . represent Silvanus as the amanuensis or the bearer of St Peter's letter, though in the Acts he nowhere appears as in any way connected with that apostle, but both in the Acts and in three Epistles (1 and 2 Thess., 2 Cor.) as the companion of St Paul? Why, above all, should a forger give to Pauline thoughts and to Pauline language a prominent place in an Epistle bearing the name of St Peter?"

Until these questions can get better answers than the advocates of non-Petrine authorship have thus far offered, there seems little reason to abandon the traditional view of the authorship of 1 Peter.

Conclusion on Authorship

It is impossible to *prove* that Peter wrote 1 Peter. It would seem that if any *proving* is to be done, it must be on the side of those who deny Petrine authorship. This raises the question of methodology in dealing with questions like this. As one writer has suggested, if one begins with "a hermeneutic of suspicion," that nothing is to be accepted until it can be proved, his method must then be to "substantiate his doubts." On the other hand, if one takes the claims of the text seriously, "the challenge is therefore not to prove that it *must* be so, but merely to make plausible what the text claims . . . . To put it differently: what he must scrutinize is not the self-identification of the text but rather the validity of the arguments brought forward against it."

I have attempted honestly to scrutinize the arguments made against Petrine authorship, and I do not find them sufficiently strong to deny to the epistle its own claim. I agree with a British scholar who sums it up thus: "The case against the Epistle does not, in fact, appear by any means compelling. It cannot be shown conclusively that Peter was the author; but it has yet to be shown convincingly that he was not."

This confronts us with a question of the ground rules to be followed in dealing with New Testament problems. Do the ordinary categories of reasoning function adequately, or are there esoteric ranges of thought involved, which are not open to common logic? A classics scholar, writing on 1 Peter, has raised this issue in a rather pointed way. He writes: "In common with that of every other document in the New Testament, the traditional authorship has, of course, been challenged, sometimes with subtlety, often perversely, seldom objectively, and nearly always on grounds which would not be regarded as valid by competent scholarship in any other sphere of historical and literary criticism." He then adds: "To a professional classicist and historian, the world of biblical scholarship so often appears a somewhat alien environment, a closed world of cultivated skepticism, where tradition is automatically rejected, and where methods of investigation are habitually used which in classical studies would be set aside as naive or irresponsible."

These are rather biting words, but they can almost be paralleled from a private letter to another scholar written by one who a generation ago was considered the dean of English-speaking New Testament scholars: "You are certainly justified," he wrote, "in questioning the whole structure of the accepted 'critical' chronology of the NT writings, which avoids putting anything earlier than 70, so that none of them are available for anything like first-generation testimony. I should agree with you that much of this late dating is quite arbitrary, even wanton, the offspring not of any argument that can be presented, but rather of the critic's prejudice that if he appears to assent to the traditional position of the early church he will be thought no better than a stick-in-the-mud. The whole business is due for radical re-examination, which demands *argument* . . . It is surely significant that when historians of the ancient world treat the gospels, they are quite unaffected by the sophistications [of some biblical scholars], and handle the documents as if they were what they professed to be . . . ."

An Old Testament scholar has recently compared the conquest account in Joshua 9-12 with other Near Eastern conquest accounts, finding similar "literary devices" in both. He then raises the question why "scholars normally give a significant degree of historical credence" to the nonbiblical Near Eastern accounts, while "at the same time regarding as of little use historically the accounts in Joshua." A reviewer of his book grants that "the biblical accounts of Israel's entry into Palestine have often been treated with a degree of skepticism applied to few other documents from the ancient Near East."

Such statements have rung in my ears again and again as I have once more gone over the ground with regard to the problems connected with 1 Peter. I do not think that the conclusion that I have reached is based either on obtuseness, or unwillingness to face evidence, or theological conservatism, or on fears of rocking the ecclesiastical boat, but rather on an open and careful consideration of the arguments. My Christian faith does not rest on the traditional view of the authorship of 1 Peter. But those who deny Petrine authorship have the burden of proof, and I am simply not convinced by their arguments.

A photographic look-alike contest for Audrey Hepburn was held some time ago, with a prize awarded to the one who was judged to resemble her most closely. Someone, for fun, sent an actual photograph of Audrey. *It was awarded fourth place!* In the judgment of many current scholars, a photograph of Peter would come out fourth—or, in some cases, would not qualify for the contest at all—as a look-alike for the author of 1 Peter. In biblical criticism, judgments often go by current styles. The last sentence of a book review in a major biblical journal recently said of the book's author: "It is perhaps unfortunate that his source theory is linked with views regarding authorship and date that are now out of vogue." It is now "out of vogue" to reach the conclusion about 1 Peter here stated. In my judgment, however, when all the contestants for the authorship of 1 Peter have been assembled, and their claims examined, and the request is made: "Will the *real* author please stand up," he would be Peter himself, the brother of Andrew, the fisherman of Galilee, who after faltering momentarily during the trial of his Lord, became the "rock" around whom the scattered flock of Christ gathered following the resurrection, who delivered the first recorded Christian sermon at Pentecost, who welcomed the first Gentile into the church, who spent his days as a "fisher of men," and who, according to tradition, ended his life as a martyr for his Lord.

Granted that difficulties with this conclusion remain, they are, in my judgment, fewer and less formidable than those confronting rival conclusions. A scholar whose credentials on 1 Peter research are impeccable, and whose "opinion is not presented from any confessional point of view," but is "a question of critical judgment," undergirds this conclusion: "it seems reasonable to accept the authorship of Peter as a working hypothesis until better evidence emerges to prove the contrary."

7

TO WHOM WAS 1 PETER WRITTEN?

The opening salutation of 1 Peter gives the only specific clue to the identity of its first readers. They were a group of Christian churches dispersed through Asia Minor (modern Turkey). Beyond that, we are left only with slight intimations to be gleaned from an examination of the letter addressed to them.

Where were the First Readers Located?

Clearly the first recipients of 1 Peter were the Christians living in the five provinces of Pontus, Galatia, Cappadocia, Asia and Bithynia (1:1). But where were these provinces, and what territory did they include? The Roman government, from time to time, made administrative shifts in the territory they controlled. Are these five provinces, therefore, the Roman provinces of that name, or do they relate to the old kingdoms prior to Roman rule, which names might still be current in popular usage? Did these names describe political divisions current at the time of writing, or ancient geographical territories?

Two objections have been raised to applying to them the current Roman political nomenclature: first, if these designated the Roman provinces, then Cilicia, Pamphylia and Lycia, which were also Roman provinces of Asia Minor, are omitted; second, neither Bithynia nor Pontus were entities in themselves, but were two parts of one province named Bithynia-Pontus.

The first objection carries little weight. Much importance was given to natural features of the country in thinking of the territory of Asia Minor. The area south of the Taurus mountains, where Cilicia, Pamphylia and Lycia were located, was referred to as "Asia without the Taurus." It was therefore, both politically and in popular thought, separated from the rest of Asia Minor. In fact, in New Testament times, Cilicia was united with Syria, the province to the east and south. Both Luke and Paul speak of "Syria and Cilicia" as one area (Acts 15:41, Gal 1:21).

The second objection is satisfactorily solved, if some adequate explanation for separating the names of the two halves of one province can be found. Such an explanation, based on the hint of an earlier German writer was put forward many years ago by one of England's most careful scholars. Though it cannot be proved, it has commended itself to many ever since. The clue was found in the order in which the provinces are named. There must have been a reason for listing them as they now stand. The order could hardly be accidental, as though the names had been placed in a bag, shaken up, and drawn from it haphazardly.

If no principle of arrangement had been in the author's mind, "the arrangement would obey unconscious promptings of association." In this case, Bithynia and Pontus would hardly have been separated, since they are one province, and Asia would likely have been given a more prominent place, either first or last, for it was the most important province of the group, both intrinsically and from a Christian standpoint. Since, therefore, the listing could hardly have been random, and since, if there had been no principle of arrangement, the unconscious "promptings of association" in the mind would have led to a different order, it must follow that "the very peculiar order of the list must have been dictated by some definite motive or occasion."

To account for the present order, as some have done, merely by its rhythmical tone is highly questionable. Nor does the suggestion solve the problem that the author began with Pontus and ended with Bithynia in order by repetition to call particular attention to the province of Bithynia-Pontus, inasmuch as the persecution there may have been most intense. It is based on a theory of a late date which is highly questionable and a type of persecution not reflected in the letter. There must have been a more "geographically luminous" reason for the order as it now stands. What was this?

The explanation proposed is that 1 Peter was an encyclical letter, carried by Silvanus, who entered Asia Minor somewhere in the region of Pontus, made a circular sweep of the whole territory north of the Taurus mountains, through the provinces of Galatia, Cappadocia and Asia, and reached his final destination in Bithynia, thus carrying the letter to all the Christian churches throughout the area. The major difficulty of this theory is that Pontus should have been chosen as the starting point of the journey. Ephesus, the most noted city in the area and the capital of perhaps the richest province in the Roman empire at that time, would seem to have been the natural place to land on a ship sailing from Rome. Furthermore, it had a Christian church to which Paul wrote one of his letters, and was the first named of the seven churches of Asia Minor addressed in the Book of Revelation.

The one who propounded the encyclical theory answered this objection with reasonable effectiveness when he pointed out that Pontus might have been the native country of Silvanus; or he may have had other *personal* reasons for beginning his tour there, having planned a trip to take care of his own affairs or the affairs of others, then adding to this a tour of Asia Minor to deliver Peter's letter. Another has reasoned from Paul's experience with the church at Antioch, which sent him and Barnabas out as missionaries and stood behind him in his efforts (Acts 13:1ff.), that the churches in Pontus may have felt led to institute a missionary project throughout the rest of Asia Minor, and called on Peter for his sanction and guidance, which he gave in this letter. If this were true, the letter would naturally be sent to Pontus first, from there to continue on its mission through the whole territory.

The truth is that there are wide gaps in our knowledge of the circumstances of the first readers of 1 Peter, and we are left to conjecture. Human curiosity continues to search for clues which might expand our knowledge. Unless further external evidence is uncovered, we shall have to be content with sanctified guesses, of which the encyclical letter is presently the most attractive.

Were the Readers Jewish or Gentile?

The effort to answer the question of whether the first readers of 1 Peter were Jewish or Gentile, as with most issues relating to this letter, has produced a difference of opinion. There was a marked division about it on the part of the church fathers. The Greek fathers of the East held the readers to be Jews, while the Latin fathers of the West held them to be Gentiles. This division of opinion continued through the Reformation and remains until our time.

Those who favor the Jews base their judgment generally on four grounds: 1) The wide use of the Old Testament in the epistle, and its priestly view of the church as the successor of the old Israel (2:4-

10); 2) its description of the readers as "exiles of the dispersion" (1:1), suggesting that they were Jews living outside of Palestine; 3) the description of their past life in terms of Gentile behavior (4:3) can be accounted for if they were Jews who had lapsed from the practice of their religion; and 4) Peter, as the one who had been "entrusted with the gospel to the circumcised" (Gal. 2:7), would more likely have written to Jews than to Gentiles.

These arguments may well be countered. The Jewish nature of the document in its use of the Old Testament, as one scholar has pointed out, may reflect the Jewish background of the *writer* of the letter, but this does not "thereby prove that the same background can be postulated of those who were to receive it." But more than that, as we have argued earlier (see p. 27), it is impossible to understand Christianity without some grasp of the Old Testament. Christianity did not abruptly arrive in the world, founded by a starry-eyed upstart without ancestry or prehistory. When a Christian evangelist told a Gentile the name of the founder of his religion, Jesus Christ, he was saying Jesus, *the Christ*. What Christ? The Christ of the Old Testament. The moment the Gentile was told that Christianity involves a *new covenant*, this could be understood only in terms of an old covenant which was transcended. The early Christians took their message to the Gentile world with an Old Testament in their hands. It was their scripture on which the whole thing was based. The Jewish synagogue had spread those scriptures throughout the Gentile world, and had made proselytes of some Gentiles. They had also attracted many "God-fearers" from among the Gentiles who had not become circumcised and keepers of the law, but who heard the law and the prophets expounded Sabbath by Sabbath and were already familiar with the Jewish scriptures. It is likely these proselytes and God-fearers were the first Gentile converts to the Christian faith. The Jewish character of the epistle, therefore, in no way demands a Jewish audience.

The expression "exiles of the dispersion" (1:1), with which the epistle opens, need not be taken any more literally than is "Babylon" (5:13) with which it closes (see pp. 43ff.). It is more likely a figurative expression describing the Christians dispersed throughout the non-Christian world than a reference to the Jewish dispersion.

Some of the expressions concerning the past behavior of the readers might conceivably be descriptive of Jews who had lapsed from their faith. On the other hand, there were hardly very many Jews, even those who had abandoned their background, of whom it could be said that they were "living in licentiousness, passions, drunkenness, revels, carousing, and lawless idolatry" (4:3). And, more, it would not likely be *those* Jews who would have been attracted to the Christian faith. Beyond that, other expressions about the readers' past hardly make sense if they were Jews. Would the Gentiles "be surprised" if the Jews did not join them in "wild profligacy" (4:4)? Rather, they would have been surprised if they had joined them, for the superior moral behavior patterns of the Jews were known to all Gentiles. And could the conduct of the Jews rightly be described as "futile ways inherited from [their] fathers" (1:18), springing from "the passions of [their] former ignorance" (1:14:)? One can imagine a Christian describing in this fashion the *beliefs* of Jews who had rejected Jesus as their Messiah, but hardly their conduct.

If the majority of the readers had been Jews, it is unlikely that the problem of slavery would have been brought to the fore as it was (2:18ff.), for slavery never flourished among the Jews as it did among the Gentiles. Few Jews either had slaves or were slaves.

The tone of the letter with regard to Christian relations with their social environment seems to reflect a church membership which had largely come out of paganism. The Jews in Asia Minor had worked out concessions from the government, which had accepted Judaism as a licit religion, whose distinctiveness from pagan society was officially accepted and protected. There is reason to believe, in fact, that the Jewish privileges granted by the government sometimes excited jealousy on the part of their pagan neighbors. The failure of the populace to understand the Christians, therefore, suggests that they were made up largely not of Jews, whom they had learned to tolerate, but of former pagans whose strangeness of life style was a new and unfamiliar experience for them.

The churches of Asia Minor, therefore, were likely made up principally of Gentile members. There were certainly Jews among them, however. We know from the missionary strategy of Paul in the Acts that he always went first to a synagogue to begin his work (Acts 13:5, 14; 14:1; 17:1, 10; 18:4). This usually resulted in a few converts, who could form the nucleus of a congregation which later became peopled with Gentiles, so that the Gentiles would be anchored by them to the Old Testament heritage out of which the church came, and thus be led more quickly into a deeper understanding of their new found faith.

It is likely, therefore, that the churches of Asia Minor consisted of a Jewish nucleus, a larger number of former Gentile proselytes and "God-fearers" who had had some prior touch with the synagogue, and the rest converts out of raw paganism.

Who Evangelized the First Readers of 1 Peter?

There is no way of determining who evangelized the readers to whom 1 Peter is addressed. Apart from small snatches of information about the churches of Asia Minor in the Book of the Acts, in Paul's epistles, and in the Book of Revelation, our only source of information is in a few letters written to the churches of the area around the beginning of the second century by Ignatius of Antioch. Did Peter ever visit the area? It is possible, but we do not know. It has been suggested that Peter's reference to "those who preached the good news to you"(1:12) excludes himself. On the other hand, if he had preached to them, they would have known it, and the expression could have been a modest way of refraining from pointing to himself. A few of the churches which Paul founded in Asia Minor were likely on the itinerary of the bearer of the letter, but we cannot be absolutely certain of that. On the Day of Pentecost, there were devout Jews dwelling in Jerusalem from at least three of the Asian provinces, "Cappadocia, Pontus and Asia" (Acts 2:9). Could it be that they subsequently took the "good news" they heard in Jerusalem back to their home countries? Or were the churches the result of "the fruitful testimony of modest and unknown Christians moving into the area for professional reasons or with a missionary intention"? It has been remarked that in days "when every Christian, whatever his trade or occupation, was necessarily a missionary many territories must have been evangelized without the aid of any outstanding leader."

We do not, and cannot, know who first brought the gospel to the Christians to whom 1 Peter is addressed. We know only that God, in His infinite and mysterious wisdom prompted someone, or several, to tell the story; and by the mysterious working of His Spirit prompted hearers to believe it; and then, in His gracious providence, provided someone to write them this jewel of a letter to instruct them in what they had already believed, and to comfort and strengthen them to "stand fast" in that belief to the end.

Were the First Readers of 1 Peter First Generation Christians?

It is impossible to answer with absolute certainty whether the readers to whom 1 Peter was originally addressed were first generation Christians. We are left to read between the lines, or to try to make a judgment from hints in the text which might indicate the level of their maturity in the faith. The impression one gets in this way seems to suggest that they were relative newcomers to Christianity.

In contrasting the prophetic age with the age of the gospel, Peter speaks of "the things which have now been announced to you" (1:12). We have already seen that the "now" here does not refer to the immediate moment, as though they were participating in a baptismal or communion service at that moment (see pp. 15ff.), but it does embody the tenor of a statement suggesting that it has not been too long since the readers had first heard the gospel. The reference to the "former ignorance" sounds as though there had not been too long a gap between that time and the present (1:14). "Conduct yourselves with fear throughout the time of your exile" (1:17) suggests that although they were off to a good start, they needed staying power for the long haul. Stress on the new birth "through the living . . . word," described as "the good news which was preached to you" (1:25), hardly sounds as though the message had been in their tradition for a generation or two. Peter's counsel that they should mimic "newborn babes" in seeking nourishment so that they may "grow up to salvation" (2:2), seems to point to an immature stage of development in the faith. The whole ethical instruction to the readers seems to reflect the fact that they are facing problems somewhat new to them in relation to their life in a pagan social environment, as though they did not have a long tradition of Christian instruction behind them. The fact that their pagan neighbors are "surprised" that they do not join in their "wild profligacy" (4:4) suggests that this is rather a new experience to the readers.

None of these considerations, in itself, can prove that the readers addressed in 1 Peter are first generation Christians. The cumulative effect, however, pictures them as a rather immature group relatively new to the faith, testing the rigors of Christian living in a hostile society for the first time, and needing the type of counsel suited to recent converts.

8

WHY WAS 1 PETER WRITTEN?

One of the major aids to understanding a document is a clear grasp of the purpose for which it was written. Rightly to appraise what an author succeeds in doing depends on a knowledge of what he intended to do. What purpose did Peter have in mind in addressing this letter to his first readers?

What Is 1 Peter's Stated Purpose?

In the postscript to his letter, Peter clearly states a twofold purpose: "I have written briefly to you, *exhorting* and *declaring* that this is the true grace of God; stand fast in it" (5:12). Peter has for some reason reversed the order of this twofold function here, for although the two are almost inseparably intertwined throughout the letter, the *declaring* usually precedes the *exhorting* as the basis on which the exhortation is made. But the purpose is manifest. Peter wants his readers to "stand fast" in the faith which has been brought to them and into which they have been baptized. To achieve this goal, he has pursued two methods: 1) "declaring," "proclaiming," "testifying," "attesting," "teaching" them once more what this faith is; and 2) "exhorting," "entreating," "stimulating," "enrcouraging," "comforting," them in ways that would help them in their task of faithfulness.

The word translated "declaring" or "testifying" is a strong word, used nowhere else in the New Testament, with a prefix which intensifies the meaning. One translator has rendered it "fully testifying." The testimony is to facts, but also to truths or views about those facts. It involves both "statements . . . about objective events," and about "personal convictions." "On the one hand the point at issue is whether a thing is or was really so, on the other whether it is true and valid from the standpoint of the one who states it." Peter is writing to confirm the faith he proclaims not only by the reality of the events which lie behind it in his objective experience with Jesus in the flesh, but also by his participation in the sufferings of his Lord in his apostolic labors. Through that testing of his faith in his own experience, he is firmly convinced of its truth. His teaching, therefore, involves both facts and convictions. When he testifies to the adequacy of the grace of his Lord to sustain his readers in their trials and rebuffs, they may be sure that he knows what he is talking about. "Take my word for it," he says, "I've been there! I know! Therefore, stand fast!"

The word rendered "exhorting" denotes in the New Testament both "missionary proclamation and also a kind of formula to introduce pastoral admonition." It includes "both the element of beseeching and also that of encouraging." This word is used in connection with Peter's sermon at Pentecost, when he "exhorted them, saying, 'Save yourselves from this crooked generation'" (Acts 2:40). In his letter, Peter was both *beseeching* and *encouraging* them to respond to the good news they had received. But this appeal was made not only to those who were hearing the gospel for the first time, but to those who had already been believers, yet were in danger of growing weary in their faith. So Peter is at one and the same time "admonishing" and "encouraging," "entreating" and comforting" the readers. This was not only a "moral appeal," but the redeeming life and death and resurrection of Jesus Christ was the "presupposition and basis" of all that he had to say. In effect, he was focusing the eyes of his readers on their dying and rising Lord, saying to them: "Whatever test you must undergo, let me not only admonish you to stand fast, but let me also encourage you to do so. *Stand, because you are able to stand—in Christ!"*

Peter's clearly stated purpose, therefore, was to address the little Christian groups of Asia Minor, who were living as strangers and aliens in a sea of paganism—misunderstood, insulted, socially ostracized, economically disadvantaged, and sometimes physically abused—by teaching them anew the meaning of their faith in Jesus Christ, and encouraging them to avail themselves of the resources of their Lord in remaining faithful to the end.

What is the Implicit Broader Purpose Of 1 Peter?

Beyond the explicitly stated purpose of 1 Peter lies the broader question which underlies much of what he writes: How should Christians relate themselves to the culture in which they are set? Should they withdraw from it, and be totally separate? Should they so emphasize their disengagement from "earthly things" (Phil 3:19) because their "commonwealth is in heaven" (Phil 3:20), that they detach themselves completely from the society of which they are a part? Does membership in the kingdom of Christ countermand one's obligations to the kingdoms of this world? Are the sons of the kingdom "free" from the exactments levied by the "kings of the earth"? (Matt 17:24ff.).

This has been a problem from the days of Moses until now. Until the Hebrews had grown strong enough in their knowledge of the one true God that they could survive pagan influences, they were to "make no covenant" with the surrounding nations nor "make marriages with them.... For they would turn away your sons from following me, to serve other gods" (Deut 7:2ff.). Yet they were set in a location which, when they matured, put them right at the crossroads of the nations, whereby they could make their faith known to the world. Their subsequent captivity drove them out into the larger world, and made them inescapably missionaries of their faith. This was a means of fulfilling the divine purpose that in Abraham "all nations" should "be blessed." The prophets caught the meaning of this. If there is really only *one* God, then He is the God of *all men*. So, said the prophet of the exile, "there is no other god besides me .... Turn to me and be saved, all the ends of the earth" (Isa 45:21f.). He added: "It is too light a thing that you should be my servant to raise up the tribes of Jacob.... I will give you as a light to the nations, that my salvation may reach to the end of the earth" (Isa 49:6). Israel was to be totally different from the other nations. "I am the Lord your God, who have separated you from the peoples" (Lev 20:24; see also 1 Kings 8:53). And yet she was to maintain this difference as she mingled with the nations. The problem is how to be separated from the world while mingling with the world.

In Jesus' day, the Zealots had "an inviolable attachment to liberty" and said "that God is to be their only Ruler and Lord"; therefore, they renounced the claims of Roman rule and revolted. Nonviolent forms of a similar impulse are to be seen in the Essenes and the Qumran community of Dead Sea Scroll fame during the first century A.D., and the various monastic groups of both the middle and modern ages, and the diversified Christian denominations which stress almost exclusively "otherworldliness" among their members. These are all wrestling with the question: What is the proper relationship of Christians to the society and culture in which they exist? In how far is the culture to be resisted, and in how far is assimilation to it acceptable?

"Conversionist" groups, whose aim it is to influence the society of which they are a part, can never put this problem to a final rest; for it crops up in different forms in unforeseen historic developments. A modern example of its difficulty may be seen in the Mennonite groups of our time. They all agree in the desirability of simplicity in life and in avoiding too great a preoccupation with "worldly concerns." But they disagree, and are divided into many groups, over the question of what form simplicity and the rejection of worldly concerns should take. Their experience sharpens the question of how a group can influence society without being too much influenced by society. If all conformity to the world is abandoned, there is little likelihood of converting the world. On the other hand, if, to convert the world, participation in it leads to too much conformity, how does the group maintain the dynamic of its reason for existing?

The most "unworldly" of the Mennonites, the Amish, are so detached from the world in customs and lifestyle that they make few, if any, converts from outside their group. Those who mingle more freely with the world, and seek to make their witness effective beyond the limits of their own society, immediately face new problems which threaten the very foundations of their existence. Some years ago, one of the Mennonite groups, under the leadership of a powerful evangelistic preacher, launched a series of tent meetings. The meetings were successful in bringing a rather large and sudden influx of new Christian converts into the Mennonite churches. But many of these converts came from non-Mennonite backgrounds, which immediately created problems which the Mennonites had not had to face on such a large scale. Some were divorcees, who brought conceptions of marriage with them which the Mennonites had not historically shared. Many of them were obviously sincere and wholesome in their conversion to Christ, but had little appreciation for the simplicities of the lifestyle of the Mennonite groups. How could these new Christians be nurtured and absorbed into the Mennonite churches without totally changing the historic character of those churches? Here, in a rather acute form, was the problem faced by all Christians in all times. What is the proper relationship of Christians to their culture. How can Christianity affect non-Christian culture without being acculturated into non-Christianity?

This age-old, and current, problem lies behind the writing of 1 Peter. The aim of New Testament Christianity was to bear a witness to the pagan world which would cleanse that world of its idolatry, superstition, immorality and inhumanity. The Christians had been "called . . . out of darkness into . . . light," in order to "declare the wonderful deeds of him" who had called them (2:9). To do this, they could not wholly withdraw from that world and live to themselves, as the Qumran community proposed. Much alike as they may have been at certain points, on this issue they differed radically. They both thought of themselves as "transplanted into a fully new existence and thereby . . . alienated from society as an Exodus community of the last days." The Qumran community, however, was based solely on an imperative. It expressed itself as a new mode of life practices according to hard and fast rules. Its exodus and estrangement was an emigration out of society into a tightly-knit community in which its opposition to the rest of the world was realized, there to await the final messianic battle in which they would be vindicated and their achievement confirmed. The Christian community, on the other hand, as a recent writer has emphasized, rooted itself in an *indicative* that issued in an *imperative*. The indicative was expressed in 1 Peter 1:3: "By his great mercy we have been born anew to a living hope through the resurrection of Jesus Christ from the dead." What appears here, however, as a *given*, must be expressed later as an *imperative*: "Set your hope fully upon the grace that is coming to you at the revelation of Jesus Christ" (1:13). We are born to a hope by a past event, yet we must set our hope on something future.

"The new is therefore not presently forthcoming." It is a future reality to be grasped only by faith. Like Abraham, the Christians sojourned "in the land of promise, as in a foreign land" (Heb.11:9f.), looking forward to what has not yet been realized. Like Moses, they had to "endure" as "seeing him who is invisible" (Heb 11:27f.). The Qumran community was sustained by an "annual covenant renewal ceremony." The Christian community was constantly renewed by Christ's resurrection life "made ever new through an attitude of faith." Here is the dialectic between the "already" and the "not yet"; between what God has heretofore accomplished in the death and resurrection of Christ and the future "end," when all God's enemies are overcome and

"God may he everything to every one" (1 Cor. 15:28).

Living in the present power of the resurrection, and in the future hope of God's final triumph, the Christian community was set down in the midst of the world to bear witness to others of the realities by which they lived. If they were to do this, they could not withdraw from society, but must manifest their estrangement from that society in the world where God had set them. As expressed in Jesus' great prayer: "They are not of the world," yet I have "sent them into the world" (John 17:16, 18). With a new source of life and a new goal for which to live, they were most certainly alienated and estranged from the world, which was still under the power of the old age, the age of sin and death (see Rom 3:9). But their participation in the life of the new age was to be lived out among those whose loyalties were still attached to the old age. Paul counseled the Christians to exclude from their group those who were "the immoral of this world, . . . the greedy and robbers, or idolaters" (1 Cor 4:10), but he insisted that he did not mean that they should avoid all contact with such outside the church. To do that, he said, they "would need to go out of the world" (1 Cor 5:10), and that he did not advocate.

The Christians had a missionary responsibility for the whole of society, so that through their life and witness God would make all men into a new and redeemed humanity. Paul's advice, then, was that "every one should remain in the state in which he was" when called into the faith (1 Cor 7:20). Peter gave similar counsel. The "genuineness of [their] faith" was to be "tested by fire" as they lived through the buffetings of hostile pagans (1:7). They were to live holy lives, manifesting among their pagan neighbors the character of the God who had redeemed them (1:14ff.). They were together to become a living temple where God would meet men, a holy priesthood to mediate between God and humanity, God's "own people" to "declare the wonderful deeds of him who called [them] out of darkness into his marvelous light" (2:4ff.). They were to "maintain good conduct among the Gentiles" so that unbelieving pagans would "glorify God on the day of visitation" (2:12, 4:1ff.). They were to live as good citizens, obeying the laws of the political orders under which they lived (2:13ff.). Servants, wives and husbands were to be models of uprightness, following the example of their Lord (2:18ff.). They were always to be ready to testify to inquirers concerning their "hope," but with appropriate "gentleness and reverence," which would "put to shame" those who "abused them"

(3:15f). They were to "rejoice" in sharing Christ's sufferings when "reproached for the name of Christ" (4:12ff.), as an opportunity to "glorify God" thereby. Here is a picture, not of withdrawal from society, but of participation in it, which might even involve suffering with it, and for it, as a participation in the sufferings of their Lord (2:19ff., 4:13ff.).

There has recently been a debate betseen two recognized scholars, both of whom have approached the question from the standpoint of current sociological analysis, as to whether the purpose of 1 Peter was to advocate "social assimilation" of the Christians with their surrounding world, or to maintain "Christian group boundaries" which would preserve "the believers' distinctive communal identity." Another writer has distinguished two types of personality in this regard: the "active" type, which resists "social pressure" in an improper way, in order to maintain their own religious identity, thus improving "social cohesion" but losing contact with the non-Christians; and the "passive" type who are "tempted to keep a low religious profile and assimilate to the non-Christian society in order to avoid further problems." He suggests a literary approach to this problem on the part of Peter, who was deliberately trying to appeal to both groups. Another writer has proposed that "social acceptability. . . is . . . necessary for survival and for outreach" into the world. Christians, therefore, although avoiding "the excesses of the worst in society," should "live in their civic, domestic, and ecclesiastical existence in terms of the highest social and cultural conventions of their time and place." But who, and what standard, determines what is either the "worst" or the "highest" in the "cultural conventions" of any time and place? Many who follow what might by some be called "the excesses of the worst in pagan society," even some religious people, think that those very patterns are the "best" for society." The church's current tendency quickly to align itself with almost every "cause" without deeper theological thought, and to manipulate the Scriptures and the central Christian tradition in a way that gives dilettantish theological approval to whatever the culture proposes, may so rob the church of its cutting edge that it will end up merely echoing back to the world its own word, with no distinctive Christian word to speak to it. It is conceivable that resistance to what some, even devout people, think are "the highest social and cultural conventions" of our time may prove to have embodied spiritual insight which time may accredit as correct.

These approaches raise the question whether the issue is to be settled finally either on sociological or literary or cultural grounds. Is there not a danger here of "modernizing" by introducing sociological or literary or cultural categories which were neither within the range of Peter's consciousness nor his concern. It is quite possible that if Peter could be asked which of these approaches he intended, he would say *neither*. He was likely thinking in theological rather than sociological or literary or cultural categories. Peter was not motivating them either to maintain their corporate life against the disintegrating forces of their culture, nor to be assimilated by the culture, nor to embody the "highest" of cultural norms because the culture approved them. He was not dealing with personality types, nor concerned to keep a "movement" alive and prosperous. He was rather trying to motivate them to seek the will of God for them in any given situation." What will best glorify God?" he was saying, is the question to be asked. And that cannot be answered theoretically, nor finally for all time, but is a question which must be faced continually, "with gentleness and reverence" (3:15), as situations arise.

Theologically, the Christian exists in the world with a new life wrought in him by the resurrection of Jesus Christ from the dead. This is a *gift*, a *given*. On the other hand, he has a "calling;" he is bound to bend every effort at his command to be what he ought to be in the world. The ethical demand, then, is: *Become what you already are in Jesus Christ*. A child is already perfect in the heart of loving parents. To the degree that he responds to this, he will strive to become what he already is in their love. His effort is not to *attain* their love. He already has that. It is this which motivates him. He says "thank you" for that love by striving to become what he already is in that love.

According to Peter, the Christian does not serve his Lord in the world to gain His love. He already has that. He has already "been born anew to a living hope through the resurrection of Jesus Christ from the dead." For that reason, he responds to his "calling" to be holy; to conduct himself with "fear;" to "love" his fellow man; to put away "all malice and all guile and insincerity and envy and all slander;" to "grow up" to maturity in the faith; to be a worthy stone in God's "spiritual" temple; "to abstain from the passions of the flesh" which war against the soul; to subject himself to human institutions ordained by God; to be willing to suffer for righteousness' sake if need be; and so to live, insofar as God's grace makes possible, "that in everything God may be glorified through Jesus Christ."

I was told by one who knew him well that Joseph Hromadka, the great Czech theologian, once stood in the public square of Prague, when the Communists there were in full power, and declared in an address to a great throng of people: "As a Christian, I share in, and work for many of the communist goals for society; but I do so for a different reason. I do it because I believe in the resurrection of Jesus Christ!" Here was no effort to sustain a beleaguered brotherhood in a hostile society; nor to be assimilated into a group to avoid misunderstanding and suffering. Here was a simple response of gratitude to God who had sent Jesus Christ into the world to die, and had raised Him from the dead; and the acceptance of the "calling" which divine love had laid upon him, to declare to others God's wonderful deeds. Could there be a better embodiment of what Peter meant for the Christian to be in society?

PART TWO
THE COMMENTARY

OUTLINE

I. THE SALUTATION—AUTHOR AND READERS (1:1-2)	101
A. The Authority of Apostleship	101
B. The Readers as God Sees Them	103
1. Chosen	104
2. Strangers	108
3. Dispersion	112
4. Chosen Strangers of the Dispersion	112
5. The Foreknowledge of God	113
6. Sanctification by the Spirit	115
7. Obedience and Sprinkling With the Blood of Jesus Christ	116
II. THE INDICATIVE OF GOD'S SALVATION (1:3-2:10)	119
A. Salvation As Living Hope (1:3-5) (*Proclamation*)	120
A Dynamic and a Destiny	120
B. Salvation as Joy in the Testing Process (1:6-9) (*Proclamation*)	135
A Method of Life	135
C. Salvation as the Consummation of God's Work in History (1:10-12) (*Proclamation*)	141
A Mystery Now Disclosed	141
III. THE IMPERATIVE OF MAN'S RESPONSE (1:13-2:3)	148
A. Hope (1:13) (*Exhortation*)	149
Life Focused on the Final Victory of Christ	149
B. Be Holy (1:14-16) (*Exhortation*)	153
Life Patterned After the Character of God	153
C. Live in Reverence (1:17-21) (*Exhortation*)	158
Life Lived in the Light of the Costliness of Redemption	158

D. Love One Another (1:22-25) (*Exhortation*)	175
Life Controlled by the Imperishable Value of Love	175
E. Grow Spiritually (2:1-3) (*Exhortation*)	179
Life Nourished By Proper Spiritual Diet	179

IV. THE COMMUNITY THAT RESULTS FROM GOD'S INITIATIVE AND MAN'S RESPONSE (2:4-10) (*Proclamation*) 185

V. THE LIFE OF THE CHRISTIAN COMMUNITY IN SOCIETY (2:11-4:11) 200
- A. The Purpose of Holy Living in the Christian Community (2:11-12) (*Exhortation*) — 201
- B. The Christians' Relation to Human Authorities (2:13-17) (*Exhortation*) — 206
- C. The Servants' Relation to Their Masters (2:18-21) (*Exhortation*) — 213
- D. The Redemptive Basis of Christian Behavior in Society (2:22-25) (*Proclamation*) — 224
- E. Wives' Relation to Their Husbands (3:1-6) (*Exhortation*) — 234
- F. Husbands' Relation to Their Wives (3:7) (*Exhortation*) — 243
- G. The Life of the Christian Community in the World (3:8-12) (*Exhortation*) — 247
- H. The Christian Community's Response to Persecution (3:13-4:6) — 258
    1. The Blessedness of Suffering for Righteousness' Sake (3:13-17) (*Exhortation*) — 258
    2. The Example of Christ Who Triumphed Through Unjust Suffering (3:18-22) (*Proclamation*) — 268
    3. Worthy Living in Response to Christ as Example and Judge (4:1-6) (*Exhortation*) — 284
- I. The Church's Witness to the Glory of God in Its Own Life (4:7-11) (*Exhortation*) — 292

VI. A CHRISTIAN INTERPRETATION OF SUFFERING
   (4:12-19) 309
   A. The Normalcy of Suffering (4:12a) (*Exhortation*) 309
   B. Suffering As a Test of Faith (4:12b) (*Exhortation*) 311
   C. Suffering as Participation in Christ's Suffering
      (4:13-16) (*Exhortation*) 311
   D. Suffering in the Light of Final Judgment (4:17-19)
      (*Exhortation*) 321

VII. FINAL ADMONITIONS (5:1-11) 329
   A. Admonitions on Congregational Life (5:1-5)
      (*Exhortation*) 330
   B. Admonitions on Spiritual Warfare (5:6-11)
      (*Exhortation*) 353

VIII. CLOSING GREETINGS (5:12-14) 369

I

THE SALUTATION—AUTHOR AND READERS (1:1, 2)

A. The Authority of Apostleship

The opening words of the epistle give it its authority for the church: **Peter, an apostle of Jesus Christ.** The basic meaning of the word **apostle** in classic Greek is "one who has been sent." The corresponding word in Hebrew refined it to refer to "one who is given full authority to represent, for some particular purpose and for a limited time, the person or persons from whom he comes." The rabbis had a saying: "a man's apostle is as himself."

In the New Testament the word **apostle** has both a broad and a particular reference. Broadly, it refers to those who were sent as representatives of another person or a church. Usually, however, it is restricted to those who were apostles in the specific sense—those sent by Jesus Christ with His authority particularly delegated to them. This involved two things: 1) to have seen the risen Christ (Luke 24:38, John 20:21, 1 Cor 9:1, 1 Cor 15:7). All "apostles" in the precise sense were witnesses of the resurrection, but not all witnesses to the resurrection were "apostles." 2) A second requirement was necessary—to have a mandate from Christ to witness to the resurrection, and to all that His life and death meant in the light of this (Matt 28:19, Rom 1:5, 1 Cor 1:17, where "send" is the verbal form of the noun "apostle.")

The "apostles," therefore, were "envoys of the risen Christ." Their testimony became a "constitutive element" of the gospel message, because they were the church's "immediate link with the one Lord whom they have seen and to whose resurrection they have been witnesses." This is the meaning of the affirmation that the church is "built upon the foundation of the apostles and prophets" (Eph 2:20).The "chief cornerstone, in whom the whole structure is joined together and grows into a holy temple" is "Christ Jesus himself." Our knowledge of Him, however, rests on the apostles' testimony that in the life, death and resurrection of Jesus, God has honored His promises to the prophets and achieved the redemption to which they looked forward. The Nicene Creed phrases this succinctly: I believe in "one holy Catholic [universal, not Roman] and Apostolic church." The true church is that which embodies the faith attested by the apostles.

The concern which the early church had with apostolic authentication may be seen in their choice of one to succeed the defected Judas. He must not only be "a witness to [Jesus'] resurrection," but he was to be "one of the men who have accompanied us during all the time that the Lord Jesus went in and out among us, beginning from the baptism of John until the day when he was taken up from us—one of these men must become with us" an apostle (Acts 1:21f.). The only exception to this requirement was Paul, who was "a witness to the resurrection" but had not companied with the group during Jesus' earthly life. This is not the place to elaborate on why Paul was especially chosen as an apostle in spite of this. But the difficulty he had in establishing the authenticity of his apostleship because he lacked these other credentials, indicates how concerned the church was to have as apostles only those who were fully conversant with all the facts about Jesus' earthly life, as well as His resurrection. Peter's undisputed apostleship, therefore, authenticates this little book.

As we have seen in the Introduction, there is no compelling reason to doubt that Peter himself was the author of this work. But even if that should be disproved, it would not impair the apostolic authority of 1 Peter. When the church created its canon—its list of works to be included with the Old Testament as its source and norm of faith, it did not do it haphazardly. It was very careful that "apostolicity" characterize the books included. This means that either the apostles wrote these books, or the books embodied the authentic faith of the apostles, thus carrying their authority even though recorded by others. Since 1 Peter was placed in the canon early and without dispute, its "apostolicity" was thereby affirmed.

Furthermore, the process by which the canon was formed was closely linked with the life and worship of the church. Had the "authoritative" books been determined merely by a Council of churchmen, their judgment could have been faulty. The "authoritative" quality of the books chosen, however, manifested itself first in the life and worship of the Christian congregations as they were read, studied, and preached. As cream rises to the top, these books surpassed the others in spiritual power as they were put to use. They authenticated themselves to the corporate Christian consciousness. They embodied the "apostolic faith," and touched the deepest nerves of spiritual intuition. The worshippers, as they used them, sensed: here is the pure overflow from the springs "welling up to eternal life;" here is water from the Rock supplied directly by God; here is nourishment from "the bread which came down from heaven." We recognize here the truth which brought us into being, and nurtures and sustains us. Here is the faith by which we live and die. It was this deep corporate spiritual intuition on the part of the general body of believers which first put the stamp of approval on these books.

There is a difference between *recognizing* and *conferring* authority. During Prohihition days, when gangsters seemed to have control of Chicago, a friend of mine was taking a leisurely evening stroll there. Sudddenly, a grim-looking figure stepped out of a dark doorway and demanded: "Give me a buck!" For some reason, my friend just happened to be fingering a folded dollar bill in his pocket. He just handed the thug the dollar, without pausing or looking at him, and walked on. My friend *recognized* a certain authority which that man had over him at that moment, but he did not *confer* authority upon him!

So, the church did not *impart* or *bestow* authority on these books. It simply *recognized* an inherent authority already there. By selecting a canon they did not confer authority on these books. Rather, they confessed, these books convey an authoritative word which we gladly acknowledge, and under which we willingly bring ourselves, as guides and norms by which all future developing tradition in the church is to be measured. All the Councils of the church did, then, was to give formal approval to what the worshipping Christian consciousness had already done. When, therefore, 1 Peter opens with the words, "Peter, an apostle of Jesus Chrlst," we may rest assured that we are in touch with the original authentic, undiluted, undistorted, authoritative "apostolic" faith.

B. The Readers as God Sees Them

The external features of the first recipients of the letter, such as their geographical location, their nationality, their state of spiritual maturity, have been discussed in the Introduction (pp. 77ff.). What Peter deals with in his initial greeting to them, however, is their situation in the eyes of God. Who are they, really, as God sees them? Forgetting for the moment their observable human circumstances in time and in history, what is the nature of their true existence in the light of eternity?

It is difficult to grasp exactly what Peter says in this regard in his salutation. The translators have made it doubly difficult by moving words out of their original order in such fashion that the structure of Peter's thought is obscured. Peter describes his readers in three words, all adjacent to one another. They are "chosen strangers of the dispersion." I have examined more than thirty English translations of 1 Peter, and in only three did I find these three words translated as one expression.

1. *Chosen*

The function of the word **chosen** in the sentence changes with the different translations. Some give it the force of a noun—"the chosen ones." Some give it the force of a verb—"chosen and destined." Some translate it as an adjective—"chosen exiles." What difference does this make? Simply this. If it functions as a noun or a verb, the phrases that follow in verse 2 can apply to it alone, but not to the total three-word description of who these people are. If, on the other hand, this word has the force of an adjective, the phrases in verse 2 refer not only to **chosen**, but to the entire expression of which that word is a part. They are not only **chosen by God the Father**. They are **chosen strangers of the dispersion by God the Father**. As **chosen strangers of the dispersion** they are **sanctified by the Spirit**. As **chosen strangers of the dispersion** they are to live **in obedience to Jesus Christ and for sprinkling with his blood**. In other words, the entirety of their life circumstance and experience is a part of God's gracious dealing, regardless of the situation and environment they are in, and is therefore to be lived in sanctification **by the Spirit**, in **obedience to Jesus Christ** and in accord with His own sacrificial self-giving.

Two things undergird the wisdom of giving the word **chosen** or "elect" an adjectival force. First is the parallel expression in 2:9: **you are a chosen race**. It is obviously adjectival there. Second is the position of the word in the sentence. If Peter had intended to apply the phrases of verse 2 to the word **chosen** only, he could easily have done what the modern translators do—move it down next to them. But he didn't, because he was using **chosen** as a modifier of **strangers of the dispersion.**

What, now, does **chosen** or elect mean here? In raising this question, it must be admitted that the biblical doctrine of election confronts us with mystery which is insoluble. One ultra-wise Old Testament writer once said: "The secret things belong to the Lord our God; but the things that are revealed belong to us. . . ." (Deut 29:29). Paul added his profound echo to this: "How unsearchable are his judgments and how inscrutable his ways!" (Rom 11:33). We cannot fathom the infinite depths of the divine mind. And when by our logic and rational processes we attempt to pontificate about the eternal salvation or damnation of human souls, we have arrogated to ourselves that which does not belong to us. We are "witnesses," not the judge. Luther's council on predestination is wise: "Dispute not in any case of Predestination. But if thou wilt needs dispute touching the same, then, I truly advise thee to begin first at the wounds of Christ, as then all that Disputation will cease and have an end therewith!"

In spite of the dangers involved in discussing the matter, however, it is an inescapable fact that the Bible unequivocally insists that God makes choices involving nations, individuals, and events. And the Bible writers refuse to try to "rationalize" those choices in the sense of justifying them by human logic or standards of justice. In the Bible, God's choices depend "solely upon his sovereign will." Paul insists that because of this, there can be no "injustice on God's part" (Rom 9:14). And should we say that God *seems* to be unjust according to our ideas of injustice, Paul would reply: "Who are you, a man, to answer back to God?" (Rom 9:20). But beginning with the call of Abraham, through the distinction between Cain and Abel, Isaac and Ishmael, Jacob and Esau, and Joseph and his brothers, climaxing in the call of the nation Israel, God chose individuals and the nation Israel to have a special relationship to Him.

The Old Testament writers could never understand the reason for this. It was not because Israel was great in numbers, or wealthy, or politically powerful, or meritorious in human relations. "Behold, to the Lord your God belong heaven and the heaven of heavens, the earth with all that is in it." He owns everything. Why, then, should He be concerned about Israel? "Yet the Lord set his heart in love upon your fathers and chose their descendants after them, you above all peoples" (Deut 10:14f.). Why? Simply, "because the Lord your God loved you" (Deut 23:5). God's choice seemed irrational and arbitrary in human ways of thinking, in that it depended "solely upon his sovereign will." The reason was "found in God alone, not in Israel." Is this not true, also, in the New Testament? Jesus said: "You did not choose me, but I chose you and appointed you . . . ." (John 15:16).

Although our passage is dealing with the Christian group as a whole, the truth functions just as well with individuals. Our initial acceptance of Christ, for example, may seem like solely *our* choice, but the more mature we become in the faith, the more certain it appears to us that our decision was not so much ours, as Christ's decision for us. *We* make the decision, but there were many factors over which we have no control which went into the process. We did not choose our grandparents, nor our parents, who most certainly had much to do with our decision of faith. We did not determine whether we should be born in a country where the gospel is openly proclaimed or in one where it may never have been heard. We did not determine who our neighbors were, who were our early teachers, what our childhood experiences of Sunday School and church were like, with whom we went to school, what books may have come into the circle of our attention, and a dozen other things which entered into our decision. In the light of all these things, our decision was made for us by countless influences with which we had nothing to do. The anonymous poet caught this truth:

> I sought the Lord, and afterwards I knew,
> He taught my soul to seek Him, seeking me;
> It was not I who found, O Savior true,
> No, I was found of Thee.

As someone has pointed out, God's choosing may to us seem irrational and arbitrary, but it is not capricious. It has meaning and purpose in the mind of God, and could we see reality as He does, this would be plain. Why should we men be able to fathom the mind of God? When Job was finally confronted with the living God, after arguing with Him at great length, he said: "I lay my hand on my mouth . . . . I have uttered what I did not understand, things too wonderful for me, which I did not know" (Job 40:4, 42:3). "For my thoughts are not your thoughts, neither are your ways my ways, says the Lord. For as the heavens are higher than the earth, so are my ways higher than your ways and my thoughts than your thoughts" (Isa 55:8f.). God's choice of Israel is rational in that it accords with His nature as transcendent Deity. God has His own reasons for doing things.

We are not dealing here with the question of individual salvation, but rather with God's choice of people in the fulfillment of His purpose. Peter's use of the word **chosen** in connection with Jesus as the **chosen and precious** cornerstone confirms that he is not using it in connection with individual salvation (2:4, 6). A good description of what the Bible means by God's determination of things is His "ordering of events . . . and men . . . in accordance with his will . . . for the fulfillment of his purpose . . ., and to the accomplishment of good." God is a holy God, who, as the Old Testament describes Him, "is not partial and takes no bribes" and "executes justice" (Deut 10:17f.). He can act only in accord with His holy nature. His choices embody His holiness and His justice. The Bible clears Him of capriciousness, too, in its picture of His dealing with His chosen instruments when they do not respond to His choice. If He chose them for their sake alone, He would have indulged them when they were unresponsive. But, listen to Amos, who has God saying to Israel with regard to His choice of them: "You only have I known of all the families of the earth; therefore [for that very reason!] *I will punish you for all your iniquities*" (Amos 3:2, emphasis added). It is not only to privilege, but to a *task* that God chooses people! And when the task is shunned, the choice becomes a liability! Israel was chosen that through its witness and service "all the nations" would be blessed (Gen 12:1ff., Gal 3:8). When that choice was interpreted selfishly, as a privilege and not a responsibility, it meant exile and judgment.

When, therefore, Peter described his first readers as **chosen**, he was speaking of the church in Old Testament terms as "the chosen people" of God. They bore a special relationship to God, as did ancient Israel, which, with no merit on their part nor worthiness of the privilege, gave them "the power to become children of God" (John 1:12). But this laid on them the task of showing to all the world what kinship to God involves by rejoicing in suffering, hoping for the life of the world to come, living lives worthy of the character of the One who had chosen them, loving their fellow man, declaring the wonderful deeds of

God, living quiet and peaceful lives in their homes and in society, and being ready to give to those who asked them a reason for their orientation to a higher, unseen world.

2. *Strangers*

The readers are also described as **exiles**, "aliens" "sojourners," or "strangers"—those who settle "in a town or region without making it their permanent place of residence." It is usual to give the term here a figurative interpretation, as a description of a Christian who "is an exile from heaven, his true home." This is undoubtedly the meaning of the word in its only use in the New Testament outside of 1 Peter. The writer to the Hebrews speaks of the men of faith in the Old Testament as "strangers and exiles on the earth" who "are seeking a homeland . . . a better country, that is, a heavenly one" (Heb 11:13ff.). From this, it is natural to conclude that Peter, too, was affirming that "the true homeland of Christians is in heaven and that on earth they are in a foreign territory." This would be but another Old Testament description of Christians as successors to ancient Israel, for Abraham is described as "a stranger and a sojourner" (Gen 23:4), and a Psalmist speaks of his "fleeting" life in time as that of a "passing guest, a sojourner, like all my fathers" (Ps 39:4, 12).

This view has been strongly challenged by a very scholarly work, based on sociological analysis, insisting that Peter is speaking literally of noncitizens of the Roman empire, "resident aliens and visiting strangers" who, cut off from social acceptance in society, "since their conversion to Christianity, still find themselves estranged from any place of belonging," and were seeking a "home" which Peter offers them in the "household of God." The alternative to the predicament of being "strangers" was "not a future home in heaven but a place within the Christian fraternity here and now"—the "possibility of a home in the believing community."

Although skillfully presented and persuasively argued, this view does not seem valid. Apart from the fact, as one scholar has pointed out, that there are some passages in the Greek version of the Old Testament where the idea is symbolic rather than literal, and that the first century Jewish writer, Philo, "depicts the righteous man as a stranger on earth, separated from his heavenly home," the theory does not, in my judgment, satisfy the general orientation of 1 Peter nor the tone of early Christianity in general.

As the letter to the Ephesians indicates, Gentile Christians, who were once "'strangers and sojourners," "alienated from the commonwealth of Israel, strangers to the covenants of promise," are now "fellow citizens with the saints and members of the household of God" (2:19) But, as Paul indicates in Philippians 3:20, the Christian "commonwealth is in heaven." As long as the Christian is in this world, however much fellowship he may find in the Christian community, both he and his fellow Christians are away from home. They resemble British civil servants in the days when the sun never set on the British empire; although they may have met in small conclaves for mutual fellowship, the roots of their existence lay in far-off London; and however settled in they may have been in their places of service, they were not *at home* there. As the Jews of the Diaspora, wherever they were, would greet one another with the greeting, "Next year in Jerusalem!", so the Christians greeted one another, in effect, "Next year in the heavenly Jerusalem!" They were *never* at home in this world. "Amen. Come, Lord Jesus" (Rev 22:20), with which the New Testament ends, expresses the desire of the early Christians to be "at home."

This religious orientation toward the end of history, so plainly expressed by Paul and the writers of Hebrews and the Revelation, is characteristic of Peter's letter from start to finish. The faith is a **living hope** (1:3)—a hope not yet realized; it involves **an inheritance** (1.4)— a treasure not yet possessed. As the Christian awaits this inheritance, he is **guarded through faith for a salvation ready to be revealed in the last time** (1:5), which faith will **redound to praise and glory and honor at the revelation of Jesus Christ** (1:7)—yet to come. Salvation is yet a future outcome (1:9). The Christians are to set [their] **hope fully upon the grace that is coming to [them] at the revelation of Jesus Christ** (1:13)—still future. They are to live so that gainsayers will **glorify God on the day of visitation** (2:12), and **put to silence the ignorance of foolish men** at the final judgment (2:15). They are to put themselves under the Lordship of a judge **who has gone into heaven and is at the right hand of God, with angels, authorities, and powers subject to him** (3:22), and who **is ready to judge the living and the dead** (4:5). They are to share in their Lord's **sufferings so that they may also rejoice and be glad when his glory is revealed** (4:13). Church leaders are to discharge their responsibilities in such fashion that **when the chief Shepherd is manifested** [they] **will obtain the unfading crown of glory** (5:4). And the outcome of it all will be that, after they have been faithful at whatever cost, they will finally enter into the **eternal glory in Christ** to which God has called them (5:10). However much Peter's readers may have found a home in the "household of God," it was a temporary shelter along the way. They were not indifferent to their impermanent abode, for it, too, belonged to their Lord. It was an outpost of His kingdom, where opposition to His rule was to he overcome, and where His holy love was to be the standard of excellence and the measure of reality, so that the outpost would be made as much like the homeland as possible. But they were not *at home* here.

And the family to which they belonged was a numerous one, the "great cloud of witnesses" of whom Hebrews speaks (12:1)—including "the assembly of the first-born who are enrolled in heaven, ... the spirits of just men made perfect, and . . . Jesus, the mediator of a new covenant," all of whom are *at home* in the City of the living God, the heavenly Jerusalem" (Heb 12:22ff., emphasis added). In the light of all this, it is difficult to deny 1 Peter "a theology of an earthly pilgrimage of God's people" who are *seekers*—the seekers of whom the poet spoke in his poem by that title:

> Friends and loves we have none, nor wealth nor blest abode,
> But the hope, the burning hope, and the road, the lonely road.
>
> Not for us are content, and quiet, and peace of mind,
> For we go seeking the city that we shall never find.
>
> There is no solace on earth for us—for such as we—
> Who search for the hidden beauty that eyes may never see.
>
> Only the road and the dawn, the sun, the wind, and the rain,
> And the watch-fire under stars, and sleep, and the road again.

*   *   *   *   *

> We travel from dawn to dusk, till the day is past and by,
> Seeking the Holy City beyond the rim of the sky.

Friends and loves we have none, nor wealth nor blessed abode,
But the hope of the City of God at the other end of the road.
(slightly altered)

This captures the mood of 1 Peter. The writer who denies this orientation to Peter admits that it is "central to the Epistle to the Hebrews." I believe that Peter and the writer to the Hebrews would have understood one another perfectly!

This same orientation is to be found in extrabiblical writings from the early Christian church. In the early years of the second century an anonymous author wrote to one named Diognetus: "For the Christians are distinguished from other men neither by country, nor language, nor the customs which they observe. For they neither inhabit cities of their own, nor employ a peculiar form of speech, nor lead a life which is marked out by any singularity. . . . But, inhabiting Greek as well as barbarian cities, . . . and following the custom of the natives in respect to clothing, food, and the rest of their ordinary conduct, they display to us their wonderful and confessedly striking [literally, "paradoxical"] method of life. *They dwell in their own countries, but simply as sojourners.* As citizens, they are in all things with others, and yet endure all things as if foreigners. *Every foreign land is to them as their native country, and every land of their birth as a land of strangers. . . . They pass their days on earth, but they are citizens of heaven"* (emphases added). These words have the accent of 1 Peter!

Two of the earliest church fathers whose words are recorded used similar language. Clement of Rome began his work: "The Church of God which *sojourns* at Rome, to the Church of God *sojourning* at Corinth" (emphases added). Polycarp, of Smyrna, wrote a letter to the "Church of God *sojourning* at Philippi" (emphasis added). These uses of the word "sojourners" are surely not sociological, but theological, indicating the widespread awareness of the early church that they were merely sojourning on earth, with heaven as their true home.

A recent Polish writer, exiled from his homeland for political reasons, has captured the flavor of Peter's use of the word "strangers," or "exiles." He describes "exile" as "an existential manner of being." Whether men are literally "refugees, . . . migrants, vagrants, nomads, roaming about the continents and warming their souls with the memory of their—spiritual or ethnic, divine or geographic, real or imaginary—homes," or "while remaining in their ancestral homes—have been exiled within, estranged from their own cultures, histories, and personal realities," they are discovering "that exile is the permanent human condition." He raises the question whether the "homelessness" of our time may not be God's "brutal" reminder that man's "earthly existence is temporary and that he has been placed here for reasons he is not meant to understand." Peter helps us to grasp this by interpreting Christian existence in this fashion: "In the world, Christians are foreigners; their true place is in heaven."

3. *Dispersion*

The third word used to describe the readers is **dispersion.** This word is derived from the word "to sow,"and became the usual word to describe the entire body of Jews who were away from the Holy Land, "sowed" or "scattered" among the pagans throughout the world. Since Peter was writing mainly to Gentiles, and since he freely adapted Old Testament descriptions of Israel to the Church, it is likely that he was here thinking of the Christians scattered in all parts of the world as "salt" and "light" and "leaven" among their pagan neighbors. The writer of the Epistle to Diognetus, in the first third of the second century, likened Christians to what the soul is in the body. "The soul," he said, "is *dispersed* through all the members of the body, and Christians are *scattered* through all the cities of the world" (emphases added). Like the Jews of the dispersion, the Christians formed little communities within the various secular communities in which they were placed, to bear witness to the uniqueness of the God whom they worshipped, to persuade their neighbors to acknowledge this God, and to center their loyalties and their hopes on a distant city, the New Jerusalem, "the Jerusalem above" (Gal 4:26).

4. *Chosen Strangers of the Dispersion*

The total expression, "chosen strangers of the dispersion," describes who Peter's readers were as seen from God's viewpoint. Outwardly, they lived as ordinary normal human beings in various parts of ancient Aaia Minor, tradesmen, farmers, tanners, builders, herdsmen,

Commentary 1:1-2

tent makers—just ordinary human beings as seen by men. But as seen by God, they were **chosen,** "choice," precious in His sight. They shared the wonder of ancient Israel at God's choice of them. They could say, as did Moses: "ask . . . since the day that God created man upon the earth, and ask from one end of heaven to the other, whether such a great thing as this has ever happened or was ever heard of. . . . has any god ever attempted to go and take a nation for himself," just because He loved them (Deut 4:32ff.)? But since this God is "God in heaven above and on the earth beneath; there is no other" (Deut 4:39), the Christians, like Israel of old, were bound to obey Him and serve His purposes. This set them apart from the nations who worshipped other gods, and made them **exiles,** "strangers," "aliens," misfits who, living among men at the ordinary level, marched to the beat of a different drummer, followed customs and lived by values set in an unseen kingdom, the spires of whose capital lie "beyond the rim of the sky." And amid the crumbling hopes of the kingdoms of this world, they pointed to the unseen and abiding realities of that "kingdom that cannot be shaken"(Heb 12:28). Even though, in the discharging of their tasks, they were suffering, they were to endure their suffering faithfully and joyously, knowing that in so doing they were united to their Lord who suffered, that their real inheritance awaited them when their suffering was over, and that they were comrades of their suffering brothers throughout the world who, together with them, made up the household of faith. As one has well summed it up: "Behind the visible strangership and scattering in the midst of the world were the one invisible and universal commonwealth, of whom the Asiatic Christians were members, and the God who had chosen it and them out of the world."

It is to this total reality that the three prepositional phrases of verse 2 refer. They are "chosen strangers of the dispersion . . . according to the foreknowledge of God the Father." They are"chosen strangers of the dispersion . . . in sanctification of the Spirit." They are "chosen strangers of the dispersion . . . **for obedience to Jesus Christ and for sprinkling with his blood.**" The totality of their situation is gathered up in these phrases.

5. *The Foreknowledge of God*

The first phrase, translated in the *Revised Standard Version* as

destined by God the Father, is literally, "according to the foreknowledge of God the Father." The preposition involved in the original has several meanings, but here it seems to have the sense of *motivating occasion* or *origin* or *ground* of the situation of the readers. The circumstances in which they were now living did not originate by chance. There was purpose behind them, a purpose hidden in the mind of God. This is simply a way of expressing the idea of providence. Was Shakespear right when he said: "There's a divinity that shapes our ends/ Rough-hew them how we will"? Or, do things happen mostly by chance? According to Peter, our life situations are known ahead of time by God, who plans them in accord with His purpose.

Peter makes plain what he means when he tells us that Christ was **destined before the foundation of the world but was made manifest at the end of the times for your sake** (1:20). What happened in the life and death and resurrection of Jesus at a specific era in time and a locatable place in history was, from one standpoint, determined by the free action of "lawless men;" nonetheless it was in accord with "the definite plan and foreknowledge of God" (Acts 2:23). "The kings of the earth set themselves in array, and the rulers were gathered together, against the Lord and against his Anointed," to put Jesus to death; but what they did was "whatever [God's] hand and [God's] plan had predestined to take place" (Acts 4:26, 28). As a great British scholar put it: "God thought about Jesus ahead of time." In so asserting, he raised the alternative. "Can we really picture God in the style of a celestial Mr. Macawber, 'waiting for something to turn up,' till, unexpectedly, through the unforeseen action, I suppose of natural laws, Jesus is thrown up on the surface of things, a happy chance, that enables some of God's ideas to be fulfilled, a great piece of luck for God? The thought is impossible; it negates the very idea of God . . . . the death of Jesus was no accident, no blunder, no patch on a mistake; it was the design of God Himself."

Argue as we may that the design of God cannot be squared with the free will of man, the biblical writers were not willing to surrender God's freedom to save man's freedom. And to them, the reason God was God was His capacity to use that which was set against His purposes to fulfill them. But what keeps God's purposes from being capricious is His nature. He is **God the Father**. As one translator phrases our passage: "according to the predetermination of a Father God."

If God thus predetermined Jesus' coming and accomplishment, is it asking too much to believe that such a providence determines the course of our lives? As a French writer has said: "It is not a question of an implacable decree, of a blind or capricious design (the *fate* of the Romans or the *chance* of the Greeks), but the will of a God revealed as Father, therefore rich in a love which he desires to share." Peter is not dealing here with theoretical theology, but with the actual life situation of his readers. So, he says: Your lot is not outside the cognizance of God. Do not think in your despair that God has either forgotten or forsaken you. He has known all about your difficult circumstances from the beginning. And more than that, He is your Father. You are choice in His sight. He who notices the sparrow's fall will show even more concern about you. And "**after you have suffered a little while . . . will himself restore, establish, and strengthen you. To him be the dominion for ever and ever. Amen**" (5:10ff.).

6. *Sanctification By The Spirit*

The second phrase, "in sanctification by the Spirit," describes either the sphere in which God's gracious superintendence of their lives operates, or the m114eans or instrument by which this is done. The Revised Standard Version translates the phrase **sanctified by the Spirit**, indicating that the translators have chosen the latter. One responsible commentator has combined the two, suggesting that the Christian both lives in the sphere, or the domain, of holiness and is enabled to live the life he does "by means of the sanctification wrought by the Holy Spirit in his heart." Experientially, both are true. It is difficult to be sure which Peter had in mind.

The word "'sanctification" in itself means basically "separation to holy uses," things set apart from ordinary secular life for the purpose of worship, as Aaron and his sons were "dedicated" or "consecrated" to preside over the worship of God's people. God was "holy" in the sense of being the "wholly Other," and those who ministered to Him, and even the vessels of worship used in that ministry, were "set apart" from all common uses to symbolize the "otherness" of God, "the world of the sacred." As time went on, however, the idea of the "otherness" of God began to evolve into a moral and ethical "otherness." God became the One who was "of purer eyes than to behold evil" and could "not look on wrong" (Hab 1:13). He was the thrice-holy One, in whose presence men became painfully aware of their "lostness" and moral "uncleanness" and "guilt" and "sin" (Isa 6:1ff.). Sanctification, therefore, involved the "development of moral character."

There are those who would limit the term here to the first meaning, denying that it means "spiritual sanctity of character." Since exactly the same phrase is found in 2 Thessalonians 2:13, where "sanctification by the Spirit" is associated with "belief in the truth," it is argued that Peter is referring to the action of the Spirit which initially led his readers to believe the gospel, rather than to the ongoing work of the Spirit in renovating the believer's character. In the light of the fact, however, that later, Peter explicitly tells his readers to **be holy ... in all your conduct** because the God they worship is **holy** (1:15f.), it seems difficult to sustain the view that the element of character development is lacking here. When Peter's readers were unbelievers, they were dwelling in the sphere of the **futile ways** of moral and spiritual **darkness**, led about by the **passions of the flesh, living in licentiousness, passions, drunkenness, revels, carousing and lawless idolatry** (1:18; 2:11; 4:3). Now, the Holy Spirit had transferred them into the domain of light and moral sanctity, consonant with that world toward which they journeyed, where everything reflects the beauty of holiness.

7. *Obedience And Sprinkling With The Blood Of Jesus Christ*

The third phrase of verse 2, **for obedience to Jesus Christ and for sprinkling with his blood**, describes the **end** or the **goal** for which "the chosen strangers of the dispersion" were to live. The translators of the *Revised Standard Version* reflect a grammatical choice they have made which makes both **obedience** and **sprinkling with his blood** refer to Jesus Christ. This is a highly questionable decision. Grammatically, it makes Jesus Christ both an objective genitive in relation to **obedience** and a subjective genitive in relation to **blood**, which would be strange syntax. Furthermore, **obedience** stands by itself in 1 Peter 1:14: literally, **children of obedience**. The same is true in Romans 16:19 and 2 Corinthians 7:15, where **obedience** stands alone, without reference to what or who is being obeyed. The term here, therefore, seems to refer to their general obedience to the truth of the gospel, and the will of God, as they understood them.

The word **obedience** has some interesting nuances. The one instance of its use in the Greek Old Testament is in 2 Samuel 22:36, which the *Revised Standard Version* translators render: "thy help made me great." The Hebrew word for "help" is translated into the Greek by the word that is rendered "obedience" in the New Testament. The literal meaning of it seems to be "hearing," in the sense of a "favorable acceptance of a request." In other words, God had heard David's cry and acted upon it. This passage is repeated in Psalm 18:35, where the Hebrew word "condescension" is put in place of "hearing." The two words seem to have a close connection. One must be humble enough to recognize the claim of another in hearing his call. Personal interests must be set aside to respond to the interests of the other. This combination of meaning must be close to what Peter had in mind when he spoke of **obedience**. The readers were to set aside personal interests and inclinations, listen to what God was saying to them, and respond by an active obedience. Paul's expression "obedience to the faith" (Rom 1:5, 16:26) throws light on Peter's meaning. As one writer has said: This is not "the mental acceptance of a belief but action consequent on such acceptance, open profession in the first instance and afterwards a life in accord with it."

Peter has told his readers first that God, who is their loving Father, knows all about their present condition; secondly, that He has given them the Holy Spirit to separate them from their wicked environment and to hallow their lives. Now, he asks: What is the purpose of this? What is the end to be accomplished? The answer is: **obedience.** You are humbly to respond to what you have heard about God in Christ by putting God's truth in action. Every reference to their manner of life throughout the rest of the epistle is a commentary on this expression in the salutation.

Peter now follows his customary practice of placing this in an Old Testament setting, illustrating the meaning of the New Covenant from a vivid reminder of the inauguration of the Old Covenant. After the Israelites had been freed from Egyptian bondage, they entered into a covenant with God to be His people. In the covenantal ceremony, Moses threw half of the blood of the sacrificial animals on the altar. Then, he read the Book of the Covenant to the people, to which they responded: "all that the Lord has spoken we will do, and we will be obedient." Then Moses sprinkled the rest of the blood upon the people, saying: "Behold the blood of the covenant which the Lord has made with you in accordance with all these words" (Exod 24:6ff.). In this fashion the unity between God and His people was symbolized through their sharing the life that was inherent in the blood of the sacrificial victims. The death of the victims indicated that the pledge between God and His people was total and irrevocable. The blood placed on the altar symbolized the total dedication of the people to God. The blood sprinkled on the people symbolized the fact that God was now placing them under His power and protection.

Unfortunately, the ancient people of Israel were not able to fulfill their part of the covenant. Jeremiah, rather than concluding that the broken covenant was irreparable, foresaw a day when a "new covenant" would be made by God with His people. It would be a different type of covenant, the terms of which would not be written on tables of stone. "I will put my law within them, and I will write it upon their hearts." And the final outcome would be: "I will forgive their iniquity, and I will remember their sin no more" (Jer 31:34). Mark, who was "the interpreter of Peter," indicates that Peter understood the death of Jesus as the establishment of the New Covenant which replaced the Old Covenant. He tells us that at the Last Supper on the night in which Jesus was betrayed, He gave them a cup, and said: "This is my blood of the covenant" (Mark 14:22ff.).

It is to that moment which Peter points when he adds to the word **obedience** the **sprinkling with the blood of Jesus Christ**. As the ancient Israelites, at the making of the Old Covenant, pledged obedience, then sealed the covenant by being sprinkled with blood, so the New Israel, made up in part by Peter's readers throughout Asia Minor, were to pledge their obedience, knowing that it was now sealed by Him who "entered once for all into the Holy Place, taking not the blood of goats and calves but his own blood, thus securing an eternal redemption" (Heb 9:12). Peter was stimulating them to **obedience** by the remembrance that they **were ransomed** from **"their futile ways ... not with perishable things such as silver and gold, but with the precious blood of Christ"** (1:18)—the Christ who **"died for sins once for all, the righteous for the unrighteous, that he might bring us to God"** (3:18).

One other association may have been in Peter's mind as he wrote these words. This has been phrased by a perceptive commentator:

"Fulfillment of the New Covenant rested on union with Him who had died and now lived again, and on a life conformed to His in the strength of that union, that is, on the life of sacrifice. To be sprinkled with His blood was to be pledged to the absolute and perpetual abnegation of self, culminating, if need be, in a violent death, for the good of men and the glory of God." In the salutation of his letter, therefore, Peter may have been gently introducing that of which he spoke frankly later on, when speaking of their suffering: **For to this you have been called, because Christ also suffered for you, leaving you an example, that you should follow in his steps** (2:21). They were being buffeted for their loyalty to Christ. This was to be expected. And, with their Master as their example, they should remain faithful, even if they should have to seal their obedience with their blood.

The salutation ends: **May grace and peace be multiplied to you** (1:2c). This was patterned after the ordinary greetings of letters in Peter's time. The terms he used, however, had more than ordinary meaning. The "pagan" idea of **grace** would have been something like "*joie vivre*" merrymaking, pleasure. The **grace** of which Peter speaks is the unmerited favor of a gracious God expressed in the costly giving of His all—His Son. **Peace** was not a psychological term, suggesting an "inner tranquillity or repose," the "Have a nice day!" of our time. It was rather the awareness that things are right between us and God, because He has "reconciled" us to Himself "by the death of his Son" (Rom 5:10).

II

THE INDICATIVE OF GOD'S SALVATION (1:3-2:10)

Following his initial greeting, Peter opens with one of the twofold purposes of his letter: namely, a "proclamation" or "declaration" of the "good news" which forms the basis of his writing. He focuses the attention of his readers on God's gracious saving action on their behalf throughout history, culminating in Jesus Christ. The word **salvation** is repeated three times. The readers are **guarded through faith for a salvation ready to be revealed in the last time** (1:5); the outcome of this faith is that they **obtain the salvation of** [their] **souls** (1:9); and this salvation was that to which the prophets were pointing and into which angels long to look (1:10).

A. Salvation As Living Hope *(1:3-5)* (Proclamation)

A Dynamic and a Destiny

It is significant that Peter begins his discussion with *worship*: **Blessed be God,** or "Let us praise God." Thinking about God can be done rightly only in an atmosphere appropriate to deity—reverence and devotion. In the Bible, praise to God has a distinctive quality separating it from pagan worship. One who has made a study of ancient pagan prayers has concluded that most of them "are man-centered. The gods are praised because man wants something from them. The one who prays hopes that his expressions of gratitude will so please the deity that he will respond benevolently." In biblical praise, however, "God occupies . . . the center of man's attention." God has already shown His graciousness in giving His gifts, even though man is wholly undeserving of them, and is praised less for the value of the gifts than for what He has shown Himself to be in the act of giving.

What is more, in imparting His blessings, God gives Himself along with His gifts, so that the center of biblical praise is in the warm personal relationship that the gift has established between Giver and receiver. The gift has established a bond that cannot be broken. This may be seen in Isaac's mistaken "blessing" of Jacob (Gen 27:1ff.). Isaac was deceived into giving the blessing reserved for the first-born son to Jacob instead of Esau. But once the blessing had been given, it was irreversible. The father had passed on the headship of the family to the second son. Having pledged himself to that, even mistakenly, he could not recant. So, in blessing His people in the gift of His Son, God had pledged Himself to them in an unbreakable fashion. To "bless" or "praise" Him in return was not merely to express a subjective feeling of gratitude because something pleasant or useful had been given, but to exalt Him as the Giver, who without any obligation on His part, had shown Himself generous.

To "bless" God for having been **chosen** by Him, therefore, was to exalt *God's graciousness*. Divine election "is not a device by which man elates himself but rather the supreme reason for man's humility." Paul expressed this when he said: "Jesus Christ came into the world to save all sinners. I know, I am the worst of them all. But I found mercy for this very reason: Jesus Christ wanted to manifest all his long-suffering to me first. He singled me out as a typical example, in order to encourage those who in the future would believe in him and inherit eternal life" (1 Tim 1:15f. in modern translation).

The worth of beginning a theological discourse with praise came home to me forcefully in a conversation with a Chinese convert to Christianity. Following his conversion, he came to this country to study theology. He was dissatisfied with the theological approach of his mentors, whose answers to his questions seemed inadequate. This drove him to the study of some modern philosophical thinkers whose works almost undermined his Christian faith. Tempted to give it all up, he turned in desperation to Barth and Calvin. What gripped him in them, particularly in Calvin, was that their theology was grounded in devotion. They *worshipped* as they thought. Recapturing from them the principle of *faith seeking understanding*, he recovered his faith. He learned what Peter meant, when he began his letter: **Blessed** or "praised" be God!

But who is this God who is praised? He is **the God and Father of our Lord Jesus Christ!** (1:3). God is not just God in a general sense. He is specifically defined for Christians by Jesus Christ. In Peter's day, as in ours, there were "many 'gods' and many 'lords'—yet for us there is one God, the Father, and one Lord, Jesus Christ, through whom are all things and through whom we exist" (1 Cor 8:5f.).

This means that, for Christians, Jesus Christ becomes the starting point of all thinking about God. "No one has ever seen God," says John; "the only Son, who is in the bosom of the Father, he has made him known," or "explained" or "interpreted" Him (John 1:18). It is, therefore, a questionable statement to say of Jesus, "How godlike He is!" This assumes that we know what God is like and find Jesus to be that. Apart from Jesus, however—including all that the Bible tells us of Him leading up to Him in the Old Testament, as well as the New—we do not know what God is like. Our knowledge would be mere guesswork. What we can rightly say, though, is this: "How Christlike is God!" God is not just God, a vague Being, inhabiting the unseen world, who we hope would be on our side in a crisis. He is made known to us in the life and death and resurrection of Jesus, who in His exaltation as

Lord bears divine authority in the universe. It is well to remember this when, for example, we heartily sing: "God bless America!" (I once heard a great preacher say that the Jews once prayed "God bless Jerusalem," and He did—He sent them into captivity!) Or when our politicans or entertainers, who perhaps seldom think of Jesus Christ, commend us to God. Or, when our athletes tell us that they hit the home run or made the touchdown because the "Man upstairs" was with them. Who is this "Man upstairs"?

The possessive **our** before **Lord Jesus Christ**, in the mystery of grace, includes us in the relation between God the Father and His Son. One has pointed out that we may well marvel at the **great mercy** of Him who has made this possible. As Paul phrased it, "He destined us in love to be his sons" (Eph 1:5), to receive "the spirit of sonship" (Rom 8:15), "that we might receive adoption as sons" (Gal 4:5).

What is it for which God is praised? That we are **born anew**, brought into a radically new existence. This particular word is used only here and in 1 Peter 1:23, but similar expressions are found in other parts of the New Testament. "Regeneration" (Titus 3:5), "born from above" (John 3:3, 7), "brought us forth," or "brought us into being," (James 1:18), "born of God" (John 1:13), are all cognate expressions. "In him was life," says the prologue of John's Gospel (1:4). And Jesus Himself tells us: "I came that they may have life, and have it abundantly" (John 10:10). He also said that those who follow Him should "inherit eternal life" (Matt 19:29). Is it possible that Peter is recollecting this word when he says that Christians are **born anew . . . to an inheritance**, the noun of the same word of which Jesus had used the verb?

A French commentator has well described the entire New Testament confirmation of Peter's thought here: "From the earliest beginning of the church, the Christians launched on the world their certitude: the ancient promises relative to the inbreaking of authentic life have been made a reality *by the resurrection of Jesus Christ from the dead!* The Messianic Age has dawned and makes possible, from now on, new existences for men. The commingling of the two 'ages,' so well expressed by Paul (the old world or age is condemned and the new inaugurated), makes it possible for believers to have access to life before the upheaval which will bring in the new creation yet awaited."

There is wide use today of the term "born again Christians," in an effort to differentiate a certain type of Christianity from others. Insofar as those who use this pet phrase to suggest that it is possible to be outwardly tied to the Christian faith without having seriously and personally appropriated it for one's self, it has some validity. On the other hand, every genuine Christian is a "born again Christian" in the sense that he has entered into "a new order of existence" into which he was not biologically born, and is a partaker of spiritual realities which have to do with Jesus Christ, which transcend the things of time and space.

There have been many who were introduced to the Christian faith by their parents from their earliest childhood, who cannot remember a time when they did not love their Lord, who never had a sense of rebellion in their hearts against God, and whose lives manifest the marks of a robust, living faith. Just as we have no psychological remembrance of our physical birth, so they have no conscious awareness of a particular time when they were "born from above"; but they are born—*they live spiritually.* Shall they be ruled out of the faith? The genuine meaning of the expression "born again" is worthy; its use as a "party cry" is divisive, distorting, and to be regretted.

What is the *nature* of the life into which the "new birth" brings us? It is a **living hope**—a hope that has vitality, substance, reality, a hope that cannot be killed. **Hope** was not in good standing in the pagan world of Peter's day. The word itself, to the pagans, meant mere "expectation," and could relate either to good or to bad expectations. Hope to them, then, was "a subjective expectation . . . whose content arises from what man considers to be his own possibilities. . . . Expectations and hopes are man's own projections of his future." An instance of this may be seen in a letter of a soldier to his father, found on a papyrus fragment: "I hope to be quickly promoted, if the gods will." Hopes are dependent on conjecture and contingency, with no solid basis on which to rest. With few exceptions, the pagans did not know "the power of a glad sense of the future." Paul described the Gentiles as "having no hope and without God in the world" (Eph 2:12)—a condition of true "spiritual exhaustion."

The Jews of Peter's days knew from their Old Testament that "the future belongs to God." Their hope in God's future, however, was "stultified by the fact that, since the Messianic Age could not dawn until all Israel kept the Law—one rabbi saying, 'The redemption of Israel will come when Israelites have really kept the Sabbath for two Sabbaths'—redemption then was not dependent on God alone." Messiah's coming can be "arrested or delayed" by man's lack of response. For this reason, there is "a certain note of weariness and especially of uncertainty in Rabbinic expectations of the end." And for individuals, although pictures of the rewards of the righteous were alluring, one could never be sure that he had made the grade. A famous rabbi, who was called the "lamp of Israel," when asked why he was weeping when dying, replied: "There are two ways before me, the one to the Garden of Eden, the other to Gehinnom, and I do not know on which they lead me." Another famous rabbi asked to be buried neither in white nor in black, but in neutral colors, so that his clothing would not shame him if he were numbered among the righteous or the wicked. Of this, one has remarked: "Confidence based on works cannot be assurance, and fear triumphs over faith."

We might contrast the Jewish "hope" with the Christian "hope" by saying that the first is an *undying* hope, while the latter is a *living* hope. The Jewish hope is "undying" in that it has survived twenty-five hundred years, ever since the Jewish captivity in 587 B.C. The first returnees from captivity went back to Jerusalem with great hopes that the ancient glories of David's day would be restored; but the realization was far less than the dream. Then the Greeks took over Jerusalem, then the Romans, who finally destroyed it. Then, for nineteen centuries, the city was not under Jewish control. In 1947, their old land partially was restored to their control, then more of it in 1961. But, although their hopes refused to die through all those centuries, what a forlorn fulfillment it has been. No peace, nothing but strife, turmoil, war, destruction, with their entire existence centered on surviving as a people. The faithful, through all those centuries, have continued, in their famous "eighteen benedictions," as well as otherwise, to "bless" God.

> "To Jerusalem Thy City," they have prayed, "return Thou in mercy and dwell in her midst as Thou hast spoken, and build her speedily in our days as an everlasting structure and soon establish there the throne of David. Blessed be Thou, O Lord, the builder of Jerusalem." (Benediction 14)

> "The sprout of David Thy servant speedily cause Thou to sprout up, and his horn do Thou uplift through Thy victorious salvation; for Thy salvation we are hoping every day! Blessed be Thou, O Lord, who causest the horn of salvation to sprout forth." (Benediction 15)

One has contrasted these benedictions, "national, imploring and sorrowful, attaching themselves in spite of depressing evidence to the promises," with the "song of certitude and joy sung by Peter, even if the full realization is yet awaited." The difference is this: the God blessed is named **the Father of our Lord Jesus Christ.** The "undying" hope, repeated so long without fulfillment, tended to become "languid and conventional," whereas the "living" hope was abounding in vigor inasmuch as it had already been partially fulfilled in a historic "demonstration" of its outcome in the resurrection of Jesus Christ. In Him the "end" toward which God was moving had already happened. His resurrection was a proleptic fulfillment of the final outcome of God's purpose. Hope is certain, because the goal of that hope has already come. We need not hope in man, nor in rulers, nor in military might, nor in religion as such, nor in our own righteous achievements, but solely in God who has already brought our hopes to fruition.

Herein lies the difference between a living hope and an *undying* hope. An undying hope heroically focuses solely on *a future yet to be,* clinging to the promise of something *yet to come.* A *living* hope focuses on a future that has *already happened,* but is *incomplete;* something *not solely yet to be,* but something which is *already in existence.* The *undying* hope peers out of the midnight blackness toward the first inkling of light which will herald a coming sunrise. The *living* hope has already seen "the dawn's early light." The sun has not yet burst the horizon in full splendor, but its beams have *already* scattered the darkness and cast its light on life; it has chased "the gloom of night" away, and turned our "darkness into day"; it has dispersed "the gloomy clouds of night," and "death's dark shadows put to flight." "The people who walked in darkness" have *already* seen a great light" (Isa 9:2), that "light of the knowledge of the glory of God in the face of Jesus Christ" (II Cor. 4:6). The *living* hope is not a will'-o'-the-wisp', a mere wish, a pious dream. It is a confidence in the future born of an event in the past. What *will be* already *is!* As the writer of the Fourth Gospel tells us: "In him" who has *already* come "was life, and the life was the light of men" (John 1:4). And that light has *already* shined "in the darkness," and Easter morning—something *already* taken place—is the evidence that the darkness will never "overcome it," or "put it out" (John 1:5).

We cannot, therefore, specify nor conjecture what specific form our hope will finally take. This is in the hands of a merciful God who has raised Jesus Christ from the dead. We cannot describe what we hope for, but *we know in Whom we hope*. We may, therefore leave the future entirely in His hands, knowing that His love and His power are both adequate and trustworthy, even though worse should come to worst. A poet expressed this well:

> What can we do, o'er whom the unbeholden
> Hangs in a night with which we cannot cope?
> What but look sunward, and with faces golden,
> Speak to each other softly of a hope.

The instrument, or means, through which our **living hope** is kindled is **the resurrection of Jesus Christ from the dead.** Our hope "lives" because He "lives." The fact of the resurrection, therefore, is pivotal for the Christian faith. Rightly did Paul say: "If Christ has not been raised, your faith is futile and you are still in your sins" (1 Cor 15:17). It all stands or falls at this point.

It is well to ponder that the resurrection was, first of all, something that happened to Jesus—not to us. It has consequences for us, but it happened to **Him**! This is a truth frequently forgotten in our time.

A half century ago, I heard a famous American preacher deliver an Easter sermon on the text in Psalm 138:8: "The Lord will perfect [or complete] that which concerneth me." The sermon began with depicting the desolation of the disciples upon the death of Jesus. But they went fishing thereafter, and during the long night of toil were contemplating their loss. Suddenly, it occurred to them that God is not the kind of God who does half jobs. He would hardly start something as wonderful as Jesus, and not finish it. God completes things! So, they mused, Jesus, in spite of His death, must still somehow be *alive*. This they went forth to tell the world. Jesus was put to an untimely death by His enemies, but He lives on, in His words, His memory and His influence! You can't destroy an idea, and you can't destroy a person with an idea!

While I was writing this, a magazine came into my hands reviewing a recent book on theology, where a couple of Christian monks are trying to smooth the edges of the faith so that it will not offend the sensibilities of modern man. Is the resurrection of Jesus a difficulty? Well, no problem, says one of the monks. Jesus' victory over death on Easter is not theology! "No responsible theologian is going to dredge that up today!" The resurrection was just a mental "experience" the dis-

Commentary 1:3

ciples underwent, because they couldn't bear the thought of "a wonderful, lovable person . . . being subjected to capital punishment on the basis of ambiguous allegations." The reviewer added. "He didn't have a jury trial, either." In both the sermon and the book, the resurrection did not happen to Jesus—it was something that happened to the disciples!

I wonder if either of them thought of trying this on for size on the Apostles' Creed. "I believe in Jesus Christ His only Son, our Lord, who was conceived by the Holy Ghost, born of the Virgin Mary, suffered under Pontius Pilate, was crucified, dead, and buried; later on the disciples, who just couldn't bear the thought of the unjust way He was put to death, concocted the story of His resurrection to give Him some lasting value to mankind in spite of His untimely and tragic ending!" One is tempted to say, with a great nineteenth century Scottish social critic: "O man, great is thy infidel faith!"

The Creed, in speaking of Jesus, is enumerating things that *happened to Him*. He was *born,*—at a locatable place in time and space, under Caesar Augustus; in Bethlehem, of Judea. He *suffered* under Pontius Pilate—an event which took His life at a locatable and datable place and time; in Jerusalsm, under the then ruling Roman official. He was crucified—an historic act carried out by Roman soldiers, outside Jerusalem at a then familiar place called "the place of a skull." He *died*—that is, He stopped breathing and His heart ceased beating and what we call life left His body. He was buried—lovingly wrapped in graveclothes by a man named Joseph, of a place called Arimathea, who wrapped Jesus' dead body "in a linen shroud" and placed it in a rocky tomb which was easily locatable at that tIme. Then, "the third day"—not the second nor the fourth, but the third , the next event took place—*he rose again from the dead*." Grammatically there is no switching here; it is still describing what happened *to Jesus,* not someone else. *He* rose! This, of course, had profound significance for the disciples, and for all mnnkind, but it did not happen to them. *It happened to Him*! To shift, at this point, from Jesus to the consciousness of the disciples, not only defies grammar, but common sense, as well as proper theological thinking.

I know that this may be countered with the charge of naïvete—a failure to distinguish between observable, historic actions, such as crucifixion and burial, from the supra-historical character of the resurrection. Of this I am not so sure. Of course, the resurrection story, if true, involves supra-historical features which are not observable to the five senses. But was this not true of the other events in the story? There were supra-historical cosmic things going on, which no eye could see, while Jesus was wrestling in the Garden of Gethsemane. There began an unseen and unseeable struggle with evil which "greatly distressed and troubled" Him (Mark 14:33). The first of these expressions describes the suddenness of a shock too great to be borne, and the latter the settled-in misery of unbearable agony which follows initial shock. "My soul is very sorrowful, even to death," said Jesus (Mark 14:34). Here is moral struggle of an intensity that "well-nigh kills." And, when a few hours later, after agonies of spirit which no camera could capture, nor artist depict, nor the mind of man imagine, he cried out in despair: "My God, my God, why hast thou forsaken me?" (Mark 15:34), something transcendent and supra-historical was taking place of cosmic dimensions. No categories of time and space can capture it. But, though it involved the final moral struggle of God with evil in dimensions which involved the entire universe, *it was taking place in history*. Super-history and history met in that struggle. The eternal moral battle which involved the whole universe, material and spiritual, was taking place there *in history*. The timeless had invaded time. The supra-historical had chosen to unmask itself at an identifiable spot in history. In the light of this, why was it not possible that the supra-historical character of the resurrection could not have bound itself up with historical elements, such as rocky tombs, burial shroud, and massive stones which can thwart tomb-robbers but cannot inhibit a transformed, resurrected body from exiting? Could it not be naïve to think otherwise?

To rob the resurrection of its historic nature as an event, it is often pointed out that nobody saw the transformation of the corporeal body of Jesus into a resurrection body, and that the postresurrection appearances were visible only to believers. Was there not one exception to this, however. Was Paul a believer while on his way to Damascus, "so that if he found any belonging to the Way, men or women, he might bring them bound to Jerusalem" (Acts 9:2)? And yet, much against his will, the risen Lord "appeared" to him, an event which Paul himself listed among the postresurrection appearances. Here, apparently, it is plain that the Risen One could make Himself known *in history*, at a particular time and place, if it were consonant with His purpose. For the rest of us, He says: "Blessed are those who have not seen and yet believe" (John 20:29), but He is free to act as He will.

A careful examination of the records of the "appearance to

Paul reinforces the objective nature of that event. In one of the three accounts of it, the record tells us that the "light from heaven, brighter than the sun," shone not only round Paul but "those who journeyed" with him, and that they "'all" fell to the ground (Acts 26:13f.). The other two accounts include the travellng party in the event. One says that "the men who were traveling with [Paul] stood speechless, hearing the voice but seeing no one" (Acts 9:7). The other says that Paul's companions "saw the light but did not hear the voice of the one who was speaking" (Acts 22:9).

There is a discrepancy here between the accounts, and it is interesting to note what is often made of this. The contradiction, for many, not only discounts the meaning of the entire episode, but turns Luke into an untrustworthy guide. One would think that anyone with the intellectual acumen to write Luke-Acts would be bright enough to have noticed this contradiction, as we do, and to have eliminated it if he had wanted to. The fact that he did not correct it must have had a reason. Could it be that he has a higher purpose in including two accounts contradictory in one detail because both of them had a common feature which he thought was important. They both stress the *objectivity* of the experience. Although Paul's companions did not understand what was happening, they were aware that *something was happening, something was transpiring, something was taking place* which transcended the limits of Paul's inner consciousness. This was no hallucination, no delusion, but confrontation with an objective unseen Presence which cannot be dismissed on purely subjective psychological grounds. Granted its mysteriousness and inexplicability, this was an *event, not a phantasm.*

The necessity of some sort of objective reality to the resurrection may be seen in connection with the disciples' initial response to the death of Jesus. Instead of inspiring happy thoughts that, even though He had died, Jesus must somehow still be alive through His words, His memory, His influence, the records, prompted by the disciples themselves, tell us what Jesus' tragic death did to them. They did not have the benefit of thinking nice thoughts in scholar's studies. They knew life. *And they knew death!* They knew that dead people are dead! And however much they may have revered Jesus' memory, they knew that what they had expected Him to do for them, He could never do from that cold rock tomb. For hard-bitten people such as they, sepulchers and corpses and winding-sheets, and the memory of countless loved ones and friends who had entered the world of the dead never to return, do not kindle happy thoughts of the immortality of influence, nor the hope of seeing them again some time, nor visions of imaginary delights in the elysian fields of some never-never land, nor of triumph over unjust capital punishment on the part of innocent victims. No—dead Messiahs simply will not do! When some women came to them with excited news about an experience they had had at the empty tomb with "two men . . . in dazzling apparel," their words "seemed to them an idle tale, and they did not believe them" (Luke 24:4, 11). The dream shattered by His death brought *total disillusionment,* not happy thoughts of how He might still be alive in the "beautiful isle of somewhere."

Furthermore, this all left them *hopeless.* They were young men, devout and idealistic, eager to see their national hopes fulfilled through One whom they thought God had sent as their deliverer. But His death demolished their hopes. "But we had hoped that he was the one to redeem Israel," they said disappointedly. *But their hope was gone*! And any mood to try to rekindle their hopes on pleasant memories was bludgeoned into pulp by that grim cross and the echo of those pounded nails, and that coagulating blood, and that cry of despair, "My God, my God, why hast thou forsaken me?"

And they were *afraid.* If Jesus' enemies had done Him in as they had, what was to keep them from turning on His followers. *It could be their turn next!* So, they retreated behind locked doors, "for fear" (John 20:19). Never was there a more forlorn, beaten, dejected, lamentable, disspirited group of men than those.

And yet—*and yet*—not long thereafter, these same men came forth to the public with seemingly irresistible power (Acts 1:8, 4:33). Their *disillusionment* was gone—the promises spoken by the prophets had been fulfilled, they said (Acts 2:16ff., 3:18). Their *hopes,* recently killed, were reborn and deathlessly alive—the risen Jesus was the pledge that "all that God spoke by the mouth of his holy prophets from of old" will finally come to pass (Acts 3:21). Their fear had vanished— no more hiding behind closed doors, but facing opposition with boldness (4:13, 31). Obviously, *something had happened*, between the death of Jesus and this transformation, to cause it. To find disillusioned, hopeless, cowed men rejoicing to be beaten, imprisoned and put to death, requires an explanation. We have to explain "a new life—a new life of prayer and joy and power, a new indifference to physical death, in a new relation to God." What was it? They themselves explained it by **the resurrection of Jesus. They were born anew to a living hope**

through the resurrection of Jesus Christ from the dead (1 Pet. 1:3).

Would it not be expected that the participants in this incredible change would have the most trustworthy explanation of its cause. Modern men seem to want to reverse their story. They make the resurrection of Jesus the result of an inner psychological experience on the part of these men. The men themselves say that the inner change was the result of the outer fact of the resurrection. On the ground that an effect is not likely to be greater than its cause, it would seem wise to accept the mighty fact of the resurrection of Jesus as the cause of the disciples' change, rather than vice versa. It seems saner, too, to accept the explanation of those involved rather than that of onlookers centuries later.

By resurrection, these early Christians were not thinking in terms of mere spiritual survival, but of what the Apostles' Creed means when it speaks of the "resurrection of the body"—an actual transformation of the historical, fleshly body of Jesus into another body, a "spiritual body" (1 Cor 15:44), not subject to the laws of nature as we know them in this world. This body was not a body of "flesh and blood," which "cannot inherit the kingdom of God" (1 Cor 15:50), *but it was a body*!

At this point, the Christians parted company with the Greek ideas of "the immortality of the soul." To the Greeks, survival after death meant the freeing of the spirit which had been imprisoned within the body, to exist henceforth without a body. To the Christians and the Jews before them, a human being was thought of rather as an animated body, with the body being as much a part of the person as the spirit. Resurrection, therefore, was the transformation of the *whole person,* body and spirit, into an order of life fit for the world beyond, just as the body and spirit as we now know them, are fit for life in this world.

If not, why would Paul be dealing at all with the question of the Corinthians: "With what kind of body do they come?" (1 Cor 15:35). And what did Paul mean when he spoke of the risen Jesus "appearing" to Peter, to the twelve, to five hundred brothers at one time, to James, and "last of all" to him (1 Cor 15:8). He certainly was not speaking of spiritual, psychic experiences which any Christian could have. And they were not hallucinations, on the order of deranged people seeing pink elephants on the wall. There is no such thing as group hallucination. Five hundred people could not see the same pink elephants at the same time! Whatever these appearances were, they were special occasions when the risen Christ made Himself known as alive to certain people chosen by Him, in a way that is not open to all. As Peter put it: "God raised him on the third day and made him manifest; not to all the people but to us who were chosen by God as witnesses, who ate and drank with him after he rose from the dead" (Acts 10:40f.). This hardly describes a mere vision or hallucination. And Paul visited with Peter in Jerusalem for two weeks within six or seven years of Jesus' death, when memories were still fresh (Gal 1:18). Surely, as someone remarked: "They were hardly talking about the weather during those days." So Paul was well informed about Jesus' appearances to Peter and the others, as well as having "seen" the risen Christ himself (1 Cor 9:1). Mysterious though these appearances may have been, they were actual manifestations of the risen Lord to special people in such a fashion as to assure them that He who died had not only survived in a spiritual sense, but had been raised from the dead and had some sort of a resurrection body.

To dismiss the resurrection with a wave of the hand, as one very influential scholar has done not too long ago, with the observation that we all know that dead men do not get up and walk around, has little relevance to the problem. Of course, we know that. But, if once, God, who in Himself is life, wanted to solve the problem of death for His hapless creatures "who through fear of death were subject to lifelong bondage" (Heb 2:15)—wanted to break the endless treadmill of death and give "assurance to all men by raising [Jesus] from the dead" (Acts 17:31), why should He not do so? It is *because* we know that dead men do not get up and walk around that we believe that God, in His mercy, solved the problem which that fact embodies. If we were told it of anyone else, we would not believe it. The one *exception* is the "good news." Once, it happened! And because of that, it finally can happen for all!

The decisiveness of the resurrection can be seen in a word of Paul which may seem to have an oblique relationship to it, but rightly understood, gives it its significance. Paul says that the raising of Jesus from the dead has "given assurance" that God "has fixed a day in which he will judge the world in righteousness" (Acts 17:31). That means that the "death" of this man whom He has raised, now vindicated by His resurrection, is the standard by which the world is finally to be judged. As Jesus said, recorded by the Fourth Gospel, in speaking of His death: "*Now* is the judgment of *this world*, now shall the ruler of *this world* be cast out" (John 12:31, emphases added). Henceforth, the "world that killed Jesus" is doomed. Everything that belongs to the world that clamors for the death of Jesus is judged. The "assurance" of that is the resurrection. He was the victim of the old world, a world that is passing away, and only that which can be squared with that risen victim lasts. As a poet has put it: "Fame——and you could add, wealth, pleasure, status, power, pride, intellectual notoriety —

> Fame is a food that dead men eat,
> I have no stomach for such meat."

The new age has dawned in the risen Christ, and only that which belongs to the "new creation" He inaugurated endures (2 Cor 5:17). The cross without resurrection, therefore, merely adds one more statistic to the endless list of human victims of the old order of death. The resurrection, though, vindicates the death of this one "righteous" victim as a judgment on that old order, and inaugurates the new order, so that "if any one is in Christ, he is a new creation; the old has passed away, behold, the new has come" (2 Cor 5:17). This is what Peter means when he says: **we have been born anew to a living hope through the resurrection of Jesus Christ from the dead** (1:3).

Peter goes on to describe the outcome of the new birth as an **inheritance.** An inheritance consists of something which one himself has not earned or achieved, but is his by right of the choice of another. It is imparted to him as an heir, or assigned to him in a will, by the good graces of an earlier possessor. To be born again as children of God, then, puts us in a position to have our share in all of God's riches. As the Promised Land was "given," "assigned" to Israel by the decision of God, so is salvation given to His children. But, in contrast to the ancient inheritance of Israel, the Christian inheritance has certain characteristics which set it off. The ancient inheritance could be taken away, and was. It fell into the hands of enemies and was destroyed. Everything in this world is subject to the law of decay. This inheritance, by contrast, is **imperishable.** The old inheritance, given to Israel as a place where obedience to God's will should be carried out, became defiled with an intermixture of pagan and selfish behavior, as do all human enterprises. This inheritance, by contrast, is **undefiled.** The Holy Land, although a land "flowing with milk and honey," had its droughts and blights and locusts to rob it of its beauty and fruitfulness. This inheritance, by contrast, is **unfading,** its "leaves and blossoms and fruits are immortal."

But although the **inheritance** is already in our name, we have not yet entered into its full possession. It is reserved, **kept in heaven**, so that, as a perceptible commentator has phrased it, "we may know that it is beyond the reach of danger. For, were it not in God's hand, it might be exposed to endless dangers." It is placed in safety, however, beyond all the risks and harms of this present order. Peter personalizes this by adding that it is kept there **for you**. This is an inheritance recorded in the heavenly court with our name inscribed on it.

But, as one asks: "What does it avail us that our salvation is laid up in heaven, when we are tossed here and there in this world as in a turbulent sea? What can it avail us that our salvation is secured in a quiet harbor, when we are driven to and fro amidst a thousand shipwrecks?" Peter answers this by reminding us that by **God's power** we **are guarded through faith** (1:5). The word **guarded** customarily refers to the defense of a fortress. We are safe and secure in God's fortress, with faith as the weapon of our defense. There is paradox here. We depend on **God's** power, but it functions through our faith. As one has commented: "It would go beyond biblical teaching to say that our faith is wholly due to the power of God, and it would be equally mistaken to say that God's power comes into action in our lives only as a result of our faith." They are two sides of one coin. God gives us faith, but we must exercise it—God's gifts are not forced on us; yet "faith itself receives its stability from God's power." We stand constantly before the dilemma faced by the father of the epileptic boy who said to Jesus in a crisis: "I believe; help my unbelief'" (Mark 9:24). As one writer has put it: "To know that God is capable of conducting His pilgrims to the very end, to the promised land, should, precisely, stimulate the necessary fidelity in believing." *God's fidelity quickens our fidelity.*

The final outcome of the new birth, and the living hope, and the inheritance, is the **salvation ready to be revealed in the last time** (1:5b). The word *salvation* implies "liberation from a menace, a danger, a domination." The deliverance of the Israelites from Egypt is the standard pattern in the Old Testament (Exod 12). Peter also uses Noah's rescue in the flood (1 Pet 3:20). Its full meaning refers to the final deliverance of humanity from everything that interferes with wholeness of life, both to body and to spirit, which God has purposed in Jesus Christ. This final deliverance has not yet been experienced, but it is **ready**. It is accomplished, it is prepared. It is present in Jesus, through whose life, death, resurrection and ascension it was achieved. But He is in **heaven, holding in readiness the salvation which will be revealed in the last time.**

We have here three dimensions of salvation. First, our salvation is something achieved in the past—it is accomplished **through the resurrection of Jesus Christ from the dead.** It was achieved long ago. We have been **born anew.** And yet, this Jesus who acted so long ago in the past, is with us now. He is present as the object of our trust. We are now **guarded through faith.** And He will be fully revealed only at the last time. He is the object of our hope for the **future.** Salvation has a "then," and a "now," and a "one day." The dynamic of the saved life is the "then" and the "now"—the living hope and the guarding **by God's power through faith.** The destiny is the "one day," when our **inheritance** is fully received.

B. Salvation As Joy In The Testing Process *(1:6-9)*
(Proclamation)

A Method of Life

Peter now gives us a look at salvation in terms of its relation to life's experiences. How does it function in the day to day pressure of events that make up our lives?

The answer begins in a mood of joy. **In this you rejoice** (1:6). There are some grammatical ambiguities worthy of mention before attempting to get at the meaning of the passage. First, to what does the "this" refer? Grammatically, there are three possibilities. It could refer to the closing words of the earlier verse—**the last time** (1:5), as though the joy arose out of contemplation of the final victory of our faith. Or, it could refer to the subject of the former sentence, **God the Father,** or to the **Lord Jesus Christ,** thus making the joy the outcome of contemplating the excellencies of the Redeemer. Or, it could refer to the entire passage, verses 3-5, attributing the joy to a reflection upon the wonders of the salvation which involves a **living hope** and an indestructible **inheritance.** The latter seems preferable. It is a more comprehensive view, which can include the others. The Joy does not depend only on the thought of the Author of salvation, or the final outcome of His redemptive work, but includes them in the total range of salvation with which the former verses deal.

Second, is the **rejoice** indicative or imperative? Does it mean "you are rejoicing," or is it urging the readers to "rejoice"? Inasmuch as this comes in a doctrinal, or declarative, rather than a hortatory section of the epistle, it would seem better to take it as indicative. The author is continuing to expound the meaning of salvation which has occupied his thought throughout the former verses. He is not urging them to rejoice, but describing their joy in experienced redemption. He uses the same expression in verse 8—**though you do not now see him you . . . rejoice with unutterable and exalted joy,** where obviously the use is indicative rather than imperative.

Third, is **rejoice** a present or a future tense? Does it mean that the reader is now rejoicing as an outcome of his present knowledge of salvation, or that he will rejoice at the end of time, when his salvation is complete? The former seems preferable. A very learned attempt has lately been made to revive a very ancient interpretation of this passage, where the present tense was given a future meaning. In this case, the **this** of verse 6 would refer to **the last time** in verse 5. The resultant meaning, then, would be "at which end time you will rejoice." To be consistent, then, verse 8, too, would be translated "you will rejoice." Although the possibility of this is demonstrable from other New Testament passages, the tone of the context does not seem consonant with such a future interpretation. As one commentator has put it: "the praise does not proceed only from the contemplation in advance of final realities, but arises from a present already largely transfigured by them."

The word **rejoice** is a strong one. Its force may be seen at the conclusion of the Beatitudes, where it is also set in a context of persecution and suffering: "Rejoice and be glad" (Matt 5:12); or, as some translate it, to bring out the force of the word, "Rejoice, and be exceeding glad." The word is found in the New Testament and the Greek translation of the Old Testament, but nowhere in classical or common Greek. Apparently, for religious purposes, the Jewish-Christian believers had to coin a new word for joy to avoid the pitfalls of contaminating it with pagan conceptions.

This joy is closely related to **salvation,** and is an outcome of being in right relation to God, the gracious redeemer. When, in verse 8, Peter describes the rejoicing as **unutterable and exalted,** he is not speaking of its intensity so much as of its nature. He is not saying, "Oh, I'm just so happy I can't find words to express how wonderful I feel." Rather, he is saying that this joy of which he speaks belongs to another world, for which human words are inadequate. The contrast is not so much in the *measure* of the joy as in its *quality*. The verb is in the present tense, which in the Greek involves continuing action. Peter was saying, "You are constantly, or continually, rejoicing." Joy, genuine joy—not hilarity, not boisterousness, not glee, not emotional bliss, not mystic ecstasy, not transporting merry-making—should be the characteristic mood of the Christian. It is the joy of a continual spirit of worship as one goes about the commonest tasks. It is well phrased in the Revelation:

> Hallelujah! For the Lord our God
> the Almighty reigns.
>
> Let us rejoice and exult and give
> him the glory.
> (19:6f.)

But the Christian faith involves no utopia. It is not a formula for escaping the burdens of life. The very next words of our passage seem to be contradictory to what Peter has just been saying: **though now for a little while you may have to suffer various trials.** The translation here does not quite capture the strange contrast depicted by Peter. The passage literally means: "you are grieved, pained, sad, in sorrow, distressed, because of various trials." How can one be unutterably joyful and yet sad at the same time? The answer is that the contemplation of God's rich blessings depicted in verses 3-5 makes it possible for faith to rise above circumstance and "calmly to bear all evils." Faith does not transform our humanity, and place us above all feeling. As another has put it: "the faithful are not logs of wood, nor have they so divested themselves of human feelings, but that they are affected with sorrow, fear, danger, and feel poverty as an evil, and persecutions as hard and difficult to be borne." But in spite of heaviness of spirit, the deep, fundamental joy abides. Paul experienced this: "as sorrowful, yet always rejoicing" (2 Cor 6:10). Profound joy is the *life attitude* of the Christian even in the midst of the *life experience* of heaviness and trial.

This attitude can abide this experience through a Christian *in-*

terpretation of it. For one thing, the trials are **for a little while**, not permanent—a relatively short period compared to the eternal destiny of the believers. Or, the expression may be one of degree, referring not to duration, but to importance—the trials are relatively of little consequence, thus depreciating "the intrinsic importance of the sufferings endured" in relation to the *purpose* for which they are imposed. The process of refining, although it involves the white heat of the crucible, is designed by the refiner to rid the metal of all alloy and leave a pure deposit of gold. So, with faith. Although it is not stated, it is implied that the refiner is God; therefore, the Christian may be certain that the refining process, excruciating though it may be, is not the result either of chance, or the maliciousness of men, nor the harshness of circumstance, but arises out of the kindly providence of God. It can, therefore, be neither "absurd nor revolting." It is not the test that is **precious**, but "the thing tested"— your **faith**. When the purging fires have removed all the alloy, the "proved," the "genuine" deposit that is left in the crucible is the bright, pure, refined residue of faith. That is the purpose of the testing, to demonstrate the excellence of that which the testing produces. If such a radical process is necessary to refine precious metal, how much more is it acceptable to refine faith which is **more precious than gold** (1:7). If perishable things must be purified by fire, how much more our imperishable "confident attachment to God."

The testing may be gladly endured, too, in the light of its relationship to God, the Judge, at the final judgment. The word **redound** is better translated "be found." The expression "to find" often refers merely to locating or coming across something. Its preponderant use in the New Testament in its passive form, however, is to describe "the surprising discovery and mysterious understanding of human existence" in its "hidden relationships as seen from the standpoint of . . . the kingdom of God." For example, in Philippians Paul speaks of his ambition to "be found in [Christ], not having a righteousness of my own, based on law, but that which is through faith in Christ" (3:9). He wants **God** to find him thus at the last judgment. So here, Peter says that the residue of the believer's faith, which survives the fires of trial, will be found by God and will be "praised" or approved by Him. And, as Jesus is "crowned with glory and honor" in the presence of God because of His willing endurance of suffering (Heb 2:9), believers who joyously submit to life's testing will share that at the last day. This means "participation in the divine privileges" which "God has prepared for those who love him" (1 Cor 2:9). As one writer has remarked, the nature of spiritual reality is such that "the realization of the insecurity of a material basis of life is the only sure way of gaining a dependable knowledge of God," who has "intentionally embedded our lives in a very contingent environment, for the definite purpose of making us realize that we belong to an eternal and not a temporal world." Does this not embody the nuance embedded in Peter's expression **you may have to suffer**? Or, as other translations have it: "if need be," or "if it has been necessary," or "if. . .you are compelled" to suffer. The necessity of suffering under the circumstances here depicted is "the compulsion of what is fitting," or "proper, to remind us of our spiritual destiny—that we are not "all flesh."

Having mentioned the last judgment as **the revelation of Jesus Christ**, where God will judge all things by their relationship to Him, Peter's mind naturally turns again to the believer's present relationship to Christ. What is the *motivation* that would lead men to remain joyful in tribulation, gladly enduring the testing process for the sake of a higher end? This is hardly possible on the basis of cold, calculated principles. There must be something personal about it. Hence, Peter turns the thought of his readers to the person, Jesus, who now, for them, stands in the place of God. The certainty of **salvation** was the cause for "rejoicing" in verse 5; here the cause of their joy is a person, the *author* of that **salvation**.

Although they had not **seen** Him in the flesh, they had, in a sense, seen Him through Peter's eyes and the eyes of those who told them of what He had done for them in dying and rising. What they had seen with their mind's eyes, led them to respond to Him by continually loving Him. And even though now He was physically absent, they were continuing to believe on Him with **unutterable and exalted joy**, and were daily receiving tokens of the **outcome of** [their] **faith**, the **salvation of** [their] **souls** (1:8f.). Here is the paradox of the believer's life: he does not *see*; sometimes he "walks in darkness and has no light," yet "his difficult existence is brightened by glimpses of the dawn." This is because he loves Christ, and "trusts in the name of the Lord and relies upon his God" (Isa 50:10). Genuine love and faith bring the future into the present, and enable the believer to endure as though he were already living in the end time, participating proleptically in his redeemer's final victory. As one has illustrated it: it is akin to the excitement and joy of children on Christmas eve. The expectation of what awaits them on the following morning spills over into the evening before and, in a way, is as real as that of the day when gifts are really given and received. Love and faith bridge the gap between the believer and the unseen Lord.

What is love? It is not mere sentiment; a feeling. "God's hiddenness is not surmounted by sentimental effusions or mystic raptures." Love is less "feeling" than "will"—to will the good of another, even when it costs. Love to God, then, is commitment to His purposes, obedience to His intentions, the abandonment of self in furthering His cause. Said Jesus: "If you love me, you will keep my commandments" (John 14:15). That one can do without ever having seen Him, and without seeing Him now. We can "see" Him through the eyes of the apostles in the record they have left in the New Testament. And if, responding to Him as He is there depicted, we seek to do His will, He and His Father will "make [their] home" with us, and "abide" with us, and by their Spirit will "guide [us] into all the truth" (John 14:23, 15:1ff., 16:13).

We often sing a children's hymn which has fine sentiment, but questionable theology.

> I think when I read that sweet story of old,
> When Jesus was here among men,
> How He called little children as lambs to His fold,
> I should like to have been with Him then.
>
> I wish that His hands had been placed on my head,
> That His arm had been thrown around me,
> And that I might have seen His kind look when He said,
> "Let the little ones come unto me."

This implies that to have been with Jesus in the flesh is preferable to the relationship we now have to Him. But that was all pre-Cross, pre-Resurrection, pre-Pentecost. Now that He has died, risen, ascended, and returned to dwell in His church by the Holy Spirit, we are much more highly blessed than were those who knew Him in the flesh. **Without having seen him we love him, and though we do not now see him we believe in Him and rejoice with unutterable and exalted joy.** Many who saw Him in the flesh did not believe in Him. It is faith, therefore, that opens our eyes to who He really is. From the ascension on, when "a cloud took him out of their sight" (Acts 1:9), until we are with Him beyond death, we live by faith, and hope, and joy. One day, we shall see Him again—not as He was in the flesh, but as He is now—the glorified and exalted Lord. "For now we see in a mirror darkly, but then face to face" (1 Cor 13:12). Then, "we shall see him as he is." Then, we shall **obtain the salvation of [our] souls**, (1 Pet 1:9), for "we shall be like him" (1 John 3:2).

One leading commentator notes four stages in our apprehension of Christ. 1) Hope, or desire, represented by the prophets. Of them, Jesus said: "many prophets and kings desired to see what you see, and did not see it" (Luke 10:24). 2) Physical sight, when Jesus was here in the flesh. 3) The apprehension of faith. Of these, Jesus said: "Blessed are those who have not seen and yet believe" (John 20:29). And 4) The beatific vision, when faith gives way to sight.

What does Peter mean by the last expression in this section, **the salvation of your souls**? What is the "soul"? A French writer has grasped its meaning well when he wrote: he does not "mean a purely spiritual, incorporeal reality: [he] means by the 'soul' the 'I,' that is to say the whole human person." The same word is used by Peter when, on the last night of Jesus' life, he said: "I will lay down my *life* for you" (John 3:37, emphasis added). This can mean only "my whole self," spirit and body. Salvation, then, is the "outflowering" of the whole person in eternity, in a quality of life that death cannot touch. The plural **souls** suggests that "eternal glory for the chosen of God can only exist in union with Christ and in the community of the saints."

C. Salvation As The Consummation Of God's Work In History *(1:10-12)* (Proclamation)

A Mystery Now Disclosed

Peter concludes his great benediction (1:3-12) by directing his readers to the cosmic dimensions of God's salvation in Christ. In doing so, he underlines "the immense privilege" of the readers, the Christians of the **now** (vs 12). **Yours, you, to you** twice—all focus on the amazing position in which they stand (vss. 10ff.). Peter sets the cross and resurrrection of Jesus in the very center of history, with all that happened before them as preparation, and makes them the pivot of all reality since. They involve a mystery now revealed. They explain the whole prophetic movement of the past, and are a subject of wonder to cosmic beings—**things into which angels long to look** (1:12) Here was the point at which eternity intersected time, the moment at which God's world and man's world met in a unique way, forever transforming the latter, and achieving in principle what God intends finally to do with His world.

The **salvation** which the readers now enjoy and to whose fulfillment they look forward, was the subject of search on the part of the **prophets**. The fact that none of them is singled out suggests that Peter has the entire prophetic movement in mind. He is thinking of all that God was doing through the entire Old Testament period in preparation for Him who came "when the time [that God had in mind] had fully come" (Gal. 4:4).

One outstanding English commentator has interpreted this passage as referring to the New Testament prophets, mentioned frequently in other passages (Acts 11:27f.; 13:1; 21:10f.; 1 Cor 12:28f.; 14:29ff., 37; Eph 4:11), rather than to the prophets of the Old Testament. The view is based on the opinion that **searched** and **inquired** did not seem characteristic of the method of the Old Testament prophets; that the expression the **Spirit of Christ within them** would be more natural with the New Testament prophets after the Holy Spirit had been given to the church; and that the lack of the definite article with prophets in the original Greek would seem to point to people more familiar with the readers than the Old Testament prophets were.

More than one scholar has successfully countered these arguments. Peter was not giving a description of the complete activity of the ancient prophets when he said they **searched** and **inquired** about the future. Their main function, of course, was "to announce God's verdict on the world in which they lived." In so doing, however, they inevitably turned their attention at times to the coming Day of the Lord "when the condemnation of the wicked and the salvation of God's chosen would be finally accomplished." In so doing, as part of their total activity, "they scanned the horizon for signs of its advent." And as the Day of the Lord was delayed, the intensity of the interest in its coming heightened, until it took center stage in the thinking of some of the apocalyptic writers. Peter's description of the prophetic activity, therefore, is not exhaustive but descriptive of only one part of their work. He is not limiting their activity solely to casting an eye on the future.

The passage, too, seems to call for a contrast in time between the prophetic activity described and the preaching of the gospel which has **now been announced** to the readers (vs 12). This lapse of time would fit the Old Testament prophets better than those of the New Testament.

There is also a contrast between the prophets and those who **preached the good news** to Peter's readers. They were two different groups—one "prophets," the other "preachers." If they were New Testament prophets, they would seem to have been a "core of scholars who inquire[d] about the time of the End, whose results were then conveyed to the church by preaching missionaries". There is no hint of any such group in the early church.

The lack of an article before **prophets** could well be a stylistic characteristic. Better still, however, it might suggest that Peter had in mind, not only the prophets of the Old Testament, in distinction from the other Old Testament writers, but rather the entire body of Old Testament literature—Law, Prophets and Writings. The church believed that all of them pointed forward to Christ. Jesus said to His enemies: "If you believed Moses, you would believe me, for he wrote of me" (John 5:46). Matthew, in one place, says: "This was to fulfill what was spoken by the prophet," and then quotes from Psalm 78:2 (Matt 13:35). These indicate that Law and Writings were considered to be "prophetic" of Jesus. Peter, therefore in using **prophets** without the definite article likely had in mind the "total Christological testimony" of the entire Old Testament.

Two descriptions of the prophetic activity are given. They **searched** and **inquired**. These terms are almost synonymous, literally "seeking out" and "searching out." The first is "the more general term," while the "searching out" is perhaps a stronger term, describing the minute and diligent aspects of the seeking. Together, they describe the intensity with which the Old Testament writers sought to understand all the implications of the word that was stirring in their souls. They were aware that they were speaking more than they knew (see pp. 25ff.), that what God was saying to them and through them was depicting something grander and more decisive than anything they were experiencing in their own time. It was **revealed to them** that they were depicting "what no eye has seen, nor ear heard, nor the heart of men conceived, what God has prepared for those who love him" (1 Cor 2:9), and that the fulfillment of these things would come far beyond their own time. They could only long, and wonder, and wait. What they were speaking of took place **in the things which have now been announced to** [Peter's first readers] **by those who preached the good news to** [them] **through the Holy Spirit sent from heaven** (1:12). This is perhaps the "most complete and the most interesting" passage in the New Testament which speaks of the testimony made to Jesus Christ by the Old Testament.

The Old Testament writers were inquiring **what person or time** their message was pointing to. The word **person** is not in the original text. It reads merely "what or what time." Some have translated the expression to mean "what time" and "what sort of circumstances." Peter's meaning is somewhat ambiguous. He affirms quite unambiguously, however, that the answer to their inquiry is to be found in the New Testament gospel. *The prophets and the apostles were announcing the same things.* "The prophet differs from the apostle in that he is trying to understand what he announces, without being able to participate in it." But he knows that "what God says to him is not a word in the air, but that it will find its accomplishment at a precise moment of history and in a particular event, that the grace and the judgment, the power and the compassion of God that he proclaims, will come to pass one day on the earth, not remaining mere words, but will be embodied in the Christ, in the King of Israel, the expected Son of David. . . . only the apostles, having known Jesus of Nazareth, could understand the prophets, and in their turn could only understand themselves through the prophets." These profound words were written by a French pastor imprisoned by Hitler's forces during the war, writing surreptitiously on scraps of paper from food packages with a bit of a pencil kept under pain of death, which had to be hidden in the mattress every time steps were heard in the corridor.

What is meant by Peter's expression concerning the prophets: **the Spirit of Christ within them?** It is likely not the Holy Spirit, distinct from Christ in trinitarian terms, but "Christ Himself conceived of as divine spirit." In other words, Peter considered that Christ was active in the Old Testament days. He was pre-existent. He did not come into being at His birth into human flesh, but existed prior to that. He did not begin His work in the world at His baptism into His mission at the beginning of His earthly ministry. He was at work throughout the Old Testament days. Paul speaks of the Old Testament people having drunk "from the supernatural Rock which followed them, and the Rock was Christ" (1 Cor 10:4). The writer to the Hebrews says that Moses "considered abuse suffered for the Christ greater wealth than the treasures of Egypt, for he looked to the reward" (11:26). John says that "Isaiah . . . saw [Christ's] glory and spoke of him" (12:41). These passages are difficult to understand or explain, but they speak of a pre-existent Christ who was active in the world before His birth at Bethlehem. Peter was in good New Testament company, then, in expressing this belief. Both he and the others would have responded wholeheartedly to Jesus statement: "Before Abraham was, I am" (John 8:58).

What was the message of the pre-existent Christ to the prophets which so perplexed them, and made them "search" and "inquire": It was **the sufferings of Christ and the subsequent glory**. It was the principle of the Cross as the pathway by which the Messiah was "highly exalted" and given "the name which is above every name" (Phil 2:9).

The translation of the *Revised Standard Version* here obscures a problem. After **sufferings of Christ** in the plural, it speaks of **the subsequent glory**, as though **glory** were singular. In the original, however, **glory** is also plural—"glories." Here the translators have sacrificed grammar for meaning, and have permitted their interpretation of the meaning to defy the grammar. The first part of the expression also is difficult. It does not say the **sufferings of Christ**, but literally "the sufferings to Christ," sufferings in His direction. Some have sought to solve the problem by translating this, "the suffering road," or "the sufferings in Christ's cause," meaning the sufferings of Christians as they follow Christ.

Here is a problem where grammar and meaning are difficult to put together. It is difficult to refer the **sufferings** to Christians rather than to Christ, for the latter is in accord with so much of the New Testament rooted in Isaiah's picture of the Suffering Servant (especially Isa 53). The risen Lord, speaking to the two travelers on the road to Emmaus on the first Easter, "interpreted to them in all the scriptures the things concerning himself" (Luke 24:27), by using Isaiah's clue: "Was it not necessary that the Christ should suffer these things and enter into his glory?" (Luke 24:26). In Peter's sermon at the Beautiful Gate shortly after Pentecost, he said: "But what God foretold by the mouth of all the prophets, that his Christ should suffer, he thus fulfilled" (Acts 3:18). This is consonant with Paul's humiliation-exaltation theology in Philippians 2:5ff.) where the "servant" who "humbled himself . . . unto death . . . on a cross" was "highly exalted" and given "the name which is above every name." As one perceptive commentator has said: "What reconciled Christians of the apostolic age to the initially shocking enigma of a crucified Messiah was their persuasion, confirmed by the resurrection, . . . that it was an essential element in God's saving plan as attested by prophecy."

Furthermore, Peter in his letter refers so frequently to the **sufferings of Christ** that it is difficult to rule them out of his reference here. He tells his readers, **Christ . . . suffered for you** (2:21); **Christ also died for sins once for all** (3:18); **Christ suffered in the flesh** (4:1); **rejoice in so far as you share Christ's sufferings** (4:13). **I . . . [am] a witness of the sufferings of Christ** (5:1). Peter also relates *glory* to Christ's sufferings. God raised Christ **from the dead and gave him glory** (1:21); he counsels his readers to **rejoice in Christ's sufferings, that they may also rejoice and be glad when his glory is revealed** (4:13). When he reminds them that he is a witness of the sufferings of Christ he says that he is also **a partaker in the glory that is to be revealed** (5:1). In the light of this incessant connecting of glory with Christ's **sufferings**, it is difficult to believe that Peter is not including Christ's sufferings in what the Spirit of Christ was quickening in the thought of the prophets. In all these other cases, however, **glory** is in the singular, whereas in 1:11 it is in the plural—"glories."

The possible solution to this dilemma is to include both the sufferings of Christ and those of His followers, and the glories which followed not only Christ's triumph, but those which have followed and will continue to follow the triumphs of the church. In the Old Testament, as well as in the Intertestamental Period, there was a strong strain of identification of God's people with the Messiah so closely that they would have to share in the "woes" which were to accompany the Messiah's coming. This is also carried over into the New Testament, and Peter places great emphasis on it. **For to this you have been called,** he writes, **because Christ also suffered for you, leaving you an example, that you should follow in his steps** (2:21). **It is better to suffer for doing right . . . than for doing wrong. For Christ also died for** sins once for all, the righteous for the unrighteous (3:17f.). Since therefore Christ suffered in the flesh, arm yourselves with the same thought (4:1). But rejoice in so far as you share Christ's sufferings (4:13). It is perhaps well, then, to conclude that Peter is including both the sufferings of Christ and of His people, and the joint glories that they share.

The mention of the angelic beings at the end is meant to stress the privilege of his hearers to whom the gospel of their salvation has come. They are more privileged than the prophets, for they have now experienced that to which the prophets were looking, but for which they had to wait. They are equally, if not more, privileged than the heavenly beings. The pure, unsullied spirits of the angels may find satisfaction in pondering the wonders of God's redeeming love for sinners. But can it be that the readers are even more privileged than the angels? The gospel is for the angels a subject of wonder. Peter suggests that they are "peering," "stooping down to look." The verb he uses, translated **long** implies "eager" or "intense desire." This eagerness may imply that there is an element in the gospel which transcends their experience and understanding, into which they "would like to gain insight." Privileged though they are to live in the divine presence, yet perhaps they cannot quite comprehend what it is to be a "redeemed" sinner. To know the love of God against which we have rebelled, and to know something of the costliness to Himself which was involved in God's making that love redemptive and reclaiming in the death of His Son, is perhaps an experience which only those who have been involved in it can know.

> The love of Jesus, what it is,
> None but His loved ones know.

A gospel song of long ago, inspired by Peter's words, **things into which angels long to look,** may have captured its meaning as well as it can be put. After describing some imaginary celestial delights in which the angels might be joined, it concludes:

> But when we sing redemption's story,
> They will fold their wings;
> For angels never knew the joy
> That our salvation brings.

Could that be what Peter means? If so, and if it is true, isn't it a wonder that we are not more excited about our redemption?

III

THE IMPERATIVE OF MAN'S RESPONSE (1:13-2:3)

The next five units of thought embody Peter's first hortatory section. Each of them contains an *imperative*, delineating the sort of responses which the salvation he has just elucidated should draw from his readers. **Therefore**, he begins. In the light of what we have just been pondering, this is the sort of behavior toward which you should be striving. In the light of what God has done for you, this is what you should be doing for Him. This is how you say "Thanks!"

In the daily struggle of the Christian with the enemies of the soul, both within and without, it is well to remember that the *imperatives* of the faith always rest on the *indicatives* of the gospel. **Therefore** is a powerful theological word. "You can do this for God," it says, "only because of what God has already done for you!" As we said earlier, the imperative of the gospel is always: *become what you already are in Christ*! "The legitimate demand which [the Christian imperative] places on the Christian life," says one, "is neither autonomous, nor despotic, demanding moral and spiritual performance of the unaided human will, but it is imbedded in an ensemble of ideas determined by the merciful intervention of God in Jesus Christ. The imperative accompanies the 'for us,' the objective of salvation, along with the 'in us,' the creation of a new being .... Without the indicative of that which God has done, the imperative addresses itself to a sinner without power, a victim of his illusions, and becomes a commandment which crushes or drives to vain and presumptious efforts."

The early Luther was perhaps the classic example of separating the imperative from the indicative of the gospel. The demand of God laid on his conscience an unbearable burden which issued in a dramatic moral struggle which he could not win, and drove him more and more to despair, and even toward insanity. When he finally discovered that God had met the demand of His own law in Jesus Christ, and of-

His problem was: "How can I make myself righteous, in order that God may be gracious?" The answer he found was: "God is already gracious, and *He* makes men righteous!" *God's demand is God's gift!*

But a gift cannot be given until it is received. The antinomianism must be avoided which says: Since God is gracious and gives Himself to man, there is nothing for us to do. This does not root the imperative in the indicative, but does away with it. God has acted "not only in place of man and in his favor but 'with him.' The creature is truly a partner in the covenant." The indicative, that God makes men righteous, draws forth the response of grateful man: *Since God makes me righteous, I will strive with all my might to be made righteous!*

A. Hope *(1:13)* (Exhortation)

Life Focused on the Final Victory of Christ

The imperative of verse 13 is to **hope.** This means that the objective **living hope** of **an inheritance ... kept in heaven** mentioned in verses 3 and 4, should now transform our lives into a constant mood of expectancy, a subjective yearning for that which awaits us. This may be seen in the early stage of God's saving activity for His people. The exodus was an objective deliverance wrought for them by God Himself which they could in no way have achieved by their own efforts. But they were delivered from Egypt in order to he brought into the Promised Land. The objective hope created by the deliverance from Egypt now became a subjective turning toward the gift yet awaiting them, the Promised Land. So, says Peter, make the objective **living hope** created in you by God's action in Christ the inspiration to focus your attention on the **grace** that is yet to be brought to you at the final **revelation of Jesus Christ** at the last day. Since the verb in the expression **the grace that is coming to you** is in the present tense, as though the coming is now in process rather than a future thing, some have interpreted the revelation of Jesus Christ as the present unfolding of the meaning of Christ in daily experience, rather than a reference to His future coming. The fact that the two other appearances of the expression, in 1:7 and 4:13, refer unmistakably to the future coming of Christ, it would seem to commend a similar meaning here as consistent with Peter's thought.

Two participles relate to this **hope.** The first, **gird up your minds,** is reminiscent of the intense preparations made by the Israelites when they fled Egypt. They were instructed: Have "your loins girded" (Exod 12:11); that is, have your long flowing garments tightly pulled up for unhampered speedy action. In this case, Peter is counseling his readers: Have your **minds** "stripped for action and fully alert."

Minds does not portray merely the "reason," the "thinking capacity." It describes rather an inner attitude when "resolution counts as much as comprehension," where the will is involved as well as thought—"a tension of the entire being in a given direction." It could best be depicted by the dedicated athlete whose whole being—thought, will, energy—is devoted to making a record heretofore unattained. Or, it might be thought of as the inner state of one who says to himself: "I have a 'mind' to sail around the world alone in a small boat." All the energies of thought, will and ingenuity are bent to that one goal. The word **minds** here is broad enough to include the springs of action in the human personality that transcend mere rational thought. A poet sought to state it thus:

> Reason . . . should be my counsellor
> But not my tyrant. For the spirit needs
> Impulses from a deeper source than hers;
> And there are notions in the mind of man,
> That she must look upon with awe.

This is strengthened by the second participle, **be sober**. This word is used only six times in the New Testament, three of which are in 1 Peter. It is always used metaphorically: "be free from every form of mental and spiritual 'drunkenness,' from excess, passion, rashness, confusion." It describes a life "well-balanced, self-controlled." Again, it may he likened to the self-control or self-discipline of athletes, who avoid all that would impede progress toward their goal. It is the opposite of "intoxication," figuratively referring to "states of spiritual intoxication." This involves the avoidance of "mental fuzziness," the ability to size things up aright, to make spiritual judgments which accord with the mind of God in the light of the revelation of Himself in His Son, to judge moral issues in the light of ultimate reality.

The inebriated man loses, one after the other, "his rhythm, his sensitivity, his thriftiness, his modesty, his power of discriminating between decency and indecency, the mastery of his sensory impulses." He has temporarily lost those aspects of the "image of God" in him which set him off from the animal order. How easy it is to become spiritually "drunk." When the Berlin wall fell, a young man was interviewed on television. When asked about his new found freedom, he replied: "It's great! Now we can have discotheques!" How "blurred" the human vision when spiritually intoxicated, to think that the innate yearning of the human spirit for freedom can be satisfied with discotheques! It is conceivable, of course, that one could be rightly related to God and be living a **sober** life, and still enjoy discotheques. Only God can judge that in individual instances. Since discotheques have lights, music and lyrics which, by the admission of those who design them, are intended to "turn on" the sex impulses, it is difficult to understand how that atmosphere can be intermixed with Paul's counsel to concentrate on "whatever is true, . . . honorable, . . . just, . . . pure, . . . lovely, . . . gracious" (Phil 4:8). But even if that can be done, to make that world, when it is forbidden, the zenith of one's hope, bespeaks a sort of "drunkenness" of spirit which has fatally damaged one's vision of life's meaning.

The **hope** of which Peter is speaking, therefore, must be both intense and controlled, both sharply focused and yet sanely reined in at the same time. It is set **fully** ["perfectly," "completely"] **upon the grace that is coming to you at the revelation of Jesus Christ.** The central core of the Christian's life should be the continuing awareness of the great mercy of God in His Son, of which we now have splendid foretastes, but which will be fully known at the end of time. I once heard a minister say that he had no time to deal with the Second Coming of Christ, because he was so greatly obsessed with His first coming. When I heard that as a young man, I thought it was clever. I have since decided, however, that it expressed a failure to grasp the full meaning of the Christian faith. The longer one tries to live the Christian life, the more he sees the inadequacy of his present state of grace. Marvelous as God's grace is, does not one often have to ask himself: Is this *all* that God is going to do for me? If so, it is not enough.

Surely there are depths of redemption yet awaiting us which will far surpass anything that we now experience. Surely there is an **inheritance** awaiting us in the light of which the supplies of grace now given will seem very small. For that reason, Christians should focus their **hope** on that coming, overwhelming, decisive moment, when the final purpose of God for His universe will be achieved. To change the figure, the daily lot of a soldier should be transfigured by the hope of coming victory. And although he has to sleep to survive, he even sleeps in the posture of readiness to respond to the call to service at any time, and with the hope that victory will arrive at any moment. It is the controlled focus on this coming victory that keeps hope alive.

When this **hope** becomes all-consuming, it pales into insignificance all other hopes. It is this which distinguishes the Christian from others, enabling him to share the common joys of life with his fellows, but to see them in a totally different light. "A cardinal biblical virtue," says our commentator who wrote from his French prison, "is the temporary and relative character of all present things." One whose hope is fully set on the final victory of Jesus Christ takes a similar attitude toward all material and human values. This is what Paul meant when he wrote to the Corinthians: "From now on, let those who have wives live as though they had none, and those who mourn as though they were not mourning, and those who rejoice as though they were not rejoicing, and those who buy as though they had no goods, and those who deal with the world as though they had no dealings with it. For the form of this world [of "the present scheme of things"] is passing away" (1 Cor 7:29ff.). This is not "disdain" of ordinary things, but "on the contrary, a just measure and authentic use of passing things."

The "sobriety" of the **hope** saves it from fanaticism. The clear-headedness, the self-mastery, the avoidance of excess, keeps the Christian, with his sole focus on the end of things, from the wild-eyed fanaticism and utopian folly of many "one cause" people, who put the whole of reality at the mercy of the one thing about which they are concerned. The Christian focuses on a goal broad enough to include all other worthy goals. This saves from religious fanaticism. To quote our prison commentator again: "Sobriety implies that we remain the master of all things and acknowledge the lordship of no one save the king of the kingdom to come." The "sober intoxication" of the Christian faith distinguishes it from the uncontrolled psychic states of enthusiasm embodied in many non-Christian cults and the emotional excesses stimulated by the frenzied dances and frantic music of the entertainment world. Christian sobriety develops the spiritual, rather than the animal, aspect of life.

B. Be Holy *(1:14-16)* (Exhortation)

Life Patterned After the Character of God

Peter's second imperative here has to do not with mood or attitude, but with action, behavior—**be holy . . . in all your conduct.** As we have seen (pp. 115f.) "holiness" has more than one meaning in the Bible. Basically, it describes that which makes God to be God—His transcendence, His otherness, that which places Him above all created things. But to this the Old Testament adds a moral dimension to God's holiness. He is not only above all created things, but He is the opposite of all that is evil and corrupt. He is the only One who is perfectly "pure, just, faithful, and merciful." The pagan gods were above men, but shared in their evils. In fact, they outdid men in evil. As deity is superior to humanity, so the pagan gods could surpass men in evil. Not so the biblical God. As Isaiah described Him: "the Holy God shows himself holy in righteousness" (5:16). Since God's people belonged to Him, they were to make His moral perfection the ethical standard of their own conduct. "Who shall stand in [God's] holy place?" asks the Psalmist. "He who has clean hands and a pure heart, who does not lift up his soul to what is false, and does not swear deceitfully. He will receive blessing from the Lord, and vindication from the God of his salvation" (24:3ff). Peter takes up this theme, and here affirms that **in all** [their] **conduct** Christians should conform to the holy nature of the God to whom they belong.

Conduct has been defined as "a totality of attitudes, gestures, words which have consequences for others, which belong to the sphere of the visible and are exposed to the judgment of society." One's whole public behavior should be expressive of his faith. This has been contrasted with the outlook of the Qumram community, where "holiness is strict, distant, separated, with the intention of a total concentration on the religious. For Peter, attachment to God should manifest itself in the sphere of the world of men."

Behavior, however, needs a pattern, a standard by which life is to be shaped. Peter presents a pattern by the use of a strong antithesis—not *this*, but *this!* **Do not be conformed to the passions of your former ignorance.** Ignorance, as applied to the Gentiles in the New Testament, refers to their lack of the knowledge of God. When Paul addressed the Athenian philosophers, he referred to the pagans' thinking of the deity in terms of the "art and imagination of man," in the shape of "gold, or silver, or stone," as the "times of *ignorance*" (Acts 17:29f., emphasis added). In Ephesians he speaks of "the Gentiles" as living "in the futility of their minds, . . . darkened in their understanding, alienated from the life of God because of the *ignorance* that is in them (4:17f., emphasis added). **Ignorance**, then, is a euphemism for "paganism"— both the ruder types of sensuality and the more refined forms of "the worship of self and the looking out for one's own interests." Smash all the models of your former "pagan" life, says Peter.

He replaces these old patterns with a new one: **as he who called you is holy, be holy yourselves in all your conduct.** The moral perfection of God is to be the pattern after which the Christian should shape his life. This is not an invitation to draw up a set of rules to be followed in a dogged, moralistic way, but rather to enter into a very personal relationship with the holy God, who has **called** the Christian to Himself. As a child grows in maturity by fellowship with a parent who, in his or her person embodies what an adult ought to be, so the Christian's life is shaped by constant fellowship with God. The fact that God has **called** us indicates "that the God of the Bible is a person confronting persons." How clear this is when Isaiah says: "I have *called* you by name, you are mine" (43:1, emphasis added).

And this "calling" is closely associated with "creation" and "redemption." "But thus says the Lord, he who *created* you, O Jacob, he who formed you, O Israel: 'Fear not, for I have *redeemed* you'" (Isa. 43:1, emphases added). In typical poetic Hebrew parallelism, it is clear that Isaiah used "'called" as another way of saying "created" and "redeemed." This reminds us of the Genesis story of creation: "And God said" (1:3 et al), which was carried forward into the New Testament, when Paul speaks of "God . . . who gives life to the dead and *calls* into existence the things that do not exist" (Rom 4:17, emphasis add). When God "calls," things happen! His creative word is efficacious. To be **called** by God, therefore, is to be **born anew** (1 Pet 1:3), "re-created" by a heavenly Father (1 Pet 1:2, 17), who has **called** us into His family to live with Him a "redeemed" life, making Him personally the pattern of our daily conduct.

This counsel to the Christian to **be holy**, therefore, is not mere moralism, adding a burden of legalism to our behavior, of which Peter on another occasion said "neither our fathers nor we have been able to bear" (Acts 15:10). It is rather to lay upon us the joyous freedom of the Psalmist who said "I delight to do thy will, O my God; thy law is within my heart" (Ps 40:8). At a wedding rehearsal, when the bride and the bride's mother and the professional advisor had attended to a dozen details without consulting the groom, the minister, trying to draw him into the decisions, said: "Isn't there something you would like to suggest, George?" George just smiled and, pointing to the bride, said: "No, her will is law to me!" What *she* wants is what *I* want! This is what Peter meant when he spoke of Christians as **obedient children,** patterning their lives after Him who had **called** them into His fellowship, and replacing their former desires, ruled by self, with the desire to please Him.

Conduct now becomes the outgrowth of the new relationship that Christians bear to God. They have been **born anew,** they have become **children** of a heavenly Father, and should therefore acquire the characteristics of their new family. We often say of someone, with regard to some aspect of his behavior: "He is true to his father." Or, we say of another: "He is a true Scotsman," meaning, he manifested a characteristic for which Scots are known. So, Peter proposes that Christian **conduct** should reflect the character of their Father, God. Let your behavior remind others of the Father and the family to whom you belong.

The grammar of the passage confirms the fact that the demand for holiness of life is not a mere moral counsel devoid of gospel, a self-help advice directed to human effort alone. The word translated be is not a form of the word "be" or "exist." It rather means "become." But of the many nuances of this word, the one that may have been in Peter's mind here involves less a description of the "essence" of something than of its "manifestation"—"show yourselves holy, as you are," "show forth in your lives the character of holiness which you possess. Be worthy of it." A parallel use of the word would be Paul's reminder to the Thessalonian church: "You are witnesses, and God also, how holy and righteous and blameless was our behavior to you believers" (1 Thess 2:10). He is telling them that he had lived among them "like a father with his children" (2:11), and his behavior "manifested" or "proved" this. So, says Peter, let your **conduct** be a visible illustration of that holiness which you already have as God's gift in Christ. As one writer has put it: through his exhortations the "Apostle . . . becomes an evangelist." He reminds them that "God's gift of grace is life. . . .Between his admonitions and his gospel there is no breach. . . .This gives the exhortations a double significance; they are at the same time an indicative and an imperative, they say what should be, and they say what is."

Furthermore, the verb **be**, "become" or "show," is in the passive voice, which suggests that in manifesting his redeemed nature in life, the believer is *acted upon* by God's grace rather than merely acting by his own effort. In fact, in one Old Testament passage, after the admonition: "Consecrate yourselves therefore, and be holy; for I am the Lord your God" (Lev 20:7), the statement is added: "I am the Lord who sanctify you" (Lev 20:8). This means in effect, "sanctify yourselves, for I have sanctified you." One writer remarks of this: "It is God Himself who proves His name holy." Another insists: God "sanctifies men . . . . They have to deduce the consequences of it. But the sanctifying by which He claims and makes them and their actions usable in His service . . . is a 'manifestation of His own divine power' . . . and as such it is wholly and exclusively His own act, and not theirs." Paul echoes this in writing to the Thessalonians: "May the God of peace himself sanctify you wholly; and may your spirit and soul and body be kept sound and blameless at the coming of our Lord Jesus Christ. He who calls you is faithful, *and he will do it*" (1 Thess 5:23f., emphasis added). Through prayer, we are to put ourselves at His disposal, and *let Him do it!*

The ability to make great music on the piano is a gift. It cannot be achieved. If the gift is not there, no amount of effort can enable one to be a great musician. Horowitzes are born, created by God with their gift. If the gift is there, however, the one to whom it is given must develop it and keep it alive by practice. Yet, even if he should have the gift, and develop it by practice, then never play in public, the gift would be worthless to others. He must "show" to others that he has the gift by playing for them. So, in sanctification, God gives it to us. We must deduce its consequences, use our own efforts by practicing it and more and more becoming what we already are, then "showing" to others what the gift is by lives which reflect the Giver. This does not, of course, suggest that by self-conscious acts of contrived and artificial piousness we parade our poor virtues "before men in order to be seen by them" (Matt 6:1). The One who warned us against all such vain posturing, however, also admonished: "Let your light so shine before men, that they may see your good works and give glory to your Father who is in heaven" (Matt 5:16). The quiet, modest effort to pattern life after the character of the God revealed in Jesus Christ will shine as light from a higher world into the darkness of the world in which we live.

Peter's words might almost be translated: "Let yourselves be made holy," or "Let yourselves be shown to be holy." The verb form suggests surrender to God's action in us rather than initiative action on our part.

Peter continues his discussion of holiness with an Old Testament reference which fulfills a double purpose: 1) it reiterates one of his favorite themes, that the church is now the "new Israel," the successor to the promises of the Old Covenant; and 2) it warns them to take what he is saying seriously, in the light of the failure of their forefathers in the faith. **You shall be holy, for I am holy** is repeated in almost the same form five times in the Book of Leviticus (11:44, 45; 19:2; 20:7, 26). This venerable counsel is now laid upon the church. Ancient Israel, however, failed to come up to the level of God's expectation for them through unbelief and disobedience. Let the church beware lest it, too, fail of its goal.

While working on this passage, a striking illustration of how deeply its message is needed by our generation came into view. A television news broadcast presented a brief interview with a well-known movie star. She had had one or two children out of wedlock, and was now living with a man to whom she was not married, but to whom she bore a child. The interviewer raised the question of marriage. "Not on your life" was the mood of the reply. Furthermore, it was nobody else's business what she and her live-in lover did, least of all the government's, she insisted. Why should the government have anything to do with whether she was married or not? But above all, she had a "relationship with God," and she was sure that He, or She, as the case may be, fully approved of what she and her alleged lover were doing! If God approves, whose else business is it?

This was out-paganing the pagans. Every society, including the most primitive, considers the establishment of families of concern to more than the individuals involved, and have social regulations of one sort of another with regard to marriage. And there is pretty general agreement among thinkers today, that however complex or baffling society's problems may be, the likely major cause of our streets and schools resembling jungles of wild animals more than places of civilized social relations is the breakdown of the family. But quite apart from the questionable sociology of the actress's attitude—unfortunately, very widespread in our "enlightened" West today, the religious assumptions underlying it are pagan to the core, molded by **passions**, "desires," "self-interest." Peter's word translated **passions** means to be "without objective moral standards," to behave with no guidance beyond one's own whims. Anything goes, on which "consenting adults" agree. Experience exists "for its own sake, as its own validation. If it works, its right; if it feels good, do it." And one can be "chummy" enough with God to persuade Him, or Her, or It, or the Universal Spirit, as the case may be, to agree that whatever I prefer is right. When God agrees with me on what is right, there are no restraints, no limits. This attitude reigns, not only in the realm of behavior but in the "epistemological despair" of "cultural relativism," "poststructuralism," and "deconstructionism."

This is exactly the opposite of that for which Peter is pleading. Instead of fashioning life by the holy character of God, God's character is fashioned by my unholy desires. And when I can get God's agreement on my depraved wishes, morality is at an end. There is no objective standard of measurement outside my own self-interest by which behavior is to be tested. Peter has the only cure for this: to respond in faith and obedience to the costly redemptive act of the holy God in Christ's death and resurrection, in the light of which we set out on the journey of life as ancient Israel set out from the slavery of Egypt toward the freedom of the Promised Land, with life's highest and most joyous task finding and embodying in life the will of the God who has redeemed us, setting our own desires aside to become like Him in character; rather than self-will, self-expression, self-discovery, the raising of self-consciousness, to know that we have "died with Christ," that we now "live" with Him (Rom 6:8), that "[we] are not [our] own; [we] were bought with a price" (1 Cor 6:19f.), and that "whatever [we] do" is to be done "to the glory of God" (1 Cor 10:31).

C. **Live in Reverence** *(1:17-21)* (Exhortation)

Life Lived in Light of the Costliness of Redemption

The next long sentence, consisting of five verses, has another imperative as its central verb—**conduct yourselves with fear**. Both in Greek and in English, the word **fear** has more than one meaning. The usual meaning suggests "fright," "alarm," "terror," "slavish fear." It can, on the other hand, depict "reverence," "awe," "respect," "honor." It carries with it the flavor of "worship," describing the attitude one has toward God when He is properly approached in prayer. It is to sense the *"mysterium tremendum,"* the wholly Otherness of the Deity, the unsurpassable greatness, majesty, splendor, infinity of the Supreme Being. It is the overpowering experience of being in the presence of the Sacred. Peter is here admonishing: "Let the reverence and awe with which you approach God in prayer carry over into the total round of your daily doings. Journey through life as though you were journeying in the presence of God—*because you are.*"

A major characteristic of modern life is the loss of reverence. Nothing is sacred. This is the result of at least two things. First, in a worthy effort to erase the artificial line between the sacred and the secular, to expose the hypocrisy which arises when we are "religious" only on stated occasions marked off for spiritual development, but totally detached from that in daily living, the effort was to bring God into the whole of life and make all of life sacred. Worthy though this goal may have been, it has backfired and achieved exactly the opposite of its intention. By effacing the line between the sacred and the secular, instead of raising the level of ordinary living to the sacred, the result has been to drag the sacred down to the level of the secular. In an effort to bring God into the whole of life, we have forgotten who He is. The God who accompanies us on the common round has become an idol of our own making. The line between the divine and the human has been blurred. God has become the extension of our secularity, the pale embodiment of that which is no longer numinous, the mythic projection of ourselves who, when we look with Him into a mirror, is only another person standing beside us, with no distinguishing marks which set Him off from the human. It is paradoxical but true,—we shall never know how really close God may be to us until we discover how far beyond us He is. It is only He who "determines the number of the stars" who "heals the brokenhearted, and binds up their wounds" (Ps 147:3f.).

The second source of the dethronement of God from His position as the Absolute has been our modern egalitarianism. To give all persons equal opportunity, we have defined reality by assuming that all are equal in every respect. Our democratic principle of "one man one vote" places on the same level of worth the vote of the ignorant and the learned, the depraved and the upright, the man of folly and the man of good judgment. This then moves from equal rights to the assumption of equal achievement; that whatever anyone does is equally worthy with the doings of superior people. This is, of course, a denial of reality. Some people are stronger than others; some are smarter; some are better looking; some can run faster than others; some can handle money better than others; some can acquire skills that others cannot. Defying this aspect of reality, we have tended to develop a society which drifts toward the level of the lowest common denominator.

This egalitarian tendency has invaded our spiritual outlook. We have tended to turn the Kingdom of God into a democracy. God has no rights which man does not have. We tend to make our own democratic God who comes into being and rules by popular vote. He governs only with the consent of the governed. If He does not keep up with the trends in the culture, He may be voted out of office and another put in His place. If He should make demands on us which we do not approve, they can be defied and set aside by majority opinion. For many modern men, God has ceased to be God. "A workman made [Him]; [He] is not God" (Hos 8:6). He is the sum-total of men's own ideas, of what man likes or dislikes in morals, of what part man will allow Him to play in life.

How different the God of the Bible! As He said, through Hosea: "I am God and not man" (11:9). "It is he who sits above the circle of the earth, and its inhabitants are like grasshoppers; . . . who brings princes to nought, and makes the rulers of the earth as nothing. . . . To whom then will you compare me, that I should be like him? . . . Have you not known? Have you not heard? The Lord is the everlasting God, the Creator of the ends of the earth. He does not faint or grow weary, his understanding is unsearchable" (Isa 40:22, 23, 25, 28). And the God of the New Testament, revealed in Jesus, is no less a God. As a poet phrased it:

> Jesus, the name high over all,
> In hell, or earth, or sky;
> Angels and men before it fall
> And devils fear and fly.

If we do not like the poet's words, we may change them; but if in so doing, we mean anything less than he meant, we have missed the God of the Bible.

This God is to be held in *reverence*—He is to be *feared* in the sense meant by the writer of the Proverbs: "The fear of the Lord is the beginning of knowledge" (1:7). Until God becomes God, there is no true knowledge of Him. And if our faith and hope are in any other God than this, they are vain. Until we discover that God is not man, that He is above and beyond anything that we can think or imagine, we are not dealing with the God of the Bible. And when we worship *this* God, we do not get "chummy" and familiar with Him, and approach Him as though He were on our own level. We approach Him with awe and respect, and tread softly in His presence. And who would want a God other than One who commands our highest? The **fear** here commended, therefore, is not the fear "of pain and punishment . . . but lest [God] forsake you and withdraw His hand; just as a dutiful child is afraid lest he provoke his father, and do something that might not please him. Such a fear would God have within us, that we guard ourselves against sin, and serve our neighbor, while we live here upon the earth."

Charles Lamb, discussing Jesus with a group of literary friends in London, said to them: "If another man came into this room, we should all rise to greet him; but if *that* man appeared, we should all kneel." I fear today that, instead of kneeling, we would slap Him on the back, call Him by His first name, and tell Him the latest joke we had heard. One of the greatest preachers I have ever known once said: "I do not want a Savior whom I can wholly understand, least of all one with whom I can be familiar. . . . Show me, in the tragic hours of my life, not a good companion to put his hand on my shoulder and call me by my name and go along life's pathway as a jolly good friend. I don't want that kind of Savior. I can find plenty of men and women like that among my own friends. I want a Savior that puts fear in my heart, and fear lies at the basis of confidence. Fear is the acknowledgment of power, not terror."

In the Bible, the acknowledgment of power has to do with the power of the Creator in relation to us, His creatures. The One who had the power to create us is to be revered by those whom He has made. This is clear in Psalm 9:19f.: "Arise, O Lord! Let not man prevail; let the nations be judged before thee! Put them in fear, O Lord! Let the nations know that they are but men!" Here, **fear** is "the acknowledgment of creaturehood."

Peter rests **fear** on two bases, one given before the exhortation, and the other after. The prior basis is set forth in verse 17: **if you invoke as Father him who judges each one impartially according to his deeds, conduct yourselves with fear.** The **if** here would better be translated "since." It does "not introduce an eventuality, but underlines a reality"—you *do* call God **Father.** Since you do, live in fear! It is the character of this Father-God that demands the reverential life.

Even in the Old Testament, the Bible was foreshadowing the ultimate title for God as **Father.** A Psalmist, speaking of King David, says: "He shall cry to me, 'Thou art my Father . . .'." (89: 26). Jeremiah has God lamenting the unfaithfulness of His people: "And I thought you would call me, My Father, and would not turn from following me" (3:19). The prophet Malachi depicts God lamenting to His people: "If then I am a father, where is my honor" (1:6)? The Jews, however, at least ritually if not in behavior, so revered God and thought Him so transcendently beyond them that they avoided even pronouncing God's name, and, according to one scholar, no search through Jewish literature has ever turned up the title Father for God outside the Bible. Jesus, however, called God "Father" in the most intimate term possible, "Abba," meaning in His language, Aramaic, "Daddy," and taught His disciples to call God "Father" (Matt 6:6, 9). This, then, became the customary mode of address to God for the Christians.

There is danger, however, in this title, far more so in our culture than was so in Jesus' day. In the Jewish culture of His time, the father of the family "embodied the authority which ruled there and which taught children the law of the Lord." We have tended to derive from that title only the tender concern for children that the title implies. Did not the Psalmist say: "As a father pities his children, so the Lord pities those who fear him. For he knows our frame; he remembers that we are dust" (103:13f.). From such statements, and from our experience of playing on the softness in our own father's nature to get what we want, we have developed an idea of fatherhood which is largely dominated by indulgence, leniency, complacency. God has become for many moderns, if they think of Him at all, a sort of long-whiskered grandfather, past His active days of responsibility, watching His children at play and indulging their sins with the philosophy, "Oh, boys will be boys." He is a Being who makes few demands, and with whom we may be sure that, if we get caught in our misdeeds, we will "get by!" Most contemporary men are so sure of themselves, and of human abilities, and of man's control over the forces of nature, and of his command over physical powers, that they have lost any conception of supranatural realities which once struck terror into men's hearts. Contemporary man knows nothing of which to be afraid but other men, and the forces they control, and fears no power beyond the material. He has no conception of what Jacob experienced when he had an encounter with the living God, saying: "'Surely the Lord is in this place, and I did not know it.' And he was afraid, and said, 'How awesome is this place!'" (Gen 28:16f.); or, when on another occasion, in which an encounter with the Almighty left him crippled for the rest of his life, he shuddered in dismay, saying: "I have seen God face to face, and yet my life is preserved" (Gen 32:30). In other words, "I had an encounter with the living God, and the marvel is, I lived through it!"

Aware of this danger, the danger of irreverence growing out of a false view of God, Peter seeks to jar his readers into ethical and moral reality by cautioning them against thinking of God as indulgent. Although the Bible tells us that "God is love" (1 John 4:8), it refuses to allow us to define "love" as sentimental indulgence, tolerance of evil, indifference to matters of right and wrong. Many years ago, a great British theologian reminded the Protestant world that "love" is not the first category of thinking about God in the Bible. It is rather "holiness." God is *holy* love. To leave out the adjective and to say "God is love," allowing our modern Hollywood-contaminated ideas of love to define the word, is to make a statement far wide of the truth. "When men demand a God in whom there is nothing to fear, they demand an idol who does not exist."

It is the **holy** character of our **Father** God which defines Him for us. Therefore, says Peter, since you are to be **obedient children** (1:14) of a holy **Father who judges each one impartially according to his deeds, conduct yourselves with fear.** You are a child of God, you have the right to bear God's name; but remember that he is not only **Father,** He is also a judge, who **judges** "without favoritism." He does not "permit himself to be affected by human evaluations, situations and privileges, and, perfectly informed, he judges according to the work of each one." The translators make a plural out of **deeds,** but it is singular in the original. This stresses not so much individual deeds as the composite worth of one's total behavior in contrast to "appearances and beautiful words."

Peter's combination of *grace* and *judgment* is one of the paradoxical elements of the Bible, in both the Old and New Testaments. The juxtaposition of these terms presents two aspects of reality which would seem to cancel one another out, but neither of which can be discarded. Judgment without grace would destroy our salvation. Grace without judgment would make our salvation into a moral mockery. As one has stated it: "Ethics is only Christian if, on the one hand, it leaves a place for the past, present, and future work of grace, and on the other hand, exposes each thought, word and act of the believer to the gaze of the Judge and His verdict." Paul, who renounced decisively any effort to attain salvation by good works, insisted at the same time that "we shall all stand before the judgment seat of God" where "each of us shall give account of himself to God" (Rom 14:10, 12). Grace and moral seriousness must go together.

The Jewish mind, unlike the Greek, which tended to think more in categories of human logic, was able to entertain seemingly contradictory truths, and cling to both. An example of this, on the very theme we are now discussing, is to be found in a nonbiblical Jewish writing, in the Psalms of Solomon. "Thou art a just judge over all the peoples of the earth," says the writer, for "from Thy knowledge none that doeth unjustly is hidden." According to this writer, man's status before this just Judge is determined, on the one hand, by faithfulness to His commandments—"He that doeth righteousness layeth up life for himself with the Lord"—or by adequate repentance when he fails—"Thy goodness is upon them that sin, when they repent." On the other hand, the writer finds his standing before God based on God's election of Israel—"Thou art our God, and we the people whom Thou hast loved.... For Thou didst choose the seed of Ahraham before all the nations, and didst set Thy name upon us, O God." Here God's law demands repentance, but His grace is independent of human achievement. So, Peter insists that our standing with God rests on His call, His mercy, His choice of us, and yet warns against playing fast and loose with this by ignoring the demands this mercy lays upon us. Since you call God *Father,* remember His inflexible moral judgment and live reverently. One's faith in God's grace issues in good works, so that a judgment on the sum-total of our works is finally a judgment on the reality of our faith. One has illustrated it thus: As a liar is judged by his words, which are the evidence of his inner condition, so good deeds are evidence of faith in the heart. A judgment, therefore, on the total bent of one's behavior is ultimately a judgment on how far he has turned his inner life over to God. To know that God so judges means that He takes our human life seriously; and this, in turn, enables us to take our own lives seriously.

The second basis for a life of reverent awe is an awareness of the wonder and costliness of our redemption. **You know** begins a new sentence in the English translation, but in the Greek it is a participle continuing the same sentence. **Conduct yourselves with fear throughout the time of your exile, "knowing that. . . ."** The expression "knowing that" is a formula "frequently used to introduce a well-known fact that is generally accepted." It may reflect here a "standardized teaching" in which these Gentile Christians had been instructed following their conversion. It introduces the generally accepted view of Christian redemption at that time. "Knowing what you do about your redemption," says Peter, "is all the more reason for living in reverential awe." And that of which he reminds them could well quicken reverential awe in us, if we could be even lightly grasped by its meaning. We Christians go about theologically poverty-stricken, when abundant riches are ours merely for the taking. If we only knew what we should know, as Christians, how different life would be!

First, is the fact that we were **ransomed**. The force of this word is softened by some translators, who render it "redeemed" or "delivered," to avoid any idea of a price paid, or a legal transaction being involved, in our redemption. Others, however, come nearer conveying its true meaning by rendering it **ransomed,** "bought," "payment." The Greek background of the word has "the sense of payment for something"—such as instruction or information; and most of all, "money paid to ransom prisoners of war, . . . slaves, or for release from a bond." The Jewish background involves a price paid for the redemption of the first-born sons, as a memorial to the fact that they were spared in Egypt (Exod 13:12f.), or the price offered to release a member of one's family who had sold himself into slavery (Lev 25:47ff.). The redemption of Israel from Egypt involved no price paid, either by God or the Israelites, and from this it is argued that the idea of "price" is not essential to redemption.

The New Testament writers, however, do not hesitate to speak of God's redemption in terms of a ransom. "You are not your own," said Paul, "you were bought with a price" (1 Cor 6:19). In the same letter, he associates this with the ransom price of freeing a slave—"You were bought with a price; do not become slaves of men" (7:23). Jesus is referred to as "the Master who bought them" (2 Pet 2:1). The Revelation says that Jesus "ransomed," literally "bought," men for God (5:9, 14:3). In the passage we are discussing, Peter is obviously dealing with a "price" paid, for he contrasts it with the normal payments of **silver or gold.** This is confirmed by the pungent statement placed on the lips of Jesus in the Gospel which tradition holds is Peter's own story through the pen of Mark: "For the Son of man also came not to be served but to serve, and to give his life as a ransom for many" (Mark 10:45). Here the "ransom" is related to "serving," which is reminiscent of the Suffering Servant of Isaiah, who innocently and vicariously "bore the sin of many," with "the iniquity of us all" laid on Him who "made us whole" (Isa 53:12, 6, 5). Added to this is the lamb-like nature of Jesus, whom Isaiah likens to a "lamb led to the slaughter" (Isa 53:7).

With all this as background, it is difficult to believe that Peter, by his use of the word **ransomed,** means anything other than that in the death of Jesus, God paid a costly price to release us from the bondage of evil, the contemplation of which shows how seriously He took our evil, and lays upon us the obligation to respond equally seriously by living in reverential awe lest we trample under foot the blood that bought us.

From what did this costly action on God's part ransom us? **The futile ways inherited from your fathers** is Peter's answer. Various translators have pressed language to the limits in trying to convey what is meant here. "Empty way of life," "worthless life," "slavery of your ancestral folks," "futile" or "worthless" or "vain" or "useless" or "fruitless form of conduct," are some of the attempts made. This may seem like a harsh judgment on paganism, but could it be true?

Some years ago, a worker with college students administered a carefully designed questionnaire to thousands of them. After long experience, he said that the question most often left unanswered, or answered most unsatisfactorily, was this: "What is the meaning of your life?" College students simply did not know. I suspect that an even more marked result of this sort would characterize the college students of the present generation. The restlessness and frantic search for pleasure symptomatic of our time, and the frenzied turning to self-centered and fraudulent gurus, and mystical cults, and consciousness-raising self-help fads, testify to the meaningless of life for vast numbers of people. The thirst for meaning is witnessed by the desperate efforts to quench it at "broken cisterns, that can hold no water" (Jer 2:13). Paul held that even many of the customs handed down from his Jewish "fathers" were "vain," a "loss," "refuse" (Phil 3:4ff). As he put it in another letter: everything that is rooted in the created order, anchored to man alone, has been "subjected to futility," a futility overcome only by the "hope" of being "set free from its bondage to decay" in the new creation (Rom 8:28f.).

By what are we **ransomed**? Peter answers: **with the precious blood of Christ, like that of a lamb without blemish or spot.** Both Old and New Testaments relate blood to human redemption. In some sense, the writer to the Hebrews sums up the entire message of both Testaments in the simple statement: "without the shedding of blood there is no forgiveness of sins" (9:22).

To make sense of the relationship between "blood" and "redemption," however, it is necessary to take careful note of the meaning of **blood** in the Bible. Otherwise, it can be understood crudely and materially, and become an offense to sensitive folk. One understands well how perceptive and refined people can be turned away from the Christian faith by inelegant and crassly materialistic uses of the word **blood** as a vehicle of Christian truth. A much-loved gospel song raises the question: "Are you washed in the blood of the Lamb?" It goes on to query: "Are your garments spotless, are they white as snow?" This is based on a biblical passage: "the blood of Jesus his Son cleanses us from all sin" (1 John 1:7). If thought of materialistically, this involves an unintelligible contradiction. **Blood,** rather than washing or cleansing, makes spots, which, if allowed to dry, often become irremovable. Over-enthusiastic ministers sometimes indulge in rash statements, such as: "There is enough efficacy in one drop of Jesus' blood to save the whole world," as though the blood of Jesus could be considered in a quantitative sense. If this were literally true, then a crucifixion was hardly necessary—a thorn prick from the crown of thorns could have done the job, or the struggle in Gethsemane, where his "sweat became like great drops of blood" (Luke 22:44), might have ended the story. And, continuing in the same literalistic and quantitative analysis, presumably all the blood Jesus shed beyond the "one drop" which could have redeemed the world was superfluous and wasted.

Let us suppose that in the days when Jesus was crucified, the Romans had thought of hanging as a more disgraceful and stigmatizing form of execution than crucifixion, and would have hung Him by the neck rather than nailing Him to a cross. In this case, he would not have shed one drop of blood in dying. Would His death by that means have had no saving significance for the world? To phrase the question in this rather crass way suggests that the relation of the shedding of Jesus' blood to the world's redemption must be lifted above the materialistic and quantitative level into the realm of metaphor, and be thought of in spiritual and qualitative terms.

In the Bible, **blood**, both in Old Testament and New Testament, is a metaphor for "life." The Jews were forbidden to eat blood, "for the *life* of the flesh is in the blood; and I have given it for you upon the altar to make *atonement* for your souls; for it is the *blood that makes atonement, by reason of the life*" (Lev 17:11; Deut 12:16,23f., emphasis added). The atoning virtue of the blood "lies not in its material substance, but in the life of which it is the 'vehicle'." And when the blood was shed, "the life which was in it was not destroyed, though it was separated from the organism which it had before quickened" (Gen 4:10, Rev 6:9f.). When the priests sprinkled blood on the altar, it was "distinctly treated as living. . . . it makes atonement in virtue of the 'life' which is in it." The death of the victim was the "liberation" of the life, so that it "became available for another end."

In the Old Testament sacrificial system, however, the sacrifices were "imperfect and transitional," "conventional and not real." They were "sacrifices . . . which cannot perfect the conscience of the worshipper, but deal only with food and drink and various ablutions, regulations for the body imposed until the time of reformation" (Heb 9:9f.). There could be no fellowship between the offering and the one who offered it, and the sacrifice made by the victim offered was not voluntary, and had, therefore, no moral involvement in the surrender of the life laid down. In Jesus, both these inadequacies are rectified. We may have vital personal union with the One offered, and His offering was purely voluntary, an act of ultimate obedience to His Father's will (Heb 9 12). And this life voluntarily laid down continued to live beyond death, as demonstrated by the resurrection. Therefore, the offering of this lamb-like Being, **without blemish or spot**, whose imperishable life, more **precious than perishable things such as silver or gold**, was laid down, has wrought for us all "an eternal redemption,"and He "always lives to make intercession" for us (Heb 9:12, 7:25).

But why was the offering of Christ's life necessary to reconcile us to God? Why did we have to be **ransomed . . . with the precious blood of Christ**? Why could not God just simply forgive us, and let it go at that? If God could have done that, then Jesus' death was surely a mistake. I was approached once after an Easter sunrise service by a young woman who said to me: "How tragic Jesus' death was! To think that all He had to offer the world was snuffed out at the early age of 33! If He had not gone to Jerusalem as He did, He might have continued teaching the world down to a ripe old age!" Why not? If the world could have been saved by teaching, His death was irreparable folly. But if the world could have been saved by teaching, it would have been saved even before He came. The world suffers from a malady too deep to be cured by teaching. It needs a Savior! And nobody could save the world who did not participate in a tragedy equal, or more than equal, to that in which the world is caught. To save the world, God had to deal with the alienation of man from Himself—a rebellion which has violated the moral structure of the universe and challenged God's holy love at a level which only cosmic tragedy can touch.

Why cannot God just forgive by fiat—by merely saying: "I forgive you"? A little boy once told his mother a lie. After dealing with the situation as best she could, the mother finally said: "It's all right; I forgive you." The little boy replied: "But I still told a lie!" No mere words of forgiveness could undo that fact. And the little boy had some vague sense that by lying, he had not only wronged his mother, but had violated the moral law of the universe, which his mother's kindly disposition toward him could not cancel. Human rebellion against God is a violation of God's holy nature which can only be forgiven when it is set right. If God could forgive without doing something to right that violation, we would not be living in a universe we could trust. If God even once overlooked one sin against His holiness, we could never again be sure that He would not do so again, and would be hopelessly lost in a nonmoral universe which we could not trust to be on the side of the right. Only moral chaos could result from such a world. And regardless of God's kindly feelings toward us, His wayward children, we could neither trust nor respect Him if He once winked at our disobedience to His will, and said: "It doesn't matter. Let it go!" Could we really live with any confidence in a universe run by a God like that? Some years ago, a judge in this country became quite notorious because he had to inflict the penalty of the law on his own son whose case came before him. He was bound by oath to uphold the law. To have permitted his sentimental feelings for his own son to violate duty would have been reprehensible. Had he wavered in that instance, none of his other judgments would have been viable. If the penalties of the law had to be imposed on other fathers' sons, the judge had to impose them on his own son. And in so doing, he was not merely legalistically following the book, but was honoring the very idea of law without which societies of men could not adequately function. Law is the necessity laid down by *reality*, not merely by the decisions of fallible men.

But another element enters the picture. The imposition of the penalties of law, even though it may honor the moral necessity of law to avoid anarchism, thus satisfying some abstract law of justice; and even though it may be a deterrent to other violators of the law; it cannot undo the wrong for which the penalties are imposed. John Wilkes Booth assassinated President Lincoln. He was shortly thereafter, in a burning barn, either shot for so doing or shot himself rather than surrender. He paid the extremest penalty society can impose for wrongdoing—the giving of his life for the life he took. This may have satisfied the law of justice, but did nothing to set right the wrong he had done. It did not restore Lincoln to life, soothe the sorrow of his loved ones, nor restore him to his place in the nation and the world. The extremest form of punishment is powerless to undo the wrong for which it is imposed. If there is a moral Being behind the universe, He had to take human rebellion seriously; and to maintain the trustworthiness of the universe, He had to exact the extremest form of punishment—death. As both the Old and New Testament plainly affirm: "the wages of sin is death" (Gen 2:17, 3:3; Rom. 6:23).

It is often said that God imposed death on Jesus so that man could be freed from it. This raises as many problems for the thoughtful mind as it raises hopes for humanity. What would one think of a human judge who imposed the penalty of law upon an innocent person in order to let a guilty person go free? This would be monstrous *human* justice; much more monstrous *divine* justice. The effort to solve the problem here posed involves the prior question of who Jesus is. If Jesus were merely a man, not even God could make moral the imposition of penalty on Him to allow others to go free. If, on the other hand, Jesus were divine, a part of the Godhead Himself, then His death was not God's imposing penalty on another in place of the criminal, but rather the taking of the penalty on to Himself. In the death of Jesus, "God was in Christ, reconciling the world to himself, not counting their trespasses against them" (2 Cor 5:19). This is supremely moral. But moral as it is—could God undo our wrong merely by imposing on Himself the penalty due to us?

One thing deeper yet remains to be done. If God is to undo our wrong, He must not only impose the punishment incurred by it, but must *do something positive to replace it*. The murderer, so to speak, must not only be brought to justice, but the one murdered must be restored to life! The wrong of human disobedience must be replaced by the re-creation of that which it has destroyed. What is the central reality at the heart of our alienation from God? Is it not human disobedience? In simplest form it is pictured in the creation story of Genesis. God said to Adam: "you shall not" (2:17). Adam said: "I will." At heart, sin is the refusal of man to submit his will to the will of God; the refusal to live as a dependent creature under the sovereign lordship of his Creator; the proud effort of man to be God himself. Sin is basically human disobedience to the will of God. To overcome this, the fundamental nature of moral reality, to which God must conform to remain God, demands that it must be replaced by its opposite; namely, humble human obedience to the will of God. Neither our sorrow for past rebellion, nor God's kindly disposition toward us as a heavenly Father, can undo moral reality. No penitence or no punishment will set right human disobedience to the will of God. To overcome this, the fundamental nature of moral reality, to which God must conform to remain God, demands that it must be replaced by its opposite; namely, humble human obedience to the will of God. Neither our sorrow for past rebellion, nor God's kindly disposition toward us as a heavenly Father, can undo moral reality. No penitence or punishment will set right human disobedience to the will of God.

An illustration may help at this point. Many years ago, before Thomas Carlyle had published his first volume of *The French Revolution,* his friend John Stuart Mill borrowed the manuscript to read it. Some days later, in abject mortification, Mill returned with the shattering news that a maid had inadvertently gotten the manuscript mixed up with some scrap papers, and thrown it into the fire. It was gone! What could be done to set this right? Be sorry? Mill was disturbingly sorry. He took it so hard that Carlyle told his wife that they must try to shield from him how very serious it was, for it involved their necessary income at that time. But he could be sorry till doom's day, yet that would not restore the lost manuscript. Mill could offer to pay Carlyle money to compensate for the loss, which he did. But no amount of money would undo the wrong that Mill had inadvertently done against Carlyle, and against the human race, in robbing us all of that volume. No penitence, nor penalty, nor forgiving good will, would suffice. There was but one thing that could undo the wrong—replace it! And that is exactly what Carlyle did. He gathered up his books again, and set himself to the toilsome task of rewriting the lost volume.

If God were to overcome the tragic consequences of human

disobedience, there was but one way to do it—by the costly task of replacing it with perfect human obedience. This He did in the perfect human obedience of Jesus, both in His life and in His death. That which gives Jesus' death saving significance is not merely that He died. Everybody dies. There is nothing unique about that. Nor is it that He died for a good cause. Many martyrs have died in good causes. We revere them for that, and wish we had the courage to emulate them; but we do not look to their deaths for saving efficacy. Nor is it that He died on a cross. So many Jews were crucified by the Romans within a long generation of Jesus' death that they ran out of trees to make crosses. What is unique about the death of Jesus? *It is the perfection of the life He laid down in His death.* It was the fact that He was like **a lamb without blemish or spot** that made His death unique.

The writer of the letter to the Hebrews captured this when he wrote: "When Christ came into the world, he said . . . 'Lo, I have come to do thy will, O God'" (10:5, 7). Quoting here from Psalm 40, he did not take the space to add what else the Psalmist said on this: "thy law is within my heart" (vs. 8). Is this not exactly what Jeremiah looked forward to in the New Covenant?: "I will put my law within them, and I will write it upon their hearts" (31:33). And did not Jesus Himself make this the central key to His life when he said: "I always do what is pleasing to him" (John 8:29), and when He prayed in the Garden in great agony of spirit "remove this cup from me; yet not what I will, but what thou wilt" (Mark 14:36)?

Jesus came into the world, born of a human mother, living through all the psychologically and physically dangerous years of boyhood and adolescence; exposing Himself to the tests of human life at every level; "made like his brethren in every respect" (Heb 2:17), "in every respect . . . tempted as we are, *yet without sinning*" (Heb 4:15, emphasis added). Behind Jesus' death lay a perfect life of human obedience to the will of God. His death was part and parcel of this, the last act of obedience to His Father's will. In Christ, therefore, God achieved human redemption, not only by taking on Himself the consequences of our sin, but also by replacing our disobedience with His perfect obedience. *In Christ, man has obeyed God!* He is "the last Adam" (1 Cor 15:45), a new Adam, the fountainhead of a new humanity. "For as in Adam"—the fountainhead of the old humanity, "all die, so also in Christ"—the fountainhead of the new humanity, "shall all be made alive" (I Cor 15:22). Or, as Paul phrased it elsewhere: "For as by one man's disobedience many were made sinners, so by one man's obedience many will be made righteous" (Rom 5:19). Jesus' whole life, climaxed in His death, was the "obedience" by which many were "made righteous."

Peter insisted that through the obedient response of this **lamb without blemish or spot** his readers had been **ransomed** from the consequences of their disobedience, which he describes as **the futile ways inherited from your fathers.** Here is an echo of what Peter likely remembered from His Lord's own lips: "For the Son of man also came not to be served but to serve, and to give his life as a *ransom* for many" (Mark 10:45, emphasis added). Jesus' obedient life and death were not only a demonstration to be imitated, but were the means of redemption. Jesus was a representative of humanity, acting in our stead. The "ransom for many" was not only "to the advantage of many," but the obedient giving of His life in His death was "what would have had to happen to the many" had He not done it. Here the Hebrew idea of "corporate personality" comes into play, where the *one* can represent the *many*. Nowhere in the Old Testament is this set forth more clearly than in the picture of the Suffering Servant drawn by the Second Isaiah, where "the righteous *one,* my servant, make[s] *many* to be accounted righteous" (53:11, emphasis added). There, the innocent servant was "stricken for the transgression of my people" and "bore the sin of many," with "the iniquity of us all" "laid on him" (53:8, 12, 6). It was this total obedience, climaxed in the obedience of the Cross, which gave, and gives, Jesus the right to forgive sins. Otherwise, His enemies were right in accusing Him of blasphemy in His claim to do so (Mark 2:5ff.).

Jesus' death was neither "an example of punishment which serves as a deterrent" to evil, nor merely a "demonstration of the infinite love of God," to exert a moral influence upon sinners, but an objective achievement which, as Paul said, "was to show God's righteousness, . . . to prove that . . . he himself is righteous and that he justifies him who has faith in Jesus" (Rom. 3:25f.) This accords well with the immediate context of Peter's thought here, as it does with his continuing stress throughout his letter on the desired holiness of the Christian life and the abiding demand to demonstrate the reality of faith by obedience to the will of God. If the obedience of Jesus to the will of God was necessary for the establishment of God's holy character; if our Redeemer were like a lamb without blemish or spot, enabling God to maintain His holiness while at the same time forgiving unholy men; an obligation is laid upon those who have been **ransomed** to manifest that holiness which Christ has achieved for them—**as he who called you is holy, be holy yourselves in all your conduct**—and to conduct [themselves] **with fear as obedient children in obedience to the truth** (1:15, 17, 14, 22).

As Peter has done earlier (see pp, 113ff), again he insists that the achievement of Jesus was not a novelty, an unexpected accident on the moral stage of history, but the outcome of a definite divine purpose. He was **destined before the foundation of the world but was made manifest at the end of the time for your sake.** There is divine purpose behind it all, and it bespeaks God's gracious concern for His people in that its costliness was **for your sake.** How much God cares! "He who did not spare his own Son but gave him up for us all, will he not also give us all things with him" (Rom 8:32)? **Made manifest at the end of the times** suggests that Jesus existed before He came, but was **made manifest**, or "visible," when He was born in the flesh (see pp. 144ff.). It is encouraging to know that from **before the foundation of the world to the end of the times,** history is in the hands of God.

This conviction is made possible for the Christian community **through him**—through Christ. It is because of Him that our **confidence** in God is born and nurtured. And what is the basis of this **confidence? God . . . raised him from the dead and gave him glory.** The resurrection is both God's "attestation," His "affidavit" to the efficacy of Christ's death, and also the means by which He "communicates" His life to us. Both give us **confidence** that God's work in our behalf is valid. God not only **raised him from the dead** but he **gave him glory.** This is obviously a reference to Christ's ascension after which, Peter tells us in his Pentecost sermon, Jesus was "exalted at the right hand of God" (Acts 2:33; see also Phil 2:9, Eph 1:20). This exaltation has been described by one writer as both "a position of supreme authority and a manifest participation in divinity." **Through him** we know that we are in touch with God Himself and may safely rest our **faith and hope . . . in God.**

To contemplate the **futile ways** from which we have been **ransomed,** the costliness of this deliverance, the magnificence of God's control of history, and the exalted position in the universe of our Deliverer—who could ponder this with any degree of understanding and appreciation, and respond in any way other than with a continuing life of reverential awe?

D. Love One Another *(1:22-25)* (Exhortation)

Life Controlled by the Imperishable Value of Love

The fourth of the great imperatives of this chapter is to **love one another.** "Set yourself to love," Peter is saying, "realize in action the grace of your new-born life, which is first and above all a capacity of love." It is another case of "working out" in life what God has "worked in" us. The earlier exhortations to **hope, be holy, conduct yourselves with fear,** involve our relationship to grace and to the God of grace—Father, Judge, Redeemer. This one involves the interrelations of Christians in the community of faith—the "working out" toward one another that which God has "worked in" us. In this admonition, Peter is at one with other New Testament thought. Says John: "Beloved, let us love one another; for love is of God, and he who loves is born of God and knows God" (1 John 4:7). Paul says: "Owe no one anything, except to love one another . . . love is the fulfilling of the law" (Rom 13:8, 10). The writer to the Hebrews, says: "let us consider how to stir up one another to love"(10:24).

The strong imperative form of the verb **love** suggests that effort to love is necessary; that it involves discipline, thought, discernment of the needs of others, and a will to carry out its demands. Christian love, therefore, is more than feeling or sentiment. The **love of the brethren** mentioned in verse 22 might be of an affectionate nature, where the bonds which unite brothers in the faith evoke a mutual liking one for another, born of common interests and goals. A certain level of this **love** they have already achieved. But Peter wants them to go deeper; to acquire that **love** which involves willing the good of the other, whether there is a response or not, and even though it may prove costly. And it is always costly in that it means that our natural self-centeredness must be set aside and the interests of the other moved to center stage. A perceptive commentator has observed the strong connection between **purified your souls** and **love one another** in verse 22. "The personal, individual hallowing towards God," he observes, "must be followed up by a corresponding love toward men; the first precedes the second, but is also unreal in the absence of the second."

Having purified your souls contains a verb form which suggests a past action fully done, with permanently existing results. It, therefore, must refer to their initial conversion from paganism to the Christian faith whereby, "by the washing of regeneration and renewal in the Holy Spirit" (Titus 3:5), they had been cleansed from idolatry and pagan behavior. This initial step was to be implemented now by a permanent purifying of the contamination both of their background and their own personal sins, not only those of an outwardly crude expression of pagan lusts but of "all forms of selfishness." For self-centeredness is the opposite of love.

The purifying comes through **obedience to the truth**. This is in contrast to Peter's description of their earlier heathen behavior as conformity to **the passions of your former ignorance** (vs. 14), interpreted by one as the "accidental individual desires in ignorance of the realities of life." Paul describes the pagans as "darkened in their understanding, alienated from the life of God because of the *ignorance* that is in them" (Eph 4:18, emphasis added). These Gentiles have now passed from **ignorance** to **truth**. What is truth? It is not a "mere law code of commands." The truth is the gospel, the "good news" about Jesus Christ, who could say of Himself: "I am . . . the truth" (John 14:6). Whoever genuinely believes in Him "will not walk in darkness, but will have the light of life" (John 8:12). To live in obedience to Jesus Christ, then, is to live in **obedience to the truth**. Peter confirms this in stating his purpose for writing—it is to affirm that what he tells us about Jesus Christ is **the true grace of God** (1 Pet 5:12).

The conquering of self-centeredness which **obedience to the truth** involves results in **love of the brethren**. An interpreter has remarked: This "is not 'brotherly love' in the common vague sense of the term, i.e. a love like that of brothers, shown to those who are not brothers, but the actual love of brothers for each other." Classical Greek seems consistently to have used this expression for those who were "literally brothers." When the New Testament writers, therefore, expanded its use to include those of different human descent, they did not mean that they loved one another *as though* they were brothers, but really *as brothers*. Having been "**born anew . . . through the resurrection of Jesus Christ**" (1 Pet 1:3), all Christians *were born into the same family, with God as their Father*. Even when Jesus was still on earth, when told that his brothers—meaning His biological brothers—were outside, asking for Him, He replied: "'Who are . . . my brothers?' And looking around on those who sat about him, he said, 'Here are . . . my brothers'" (Mark 3:31ff.). On another occasion, He said to His followers: "You are all brethren" (Matt 23:8). And Paul could speak of the Christian group as "brethren beloved by God" (1 Thess 1:4; 2 Thess 2:13). Also, Peter refers to the entire Christian community with the delightful term **the brotherhood** (2:17).

But, just as disunity may invade the relationships of those who are biological brothers, so "a secret growth of hatreds, jealousies, and selfishness" can mar the unity of genuinely spiritual brothers. The love of the brethren, therefore, should be sincere. This word means "with no hypocrisy." All pretense, all "stage-playing," should be avoided among Christian brothers. The truth of the gospel, whose opposite is less falsehood than unreality, should conquer all unreality in brotherly relations in the Christian community.

The quality of the **love** which Peter is urging is set forth by two characteristics. The first (in the Greek, although the English translation has reversed them) is **from the heart**, or, as we might say colloquially, "from the bottom of the heart." The **heart** is the center of the person, the spring of moral action, the seat of one's very being. The apostle wants the **love** of which he speaks to be devoid of any admixture of selfishness which would lessen its purity. He wants it to express the whole being, rather than acting as an external ornament which may be detached from the person. Then, too, he wants them to **love earnestly** or "fervently." This is a word suggesting the ever-tightening tension of a rubber band as it is stretched. Or, it depicts the eager straining of a runner or a horse as they strain every ounce of energy to cross the finish line. It is **love** "with every energy on the stretch." Or, it has been likened to the tightening of a violin string, "stretched to a tighter pitch that it might yield a higher note." The apostle "urges them to ask for the superlative in the . . . kingdom of love." **Love** for the Christian brother, sourced in the heart and sublimely fervent, is the bond which holds the brotherhood together.

Is this asking too much of human nature? Is not the apostle risking in his readers the disillusionment which comes from moral failure? Yes, if we were left alone to fulfill the demand. Peter, therefore, directs his readers away from their natural reaction to an impossible demand by appealing "to the very nature of the new life" of which love is the expression. It is not based on human effort, but on divine resources. It is not something to be "whipped up" by enthusiastic determination, but by recalling the fount from whence it flows. The translators begin a new sentence in verse 23 to render the thought into more readable English. There is, however, no break here in the original; rather, a participle links the rest of the sentence to what has gone before—"having been born anew." The passive form of the verb directs attention to the initiative of God in the new life of love. It is not something we achieve, nor even decide to become, but something that originates with God. The verb is also in the perfect tense, a form which suggests completed action with permanently existing results. God is not only the initial *source* of love, but He continues to *sustain* and *renew* this love. In this, Peter was at one with other biblical writers. John writes: "Beloved, let us love one another, for love is of God" (4:7). "We love, because he first loved us" (1 John 4:19). It is God's love born in us which becomes our love to others.

Peter illustrates his meaning as the springing up of life which results from the sowing of the seed of God's word, not a **perishable seed but [an] imperishable**. An astute interpreter sees here "a seed which, though in one sense sown once for all, was also imparted by a continuous and perpetual sowing. . . . The new life of the Christians was being constantly renewed from its original source, a living stream from the living God." The **seed** was fructified by the vitality within the **word of God**, which was **living and abiding**—a continuing, steady source of new growth.

The *instrumentality* through which God imparts the life of love is the **word of God**. In simplest terms, a *word* is a medium of expressing one's self—the vehicle by which what is in the mind and heart of one intelligent being is conveyed to the mind and heart of another. In the Bible, however, the self-expression of God is not limited to "spoken words" formed by the vibration of air on sensitive ear drums. God has more to say than can be put into words of this sort. God's **word**, therefore, is God Himself in action. It is "speech in relation to the speaker, and so to the meaning in his mind which he wishes to convey." And when God has things in mind which cannot quite be put into words, He dramatizes, so to speak, and *enacts* what He means. God's **word**, then, is the totality of the means by which He conveys Himself to men. In Genesis, God "spoke" and creation came into being. A Psalmist tells us that when the Israelites were sick, God "sent forth his word, and healed them" (107:20). In his address to the family and friends of Cornelius recorded in the Acts, Peter himself uses the strange expression that God sent His "word" to Israel, "preaching good news of peace by Jesus Christ" (10:36). Here God's **word** was His "whole utterance of Himself in His incarnate Son." The event of the Incarnation was God's **word**. God is the *originating source* of life and love. His word is the *instrumentality* through which He, the originator, calls life and love into being.

Because the instrument is God's **word**, it is **living and abiding**. It is thus in contrast to **all flesh**—all that is human, which is marked by death and is impermanent. A Psalmist, speaking of humanity, says that God "remembered that they were but flesh, a wind that passes and comes not again" (78:39). Peter calls upon a quotation from Isaiah to underline his meaning here. The prophet indicates that human life may have a temporary glory, like the lush green fields of Palestine after the Spring rains, with their blanket of new-grown grass, ornamented with its "blaze of scarlet colour" from the blooming anemones, tulips, and poppies. Glorious as it is, however, it soon withers, the luscious petals fall, and the barren hills bespeak the death and desolation that the hot oriental sun and the summer drought bring. Such was the fading beauty of the pagan lives Peter's readers had left when they became Christians. But now, **through the good news which was preached** to them—the human words about God's active **word** in bringing Christ into the world to live, die, and rise again, they have been born anew into a life which is as permanent as God Himself.

What does this digression have to do with Peter's exhortation to **love one another earnestly from the heart**? One writer has summed it up well: "a love with a quality so rare, so authentic, so strong and constant, calls for a super-human origin and the strength of a life produced by an imperishable power, the word of God, both lifegiving and permanent as Isaiah 40 affirms."

E. Grow Spiritually *(2:1-3)* (Exhortation)

Life Nourished by Proper Spiritual Diet

The next imperative is introduced by the word "therefore," translated by the *Revised Standard Version* as **So**. It is a particle "denoting that what it introduces is the result of an inference from what precedes," and may be translated "consequently," or "accordingly"— meaning "because of what has just been said, so-and-so follows." Here it implies, "If what has just been said about **love** has true validity, then growth in the faith will be necessary." True Christian **love** cannot flourish in a community that is static and stunted.

The central imperative is **long for** nourishment. But this is accompanied by a *preceding condition* and an *accompanying simile*—the first negative, the second positive. The *preceding condition* is to **put away all malice and all guile and insincerity and envy and all slander.** The decisive rejection of love's opposite is essential to growth in love. The verb **put away** is used eight times in the New Testament, one of which offers a vivid literal illustration of its meaning, the others paralleling Peter's metaphorical use. At the stoning of Stephen, we are told that "the witnesses laid down their garments at the feet of a young man named Saul" (Acts 7:58). Here the literal *casting off* of clothing is pictured. The metaphorical use is clear. As one would cast off his garments, so cast off or **put away** all in the realm of the spirit that would be incompatible with mature Christian faith.

In accord with the custom of the times, both the Jews and the Christians drew up lists of virtues to be desired and of vices to be avoided (for other New Testament examples, see Rom 1:29ff.; 2 Cor 12:20; Eph 4:31; Col 3:5, 8f., 12ff.; Titus 3:3, 9). These lists are not complete in each case, but are simply typical of what the writers had in mind.

The theological question once more raises its head: If the new nature, which loves the good and resists the evil, is born in man by the **living and abiding word of God** (1 Pet 1:23), why is it necessary to admonish the newly-born to renounce evil that this **word** may produce growth? And if the Christian has already **tasted the kindness of the Lord,** why should he be vehemently exhorted to desire to take it? This "logical impasse" is perhaps more troublesome to new-born Christians than to mature Christians, who have discovered by experience that they live in two worlds at the same time. When born into the new world, one does not become totally detached from the drag of the old world in which he still lives. Or, to put it more personally, the Christian is two persons in one. Most certainly, he is a "new" man. For this "new" man, "the old has passed away, . . . the new has come" (2 Cor 5:17). But, strangely, the "old" man still lives. If a cat has nine lives, the "old" man within us has a thousand lives! He has a strange way of coming back to life again! So, Paul could say that he put the "old" self in the ring again and again, as in a boxing match (1 Cor 9:26f). And he did not shadowbox. He gave the "old" man a "black eye"; he delivered a "knockout blow," subduing him time after time. As a poet phrased the struggle:

> So let me sin, but not with my consenting;
> So let me die, but willing to be whole;
> Never, O Christ, so stay me from relenting,
> Shall there be truce 'twixt my flesh and soul.

So the battle rages, with an occasional successful skirmish, but always with the **living hope** of final victory through **our Lord Jesus Christ** (1 Pet 1:3).

What are the vices Peter wants discarded so that **love** may flourish? One writer remarks that "Christian morality does not necessarily and invariably differentiate itself from pagan ethics in its requirements, even if it is of a fundamentally and radically different nature." The radically different nature may be seen in contrasting Christian with Stoic virtues. "The Stoic virtues," we are told, "are the proud struggle of the human spirit to conform to nature and to gain the mastery over weakness; the Christian virtues emerge after the recognition of sin and the confession of human helplessness; they are the result of committal to God and dependence upon him, It is not by chance that . . . 'courage,' so prominent in pagan ethical systems is a word never occurring in the New Testament (the verb ['be courageous'] occurs once, 1 Cor. xvi. 13). The courage of the Christian martyr is not the result of the steeling of the soul to endure; it is the by-product of self-forgetfulness and abandoned loyalty—sheer dependence upon the Lord. By the same token, the Christian character is notable for just that warmth and graciousness of which the Stoa might actually have felt ashamed."

The vices pointed out here by Peter are the sort of refined evil qualities which easily invade interpersonal relationships in a closely knit group. It has been suggested that a careful examination of this list reveals that it is not haphazard, nor merely "traditional," but is "carefully constructed."

The first two vices mentioned are inclusive—**malice and . . . guile**—"ill will" and "cunning" or "deceit," the "latter being occasioned by the former." Maliciousness spawns deceit. The other three vices mentioned are put in the plural. This, along with the thrice repeated *all,* meaning "every sort of," or "every form of," suggests that they are general terms with manifold types of expression, all various forms of the inclusive first two. If one indulges in **malice**, or **guile** toward another, this is likely to breed **insincerity**—literally 'hyocrisy," all sorts of "pretense" designed to misrepresent one's true inner attitude. Likewise **malice** and **guile** stimulate all sorts of jealousies and envies of what another has that we do not; and **slander**, or "defamation," or "detraction" is a natural form of speech to cover that jealousy. These sorts of things, expressions of the old, unregenerate man within us, tend to destroy the bonds of true love in the Christian community and to stifle individual growth in the faith. They are vestiges of unredeemed nature in us which should be cast off in order to **grow up** and mature in the faith.

The positive *accompanying simile* used by Peter to stimulate longing for growth is the mental picture of **newborn babes**. The first, and almost the only thing that **newborn babes** want to do in their waking hours, after beginning to breathe and move their appendages, is to eat. The one thing **newborn babes** are well equipped to do is to drink milk from their mother's breast. For the nonce, it is a matter of life and death. They must eat or not live. Instinctively all their interest turns toward getting sustenance. So should the new life within us, born within us by Christ, almost instinctively cry out for food. We cannot maintain our spiritual life apart from it. Nourishment comes not from ourselves, but from without. It is **the living and abiding word of God** (vs. 23) which is the **spiritual milk** that nourishes us. If we have little desire for this, it could well be a sign that we are not spiritually healthy. And if we have no desire for it, it could be a sign that we are spiritually dead. Healthy babies want **milk!** So, says Peter, **like newborn babes, long for the pure spiritual milk, that by it you may grow up to salvation.** . . .

A grammatical problem faces us here. The tense form for **long**—and the same is true for all the imperatives with which we have been dealing, is one that suggests a once-for-all action rather than a continuing one. But is not the longing for the **pure spiritual milk**, of which Peter is speaking, an ongoing thing? Does not his word in verse 3, reminding them of their earlier tasting of the **milk**, suggest that he wants them to feed continually that they **may grow?** And did he not want his readers to go on hoping, being holy, living in reverence and loving?

A trusted grammarian may have untied this knot for us. After discussing the difference between the two tenses, the one describing "an action that is either transient or instantaneous . . . or to be undertaken but once," while the other "denotes an action already begun and to be continued, or one that is permanently or frequently recurring," he tells us that the Greek form for ongoing action "conveys more softness and reserve of expression, and frequently denotes merely advice." The other form, suggesting a one-time action, is "more forcible and stringent." Occasionally, the distinction between the two tenses is disregarded, and the once-for-all form used where the continuing action would be expected, because the writer is more concerned about the strength of the verb than its form of action. If he wants to go beyond merely giving advice, and insist that something be done, he may use the stronger punctiliar form in the interest of strengthening discourse where the milder ongoing form would be expected. The grammarian concludes: "the strengthening of discourse is mainly a subjective matter." It would seem that Peter, in all his exhortations here, used the punctiliar form to give force to his words, but intended the action to be ongoing.

The eager desire lying behind this passage is well illustrated in the Old Testament: "As the hart longs for flowing streams, so longs my soul for thee, O God. My soul thirsts for God, for the living God" (Ps 42:1f.). Another Psalmist wrote: "My soul is consumed with longing for thy ordinances at all times" and "I long for thy salvation, O Lord, and thy law is my delight" (119:20, 174). The depth of our desire for worship and the study of the Bible may well be an index of the health of our souls. To the healthy Christian, these are not mere duties, but delights. Says our commentator from the French prison: "One who asks a believer why he goes to church, or why he studies the Bible, might as well ask a newborn infant why he feeds from his mother's breast."

Peter's use of **milk** differs from that of Paul and the writer to the Hebrews. They used it as a symbol of elemental food for babies, rather than for grownups. Paul says to the Corinthians: "I fed you milk, not solid food, for you were not ready for it" (1 Cor 3:2). The writer to the Hebrews said: "You need milk, not solid food; for every one who lives on milk is unskilled in the word of righteousness, for he is a child. But solid food is for the mature" (5:12ff.). Peter has no such thing in mind. He uses **milk** simply as a metaphor for food.

The *purpose* of eagerly seeking the nourishment of the word is that the readers **may grow up to salvation**, needed by both spiritual babes and the spiritually mature. As one writer has stated: "The assimilation of the 'milk of the word' induces the growth . . . which is not overcast, as is corruptible life, by the fatality of old age and death. It is a question of a growth **unto salvation**, to the total outflowering which ultimate salvation will bring."

Some have argued that Peter's concern for **pure** milk suggests a background of false teaching against which he was arguing—the contamination of the gospel by heresy. Since the nature of the entire letter, however, seems not to be antiheretical in any sense, it does not seem necessary to see such a polemic here. Peter is speaking of breast milk, which "by the nature of the case cannot be adulterated." He is simply implying that "purity" is "characteristic of the spiritual sustenance which proceeds directly from God Himself."

Peter closes this particular admonition by an allusion to Psalm 34:8: "O taste and see that the Lord is good!" His purpose is to stimulate his readers to respond to his admonition to desire the nourishment of the word by recalling their past experience. He says: "**You have tasted the kindness of the Lord** already. On the basis of this experience, **long for more.**" His appeal, then, is both "logical . . . and scriptural." The logic is: "Why not continue to search for that which has already given satisfaction?" Or, as one astute interpreter has phrased it: "Such past experiences as they already had of the Divine milk would lead them up to a higher experience of the graciousness and goodness of Him from whom it came." The scriptural basis is the entire 34th Psalm, which rehearses the Psalmist's experiense in finding God's goodness adequate in every circumstance of life.

When our daughter was about a year and a half old, well able to walk about on her own, she amused us by illustrating what I think Peter meant here. We had a papier-mache box with a rather tight fitting lid on a coffee table in the living room, in which we kept some hard candy. She had played around the box often, without opening it, not knowing what was inside. One day, however, in her play, she got the lid off the box and discovered its contents. Every time thereafter, when she went into that room, she made a beeline for that box! She had tasted that it was good, and she wanted more! Does that not illustrate what Peter had in mind here?

IV

THE COMMUNITY THAT RESULTS FROM GOD'S INITIATIVE AND MAN'S RESPONSE (2:4-10) (Proclamation)

At this point, Peter seems rather abruptly to shift the direction of his thought. Rightly understood, however, there is a close connection in what he is about to say with what has gone before. In verses 1-3 he has been speaking about the spiritual nourishment that produces growth in *individual* Christians, and produces a mature outflowering of Christian love in the hearts of those who believe. He moves on now to deal with the nature of *corporate* growth in the Christian group. Maturing individuals are members of a body, the whole of which is to develop into a well coordinated and effectually functioning community. Verses 4-10 of Chapter 2 explore the question of what happens when God's initiative and man's response coincide. The fusion results in a Christian community which is built into a spiritual temple where spiritual sacrifices are offered and where witness is borne to God's wonderful deeds. The response of others to this witness determines their eternal destiny. These verses are theologically rich. They reflect the early church's understanding of Christ, of His rejection and exaltation, of the salvation He achieved, of the nature and mission of the church, and of the final judgment.

The passage opens with what sounds like an invitation to **come to him**, or "keep coming to him," or "come to him continually." The tense form involves continuous, unceasing action. It is, however, not an invitation, but an *accompanying condition*. It does not express "command, entreaty, or exhortation." It is a present participle which implies: "As you continue to do something, a certain result will follow." By continually "coming to him" you will, **like living stones, be built into a spiritual house.**

What does it mean to **come to him**? Using the same word root as here used by Peter, the Fourth Gospel quotes Jesus; "I am the bread of life; he who *comes* to me shall not hunger, and he who *believes* in me shall never thirst" (6:35, emphases added). Here, in typical Hebrew synonymous parallelism, "coming" is "believing" in the sense of a vital faith which appropriates Christ as the spiritual food and drink to nourish the soul. Again, Jesus said: "All that the Father gives me will *come* to me; and him who *comes* to me I will not cast out (6:37, emphases added). "Everyone who has heard and learned from the Father *comes* to me" (6:45, emphasis added). In these passages "coming" to Jesus is finding in Him the climax of the soul's fellowship with God. Once more, Jesus promised: "If any one thirst, let him *come* to me and drink. He who *believes* in me, as the scripture has said, 'Out of his heart shall flow rivers of living water'" (7:37f., emphases added). Here again "coming" is identified with "believing" in a vital manner which finds in Jesus the sustaining source of spiritual life. The close association of "coming" and receiving spiritual life is seen in Jesus' words, "you refuse to *come* to me that you may have *life*" (5:40, emphases added) It is clear that in the Fourth Gospel, "coming" to Jesus is equated with "believing" in Him" and finding life in Him. It involves an intimate personal fellowship with Him which makes His life ours, and enables us to trust ourselves to Him for time and eternity.

The exact word used by Peter is used seven times in Hebrews, usually with the force of a worshipper, either in the Jerusalem Temple or in the unseen Heavenly Sanctuary, "drawing near" to God to receive His benefits through the priestly ministry, either of the Levitical priests, or Jesus, the true High Priest. Once Hebrews associates "drawing near" with "confidence" (4:16); once it exhorts to "*draw near* with a true heart in full assurance of *faith* (10:22); and once it says: "whoever should *draw near* to God must *believe* that he exists and that he rewards those who seek him" (11:6, emphases added). Here again "coming" is worshipping God in Christ with faith and confidence.

The strong association of "believing" with "coming" and "drawing near," both in the Fourth Gospel and in Hebrews, accords with Peter's stress on the word **believe** (vss. 6, 7). Since Peter insists that "disbelief" is the cause of stumbling, and also describes those who **stumble** as those who **disobey the word**, we may affirm that coming to Christ is "faith in the word of Christ, the invisible Christ (cf. 1:8) being accessible only in the testimony which is rendered to him." To **come to him** is to hear the "good news" about Christ, and to believe it, by casting one's self totally on God through Him as our eternal hope.

Who is the One to whom we **come**? **A living stone.** Peter here turns to the metaphor of the community of faith as a **spiritual house,** built on Christ as the **cornerstone**. But he is not thinking of architects, plans, building supervisors, masons and carpenters. He is thinking rather in terms of living relationships where lives are being **built** and interfused into a spiritual community. The One on whom the structure rests, therefore, is **a living stone,** a living foundation, the basis of a spiritual vitality. And this **living stone** not only has life in Himself, but He imparts life to others. He is not only vital, He is vivifying. Those who **believe** in Him, therefore, are made into **living stones.** They share His life, and by Him, and with Him, they are built into **a spiritual house.** The stones of the old Temple, which signified God's presence among men, are replaced by an edifice of lives. This vitality is now eternal. It flows from His resurrection, where death was forever replaced by eternal life. This **living stone** was indeed **rejected by men,** but is **in God's sight chosen and precious. Men** includes the whole of humanity. We are told in the Acts that "there were gathered together against thy holy servant Jesus, . . . both Herod and Pontius Pilate, with the Gentiles and the peoples of Israel" (4:27). Who crucified Jesus? Both Jews and Gentiles, both rulers and ruled. And when the Negro spiritual asks: "Were you there when they crucified my Lord?" we must all answer "Yes"— we were participants in the act.

> [My] weak self-love and guilty pride
> His Pilate and His Judas were.

Nothing was more absurd to both Jew and Gentile in the first century, than to believe that the eternal destiny of the human race depends on their response to a crucified Jew. That truth would be considered equally absurd on the average University campus of our modern world. And how many of us who are outwardly identified with the Christian Church really understand what it means, and would stand by it come what may, if it again became costly to do so? This One who was **rejected by men** is still **rejected,** and often by the unregenerate "old man" who still lives within us who dare to call ourselves Christians.

But this stone **rejected by men was in God's sight chosen and precious.** These descriptive words relate to their Old Testament background in Isaiah 28:16, where God is proposing to build a new Temple with "a tested stone, a precious cornerstone, of a sure foundation." Peter, following the Greek version of the Old Testament, changes the word "tested," "tried," "proved," to **chosen**—a stone especially "choice" to God, and selected by Him as most appropriate for the purpose. The word **precious** may mean "costly," but more likely carries the meaning "held in honor." These expressions stress not only the intrinsic worth of Christ, but suggest "the unerring Divine judgment" as over against man's folly. This is a theme which emerges frequently in the Scriptures. Stephen, for example, was brought officially before the "council," the Jewish court, to be tried. He was there judged guilty, and stoned for blasphemy. At the same time, however, the Son of man was standing as his counsel "at the right hand of God," before the Judge of the heavenly court, and there the judgment was pronounced: Innocent! (Acts 7:54ff.) Whatever the judgment of human courts, the judgment of the Divine court is final, and the only one that matters.

Scholars differ as to whether the verb in the expression **be yourselves built** is passive or reflexive. Grammatically, it may be either. Is the building process purely God's work, with the **living stones** being acted upon solely by Him? Or is the building up "an act of the Christian society itself"? Whatever the grammar, the context suggests that there is an element of both involved. Surely, in the picture of the new Christian temple, God is the builder. It is only as the **living stones** keep alive, as they continually **come to him** that they can be incorporated into the new building. He gives them life, he shapes them to take their rightful place in the whole structure, He binds them together into a unity which can stand against the storms, He empowers them to fulfill their function as a living community in the life of the world. In all these senses, the **living stones** are being acted upon by the **living stone**. On the other hand, since they are **living**, since they are persons who must continually **come to him** for their life and strength, their response to His action on their behalf is a part of the entire process of being **built into a spiritual house**. This new building is "not a fabrication but a growth," so that the Life-giver and the life-receivers are somehow both involved in the process.

Into what are they to be **built**? Into **a spiritual house**. The "stone" image so carefully woven into the entire passage, and undergirded by several "stone" passages from the Old Testament, suggests that this **spiritual house** is a new "temple" which is to replace the old shrine in Jerusalem, and to discharge the functions which it was designed to perform, save at a higher level.

According to the Gospels, Jesus applied the "stone" image to Himself. In His parable of the vineyard being taken away from the Jews and given to others, He is forecasting the coming destruction of Jerusalem which will follow their rejection of Him (Matt 21:33ff.). Jerusalem was the place of the Temple. That is why all Jews from all over the world wanted to go to Jerusalem, to go to the Temple, which God had ordained as the place where He would meet man. Jesus, speaking figuratively, found the meaning of His own "rejection" in the "stone" passage in Psalm 118:22. There, after the destruction of the Jerusalem Temple, which He foresaw, the "rejected" stone becomes "the chief cornerstone" of a new temple, a new place where God would meet man. The Fourth Gospel makes this unmistakably clear. After having cleansed the Temple, Jesus said: "Destroy this temple, and in three days I will raise it up." His enemies replied: "It has taken forty-six years to build this temple, and will you raise it up in three days?" John adds: "But he spoke of the temple of his body" (2:19ff.). Here Jesus is proposing that after His death and resurrection, the place where God deigns to meet man will no longer be in the old Temple of stone. The efficacy of God's functioning then will take place in Him, in His resurrected body, in His glorified Person. The risen Lord will henceforth be the place where God meets man. When Peter speaks of a spiritual house, then, he is referring to Christ's resurrected body, which is His church, the community in which He now dwells, through which He now deigns to offer His grace to humanity. This is confirmed by Paul's word in Ephesians, where he speaks of the church as "the household of God, . . . Christ Jesus himself being the chief cornerstone, in whom the whole structure is joined together and grows into a holy temple in the Lord" (2:19ff.).

What is the function of those who together are built into this new temple of God? They are to be **a holy priesthood, to offer spiritual sacrifices acceptable to God through Jesus Christ.** A temple involves a **priesthood,** those who serve the God in whose honor the temple exists. To be holy is to be totally dedicated to the service of God. This dedication also involves the embodiment of moral excellence expressive of the character of the God who is being served (see pp. 115f.). Our passage includes in this **priesthood** all Christians, not just a special class who are set aside to be priests. That means that all who are united by faith to Jesus Christ are "priests." And even though their earthly tasks may demand that they spend a good deal of time in various professions, or trades, whatever the form by which they make a living, their true "vocation" is to be "priests" of God, to demonstrate in their other tasks what it is to be devoted to God's service.

Two things are worthy of note here, which relate to the New Testament understanding of the church. First, the only **priesthood** the New Testament acknowledges, apart from the priesthood of Christ, is "the priesthood of believers." Much stress is laid on Jesus, as our High Priest, in Hebrews. The Revelation speaks of believers as "a kingdom, priests to his God and Father"(1:6); it tells us that men "from every tribe and tongue and nation" have been made "a kingdom of priests to our God" (5:9f.); it refers to those over whom the second death has no power as those who are "priests of God and of Christ" (20:5). In the passage we are considering here, Peter twice speaks of the Christians as a **priesthood**. Aside from these five references, the New Testament *never* refers to any other priests save our Lord, and those of the Old Testament. It is both strange and unfortunate that one of the stickiest issues involved in the mutual recognition of the validity of the ministry in the various Protestant Churches should be an issue of which the New Testament knows nothing.

The second item of interest is the current stress of some scholars on the "corporate" nature of the descriptions of the church in this passage, to the exclusion of any "individual" aspects of **priesthood**. Since **priesthood** here involves a group, a "body of priests," it is argued, it is impossible "to suggest that each individual believer is being depicted as a . . . 'priest.'" This is an effort to counter Luther's doctrine of the "priesthood of all believers," which involved: "(1) The equivalent spiritual authority and dignity of each Christian; (2) the Christian's unobstructed approach to God and His word; (3) the priestly office of offering oneself to one's God; (4) the commission of proclamation given to the Christian within a certain defined area."

Does "corporateness," however, exclude "individuality"? If one is a member of "a body of priests," how can he be other than a "priest" himself? This seems like being a member of the "citizenry" without being a "citizen," or a member of a group of military air pilots without being a pilot! Granted that Peter is resting his discussion here on the passage in Exodus 19:6, where the "two basic . . . characteristics of this community were her *electedness* and her *holiness*," still the Exodus passage speaks of those who were elected to be holy as being "a kingdom of *priests*" (emphasis added). And the Exodus passage seems to suggest that God's intention was "that all members of the people of Israel should be priests, i.e. a kingdom consisting of priests." Why, then, should not Peter, transferring the task of Israel to the church, when calling them a **priesthood,** imply that every member of the church is a "priest"? The story of Ananias and Sapphira in the early church (Acts 5:1ff.) indicates that *individual* realities had some relation to the "corporateness" of the community, and that the "holy" nature of the priesthood applied to individuals as well as to the group.

Priests have functions to perform. They preside at sacrificial offerings designed to enable sinful men to approach a holy God, and they instruct people in the ways of God. The living Christ and His living followers together make the new temple, the church, where sinful men may come into the presence of God, and where they may learn of His ways. This twofold function is described by Peter as offering **spiritual sacrifices acceptable to God through Jesus Christ,** and declaring the **wonderful deeds of him who called** [them] **out of darkness into his marvelous light.** This new temple, then, was made up of worshipping human beings, knit together by the invisible Spirit of their Lord. They brought others into the presence of God by proclaiming the gospel in their common fellowship, and by offering their lives in service to this Lord and their fellow men.

This **spiritual** nature of the church was a perplexity to the pagans. They complained that the Christians could not "tolerate temples, altars, or images." Another said of them: "They despise the temples as dead-houses, they reject the gods, they laugh at sacred things; wretched, they pity, if they are allowed, the priests. . . . Why do they endeavor to conceal and to cloak whatever they worship? . . . The lonely and miserable Jew . . . worshipped one God, and one peculiar to itself; but they worshipped him openly, with temples, with altars, with victims, and with ceremonies. But the Christians . . . . They have no altars, no temples, no acknowleged images. . . Moreover, whence or who is he, or where is the one God, solitary, desolate, whom no free people, no kingdoms, and not even Roman superstition, have known?"

What the pagans did not know was that the one God whom both the Jews and the Christians worshipped, had *always* wanted a **spiritual** worship. The Temple, the altars, the victims, the ceremonies of the Jews were temporary pedagogical devices designed to assist the worshippers' self-surrender to God, and were intended to be visual aids pointing toward spiritual realities which would one day replace them. The Jewish sacrificial system was not a man-made set of ceremonies designed to placate or bribe God into being merciful, as though God needed their food offerings or could be "bought off" by their sin offerings. The whole system was *given them by God* (Lev 17:11) to teach them His holiness and their sin, and to prefigure a coming sacrifice equal in tragedy to the tragedy of their moral predicament, which would make it forever possible for God "to be just, and the justifier of unjust men" (Rom 3:26 KJV).

Those who went through the motions of the Old Testament ceremonies without using them as vehicles of *spiritually* offering themselves to God through them were, according to the prophets, an "abomination" to God (Isa 1:10ff.). "For I desire steadfast love and not sacrifice; the knowledge of God, rather than burnt offerings," said the Lord through Hosea (6:6). And God asked through Micah: "What does the Lord require of you but to do justice, and to love kindness, and to walk humbly with your God?" (6:8). Through a Psalmist, God asked: "Do I eat the flesh of bulls, or drink the blood of goats? Offer to God a sacrifice of thanksgiving" (50:13f.). "The sacrifice acceptable to God is a broken spirit; a broken and contrite heart, O God, thou wilt not despise" (Ps 51:17). The Book of Proverbs includes the clear statement: "To do righteousness and justice is more acceptable to the Lord than sacrifice" (21:3).

New Testament writers, other than Peter, grasped the significance of **spiritual sacrifices acceptable to God**. Paul, in Romans 12:1, exhorted his readers: "present your bodies as a living sacrifice . . . to God, which is your spiritual worship." He spoke of his ministry to the Gentiles as a "priestly service," an acceptable "offering" (Rom 15:16). He spoke of a gift from the Philippian church as "a fragrant offering, a sacrifice acceptable and pleasing to God" (Phil 4:18). The writer to the Hebrews spoke of offering praise to God as a "sacrifice," and branded the sharing of material gifts as "sacrifices . . . pleasing to God" (13:15f.). All of this is crowned by the word of our Lord to the Samaritan woman, who queried whether valid worship took place according to the Samaritan rites on Mt. Gerizim or the Judean rites at the Temple in Jerusalem: "God is spirit, and those who worship him must worship in spirit and truth" (John 4:24). Here, freed from all restrictions of time and place, of form and ceremony, true worship is the offering of the spirit of man to the Spirit of God. Worship is communion of the human spirit with the Divine Spirit. This does not mean the abandonment of all liturgy. Liturgy may be an aid to the spirit, a concrete vehicle through which spiritual responses are furthered. But any ritual which is not accompanied by the *spiritual* offering of the self, the person, to God is ineffective and deplorable.

Spiritual sacrifices, then, consist of the offering of one's self in genuine praise to God, of authentic spiritual communion with God, of heartfelt service to our fellowmen in the name of God, and of a life and word which together **declare the wonderful deeds** of God. One of the early church fathers, in the first half of the third century, phrased it thus: "You are a priestly people, therefore you have access to the sanctuary. Each one of us has his offering in himself, and each one kindles the fire on the altar. If I therefore renounce all that I have, if I take up my cross and follow Christ, I therefore make my offering on the altar of God. If I have love, so that I surrender my life to death by burning, and if I attain the glory of the martyrs, I sacrifice myself on the altar of God. If I so love my brother, that I sacrifice my life for him, if I fight to the death for righteousness and truth, then I make my offering on the altar of God. If I deaden my bodily members against all fleshly lust, if to me the world is crucified and I to the world, I sacrifice my offering on the altar of God, and I become a priest for my own offering. In this way I exercise my priesthood." Apparently, the cost of offering **spiritual sacrifices** in his day was high. Although we Americans are shielded from such costliness at present, there have been many of our brothers throughout the world during the past half century who have paid dearly in making their **spiritual sacrifices**. We should at least ponder how high a price we would be willing to pay if the price of commodities in the spiritual world suddenly went up.

These offerings can be made **acceptable to God** only as they are brought into being and sustained by the Holy Spirit; so they are **spiritual** also in the sense that they are Spirit-filled. They are **acceptable to God** not as human achievements but as the return of gifts given to us by God. As was true of the Old Testament sacrifices, so is it with **acceptable** Christian sacrifices—"I have given it to you," says God (Lev 17:11). Our **spiritual sacrifices** are **acceptable to God** only

through Jesus Christ, His greatest gift.

Peter now turns to the Old Testament background on which his thought is based, not so much to argue the case, nor to engage in a polemic with the Jews who did not see what he saw in the Old Testament, but rather to encourage his readers. He wants them to be reminded again that all that he has been saying was not a novelty, but was in the mind of God from the very beginning. He also wants them to understand that the rejection of his message, which is causing his readers suffering, is to be expected. And he wants them to see how privileged they are to be living at the time when all that God had planned since before the foundation of the world had reached its climax and had flowered out in its fullness.

The first reference is to Isaiah 28:16. The setting of this passage is a crisis in the life of the ancient people of God. They were caught between two great powers, Egypt and Assyria. The prophet had advised political neutrality in the struggle, and trust in God for survival. The leaders had opted for human ingenuity instead. They had made an open treaty with one power, and a secret treaty with the other, thereby thinking that they had, by this deceit, buttered their bread on both sides, and would be safe, however the struggle came out. At a banquet planned to celebrate their cleverness, the prophet showed up and upbraided them. In their drunkenness, they ridiculed him, telling him that his advice sounded like baby talk. He replied that God would utilize the same baby talk, save that He would do it with Assyrian swords and spears. For, he said, God had laid "a stone, a tested stone, a precious cornerstone, of a sure foundation" on which Israel's future rested, and that foundation was *faith in Him*. "He who believes will not be in haste," but will wait for God to act and commit the future to Him.

Those who translated the Old Testament into Greek in the third century B.C. indicate that by then, this passage from Isaiah had been given a Messianic interpretation by the Jews. They added the words "in Him" as the object of the verb "believe," thus personalizing it, proposing that belief was to be placed in a coming Messianic figure. It was natural, then, for the church to apply this passage to Jesus. The strong emphasis on believing also gave Peter opportunity to stress that his statement that his readers had **come to him** meant that they had "believed" in Him, and to encourage them to continue their believing. The measure of the "preciousness" to them, of the **cornerstone** which was precious to God, would be the indicator of the depth of their faith in Him.

The next two Old Testament passages Peter quotes are Psalm 118:22 and Isaiah 8:14f. Near the end of His life, Jesus had quoted Psalm 118:22f. in connection with His coming death, implying that He was the "stone which the builders rejected," but had been made "the head of the corner" by God (Mark 12:10f.). Here the stone is the capstone or "keystone" which crowns the arch of the building. To Peter, then, Jesus is both foundation stone and keystone. It is perhaps not pressing the figure too far to see in this that the church is founded on Jesus' death, but is completed by the crowning event of the resurrection.

Isaiah 8:14f. adds another dimension to the stone picture—the twofold function of the stone. The stone is not only the foundation stone and crowning stone of a "sanctuary," a place of safety, but is also a "rock of stumbling. . . , a trap and a snare" over which many shall "stumble . . . , fall and be broken." The rock is not only the foundation of a sanctuary of safety from fear, but also a judgment. To those who hear the word of Christ, and hearing, both believe and obey it, He becomes a haven of salvation. To those who, hearing, disbelieve and **disobey the word, He is a stone that will make [them] stumble, a rock that will make them fall.** This is "hard" doctrine to many, and becomes part of the "scandal" of the Christian faith which we moderns find difficult to accept. But Peter's thought here is based on that of Jesus Himself. He once said that He had not "come to bring peace, but a sword" (Matt 10:34). His confronting of men is a decisive thing that has to do with eternal realities. "So," He said, "every one who acknowledges me before men, I also will acknowledge before my Father who is in heaven; but whoever denies me before men, I also will deny before my Father who is in heaven" (Matt 10:32f.). One's ultimate standing before God rests on his belief or unbelief, his obedience or disobedience, to Christ. "Christ the stone is at one and the same time a symbol of salvation and perdition."

Peter stresses this decisiveness in order to help his readers understand the sufferings they are enduring as believers. There have always been, and always will be, those **who believe and those who do not believe**. His readers, therefore, should not be surprised at the fact that many of their fellows **do not believe** and look upon the faith with ridicule and oppression. This is to be expected. Said the ancient prophet: "Who has believed what we have heard? . . . He was despised and rejected of men. . . . By oppression and judgment he was taken away, and as for his generation, who considered that he was . . . stricken for the transgression of my people? . . . Yet it was the will of the Lord to bruise him; he has put him to grief" (Isa 53:1ff.). The rejection of what they **believe** was foreseen; it is typical. Do not, then, be surprised by it, but hold your faith steady in the face of it. **For those who do not believe** were **destined to stumble.**

This does not mean that they were **destined** not to **believe,** but that those who disbelieve are **destined to stumble.** The verb form for **disobey** is one of continuing action, and carries the connotation "not to allow one's self to be persuaded." In other words, by habitually resisting the persuasive power of truth, they are caused to **stumble.** The "destining" relates to the "stumbling," not to the "resistance" to truth. As one translator has put it: "Yes, they stumble at the Word of God for in their hearts they are unwilling to obey it—which makes stumbling a foregone conclusion." The response of faith determines whether the **stone** is a sanctuary, or a stumbling block. One cannot habitually resist being led **out of darkness into . . . light** with impunity.

Peter then calls upon three other Old Testament passages to depict what the church is—Exodus 19:5f., Isaiah 43:20f., and Hosea, chapter 2. The setting of the Exodus passage is the covenant God made with Israel. God reminded them of what He had done in delivering them from Egyptian bondage, and in the light of that sets forth the expectation He has of their response. "Now therefore, if you will obey my voice and keep my covenant, you shall be mine own possession among all peoples; for all the earth is mine, and you shall be to me a kingdom of priests and a holy nation." This was followed by a ceremony in which the people agreed to keep the covenant God had made with them, after which the Ten Commandments and an early elaboration of their significance in the life of Israel was given to them (Ex 19:7 through chap. 23).

The Exodus description of Israel is now applied by Peter to the church, by which Peter is affirming that the Christian community is now bound by a new covenant to God, and exists in the world to be God's special people as was ancient Israel under the old covenant.

The Isaiah passage comes from a section dealing with God's

Commentary 2:8-10

coming deliverance of His people from Babylonian captivity—a sort of second Exodus out of slavery for them. The chapter is filled with glowing pictures of their trek across the desert to their home land, in one of which God refers to them as "my chosen people, the people whom I formed for myself that they might declare my praise."

The Hosea passage is a graphic depiction of Israel playing the harlot with God, by trysting with other gods. This brings on her God's judgment, but judgment will finally give way to redemptive mercy. The mercy is symbolized by changing the name of Hosea's daughter "Not pitied" to "She has obtained pity," and his son named "Not my people" to "You are my people."

These three descriptive passages are now applied by Peter to the church. In this way, Peter affirms that the Christian community now replaces the community of the old covenant, and is bound to God by a new covenant. The Christian community replaces the old "Servant" community of Israel by a redemptive return to God far more significant than the return of the ancient Jews from Babylonian captivity. They are now delivered from the captivity of sin. And the church is now God's people, replacing the old Israel, and embodying both the privileges and responsibilities of that former community.

What are the specific descriptions which Peter selects from his Old Testament passages? The first is a **chosen race**, or perhaps better, "a chosen nation" or "chosen people" (see Isa 43:20). Peter had opened his letter by describing his readers as **chosen** (1:2, vs 1 in the Greek). This was a favorite description of Christians by Jesus Himself. Jesus spoke of "the elect, whom he chose" (Mark 13:20; see also vss 22 and 27). He said that God would "vindicate his elect, who cry to him day and night" (Lk 18:7). He told His disciples: "You did not choose me, but I chose you" (John 15:16), and on another occasion He said: "I know whom I have chosen" (John 13:18). The word "nation" or "people" suggests a common ancestry. The church, then, is made up of people commonly brought to birth by a Heavenly Father "through the resurrection of Jesus Christ from the dead" (1 Pet 1:3), who have been "chosen" or "called" to do God's work in the world.

A second description is **a royal priesthood** (see Ex 19:6, "kingdom of priests"). It has been shown that this phrase can be interpreted in at least five different ways. Peter seems to have followed the translators of the Hebrew Bible into Greek, who "put the emphasis on the priesthood more than the royalty," and thought of Israel as "a kingdom composed of priests: a whole nation with a sacerdotal status, being put apart from all other peoples, having the privilege of direct access to Jahweh." As Paul stated in Ephesians, in the church, through Christ, Gentiles and Jews "both have access in one Spirit to the Father" (2:18). This would make of the church a community of priests who are privileged to have access to God on behalf both of themselves and the world. Their task is to intercede with God for others, and to make Him known to others, both by word and life.

A holy nation is the third Old Testament description of the church (Ex 19:6). **Holy** means "set apart" or "dedicated" to God's use (see pp. 115ff.). In Exodus, the **nation** was Israel, a group bound together by a single faith, but also by common ethnic ties and a shared political experience. In the church, this **holy nation** is united solely by a single faith. Made so of people of all nations, it is bound together into a supranational unity, set apart as a group specially dedicated to serving God in whatever ethnic or political setting they find themselves.

God's own people is the fourth designation of the church taken from the Old Testament. "My own possession" is the Exodus phrase (Ex. 19:5). It is interesting that the Exodus passage from which this expression comes, immediately follows it with the affirmation: "for all the earth is mine" (5:5). God does not mean that Israel alone is His people for *all peoples* are His, but that Israel belongs to Him in a special way. Israel is His "personal property," His "reserved domain," His "private hunting ground," so to speak. One translator has rendered this: "a people God means to have for himself." This does not mean that God does not care for others than Christians. He is "not wishing that any should perish, but that all should reach repentance"(2 Pet 3:9). But He takes delight in those who repent and turn to Him. Penitent Christians, therefore, are under His care in a special way, and bring joy to the heart of God. Said Jesus: "there will be more joy in heaven over one sinner who repents than over ninety-nine righteous persons who need no repentance" (Lk 15:7).

Peter, then, drawing upon a phrase from Isaiah 43:21, "that they might declare my praise," states what the major task is of the **chosen race**, the **royal priesthood**, the **holy nation**, **God's own people**. It is **to declare the wonderful deeds of him who called you out of darkness into his marvelous light**. This declaration should be both in word and in life, a double meaning which one translator has caught in the word "demonstrate." "Since you are what you are," Peter is saying, "heirs of the Old Testament people of God, it is for you now to *demonstrate* what this means."

Wonderful deeds is the plural of a word used only four times in the New Testament. The other three places it means "virtue." This could be close to the meaning of the expression in Isaiah from whom Peter takes it. There the text reads "declare my praise" (43:21). It could mean to declare God's virtue by praising Him. Another meaning of the word, however, and the one more likely to have been in Peter's mind here, is the "manifestation of divine power," acts which show forth the might and disposition of the gods, "the intervention of gods in favor of men and the means of this intervention." This would include "not only the miracles . . . , but the prodigious manifestations of his mercy and his divine almightiness in favor of the elect." His **wonderful deeds** would include all that God has done for man as Savior.

The particular aspect of salvation here stressed is God's calling people **out of darkness into his marvelous light.** In the Bible, **light** is a favorite symbol for God. **Darkness** is an oft used symbol for evil, for all that is opposed to, or alienated from, God. The Israelites were warned that if they forsook God's ways, they would be smitten "with madness and blindness and confusion of mind, and you shall grope at noonday, as the blind grope in darkness" (Deut 28:28f). A Jewish proverb has it: "The way of the wicked is like deep darkness; they do not know over what they stumble" (Prov 4:19). Speaking of pagan gods, a Psalmist wrote: "They have neither knowledge nor understanding, they walk about in darkness" (82:5). God's deliverance of His people is cast in the symbolism of light. "The people who walked in darkness have seen a great light," said Isaiah (9:2; see also 60:1ff.). Jesus said: "I have come as light into the world, that whoever believes in me may not remain in darkness" (John 12:46). Conversion is seen in the New Testament as having the convert's eyes opened, that he "may turn from darkness to light" (Acts 26:18).

When one thinks on the **darkness** of superstition which reigned in the pagan world of Peter's time, it becomes clear what being called **out of darkness into . . . light** meant to his readers. One interpreter caught this when he wrote: "One of the most impressive features of the new life, for the recent convert, must have been the deliverance from fear—fear of witchcraft and evil spirits and the forces of evil." Rescuing the believer from "the realm of darkness" into "glorious light," and overcoming the "powers of darkness" must have been a tremendous deliverance for the pagan. I myself have seen people in pagan lands today risk their lives crossing the road in front of moving automobiles in the hope that the car might run over the demon who was pursuing them as they walked down the road. "The hagridden world of superstition" was a large part of the darkness from which Christ delivered Peter's readers, as well as from all the grip of evil on their inner lives over which they had no power. We pride ourselves into believing that our enlightened world is free from superstition. But what of those who avidly follow the astrological pages of the newspapers? What of the fortunetellers? What of the palm readers? What of the gurus to whom modern men turn in their hopeless search for deliverance from powers beyond themselves, or from the emptiness and meaninglessness and inner bondage of their daily lives? The task of the church is to announce freedom from all this by declaring **the wonderful deeds of him who** [calls men] **out of darkness into his marvelous light.**

V

THE LIFE OF THE CHRISTIAN COMMUNITY IN SOCIETY (2:11-4:11)

Having dealt largely thus far with matters relating to their God and to one another within their own fellowship, Peter now turns his attention to the involvement of the Christian community in the pagan society in which it was destined to live. What should be their relation to the official governmental institutions of pagan society? How should Christian slaves respond to the demands of pagan masters? How should Christian wives relate themselves to pagan husbands? How should Christian husbands treat their wives? How should the Christian community respond to the misunderstanding and mistreatment of their pagan neighbors? How should Christians relate to one another within their own fellowship, in order to glorify God in the non-Christian world? It is to questions such as these that Peter now addresses himself.

A. The Purpose of Holy Living in the Christian Community *(2:11-12)* (Exhortation)

Verse 11 deals with the relation of holy living to personal spiritual health, while verse 12 takes up the theme of the influence that the group of healthy Christians would have on their pagan society.

Although the letter abounds with exhortation, only here and in 5:1 does Peter address his readers in a personal way by saying **I beseech you**, or "I exhort you." This personal touch here, along with his characterizing them as **beloved**, adds a warm personal appeal to his entreaty, and gives it added force. Since he is going to counsel them about their behavior in the surrounding society, he again reminds them of who they are—**beloved** of God, a term more of dignity than of human affection; they are **aliens and exiles** in a pagan world. They are "resident foreigners" living in a country of which they are not citizens, with their loyalties and hopes set on a higher world. They are "people who are passing through"—temporary residents on their way to another place, aware that human life is transient and evanescent. This was expressed by a Psalmist in a passage which, when translated from the Hebrew into the Greek, used these same two expressions: "For I am thy passing guest, a sojourner, like all my fathers. Look away from me, that I may know gladness, before I depart and be no more!" (39:12f.). As Peter's readers pass through Vanity Fair on the way to their true home, Peter wants them to avoid becoming attached to the allurements of the land through which they are journeying, by keeping their thoughts on the home land to which they travel.

One commentator has branded this conception as "a superlative formula" for expressing Christian psychology: "a traveller does not adapt himself to the customs and manners of a country through which he passes, he keeps his own set of mind, he has another 'standard of values' than the natives with whom he trades. Thus the citizens of heaven carefully guard themselves against all that would tarnish their spiritual existence" (see 1 Pet 1:13ff.).

This demands that they **abstain from the passions of the flesh that wage war against the soul**. What are **the passions of the flesh**? They are not only the more vulgar and crude passions, but all human desires which, although "made and meant to serve," tend to usurp power and rule. They are anything which tends to lessen our awareness that we are people of an eternal destiny, with a spiritual potential that cannot be developed or satisfied with anything less than fellowship with God. In Paul's listing of the works of the flesh, which begins with "immorality, impurity, licentiousness" and ends with "drunkenness, carousing, and the like," there are imbedded such things as "jealousy, anger, selfishness, dissension" (Gal 5:19ff.). "Desires" are not necessarily wrong in themselves. What can be innately wrong with the desire promoted by the smell of coffee in the morning? Or the response to a stunning photograph of a South Sea Island or the Swiss Alps which says: "My, I would like to see those places"? Or the desire, kindled by a masterful review of a good book, to have and read the book? "Desires," in themselves, if properly mastered, can become the source of enriched living.

The human condition is such, however, that "desires" tend to master us rather than serving us. This is why one can speak of the "tyranny of desires." The **passions of the flesh,** then, are "the desires which arise from the total man in his present weakness, with his will for autonomy and his illusion of being master of his own happiness." The word **that** after **flesh** in our passage is one that means "which by its very nature." The **passions of the flesh** are those things which, by their very nature, wage war against your soul. Even things not inherently evil can do that—things which in themselves may not be demeaning but which tend to atrophy our capacity for the highest and the best. When one hears what passes for "music" in our time, on which our youth are almost exclusively fed, with its savage beat and animal-stirring lyrics, and contrasts it with the music of Bach, for example, one wonders whether it is not something that wars against the finer natures of our youth without their knowing what is happening to them. Shut off for the moment the ceaseless pounding of the air waves, and listen to this:

> Jesus, joy of man's desiring,
> Holy wisdom, love most bright;
> Drawn by Thee, our souls aspiring,
> Soar to uncreated light.

Has not one entered a totally new world? And can the two worlds congruously be put together? And does immersion in the former world not tend to atrophy one's capacity for appreciating the latter? Any cheapness, therefore, anything tawdry, anything that would tend to loosen our grasp on the true "joy of man's desiring" and dim our vision of that "uncreated light," may be that which wages war against the soul.

Peter's counsel is to "shun," "avoid," **abstain from** all that challenges the freedom of the highest that is within us—the soul, or "self." Such things vary with individuals, so that no list can be drawn up to identify them. Each must determine for himself what the enemies of his soul are. I once knew a missionary in India who loved to hunt, and always took his gun with him on his itinerations, so that if a hunting opportunity arose, he could take advantage of it. He discovered, however, that the hunting was beginning to motivate him so vitally that his itinerations began to revolve more about the hunting than about his missionary responsibilities. He did not brand hunting as a sin, nor give it up totally, nor begin a campaign to save the souls of other hunters. He rather took his gun, put it in its place in his home, and said to himself "I will not take that down again until I have mastered it, rather than allowing it to master me." Even wholesome and innocent desires may hecome that from which we must **abstain** if they no longer serve our well-being, but master us.

"Abstinence" is a much disliked word in our time. We do not take kindly to Peter's advice: "hold yourself apart," "distance yourself from" the things which tend to "steam the windows of the soul," or blur our spiritual vision, or damage our spiritual sensitivity. We do not know that there is a *war* going on. When one knows that, and knows who his enemy is, and bends every effort to avoid defeat, it is relatively easy to make the sacrifices necessary to win. But when it is a "cold war," without open battle, with the enemy unknown and using the strategy of acting like a friend, we are in grave danger. In our time, many Christians have relaxed their defenses and fraternized with the enemy until they do not know who their enemy is, and are happily consorting with a thousand enemies of the self, which have infiltrated the spiritual ramparts by way of television, advertising, sports, government-encouraged gambling for good causes, popular forms of entertainment, and a general mood which exalts sensuality, discourages excellence, deifies pleasure and deems it more important than work, and deals with us as one-dimensional creatures who exist on this earth only and have no eternal destiny. *There's a war on, and on many fronts the enemies of the soul at present are winning!* One thoughtful writer has said: "If man survives this menaced century it will be by means of a vast, cleansing return to God, and through whom can such a spiritual force find entrance into the crawling ruin of a pagan world save through the Christian Church?" A friend of mine used to say: "Every once in a while the Holy Spirit gives the human race a desire to take a bath! Somewhere down the line man will clean up!" In thinking of this, it occurred to me that if the church is the place where that bath is to take place, wouldn't it be well to keep the tub clean while we wait?

Although it is introduced here by a prohibition, the Christian ethic does not exhaust itself in a negative. Peter now turns to the positive: **Maintain good conduct among the Gentiles**. The "inner purity" honed by abstaining from fleshly passions produces "visible fruits" which are observable by the enemies of the faith and serve as a testimonial to them. The whole manner of life of the Christian should exhibit a quality which "is at once seen to be good." It should be "honorable," morally "blameless," "beyond reproach." As one translation puts it: "Let all your behavior be such as even pagans can recognize as good." The word **good** carries with it an aesthetic connotation which one translator has rendered "lovely." There is a "seducing beauty" about a wholesomely good life that even morally warped people sometimes see and envy.

Unfortunately, however, no matter how appealing simple goodness may be, it often evokes a hostile response. "The surest way to the dislike of other men," a writer once said, "is to behave well where they behave poorly." This truth has been observed at least as far back as the Book of Proverbs, where we are told that the wicked cannot "abide him whose conduct is upright" (29:27 REB). The sheer "goodness" of the Christians, either through envy, or because of the judgment which their high moral living brought on the immoral, or because of misunderstanding, often caused them to be vilified by their pagan neighbors. They were branded as "atheists," since they had no visible representation of their God. They were accused as "traitors," because they refused emperor worship on the ground that "Jesus is Lord." They were called "cannibals," on the basis of a misunderstanding of their Lord's Supper as physically eating the "body of Christ." They were accused of "abominations" and "superstitions," because their religious insights differed so widely from those of their pagan neighbors.

Peter's suggested answer to such calumnies was to **maintain**

good conduct which, when seen by their calumniators, will ultimately **glorify** or bring "praise" to God. It is quite likely that in this expression Peter is recalling the word he had heard from the lips of Jesus, when He said: "Let your light so shine before men, that they may see your good works and give glory to your Father who is in heaven" (Matt. 5:16). But like that passage, it does not define when or in what form this "glory" will be given. Does this imply that those who give the "glory" become converts to the faith, and **glorify** God as believers; or does it mean that when God's final judgment falls, even though they have continued to resist God's offer of salvation, their consciences, prompted by the **good conduct** of the Christians, will grant that the Christians were right and that God is just in His judgment? Both views have been held by creditable scholars.

One's judgment on this question is often determined by the connotation given to the **day of visitation**. The Old Testament background of this offers a choice. Sometimes God "visits" in redemption and grace. The dying Joseph said to his brothers in Egypt: "God will visit you, and bring you up out of this land" (Gen 50:24). Referring to the deliverance of Israel from their captivity, Jeremiah puts these words into God's mouth: "When seventy years are completed for Babylon, I will visit you, and I will fulfill to you my promise and bring you back to this place" (29:10). At other times, God "visits" in judgment. God said to Moses, of His people: "in the day when I visit, I will visit their sin upon them" (Ex 32:34). Some scholars hold that Peter is envisaging a **visitation** of grace, when, as he hopes for in the case of pagan husbands of Christian wives (3:1f.), the persecutors of the faith will become converts. Others hold that the **visitation** is the final judgment, when even unbelievers will admit that God's judgments are just. Some tend to combine these, suggesting that there is a hope for conversion, but failing that, judgment is inevitable. There seems, however, to be no evidence that **visitation** is ever used elsewhere with such a double meaning, where the coming is "at once penal and corrective."

There is evidence, on the other hand, that **visitation** sometimes involves the purpose of "trial and probation." A Psalmist, for example: "If thou triest my heart, if thou visitest me by night, if thou testest me, thou wilt find no wickedness in me" (17:3). And Job asks: "What is man, that thou dost . . . visit him every morning, and test him every moment?" (7:17f.). Jesus picked up this theme when, in the last week of His life He pronounced judgment on Jerusalem: "because you did not know the time of your visitation" (Lk 19:44). God had come to them, putting them on trial, and they had failed the test. It could be, therefore, that Peter's **visitation**, although it refers to the final judgment, could involve a "test," the results of which will be determined by the response of those who had been put on trial.

The apocryphal book of Enoch clearly speaks of a final judgment on kings and mighty men who **glorify God**, but are condemned nonetheless. Their mouths will be "muzzled," but too late. "We have now learnt that we should *glorify* and bless the Lord of kings," they say; "would that we had rest to *glorify* and give thanks and confess our faith before His glory" (ch. lxiii) [emphases added]. But, as one interpreter points out, "they do not find the time, for they are condemned . . . . " It is quite possible, then, for Peter to have meant that those who malign the Christians will, at the last judgment, acknowledge the **good conduct** of the Christians as right, and thus **glorify** or "praise" God, but still be condemned for their refusal to do so when they were persecuting the Christians.

It seems to me that, since Peter's thought here was not directly focused on the answer to this question, but was directed to the present believers in encouraging them to **maintain good conduct** so that God would ultimately be "glorified," it is impossible to make a final judgment on this. It must be left an open question. When we no longer "see in a mirror dimly," knowing only "in part," but understanding as we have been "fully understood" (1 Cor 13:12), **good conduct** will undoubtedly be acknowledged by all as right. If, through that acknowledgment, some who formerly maligned the faith should be converted to it, we could only be glad.

B. The Christian's Relation to Human Authorities
(2:13-17) (Exhortation)

Be subject for the Lord's sake to every human authority is a questionable translation of a difficult passage. Peter literally says "every human creature." The word translated **authority**, or "creature," is used only here in the entire letter. It is used with some frequency, however, in other parts of the New Testament. In every other instance, it is translated "creature" or "creation. " Because the immediate context here is dealing with the Christian's relation to governmental authority, most translators make it refer to "human order," or "all authority man has imposed." Some broaden it to include not only governmental authority but all "institutions of human society," including home, family, and the like. The difficulty with this is that there is no other instance of such a meaning for the word in secular Greek, nor in the Old Testament in Greek, nor in the Rabbinic writings. Since submission to others is repeatedly stressed in the following paragraphs in an inclusive way—authorities (2:13ff.), masters (2:18ff.), husbands (3:1ff.), wives (3:7), and all men, even those who revile (3: 8ff.), it seems better to think of this verse as an introduction to the entire section and translate it literally: "Be subject for the Lord's sake to men of every sort."

Be subject, or "subordinate yourself," runs counter to human nature, especially in an egalitarian democratic society where nobody is supposed to be superior to anyone else. And, as one commentator has observed: "it is not a question of submitting to the inevitable, of accepting an exterior constraint, either physical, juridical or moral because one has no choice or violence alone would permit one to avoid it, but rather of innerly consenting to recognize the authority of persons occupying definite positions, and that . . . for the sake of the Lord." It is a conscious choice to place oneself last! It is the exact opposite of being pushy, graspy, assertive, seeking the limelight, demanding center stage. To **be subject** does not mean to be innocuous, insipid, languid, colorless, grovelling. And, as with the Sermon on the Mount, exhortations like this are not to be applied literally, without exception, to every situation. Common sense and realism have their Christian uses.

To **be subject** means basically to recognize all other men as "creatures of God, as are we, and to respect them not only as having originated in God, but as placed in the world to fulfill a part of God's plan for humanity." To **be subject**, then, is to recognize this in each person we deal with. It is not a question of being a Mr. Milquetoast, who surrenders his own decision making to others, or subjects his will to the dictates of lesser men; but rather of putting the interests of others before our own. If one were dealing with a person of limited abilities, it would not necessitate surrendering to that person's impeded judgment nor even always allowing him to determine his own course. It would entail, however, placing the genuine interests of the other's welfare at the center of our responses to him, and subjecting our own interests to his good.

Peter's counsel is designed to propose the general mood of a Christian's behavior toward others. It is none other than Paul's advice: "Do nothing from selfishness or conceit, but in humility count others better than yourselves. Let each of you look not only to his own interests, but also to the interests of others. Have this mind among yourselves, which you have in Christ Jesus, who though he was in the form of God . . . emptied himself, taking the form of a servant" (Phil 2:3ff.). Genuine subordination of one's own interests to the interests of others, whoever they be, would go far toward solving human relations, and could be a tempering factor among those who represent "causes" in our time.

Does the expression **for the Lord's sake** refer to Jesus, or to God? If it is Jesus, the motivation lying behind the counsel to **be subject** would be thereby to honor Him by following His example in His behavior toward the state, or to honor Him with good behavior before the pagans. Peter, however, is likely referring to God. The function of human authorities described in verse 14 seems more likely to have been assigned to them by God rather than Jesus, and the **doing right** of verse 15 is clearly labeled as **God's will.** The motivation to **be subject** to human authorities, therefore, is that thereby one may show his subjection to God.

The function of the **emperor** and the **governors** he appoints is an ideal description of what Peter thought about government in general. Order is necessary to any society. Without government, anarchy reigns. And when governments lose control, and anarchy takes over, it is abundantly evident that human social relations can have no meaning. Even pagan authorities, the early Christians believed, were ordained by God to deter and control wrongdoing and to **praise those who do right.** This authority was exercised, of course, in terms of the pagan governors' conception of what was wrong or right, which did not always accord with Christian views. Furthermore, Peter was well aware that governors are not always upright, and often make their judgments with evil motives. In spite of the lapses, however, in general, the function of rulers is to inhibit evil and promote good.

The praising of **those who do right** was often, in Asia Minor, a public function of erecting statues, or making inscriptions on monuments, or awarding other honors evidencing the good that men do.

Some commentators see here an encouragement, on the part of Peter, to his readers to engage in such good works as would be given public notice, and thus raise the esteem of the Christians in the eyes of the pagans. This would seem, however, to conflict with the humility he elsewhere commends, and seems quite unlikely. If there were Christians of wealth, however, who were in a position to do acts of public benefaction, Peter would have approved of their doing so because this would be for the good of the public by making a "positive contribution to the everyday life of others." The motivation for this, however, was to maintain God's approval, not man's. The will of the Father who **judges . . . impartially** (1:17) is the ultimate spring of Christian good deeds.

Peter does want his readers, however, by subjecting themselves to the laws of the state, to live lives of goodness which will draw forth the moral approval of their neighbors, and thus **put to silence the ignorance of foolish men.** Insofar as the calumnies against the Christians were based on **ignorance,** Peter wanted his readers to demonstrate such unsullied lives that their detractors would be enlightened as to the true nature of the faith and see, by Christian behavior, that Christianity was not a politically subversive movement. He was well aware, however, that sheer goodness would not **silence** all criticism of the faith. Had he not seen his Lord crucified for doing good—the highest virtue eliciting the exact opposite of his intention here? In any case, truly good behavior would remove the grounds for the uninformed responses of their enemies, and insofar as their maligning was based on sheer perversity, it would, at the last judgment, rob them of any ground on which to stand. When "God judges the secrets of men by Christ Jesus . . . every mouth [will] be stopped, and the whole world . . . held accountable to God" (Rom 2:16, 3:19). The ultimate reason for conforming to the order of the State was that it was God's will. The highest Christian motivation, at long last, is not that which works, or commends the church to society, but what God wills.

Live as free men, yet . . . . The "freedom" of the Christian goes back directly to words of our Lord. When the question of paying the Temple tax came up, Jesus asked Peter: "From whom do king's of the earth take toll or tribute? From their sons or from others?" When Peter answered, "From others," Jesus said: "Then the sons are free" (Matt 17:25f.). Here is an indication that from God's standpoint, members of the kingdom of God owe their loyalty only to Him, and should therefore be free from obligations to earthly kingdoms. "However," said Jesus, "not to give offense to them," we should fulfill the obligations imposed on all. This is the way one is **subject** to all men. To be free for the Christian is to **live as servants of God.**

Herein Christian freedom differs from pagan, or secular, freedom. One of the pagan Stoics described freedom thus: "Who then is free? The wise, who is master of himself, who fears neither poverty, death nor dungeon, who can resist desires and refuse positions of honor ..., whom no misfortune can disturb." This is a self-achieved freedom, the end product of the human will seeking to overcome all human feeling and to steel itself against desires. Christian freedom, on the other hand, is a grace, a gift, resulting from placing one's self in the hands of God and seeking to serve Him rather than bludgeoning one's self into a state untouched by human feeling. It is not to stifle all human affection, but to sublimate it into a higher enchantment; to know what a famous preacher meant when he spoke of "the compulsive power of a new affection"—so to love God and be loved by Him that self-love is not so much denied as forgotten in a higher loyalty.

Voluntarily to fulfill one's obligations to earthly authorities is not to lose one's freedom. It is an opportunity to express one's "slavery" to God alone. There is no conflict between this allegiance and a secondary allegiance to the structures of society, unless the latter present themselves as ultimate authorities and thus try to take the place of God. Then the Christian's allegiance to God must take precedence (see Acts 4:19, 5:29).

Freedom, without slavery to God, is a dangerous thing. It may then become a **pretext for evil**, a "cover," or a "veil," or a "camouflage" to hide evil motives. Human urges must be mastered; otherwise life becomes like a river without banks, or a train without rails, or a car without brakes, or electric voltage without insulation, or atomic energy without adequate safeguards. "Be ruled or die" is the law of life. **Freedom** may become licentiousness, a slavery to the lower passions, where "all things are lawful" (1 Cor 6:12). The New Testament elsewhere speaks of those who "promise . . . freedom, but they themselves are slaves of corruption; for whatever overcomes a man, to that he is enslaved" (2 Pet 2:19). The writer comments: "the last state has become worse for them than the first" (2 Pet 2:20). Or **freedom** may become a prideful escape from human obligations, with the attitude: "Since I belong to God, I owe no man anything." Those who are truly **servants of God** are never free from the claims of love to their fellow men.

Verse 17 sums up what Peter has been saying throughout the paragraph from verse 13 on. The **freedom** which is expressed in **doing right** and in deference to **all men,** is now gathered up in relation to neighbors, brothers in the faith, **God,** and the **emperor.** The first three form a natural climax, while the last one, standing by itself, is given a twofold emphasis. The *Revised English Bible* makes the first the heading and the main clause to which the other three clauses are subordinated: "Give due honour to everyone: love your fellow-Christians, reverence God, honor the emperor." I prefer placing the first three as separate, and arranged in climactic order, with the fourth standing by itself. "Reverence God" could hardly be subordinated to, or explain, "give due honour to everyone." Furthermore, if "everyone" includes only the brotherhood, God and the emperor, the pagan neighbors would not be included. It seems preferable, then, to arrange the first three in climactic order—**all men, the brotherhood,** and **God,** then to set the fourth off by itself, as a return to the reference to the **emperor** previously made in verse 13.

Honor all men is a universal formula which dissolves all unworthy distinctions between men, and places them all on the same level before God. It accords with an ancient Jewish proverb: "Who is honored? He who honors mankind"; the reason for so honoring such an one is that he "thereby honors God." To deny all inherent distinctions between men, such as that some are brilliant and others dull, some are attractive and others repellent, would be to deny reality, to shut one's eyes to the variations built into human life by the Creator. This passage is not advocating a blind egalitarianism which insists that all men are of equal importance to the world. It does, however, propose that all men, however different they may be in ability, skill, accomplishment, or personal attractiveness, should be treated honorably, offered the same respect, with no "cynical contempt or sneering disdain" which cumulatively can be "worse than murder." In fact, Paul, in figurative language, seems to suggest in 1 Corinthians that, within the Christian church, "special honour in the whole organism of the community is to be granted to those Christians to whom is given no striking [charism]. By the [honour] shown them they are set on an equal footing with other members of the community." In this way, "the members may have the same care for one another" (12:22ff.). This respect and concern should, according to Peter, be directed toward **all men**.

There is a deepening of concern involved with those who are of like faith. **Love the brotherhood** is Peter's instruction. Believers are tied to one another as children of a common father, and brought to life by a common faith in the "resurrection of Jesus Christ from the dead" (1 Pet 1:3), and are therefore "in the family" in a special way. So Paul could admonish the Galatian Christians: "do good to all men, and especially to those who are of the household of faith" (6:10). The bonds of brotherhood lay a special obligation of **love** in addition to **honor** toward those who are brothers in Christ.

Fear God adds a unique dimension. **Fear** is not a slavish fear, a feeling of terror, but the acknowledgment of God as God—Creator, Redeemer, Sustainer—the unique Being in whose hands our lives rest for time and eternity, who has made us His own at great cost (1 Cor. 6:20, see pp. 160ff.). Ultimate reverence is due to Him alone.

Honor the emperor is not climactic, but returns to the first category of human relationships—**honor all men**. There is a subtle suggestion here as to what the Christians thought of the **emperor**. At the time Peter wrote, "emperor worship" was a part of the pagan consciousness. The Christian appraisal of this is to be seen in the word **honor** which Peter counsels for the **emperor**. It is the same word which is attached to the expression **all men**. In this way, Peter is classifying the emperor not as a god, but as a mere man, standing on the same level as all men. On the other hand, the fact that, after suggesting that all men should be honored, he picks out the emperor for special mention, Peter indicates that by virtue of his position as ruler he is worthy of special respect. In other words, the emperor has a different function in society from others, but shares exactly the same status. This reflects the ancient Jewish respect for political rulers as instruments of God's jurisdiction over men. Denying them deity, they thought of them as instruments of deity, therefore to be respected and prayed for (see Isa 45:1; Jer 27:6, 29:7, 43:10). The Jews offered sacrifices in the Temple for the Roman **emperor** and for the empire. Paul urged "that supplications, prayers, intercessions, and thanksgiuings be made for all men, for kings and all who are in high positions (1 Tim. 2:1f.).

C. The Servants' Relation to Their Masters *(2:18-21)*
(Exhortation)

At this point, Peter applies his counsel of "subordination" or "deference" toward all men to a specific social setting in his time—the institution of slavery. Modern commentators tend to interpret Peter's thought here in sociological terms, suggesting that he was motivated by a concern for pagan approval by urging patterns of behavior which the pagans accepted. It is clear that the Roman authorities feared new religions which fostered cultural challenges to their generally accepted standards of household behavior. The submission of slaves to masters, wives to husbands, children to parents, were issues which Plato and Aristotle both took seriously as bulwarks of stability for the state. Their view had filtered down to the first century, where they played a significant role in forming the household ethics of the Romans. Peter, it is alleged, exhorted Christian slaves and wives "to the kind of behavior that would silence the negative reactions which [their] conversions generated" among pagan masters and husbands. They were to reassure "the masters and husbands . . . that they are obedient slaves and wives, just as the culture expected them to be." It has even been suggested that the "defense" mentioned in 3:15 was this reassurance, even to the governor, that they were living in accord with customary social ethics. Such a theory, although splendidly worked out and defended, leaves a sense of uneasiness.

If Peter were basing his advice here on societal norms, why did he not discuss the parent/child relationship, which usually accompanied the discussion of slave/master and husband/wife relationships? Furthermore, why did he address husbands, as well as wives, but did not speak to masters? Even though there may have been few Christian masters, the letter to Philemon shows that there were some. The explanation that Peter was silent about masters because he "hoped that the wives would convert their husbands by laudable behavior," but the "conduct of the slaves was not expected to convert masters" seems to have been plucked out of mid-air for want of a better one! After all, Philemon was already converted! Why were not others open to conversion by the behavior of their Christian slaves? And the **defense** of which Peter speaks in 3:15 was not related to behavior, but to **the hope** which had been generated in them. Such **defense** would have something to do with testifying to **the resurrection of Jesus Christ from the dead** by which they had been **born anew** into this hope (1:3), and the **great mercy** of God which had prompted it all, rather than an explanation that they were conforming to pagan social structures.

Peter does speak of silencing pagan criticism of Christian behavior, but was that his central motivation? Was that not rather a secondary issue with him? It could well have entered his mind that good behavior might function as a commendation of the Christians to the pagans in such fashion that the heavy burden of calumny might be somewhat lifted. But was not his *chief* concern that their **good conduct** bring them God's approval, and thereby silence pagan calumny and **bring glory to God** at the last judgment? As the *Revised English Bible* puts it: "Let your conduct among unbelievers be so good that, although they now malign you as wrongdoers, reflection on your good deeds will lead them to give glory to God in the day when he comes in judgement" (2:12). Not the church's image in the world but *its standing with God* is Peter's main concern.

A hurried scanning of the entire letter, with a view to discovering the motivation to which Peter appealed, seems to confirm this. Four times he speaks of the **will of God** as the basis for Christian action (2:15; 3:17; 4:2, 19). Everything is to be done so that **God may be glorified through Jesus Christ** (4:11; see also 1:7; 4:13, 14; 5:4, 10). Christians are to live as **God's own people** (2:9). They are to be **mindful of God** in their behavior and concerned only about **God's approval** (2:19f.). They are to defer to others **for the Lord's sake**, and as servants of God (2:13, 16). Wives are to have a **gentle and quiet spirit** because this is **very precious in God's sight** (3:4). Husbands are to honor their wives because they are **joint heirs of the grace of life** (3:7). Christian lives are to be **spiritual sacrifices acceptable to God** (2:5). Christians are to lead **holy lives because the God who called [them] is holy, and because the eyes of the Lord are upon the righteous, . . . but the face of the Lord is against those that do evil** (1:15, 3:12). They are to live as **obedient children** of a heavenly Father (1:14; see also 1:22). They are to live **with humility** so that God may exalt them because **God opposes the proud, but gives grace to the humble** (5:5f.). When enduring **pain while suffering unjustly** they are to be **mindful of God** (2:19), and in all the vicissitudes of life they are to **do right and entrust their souls to a faithful creator** (4:19). They are to live as those **chosen** and **called** by God (1:2, 15). When competing lordships demand their allegiance, they are to **reverence Christ as Lord** (3:15).

This general survey suggests that, although sociological aspects of life may have had minor and secondary place in Peter's thought, the central focus of his ethical motivation was not "the image of the church in the world." It was "rooted first in faith in God as Creator, Caretaker, and Redeemer." Christian behavior in society was to be determined by "submission to the will of God as Creator and Ruler of the world, by respect for the proper roles of each 'calling' in society, involving just relationships and the willing subordination of love." Although Christians had "a new existence in Christ," they were not to withdraw from the "old" world, living as hermits unrelated to the society of which they were a part; nor were they to try to force their "new life" on those who did not share it by trying to replace the structures of society with their own. Rather, living in hope of the coming kingdom of God which He would bring in His own time, they were to work out their faith and loyalty to God in the "provisory, relative, sometimes unjust, but necessary structures of the 'old' world." This difficult, theologically rooted task, was Peter's concern more than to commend Christian behavior to pagan misunderstanding. The question often raised in this connection, of the source of Peter's ethical teaching—was it based on Greek, Jewish, or Hellenistic Jewish sources?—then becomes irrelevant. It was *Christian* ethics, sourced in the Christian faith and ultimately rooted in the teachings of Jesus (see, e.g., Mark 10:20ff., 12:13-17; Matt 17:24ff.).

It was inevitable that the relation of slaves to their masters should become an area of concern for the early Christians. "The institution of slavery was universal in the ancient world and was the foundation of ancient society and economy." It has been estimated that perhaps half of the population of the Roman empire consisted of slaves, but some have heightened that estimate to three slaves to each free man. Captives from the Roman conquests were sold into slavery. Julius Caesar sold 63,000 captives on one occasion in Gaul. The demand was so high, however, that a regular commerce in slaves was established, involving a "systematically-prosecuted hunting of men" by professional kidnappers.

Slaves had no rights at all. They were chattel. Their masters had total power of life and death over them. They could not legally hold property. Although many slaves were permitted to marry, their union had no legal status, and could be terminated at will by the master. Slave children were the master's property. Slave testimony in court was valid only when taken under torture. Effective superintendence of rural slaves was particularly difficult, so that they often wore chains in the fields, and at night. Both male and female slaves were worked, under the lash, in the mines. When old, or sick, slaves were sometimes left to die of exposure. Crucifixion was the normal means of putting slaves to death. There is a story on record of a guest who remarked at dinner that he had never seen a man die, whereupon his host brought in a slave and had him put to death to satisfy his friend's curiosity. This was in accord with the view that slaves were not human beings. They were "speaking tools." Aristotle phrased it thus: "There can be no friendship or justice toward inanimate things; indeed not even towards a horse or an ox, nor yet toward a slave as such. Master and slave have nothing in common; a slave is a living tool, just as a tool is an inanimate slave."

Needless to say, not all masters were cruel, and at times, genuine friendships and close family ties developed between masters and slaves. Many professional people, such as doctors, teachers, and secretaries, were slaves and the lot of many of them was not unpleasant. Nonetheless, they belonged to their masters, and were not free to decide life for themselves in any respect.

People who lack historic perspective are shocked to learn that the New Testament writers did not come out squarely and openly against slavery. Others, likewise without historic perspective, have used the New Testament's seeming tolerance of slavery to justify it as a worthy social institution. The New Testament, however, was not written under the conditions of twentieth century democracy. As a perceptive French commentator has stated: "The epistle does not provide a universal reflection on society as such, nor offer any 'social plan,' but demands a consistent Christian demeanor in a given milieu, that of the second half of the first century, in Asia Minor." We cannot, therefore, look for specific instructions as to how to solve current social problems. We can only seek to grasp the spirit of its teaching and examine the Christian motives to which Peter appeals, and try to apply them to our very changed conditions.

Furthermore, the purpose of the early church was not that of political revolution. It had a revolutionary gospel, but it depended on its working like leaven, finally to permeate the whole of society with a challenge to its evils, but always aware that human societies are so distorted by evil that there will never be a utopia in history. Is the world getting better or worse? The answer is: *both*! Social gains are often made, then other distortions arise which mar their value. We were reminded by one great thinker during the Second World War that it was shallow thinking to say that we had lapsed back into barbarity. There is a barbarity in human nature which always expresses itself. Our "progress" often is not real progress, but merely highly technical gains in the ability to express our innate barbarism in more sophisticated ways. The breakup of the powers of communism in eastern Europe has not suddenly led to halcyon days of restored human dignity, but to outbreaks of nationlism and tribalism which may well match the brutalities from which the long enslaved peoples were delivered. And reform movements which result from the use of the sword frequently outdo their predecessors in terror. Deliverers of humanity become their enslavers. Bastille Day is replaced by the Terror. However much individual Christians, as responsible members of society, may feel called upon to take up arms for social causes, the church, as church, does not survive in the world by violence but by love, and a willingness to suffer, as did her Lord, at the hands of those who seek her undoing. It is most significant that the fall of communism in our day did not come about by military defeat but by internal collapse. Who knows how much was contributed to that by the silent suffering of Christians during the past seventy years? At least, when every effort to destroy the church behind the iron curtain by a powerful and skilled atheistic government had run its course, the church survived! And that without the sword!

Had the church, in the first century, made a frontal attack on slavery, it would only have worsened the lot of the slaves. There were slave revolts, which resulted in their deaths in battle and in worse tortures for those who survived. The "roads far and near were lined with crosses bearing the rotting bodies of the slaves, and afterwards masters were all the more oppressive and vindictive, fearing a fresh outbreak. To incite Christian slaves—or pagan slaves, for that matter—to revolt would have been to condemn them to certain death, and to increase the hardships and sufferings of those who did not revolt."

But Peter's counsel to slaves was not based on such practical calculations. Slavery slowly began to perish in the Roman empire, even outside the bounds of the church. Countering Aristotle's statement: "A man cannot be unjust to a slave, since he is his property," the Roman Stoic Seneca, who died about the time Peter was writing, said: "What shall we say? They are slaves? But they are men." Under the influence of such thinkers, the lot of slaves was gradually ameliorated in Roman Society, and its worst features would likely have vanished without the aid of the church, although the influence of the church, as it grew, hastened the process. Peter would have been gratified at any lessening of the burdens which slavery put upon men, from whatever source it came. His deepest concern, however, was not social amelioration as such, but the doing of the will of God by the members of the church. He would have agreed with Paul, who said: "For what have I to do with judging outsiders? Is it not those inside the church whom you are to judge? God judges those outside" (1 Cor 5:12f.). Unlike our democratic governmental pattern today, the early Christians had nothing to do with making or changing the legal system. Their strategy was to apply to slavery the principle they applied to the whole of life—personal subordination to God and all men in every station of life for the sake of Him who, in His incarnation, had subordinated Himself to His Father and to all men in voluntarily accepting the Cross.

How voluntary subordination is to express itself by individual Christians in a world where we are directly responsible for governing ourselves must be decided in the light of the question: "What is the *will of God* in this situation, and how can one best demonstrate the selflessness of Christ in the situations which we face?" One thing seems plain, that Peter did not intend the Christian to exhaust his influence in society merely by religious expressions of kindness to distressed individuals, but expected his readers to do **good deeds** (2:12) which would express concern for society as a whole. He "did not set up lists of works of charity or of piety, but concerned himself with the behavior of the believer in the society he belonged to," calling him to contribute "to the well-being of all."

Servants here were household slaves, rather than field hands, although it is quite likely that what Peter has to say to them he would have applied to slaves of all types. **Be submissive** means voluntarily to place one's self under the authority of another. Here it would mean that the slave who is involuntarily placed under another's authority should accept that fact for himself and by his own choice live in a situation which has been forced upon him.

Two features of this voluntary subordination are added by Peter. The first is translated by the *Revised Standard Version* **with all respect**. This translation involves a choice as to whom the **respect** is directed. It assumes that it is to be directed toward the master. It seems better, however, to direct it toward God, and to translate the expression "with all fear." The word is the same used in verse 17 where Peter exhorts: **Fear God**, thus differentiating between the attitude one should have toward God from that toward **all men and the emperor**. Honor, or "respect" toward men is encouraged, but "fear" is reserved only for God. On the other hand, Peter twice explicitly forbids "fear" being directed toward men (3:6, 14—in each case the same word is used which here is translated **respect**). What Peter is saying here is: **Servants, be submissive to your masters** "because of," or "on account of" the fact that you "fear God." In this way, Peter bases submission to human authority on "the fear of God."

Order is necessary in human society. Hierarchies of authority exist to "limit the destructive effects of evil" in human relations. Political authority is viewed in the Bible "as a very imperfect and often terribly corrupt image of the legitimate and good power of the Lord himself over his creatures." The same may be true with other established authorities in a structured society. Unfortunately, the human reflections of God's ordering of His creation sometimes become so perverted that they cease to function as subordinate powers, and seek to become autonomous, independent of God, making themselves God. When such authorities demand the human allegiance that belongs to God alone, they must be resisted.

But, although the world is fallen and imperfect, still it is God's will that hierarchies of authority should exist for the ordering of human welfare. If, therefore, one is placed in a relationship which, unpleasant as it may be, he accepts for the sake of loyalty to God, then his primary submission is to God, while his submission to human authority is secondary. This makes him innerly a *free* man, working out his human obligations in obedience to God rather than to his master, whereby he really becomes master of his situation as God sees it. He exchanges his involuntary relation of submission to man for a voluntary relation of submission to God, the real and only Master of his inner life. To Peter, it is better to be free in one's relation to God and free from the slavery to sin while living in the social structure of slavery, then to be socially free from slavery but innerly a slave to evil and an alien from God.

Some years ago, I had a blind friend. He had lost his eyesight from damage caused by the exposure of his eyes in a sandstorm when, as a missionary doctor in Egypt, he was on an errand of mercy. In telling me of this, he said: "If I had not responded to the call of Christ to serve Him as a missionary and had stayed in this country, I would most likely not have lost my eyesight. But," he added, "I would rather have lost my eyesight and have Christ, than to have kept my eyesight and lost Him." So, with Peter, slavery to blindness with Christ was preferable to freedom from blindness without Him. As one writer has phrased this: "External freedom is valuable. Its value is only relative, however, compared with what communion with Christ brings, compared with freedom from self and all the conditions which spoil life, compared with freedom for God and His will, which is the gift of Christ . . . ." Paul phrased this clearly: "For he who was called in the Lord as a slave is a freedman of the Lord. Likewise he who was free when called is a slave of Christ. You were bought with a price; do not become slaves of men" (1 Cor 7:22ff.).

It was this primary and ultimate loyalty to God which immediately destroyed slavery within the community of the church. When Paul returned the slave Onesimus, now a converted Christian, to his owner Philemon, he sent him back "no longer as a slave but more than a slave, as a beloved brother . . . in the Lord" (Phil 16). Slaves and freemen "exchanged with each other the kiss of peace, drank from the same chalice, suffered the same martyrdom, looked forward to the same heavenly inheritance. There was nothing surprising to Christians when an ex-slave Callistus became bishop of Rome, or the lady Perpetua and the slave girl Felicitas faced death together in the arena hand in hand." This confirms the judgment of one writer, that although the apostles did not attack slavery head on, their gospel destroyed it!

This ultimate loyalty to God enabled the Christian slaves to perform their required tasks, as unto God, with no consideration of the disposition of their masters. Some masters were **kind and gentle,** "friendly," "fair," "reasonable." But some were **overbearing,** "cruel," "wicked," "unreasonable," "unjust," "perverse," "hard to please." The word **overbearing,** in the original language, seems to be a term customarily used by slaves to describe "impossible masters." Their **masters'** worthiness or unworthiness, however, was not to be the guage of their service. They were not to say: "With such a master, I am not going to burden myself with scruples." They could be equally submissive to God in the service of a reasonable or a perverse master. They could be wholly "independent of the person of their owner, of his character and his manners." Is it any wonder that one commentator says that Peter was calling "purely and simply for heroism" on the part of Christian slaves? And, we might add, an impossible heroism apart from what Peter is soon to tell us about the relationship of all this to Jesus Christ. The passage breathes the impossible demands of the Sermon on the Mount, and, if accepted only as a demand, sets before us an unattainable goal which would lead us to despair. It is only when the demand ceases to be mere demand, and one sees it as the gift of God's grace who has met His own demand in His Son, that it becomes a beckoning of hope to us. We may then strive to become what we already are in Jesus Christ. A recent commentator has applied the teaching here to the modern employer/employee relationship: "Honest and diligent work and a courteous attitude are good in themselves; we are not to be more or less honest and diligent in our work or courteous in our attitude according to whether our employer is more or less worthy; but rather to work properly and be courteous, because we want to please God."

The weight of the Christian demand presses hard when one is **suffering unjustly**. There may be some of bold nature who take pride in **suffering unjustly**, who brag about their endurance and immunity to pain. When they are **beaten** for defying their master's inordinate demands, they have their reward with their fellow slaves! They are looked upon by their companions as enviously courageous men who refuse to be broken. But if, **mindful of . . . God when you do right and suffer for it you take it patiently, you have God's approval.** In both verses 19 and 20, the word translated **approved** and **approval** is literally grace. Some have interpreted this as "merit" with God, as a "title to divine favor," or a "recompense." Others have given the word its original aesthetic value: "it is a beautiful thing," pleasing to God. It thus contrasts the **credit** of verse 20—"renown" before men, with that which is creditable with God. The deeper theological content of the word "grace," however, the unmerited granting of God's favor to us rather than a favor we do to God, seems preferable here. If we retain the customary New Testament use of the word "grace" here, then, it states the almost unbelievable truth that "this unmerited suffering . . . is a favor [a kindness] of God!" A commentator who holds this view adds: "Only the illumination cast by the following Christological section can permit us to accept, if not to comprehend, a theme so difficult." This shows how far our twentieth century understanding of the Christian faith is from that of the first century. The French commentator who, at the risk of his life, surreptitiously wrote his commentary on 1 Peter while in prison, said of this: "It is a grace of God to be made one who suffers rather than one who causes suffering . . . . Do you not know that in enduring suffering patiently, it is you who are the free man, it is you whom God keeps in his grace?" This comment might seem overdone, had it not been made from one of Hitler's prison cells!

The **pain** of **suffering unjustly** can be transformed into a blessing only as the sufferer is **mindful of God**. This is a difficult and strange expression, which has produced various interpretations. Two general lines of explanation are followed. The word here translated **mindful** can, in the original, relate either to one's "conscience" or his "consciousness" of God. If a word has two meanings, one can only try to relate each to the entire sentence and choose the one which seems to make the most sense. If "conscience" is chosen, its literal meaning would be "conscience of God." This would seem to refer to the deity rather than to man, which makes no sense in the sentence. Those who retain this meaning have to restructure the relationship of the word "conscience" to God in order to give the sentence any intelligibility. They translate it "a conscience responsive to God," or "for conscience's sake before God," or "from a sense of duty" to God. These seem to be rather forced attempts to give the expression meaning and still retain the connotation of "conscience." To translate the word involved as "consciousness" would seem to be more natural, is equally true to the innate meaning of the word, and is much easier to relate properly to "God." This view is accepted by the *Revised Standard Version*, although its rendering does not make it as clear as some other translations. **Mindful of God** does not clarify the meaning as well as "God is in his thoughts," or an "awareness of God's presence," or "continual consciousness that he is living in the presence of God." In its context, then, the expression means that **you have God's approval** if you "endure undeserved suffering on the basis that you are aware that this is God's will" for you.

At this point, Peter reaches the heart of his message to the servants by the startling suggestion that they may take unjust suffering as a *sacred vocation* motivated by the fact that they are **sharing in the vocation** of their Lord. **For to this you have been called,** he says. The daily tasks laid upon you by your masters are your work, but your real **vocation** is to endure the **pain** of **suffering unjustly** by taking it **patiently,** and finding **God's approval** in the knowledge that your current burden of **pain** is God's present will for you, and thus manifesting to your tormentors the spirit of your Lord who **also suffered for you, leaving you an example, that you should follow in his steps.** The word **example** is a vivid word, used only here in the entire New Testament. It sometimes referred to a copybook, where letters were carved in wax for students to trace with a stylus "as though along furrows" in learning to write. It also was used to describe the sketch of an artist which was left for students to complete. Peter is therefore suggesting that the behavior of Christ in his "torment as a slave" was the pattern they were to follow in submitting without resistance to **unjust suffering**.

It was as though Christ, by His suffering, had sketched in a pattern which He had left for them to fill in. One is reminded of Paul's word: "Now I rejoice in my sufferings . . . , and in my flesh I complete what is lacking in Christ's afflictions" (Col 1:24)—not that Christ's sufferings were in any sense inadequate, but that the sufferings of Christ's people were to be conjoined with His as they witnessed to Him in the world. Peter presents this in the figure of slaves filling in the picture of suffering which Christ had sketched.

To this Peter adds another illustration—that of following in **footsteps.** If one were entering a woods uncertain as to the correct way through it, he would do well to pick up the trail of another's footprints who had recently made the same journey and follow them. So Peter suggests that his readers follow the path set by their Lord in enduring undeserved suffering.

Maybe detractors of Christianity, such as Nietzsche and Rosenberg, while vilifying the faith, understood it better than many of us who claim to represent it, by calling it a "slave morality." Captured by the "modern mentality," we are inclined to minimize cross-bearing, and to see Chistianity as a tool of self-realization rather than self-abasement. It impresses us as unbelievable, but it is true—that Peter "draws the slave into the fellowship of the Son of God" by insisting that the suffering his slavery occasioned was a "gift," a "grace," of God; that his was a "privileged" vocation; that since Christ, who was "innocence itself, had been treated in the most atrocious fashion and had saved us by his indefectible patience," imitating His suffering "for righteousness' sake" was the "privileged insignia of the humble, the poor, the little people, the maltreated, who are called the first in the kingdom of heaven." One has remarked: "Nothing could more effectively give the downtrodden dignity." The heroic bearing of suffering on the part of many early Christians is evidence that it did; such as when, in Lyon, those who were placed in the arena to run the gauntlet, face gladiators and wild animals, and to be roasted in hot iron chains, looked across the vast amphitheatre to where a girl named Blandina had been suspended on a stake, and were inspired with great zeal. As Eusebius, the early church historian, described it: "because she appeared as hanging on a cross . . . they looked on her in her conflict, and beheld . . . in the form of their sister, him who was crucified for them . . . ."

Peter based his thought here on two things. One was the remembrance of what he had heard his Lord say while here in the flesh about the "necessity of redemptive suffering." When Jesus had begun "to show his disciples that he must go to Jerusalem and suffer many things . . . and be killed," Peter rebuked him: "God forbid, Lord! This shall never happen to you." Jesus replied: "Get behind me, Satan! You are a hindrance to me, for you are not on the side of God, but of men" (Matt 16 21ff.). On another occasion Jesus reminded Peter that if he wished to "have . . . part" with Him, he should be as his master (John 13:8, 16). The other basis of Peter's thought here was the Old Testament prefiguring of Christ as the Suffering Servant, to which he now turns his attention.

D. The Redemptive Basis Of Christian Behavior In Society (2:22-25) (Proclamation)

Scholars debate the process by which verses 22-25 took shape. It is one of the richest bits of writing in the New Testament, and many "hesitate to attribute directly to [Peter] the responsibility of such richness." Hence, some have suggested that Peter was quoting a Christian hymn here. Others find catechetical or liturgical material here. Some find a combination of an early Christian creed and a hymn. Others suggest a personal reworking by Peter of previous traditional materials. Much is made by some of the shift in verse 24 from "our" and "we" to "you," as though more than one source lies behind the writing. It has been pointed out that this could have been occasioned by Peter's effort to draw his hearers closer into the picture, a literary phenomenon which "is relatively frequent in the New Testament." It is not too important which theory one adopts. We may be certain that Peter's intention was not to impress his readers with his literary abilities, either in writing such an elegant passage himself or in weaving together from other sources a happy combination of thoughts. It was the truth of which he was writing that concerned him, and should be our concern as we read his words.

As Peter turned his attention to Isaiah's picture of the Servant, his mind immediately went far beyond the picture of Christ as an example, a pattern to be copied, as he had just presented Him in verse 21. His vision broadens from the servants to the Suffering Servant on whom those of every station in the church depend. Said one, of this: "It is as though the apostle could not turn his eyes for a moment to the cross without being fascinated and held by it. He saw more in it . . . than was needed to point his exhortation to the wronged slaves. It is not their interest in it, as the supreme example of suffering innocence and patience, but the interest of all sinners in it as the only source of redemption by which he is ultimately inspired."

The Old Testament Scripture immediately directs his thought to the redemptive power inherent in Christ's sufferings that makes it possible for the Christian to follow His example. Left to ourselves, we could not imitate Him in the slightest. Imitation would be an impossible goal, an unattainable end. It would be like a pole vaulter who has just cleared the bar at 20 feet handing the pole to one crippled by polio and telling him to duplicate his feat. Or like a singer of magnificent voicce reaching high C, then proposing that one who has had his larynx removed do likewise. No, gracious exhortations to moral excellence are, in themselves, futile. We are cast back on Him for the power to follow His example.

This is made clear in verse 21, where Christ's sufferings are held up not only as **example**, but are described as having been borne **for you**. Here the vicariousness of the Servant's suffering is brought into focus. As a recent commentator has put it: "Christ cannot be an example of suffering for us to follow unless he is first of all the Savior whose sufferings were endured on our behalf." Verses 22 and 23 suffice for the **example**. Verses 24 and 25 add the *redemptive* element to the **example**. "It is then no longer a matter of what Christ has done for us in leaving us an example, but in rendering us capable of following him."

Peter's use of Isaiah does not involve verbatim quotation, but a rather free use of the ideas he wishes to utilize. It has been suggested that he may have been quoting from memory, or using another manuscript of Isaiah, or following earlier Christian writers of hymns or catechetical documents where Isaiah was paraphrased. It is possible that he was making his own free use of the Isaianic material. In any case, it is plain that he was following an early Christological use of Isaiah's picture of the Suffering Servant as a paradigm of the sufferings of Christ.

This messianic interpretation of Isaiah's Servant goes back at least to our Lord Himself. He likened Himself to one who came "not to be served, but to serve, and to give his life as a ransom for many" (Mk. 10:45). Near the end of His life He said of Isaiah 53:12: "this scripture must be fulfilled in me, 'And he was reckoned with transgressors'" (Lk. 22:37). As risen Lord, he pointed His disciples to the Suffering Servant as the clue to the whole Old Testament witness to Him, by saying: "Was it not necessary that the Christ should suffer these things and enter into his glory? And beginning with Moses and all the prophets, he interpreted to them in all the scriptures the things concerning himself" (Lk. 24:26f.). The early church made use of this clue in their understanding of their Lord. In the early speeches in Acts, Peter himself applies the term "Servant" to Jesus four times (3:13, 26; 4:27, 30), three of them relating to His death or resurrection. When the Ethiopian eunuch, reading Isaiah 53 while riding in his chariot in the desert, asked Philip: "About whom, pray, does the prophet say this, about himself or about some one else?" We are told: "Then Philip opened his mouth, and beginning with this scripture he told him the good news of Jesus" (Acts 8:26ff.). The Suffering Servant, then, was "the key to [Jesus'] person and death." So, in using Isaiah 53 to interpret Jesus here, Peter was but following in his letter the clue that he and others had frequently used in their Christian proclamation.

The innocence of Christ, depicted in verse 22—**he committed no sin, no guile was found on his lips,** is based on the latter half of Isaiah 53:9: "although he had done no violence, and there was no deceit in his mouth." Peter's substitution of the word **sin** for Isaiah's word "violence" emphasizes his belief in the sinlessness of Jesus. Violence is done to men; sin is against God. The Servant was not only devoid of any transgression against his fellow men, but had no stain on his record of rebellion against God. Peter makes this indisputably plain later, when he tells us that Christ's death was that of **the righteous for the unrighteous** (3:18). He uses there the same preposition as he did in verse 21, when he says: **Christ also suffered for you.** This might well be translated: "in place of you," or "in your stead." Here is the sinless taking the place of the sinful, in an act which cannot be imitated.

It is this redemptive act which gives Christ's followers strength to try to **imitate** His silent acceptance of His suffering, depicted in verse 23: **When he was reviled, he did not revile in return: when he suffered, he did not threaten.** This was manifested in His behavior before His accusers (see Mk 14:61, 15:5, Lk 23:9, John 19:9), but was also prefigured in Isaiah 53:7: "He was oppressed, and he was afflicted, yet he opened not his mouth; like a lamb that is led to the slaughter, and like a sheep that before its shearers is dumb, so he opened not his mouth." In place of defending Himself, He placed His fate in the hands of God: **he trusted to him who judges justly.** Some see in this a reflection of Jesus' cry from the cross: "Father, into thy hands I commit my spirit!" (Lk. 23:46). That passage, however, uses a different verb, and was the commitment of His *person* to God, while Peter is speaking of the commitment of His *cause*.

This is expressive of the juridic element frequently found in the New Testament, where there is a double court scene. A court on earth condemns, while the court in heaven acquits. The point here is that Jesus put His cause totally in the hands of God, willing silently to bear the verdict of "guilty" before the earthly court in the confidence that He would be pronounced "innocent" before the heavenly court. The ultimate divine judgment is all that mattered.

It has been suggested that when Jesus **did not threaten** as He **suffered,** He was overcoming evil with good, and thereby making it possible for His persecutors to escape judgment. The one who holds to this view, however, admits that the interpretation necessarily removes it from its Old Testament background. Furthermore, elsewhere in 1 Peter, the fact of final judgment is presented. Those who resist the will of God are to **give account to him who is ready to judge the living and the** dead (4:5); and **If the righteous man is scarcely saved, where will the impious and sinner appear** (4:18)?

The first half of verse 24—**He himself bore our sins in his body on the tree**, is based on Isaiah 53:4, 6 and 12: "Surely he has borne our griefs, and carried our sorrows; . . . the Lord has laid on him the iniquity of us all. . . . he bore the sins of many, and made intercession for the transgressors." It has been pointed out that Peter adds two features to Isaiah's picture: **in his body** and **on the tree**. The first stresses the reality of Christ's humanity, and His absolute identification with us as human beings when He made His offering. It implies what the author of Hebrews had in mind when he said that He, as our High Priest, did not bring to God an animal victim, but became the victim Himself. He "offered himself without blemish to God" (9:14). The expression **on the tree** defines the means by which Peter believed that the vicarious sufferer of which Isaiah spoke fulfilled His mission It is an archaic expression for the cross. Peter himself twice used this expression for the cross (Acts 5:30, 10:39), and it is attributed to Paul once (Acts 13:29). It is an expression which enhances the ignominy of the cross. The Jews considered anyone hanged on a tree as accursed (see Deut. 21:22f.), and the Romans reserved the cross as a method of punishment only for foreign malefactors and slaves. No matter how heinous the crime, anyone good enough to be a Roman was too good to be hanged on a cross.

The preposition **on** usually has the idea of motion, and commentators have sought to find in this some likeness to Old Testament priests moving sacrifices toward the place of offering. But there is elsewhere no notion of the cross as an altar. Furthermore, Peter in another place uses the same preposition to indicate the location where something takes place rather than motion towards it (4:14). If a sense of motion were at all intended, it might be thought of as a picture such as Bunyan gives us of Christian's burden of sin strapped to his back, which he could not unloose. Since Christ was the representative of the human race, the picture might be of all the sins of the entire human race placed upon his back, which burden he bore **up on to the cross**.

The purpose of Christ's vicarious suffering in our behalf was **that we might die to sin and live to righteousness**. The word here translated **die** is used nowhere else in the New Testament. It has the flavor of "being absent," of "saying farewell," or "ceasing to exist." It seems to suggest that if we are aware that Christ's suffering **on the tree** was not for sins that He had done, but for ours, that costly sacrifice should cause us to "absent" ourselves from sin, to "say farewell" to all that is counter to the will of God, to "cease to exist" to everything that contributed to Christ's death.

But this determined avoidance of evil sets us free to **live to righteousness**. Righteousness is the same word used in the Sermon on the Mount: "Blessed are those who hunger and thirst for righteousness, for they shall be satisfied" (Matt 5: 6). The word here seems not to carry the theological idea of a righteousness which only God has and only God can impart, which man by his own moral effort cannot attain. It is rather an ethical term describing "the doing of right as acceptable conduct." It is conduct designed not to attain God's forgiveness, but to express gratitude for the fact that God has already forgiven, through the merit of Christ's act of atonement on the cross. Translators, therefore, have sought to convey this by expressions such as: "live in accord with God's will," or "live to goodness." True gratitude for redemption is to seek to live in accord with the will of the Redeemer.

The latter part of verse 24, **by his wounds you have been healed**, is based on Isaiah 53:5: "But he was wounded for our transgressions, he was bruised for our iniquities; upon him was the chastisement that made us whole, and with his stripes we are healed." The figure of redemption here is drawn from the category of illness and health. This is the only place in the New Testament where this word **wounds** is used. This, along with the fact that Peter's word translated **die** in verse 24 is used only by him, might indicate that he was following his own verbal style here rather than quoting a hymn or an early catechism.

The figure of man in his separation from God as "wounded" and "bruised" is common in the Bible. Isaiah vividly describes Israel's moral condition: "the whole head is sick, and the whole heart faint. From the sole of the foot even to the head, there is no soundness in it, but bruises and sores and bleeding wounds" (1:5f.). Jeremiah likewise says of Israel: "your hurt is incurable, and your wound is grievous. . . . I will restore health to you, and your wounds I will heal" (30:12, 17; see also Isa 30:26, Mic 1:9, Nahum 3:19). In these passages, and others like them, sin is thought of as a malady, and redemption as its cure. The word **wounds** depicts the welts, or bruises caused by blows, either from fists, or clubs, or leather lashes. The slaves among Peter's readers likely knew firsthand what this word meant, with permanent scars on their bodies to remind them of blows from their overseers' fists, or clubs, or lashes. These would eloquently call to mind what their Lord had endured for them when He was slapped, spat upon, gashed with a thorn crown, lashed with the Roman scourge, and nailed to a wooden cross. The innocent Sufferer had voluntarily subjected Himself to all that they had endured, not for His own sins, but for theirs. Christ **suffered for you**, Peter reminds them (vs 21), though **he committed no sin**.

Here is the accomplishment of Isaiah's word: "But he was wounded for our transgressions, he was bruised for our iniquities; upon him was the chastisement that made us whole" (53:5). Peter's mind must also have turned to the story told by Jesus of the Good Samaritan, who found a man lying by the roadside stripped, and beaten, and half dead. He "bound up his wounds," and took him to an inn for shelter and healing, paying the cost of his care (Lk 10:30ff.). Jesus' story had overtones of how He was to bind up the wounds of mankind, for it is told in a book which climaxes in a cross toward which Luke has already told us Jesus' had steadfastly "set his face" (9:51). Here is divine Love taking into Himself the tragic consequences of others' sins, thus making it possible for them to be forgiven. This would most certainly encourage Peter's readers to suffer for Him!

Peter then turns to another image found in Isaiah: **For you were straying like sheep.** This was brought to his mind by Isaiah's picture: "All we like sheep have gone astray; we have turned every one to his own way; and the Lord has laid on him the iniquity of us all" (53:6). Recalling their conversion, Peter tells them that they **have now returned to the Shepherd and Guardian of your souls.**

The image of sheep for Israel, and God as their shepherd, is a common one in the Old Testament, and one used also by Jesus. Sheep are rather helpless creatures in themselves, and need the constant care of a shepherd. They seem to have a tendency to stray, to go their own way, to get lost and expose themselves to the risks arising from slippery cliffs, wild animals, lack of water, and faulty pasturage. The first mention in the Old Testament of Israel as **sheep** stresses their need of a shepherd, when Moses requests the Lord to appoint a successor to him, so that "the congregation of the Lord may not be as sheep which have no shepherd" (Num 27:17). The Psalmist acknowledges this need, when he says: "For he is our God, and we are the people of his pasture, and the sheep of his hand" (Ps 95:7). The prophets sensed the tendency of the **sheep** to go astray. Added to Isaiah's word that lies behind this passage is Jeremiah's description of them: "My people have been lost sheep; . . . from mountain to hill they have gone, they have forgotten their fold . . . Israel is a hunted sheep driven away by lions" (50:6, 17). Ezekiel speaks of them as having "become a prey, . . . food for all the wild beasts" (34: 8).

The rulers of the people and their religious leaders were to be shepherds in Israel, but they failed. Ezekiel says of them: "Ho, shepherds of Israel who have been feeding yourselves! Should not the shepherds feed the sheep? . . . The weak you have not strengthened, the sick you have not healed, the crippled you have not brought back, the lost you have not sought" (34:2ff.). Since they failed, God Himself affirms that He will take over the task to search for the sheep, to feed them, to bind up their wounds. "I, I myself will search for my sheep, and will seek them out. As a shepherd seeks out his flock when some of his sheep have been scattered abroad, so will I seek out my sheep; and I will rescue them from all places where they have been scattered" (Ezek 34:11f.).

This divine promise took on a Messianic cast. Jeremiah puts these words in God's mouth: "then I will gather the remnant of my flock out of all the countries where I have driven them, and I will bring them back to their fold, . . . I will raise up for David a righteous Branch, and he shall reign as king" (23:3ff.). Ezekiel adds: "And I will set up over them one shepherd, my servant David, and he shall feed them . . . and be their shepherd. And I, the Lord, will be their God" (34:23f.).

Jesus adopted this symbolism as a paradigm of His own mission. He told the parable of searching for the lost sheep until it was found (Lk 15:3ff.). He said of Himself: "For the Son of man came to seek and to save the lost" (Lk 19:10). "I am the good shepherd. The good shepherd lays down his life for the sheep" (John 10:11). It was of Him, then, that Peter was speaking when he named Him **the Shepherd and Guardian of your souls**. The writer to the Hebrews joined him in calling Jesus "the great shepherd of the sheep" (13:20).

The coming of Peter's readers to Jesus had brought them not only healing but had rescued them from their wandering and placed them safely in the protection of the fold again. If ever a generation needed both healing and rescue from its lostness, it is ours. Having severed the chains which bound us to the anchor of the moral and spiritual heritage which had been developed through the cumulative experience of the race, men have become sick—tossed about on the stormy sea of their passions and pride and self-centeredness. Without anchor, they are drifting, with no inner compass to guide them, rushing toward a massive catastrophe which they fear too much to admit or are so spiritually insensitive that they have no inkling of its possibility. Unwilling to reattach themselves to the old anchorage, and either afraid of, or unwilling to look at, the destructive consequences of their detachment, they seek escape through alcohol, drugs, illicit sex, lavish entertainment, indulgence in finery and extravagance of thrills, without thought, meditation, wholesome culture, moral seriousness, genuine faith, or God. And many who claim a dependence on God are aliens from the God and Father of our Lord Jesus Christ, the judging and redeeming God of Calvary's Cross, and have replaced Him with an idol of their own making, whom they can control and on whom they call to bless their own desires and concerns. The healing of the wounded Savior and the recovery from lostness by the great **Shepherd and Guardian** of their souls is the "good news" our generation desperately needs.

One final word on this section. A sensitive interpreter has pointed out the beauty and tenderness of Peter's use of the word **souls** in verse 25, especially as it was related to the slaves among his readers. "When the slaves were designated as a 'thing' by the Romans, and a 'body' by the Greeks, here they are called 'souls,' or 'persons.'" The slaves likely did not miss this nuance.

The best summation of Peter's presentation of the Suffering Servant here may be a rather lengthy quotation from the French pastor who wrote his commentary at the risk of death in a Nazi prison (see p. 144). "The abandonment of Jesus on the cross does not disclose the distance that he felt from his Father, but the distance . . . from his Father in which our sins had placed Him. It is our falsehoods, our self-conceits, our lusts, our idolatry which made him ascend the cross and which cast him into death and hell—and in place of throwing all that aside and disengaging himself from it in rejoining his Father, in place of throwing back on us all the faults with which we overwhelmed him, he took them all on his shoulders, he transferred all this depravity on to his body, to carry it away, to sweep it far from us, with him into death and hell. The sword with which we have pierced him, he has taken into himself, and our hands are left empty. And behold: the triumph of our sin has deprived us of our sin. Everything with which we have overpowered our Lord has now descended into the tomb with him; there remains no longer the slightest trace of it. We are miraculously stripped of all the weapons of our victory. His death, which appeared to be the death of God's justice, the death blow of the kingdom, is in reality the death of our iniquities, the *coup de grace* given to the prince of this world. Our text has a stronger expression yet: **that we might die to sin.** On the cross, it is we who died, who ceased to exist for all the things for which we had to die, and who began to exist for those things for which we must live; in order that we should **live to righteousness,** for that righteousness for which he totally committed himself and by which we are now, in him, judged and justified, condemned and pardoned, dead and alive. **By his wounds you have been healed** . . . . By his death, you live, for it is the death of everything which causes death. **By his wounds you are healed,** for they are the **wounds** which God gives to everything that makes you ill.

"This is the eternally quivering heart of the good news. This is the unbelievable mystery of a God whose love goes to the length of taking on himself the crime of his enemies, to uproot all hatred from their heart, and makes himself responsible for their misfortunes in order to deliver them. . . . Without this death, God could have permitted us to live, but we would have filled his kingdom with unrighteousness, and God would thus have lost his kingdom. Without this death God could have saved his kingdom and his righteousness in forbidding us entrance to it and casting us far from him, but thus God would have lost us, he would have abandoned us to eternal death. In the first case, he would have renounced his righteousness; in the second, his love. But in giving his Son, God has shown that he holds to his righteousness more than to himself—and to us more than to himself. Thus the death of our sin, the crucifixion of our old man in Christ, is at one and the same time our salvation and that of the kingdom . . .

"Verse 25 recapitulates for the last time the whole of the situation: . . . . Sin had removed all meaning from our life and reduced it to an erudite rambling. 'We have turned every one to his own way' (Isa 53:6); we were going into the desert of the world without God and without neighbor, free to roam—to go where of importance? to do what that mattered? in a perpetual: to what good?—frightfully free, yes, cowards in the desert, without reason or capabilities of living, without horizon and without fold, without guide and without track, lost in the infinity of space and of time, but in fact tethered to ourselves and to our death as a nanny goat to its stake. It is there that the Lord has come to find us. 'He found him in a desert land, and in the howling waste of the wilderness' (Deut 32:10). 'Some wandered in desert wastes, finding no way to a city to dwell in' (Ps 107:4). It is there that he became our Shepherd and our Guardian, and left some clear footprints where we could place our feet. And these are precisely the footprints which we find again when we endure unjust punishments [remember that the writer was enduring unjust punishments when he wrote!]. And these punishments are a grace in the measure that they help us locate his footprints and follow them, and to live in the communion of his sufferings and to return always to the Shepherd of our souls. Everything which we have to suffer in obedience is a reminder that our wandering is ended, that our life has meaning, that we are returned to the one who is for eternity, that is to say for each one of our minutes, our sovereign High Priest, our Shepherd, and our King.

"Thus we receive once more the word of God under its double form of gospel and law, of recollection and appeal. Since you are returned to your Shepherd, follow him! Since he has put to death everything which leads you astray, since he has carried you joyously on his shoulders, 'walk united to him'" (Col 2:6).

The writer of the foregoing words, although languishing in prison for doing *right*, yet free within, understood what Peter was writing better than do many of us who, although free from political imprisonment, are enslaved to all sorts of inner bondages.

E. Wives' Relation to Their Husbands *(3:1-6)*
(Exhortation)

This passage is especially difficult to deal with in our time. Rampant feminism places gender questions beyond discussion for many, and often breeds more heat than light. There would seem to be three possible ways to approach this passage.

1) To bypass historic perspective, treating what Peter says in a historic vacuum, as though his aim was to give gender instructions to all people for all time in all situations, and make a blanket application

of his words without discrimination.

2) Again, to bypass historic perspective, as though Peter were laying down gender ethics for all situations at all times, and conclude that we do not like what he said, that we know better, and set up his thought here only to knock it down.

3) To seek to place Peter's thought in its historic setting, trying to find out what it meant for his first readers in Asia Minor in the second half of the first century A.D., then see if it has any meaning for us in our time. We shall attempt the latter approach.

Both the section on wives, and the later section on **husbands**, are bound into the larger context by the word **likewise**. The word means "in the same way." Since it is used for both **husbands** and **wives**, it likely refers not to the submission of slaves to masters, the subordination of those of lesser social status to those of higher, but to the general subordination of Christians to all men with which the entire section is introduced (2:13). Since **husbands** and **wives** are both included, it is likely that Peter is not patterning his family ethics here on pagan models but rather inculcating a *Christian* ethic, where each is to subordinate his interests to those of others. In this case, the theological affirmations of verses 21-25 would apply here also. **Because Christ also suffered for you, leaving you an example, that you should follow in his steps; because when he suffered, he did not threaten;** because **he bore our sins in his body on the tree; because by his wounds you have been healed;** you should **be submissive**, voluntarily placing yourselves under the constraints of the social order in which you find yourself. This is not, then, an effort to "keep women in their place," advocating "the conventional submissiveness that the ancient world expected of a wife . . . in reality it is to be something quite different, the expression of that Christian attitude of subordination . . . not on the level of compulsion or resignation, but something freely given, active, not passive, drawing its strength not from the fear of man but from the gospel of Christ." *Because Christ submitted Himself to far worse suffering than you know, submit yourself to the situation in which you find yourself!* This was advice to Christian wives of pagan husbands in the first century A.D., and not a philosophical discussion of the ideal relationships between the sexes in general. Christians are set apart **for obedience to Jesus Christ** (1:2); they are to live in reverential **fear** (1:17); they form a temple where they offer themselves as

spiritual sacrifices acceptable to God (2:4ff.), which take the form of "reverence, devotion and submission to their neighbor." Hence, **for the Lord's sake** (2:13) they willingly place themselves under their obligations to others as an expression of their love and obedience to Him. All of this far transcends the mere acceptance of the pagan social order of the day.

Wives, **be submissive to your husbands** must be understood in its setting. In Asia Minor, in Peter's time, **wives** were the property of their **husbands**. They were, therefore, supposed to have the same religion as their husbands, and if the husband changed religion his wife was expected to make the change with him. The gospel, however, was a universal religion, geared to all alike, in which distinctions of race, sex, and social status were overcome. "There is neither Jew nor Greek, there is neither slave nor free, there is neither male nor female; for you are all one in Christ Jesus" (Gal 3:28). Difficult though it was, and counter to social custom as it was, it was possible that a woman could learn of the Christian faith at a public laundry place beside a stream, or at a public well, while conversing with neighbor women, and accept it on her own, quite apart from her husband's religion. It is not easy for us to have a feel for the tension that this would create in a formerly pagan household. It would be similar to a Muslim woman today in a Fundamentalist Muslim part of the world becoming a Christian without her husband's consent. In such a circumstance, the woman would likely be either disowned, or killed. But if she should be permitted to remain in the home, think of the predicament she would face. It would abound in tensions from which she would want to escape. And since, according to the new faith she has embraced, she is a free woman in Christ, should she not act in this freedom to sever the marriage ties and flee, if possible? No, says Peter. As the slave, by his conversion, was made a free man, yet as a Christian he was to live out that freedom by a voluntary willingness to serve his master **mindful of God** (2:19), for the Lord's sake (2:13); so Peter counsels the Christian wife of an unbelieving husband to "remain in the state in which [she] was called" (1 Cor.7:20).

This was not to be done merely as a duty, but with a missionary motive—so that **your husbands . . . may be won** to the faith. Thus, a marriage which, although Peter does not mention it, was rooted in creation (according to Jesus, (Matt 19:4ff.), would also be rooted in redemption; and the oneness of the couple would be completed in Christ.

And thus, also, another of God's straying **sheep would be returned to the Shepherd and Guardian** of his soul.

But how was this to take place? **By the behavior of their wives, when they see your reverent and chaste behavior.** The **husbands** had already heard the gospel and did **not obey the word.** The word for disobedience could be synonymous with unbelief, but "it evokes a refusal rather than a simple incredulity." For that reason, continuing vocal efforts to press the claims of the faith could well exascerbate a tense situation, cause further disruption in the home, and turn the husband further from acceptance of the gospel. Peter, therefore, suggests the possibility that the **husbands . . . be won without a word, when they see your reverent and chaste behavior.** To use this passage to justify social work as evangelism without the accompanying proclamation of the gospel is a gross misuse of Peter's intention. The **husbands** have already heard the word, and rebelled against it! And those who believed among Peter's readers had come to that faith through **the things that have now been announced to you by those who preached the good news** . . . (1:12). Peter is not counseling evangelism through "good works" only, but warning against incessant argument in the home, against an "unseasonable apologetic."

The word **see** in verse 2 suggests a penetrating look, a thoughtful observation, a contemplation of what one is seeing with the eyes. It is rather to see with the mind, to see into the heart of a thing, to pierce the mystery of something. It is the **reverent and chaste behavior** of the **wives** which would open their husbands' eyes to the mystery of the elevating power of the gospel. **Reverent** here may be pointed toward God or toward the husband. Grammatically, it is difficult to choose which was in Peter's mind. If it is toward God, it would mean that the **husbands** are impressed with how reverent the wives are toward Him. If it is toward the husband, he would be impressed with the reverential respect displayed toward him and his will. **Chaste** not only involves sexual fidelity, but "candor, modesty, propriety," the opposite of "shameful, disgraceful." It involves "a sort of transparency of the entire life," a demeanor which is "as open as a clear sky on a May morning, an absence of all chicanery, all hidden motives. It was originally a word applied to the gods, or to persons or things which belong to the gods, such as prophets who were considered to be men very near to God."

A French commentator sees this meaning of the word **chaste** as a clue to capturing the beautiful picture of a Christian wife in our passage: "Christian spouses are a figure of consecrated beings, officiants in a temple . . . they make of their homes a sanctuary where God is present and active . . . ; their silent virtue creates there the appropriate atmosphere, from whence comes the accuracy of the word 'reverent' which can be extended to a profoundly deferential attitude toward the husband, in so far as it is inspired by the fear of God . . . This is the beauty of a perfect life which, triumphing over the opposition of an unbelieving husband, can make him accept and love the Word of God."

If Augustine's mother had lived in Peter's day, one could almost think that he was using her as a model of what he wrote here. She was married to an unbelieving husband, and sought to win him to the faith by her behavior. Augustine speaks of his father as her "husband whom she served as her lord," and speaks of her motherly love as "her slavery for me." He says to God: "She busied herself to gain him to Thee, preaching Thee unto him by her behavior; by which Thou madest her fair, and reverently amiable, and admirable unto her husband . . . . while many matrons whose husbands were more gentle, carried the marks or blows on their dishonored faces, . . . knowing what furious husband she endured, marvelled that it had never been reported, nor appeared by any indication, that Patricius [his father] had beaten his wife, or that there had been any domestic strife between them, even for a day, and asked her in confidence the reason of this, she taught them her rule." It was: "That from the hour they heard what are called the matrimonial tablets read to them, they should think of them as instruments whereby they were made servants; as being always mindful of their condition, they ought not to set themselves in opposition to their lords." The outcome is not surprising: "Finally, her own husband, . . . did she gain over unto Thee."

To modern western ears this sounds intolerable. But in the culture of her day, which was similar to that which Peter was addressing, it was a wonderful expression of the power of the Christian faith to enable women to express their Christian freedom by voluntarily living under the constraints of the social customs of the day, and thereby winning their husbands for Christ. Incidentally, had Monica sought to express her freedom in modern terms, it would have achieved nothing. Augustine remarks that other women who followed his mother's example "experienced the wisdom of it, and rejoiced; those who observed it not were kept in subjection, and suffered."

Is there any word here for today? Surely, no Christian in his right mind would want women to return to the position of being "servants" of their husbands and "slaves" to their children. But is there not still a need for the disposition of subordinating self-interests to the welfare of the family other than the total independence and aggressive self-realization which is championed by so many today? The family is the basic unit of stability and wholeness for society. And the family is based on the unity of the couple, where the two become one in starkest reality. Two individuals, going totally their own way, with no mutual interests, living wholly independent lives, do not make a couple just by spending a little time under the same roof and sleeping in the same bed. And when the inevitable strains appear in the formidable task of melding two lives into one, if the process is resisted by the insistence on maintaining one's own autonomy and freedom, and solving the problem by walking out on the obligations of mutuality and coalescence, then society loses the bonds which hold it together, and becomes a mass of units without any deep or abiding relation to one another, and dooms itself to repeating the tragedy of ancient Israel, when "every man did what was right in his own eyes" (Judg 21:25). Is it stretching the analogy too far to suggest that the chaos of our time stems at least partly, if not largely, from this?

Verses 3 and 4 have occasioned a good deal of controversy among those who are inclined to interpret the Bible literally and legalistically. **Let not yours be the outward adorning with braiding of hair, decoration of gold, and wearing of robes,** is taken by some as totally forbidding the use of such things for Christian women. The word here translated robes means literally "garments" or "clothes." The fact that Peter was not advising nudity should guard against taking all his teaching here literally. Likewise, the **braiding of hair,** in our society, would be considered by many to be one of the most plain and modest forms of hairdo.

What Peter is doing is contrasting two kinds of beauty, outer and inner, and proposing that of the two, the latter is the more important. One writer has suggested, therefore, that a fair translation of Peter's words might be: "Your beauty should *not so much* come from outward adornment . . . *but rather* it should be that of your inner self." A modern translator has embodied this by translating the passage: "Your beauty should not be dependent on" outward adornment. Efforts to make one's self attractive to one's spouse or the public by tasteful grooming are surely not in God's sight reprehensible. Sarah, who is held up as a model woman, likely did not avoid personal adornment. We are told that when her husband, Abraham, sent his servant off to find a bride for his son Isaac, he sent "jewelry of silver and of gold, and raiment . . . and costly ornaments" which he gave to Rebekah and her family (Gen 24:53). If Abraham so adorned his future daughter-in-law, it is quite likely that some such adornment was worn also by Sarah. Hence, as one has concluded: "There is no direction here . . . to wear somber garments, shun ornament or damage comeliness by austere hair styling." An ornamental gift, given out of love, may mean much to the person who receives it, becoming a tangible symbol of that love and preserving wholesome memories through the years.

Jonathan Edwards, who could hardly be justly accused of undue "worldliness," on occasional trips to Boston used to purchase bits of jewelry, which at times he could not well afford, for his wife with whom he lived in what he called an "uncommon union," which helped to seal their undying love. An attractive garment may enhance a woman's beauty in a wholesome way, artfully setting forth the delicacy and grace which God gave her, as a fine picture frame brings out the beauty of a painting. But when inordinate time and expense are invested in extravagance, with more concern for physical beauty than for **the hidden person of the heart with the imperishable jewel of a gentle and quiet spirit, which in God's sight is very precious;** when one becomes what a novelist described as "a singular framework of clothes, with nothing of any consequence inside them"; or when dress and ornaments become the source of immoderate pride, and exceed good taste by calling attention to one's self and flaunting one's affluence, the question must be faced of where one's true values lie.

Although the passage is misused to forbid all efforts at making the body attractive, yet it raises profound questions as to whether the culture has not taken over the church in our time, when Christians join the mad march toward artificial physical beauty and neglect the cultivation of the inner life. Is it Christian to foster beauty contests for little children, which early in life slant their interests toward the body alone? And what of the emphasis on physical beauty to the point of driving less attractive girls to the lack of a sense of self worth, with no appreciation of the fact that the inner beauty of spirit and personality is a treasure of much more worth than external appearance? And what of the extravagant emphasis on the body that makes countless youth victims of boulemia and anorexia? And what of the millions upon millions of dollars spent on cosmetics, and plastic surgery, and slimming devices, and muscular development schemes, and physical fitness centers, all stimulated by a fanatical emphasis on the beauty of the body, while spiritual values and aesthetic appreciations and cultural enrichments go begging? And what of the countless suicides of youth who have been convinced that physical beauty holds the key to the meaning of life, and have decided to throw in the towel because they are not endowed with it, and cannot acquire it? Watching the mad scramble for body enhancement, Paul's word often comes to mind: "Train yourself in godliness; for while bodily training *is of some value*, godliness is of value in every way, as it holds promise of the present life and also for the life to come" (I Tim 4:8, emphasis added). It is not that bodily concern has *no* value, but the relative emphasis placed upon it is misleading and finally tragic, for its value is temporary at best and has little worth in developing the real, the inner person; and the current fanatical concern for it tends to obliterate spiritual concerns. Peter adds to the Christian motivation to win the wife's pagan husband to the faith, that of developing an inner beauty which has the approval of God. A **gentle and quiet spirit**—unassuming and tranquil under the pressures of life—is an **imperishable jewel**, commended by Jesus when He said: "Blessed are the meek" (Mt 5:5), and exemplified by Him when He rode into Jerusalem on a donkey, as Zechariah foresaw, as a humble king (See Mt 21:5, Zech. 9:9; "humble" is the same word translated "gentle" in 1 Peter). This is a commodity which ranks high with God!

The third motivation presented to the Christian wives for expressing their freedom in deference to their husbands, was the example of the **holy women** of the Old Testament, **as Sarah obeyed Abraham, calling him lord.** These women were not considered **holy** by Peter in that they were of "impeccable behavior," but because they were numbered among the chosen people; not merely by virtue of their ethnicity but because they **hoped in God**; that is, they were genuine believers in God's coming deliverance, which was of more value to them than any outward beauty. The Christian women of Asia Minor were the heirs of those ancient folk if they continued to **do right and let nothing terrify them.** Doing **right** would involve expressing in behavior those moral qualities which would commend themselves to the members of the

Christian community and to morally observant inquirers from pagan society, because they are expressive of the holy nature of God. **Let nothing terrify you** likely refers to mastering fear of the consequences of living as a Christian in a pagan environment. Some translators have referred to these as "hysterical fears," or "frightened panic," or "anxious thoughts." The idea seems to be that if the women to whom Peter writes are in company with the ancient women of faith, joined to them "by similar conduct and the seeking for the same ends," and now with them are hoping **in God,** they may accept "the tyranny of a common life with a man whose orders they had to accept," with **a gentle and quiet spirit,** knowing that "the anger, menace, brutality and mental cruelty of a pagan husband" are of comparatively little importance. This was a heroism impossible to women as women, but made possible for them by grace as they were **mindful of God** (2:19).

Commentators differ as to Peter's precise meaning in introducing **Sarah** as an example. In the Greek translation of the Old Testament, **Sarah** is said to have called Abraham "lord" or "master" (Gen 18:12). In the context there, however, she is skeptical of the promise of having a son when it was biologically impossible, and Peter is hardly suggesting that the Christian **wives** imitate her skepticism. Some think that **Sarah,** as the wife of Abraham, the father of Israel's faith, is merely *idealized* here, with no reference to any particular historic event in her career. Others have held that since the event depicted in Genesis 18:12 is not what Peter had in mind, he merely "saw in her use of 'my lord' in speaking of her husband . . . a representative utterance that implied a sense of habitual subordination." Still others, refining this, have drawn attention to this "habitual subordination" in the two instances where Abraham, in fear of his life, passed **Sarah** off as his sister (Gen 12:10ff. and 20:1ff.). By Sarah's acquiescence in this, she thus is introduced "not just as a model of obedience but as a model of those wives who obey their spouses in an unjust and frightening situation . . . ." This was exactly the plight of Peter's female readers, **wives** who because of their pagan **husbands** were living in an unjust and frightening setting. This is a clever and appealing suggestion, but one wonders whether, if Peter had this in mind, he would not have indicated it more clearly. Perhaps it is better to grant that we cannot be sure of exactly what was in Peter's mind in his reference other than that **Sarah,** as the wife of Abraham, was *ideally* the representative of the entire line of holy women who followed her in the history of Israel.

F. Husbands' Relation to Their Wives *(3:7)*
(Exhortation)

Peter speaks generally of the relation of Christian **husbands** to their **wives**, with no mention of the special relation of a Christian husband to a pagan wife. In all probability, this is because, in the light of the custom of women accepting their husbands' religion, there were not many such combinations in the Christian community.

Likewise links this brief section to the foregoing exhortations. The deference of a husband toward his wife is an expression of the general respect Christians should show to all men (2:17), and **servants** should show to their masters (2:18ff.), and wives should embody toward their **husbands. Husbands, live considerately with your wives.** Although social custom in the world to which Peter was writing made the wife the property of the husband, giving him full legal control of her, the Christian faith placed on the Christian husband constraints which were foreign to the pagans. Christian **husbands** were to **live considerately** toward their **wives**. This expression means literally to live "according to knowledge," or "with discernment." This means more than mere "tact," or "discrimination." It is the discernment of "more hidden realities," such as knowledge of **the grace of life** and the reality of **prayers**. This is not the "knowledge" of which the second century Gnostics were proud, "consisting in a feeling of intellectual superiority," but in an intelligent (appreciative) consideration of the weak. The Gnostics tended to "scorn a wife as a sensual and unclean creature" and to advise continence. The apocryphal *Gospel according to the Egyptians* has this: "The Saviour himself said: 'I came to destroy the works of the female.' By *female* he means lust: by *works* birth and decay." Peter has no such low opinion of a wife, but instead accords to her "equal religious standing" with the husband.

In the initial stages of disintegrating marriages, perhaps more damage is done by thoughtlessness and ignorance than by a breakdown of love. When two become one, a true understanding of the needs and responses and desires of each by the other is a prime essential for making that oneness real and permanent. Normally, men tend to be less sensitive than women to the nuances of response in personal relationships.

Husbands, therefore, need consciously to strive to **live considerately**, or "with understanding," and with spiritual sensitivity toward their wives. It has been proposed that the expression **live considerately with your wives** might well be translated: live "with a supernatural discretion," a perception informed by the will of God and an anxious effort to apply it to the thousand details of the daily life.

The considerateness, for the Christian husband, is based on certain general Christian considerations. **Honor all men** (2:17) would include honor toward one's wife. Also, reciprocity would demand of the Christian that if a wife places herself under the will of the husband, as Peter's earlier exhortation admonishes, he should take her wishes into like consideration. It has been proposed that this may have accounted for Peter's word **bestowing** in connection with **honor**. This was a word suggesting "paying," equitably "assigning" what is due to another, making an "equal distribution" of something. In this case, it would be an equal distribution of deference between husband and wife. In the light of this, there would be no servility in a wife's deference toward her husband, for it would be repaid by a like deference on his part toward her. Then, too, the demands of Christian **love** (2:17) would lay on a Christian husband an obligation that could not be fulfilled in mere sentiment, but in countless acts prompted by insight and devotion to his wife.

Beyond these general considerations, however, are three specific items to be taken into account by the Christian husband. First, is the recognition of his wife **as the weaker sex**. One writer says of this: "It would be of little profit to submit this text of Peter to modern questions on the difference between masculine and feminine, between that which is 'natural' and that which arises from the 'culture,' between that which is permanent and that which is recognized as historically conditioned." There are countless examples of the fact that the culture to which Peter was addressing himself thought of women as both physically and psychologically "fragile." Peter, in this instance, is not addressing, as with the **slaves**, the behavior of those who were considered inferior to those who were considered superior, but exactly the reverse. He is describing the Christian attitude of the privileged to the underprivileged. In our culture, then, we are not to judge him as to his first century social views, but by the remarkable behavior he outlines toward those considered the weaker.

It is native to humanity for the stronger to dominate the weaker. When a five year old boy suddenly discovers that he can overpower his playmate, it is natural for him to dominate and force his will on the other. Although this natural tendency is brought somewhat under control in its ruder forms by social pressures, it expresses itself in more subtle ways—sometimes even in brutal ways—among the mature, in that those who have power, either among classes, races, or nations, seek to dominate the weaker. Peter demands the total reversal of this tendency in the intimacies of the home. The Christian husband, just because his wife may be physically and emotionally more fragile than he, should give her the more consideration. Her interests and needs should be all the more protected by seeking to shield her from all that would wound her delicacy. To this end, according to Paul, God has given us an example, both in the human body and in the body of Christ, by "giving the greater honor to the inferior part, that there may be no discord in the body, but that the members may have the same care for one another" (1 Cor 12:24f.).

The second motivation for considerate behavior of **husbands** toward **wives** is that **wives are joint heirs of the grace of life.** All Christians, according to Peter are heirs of an **imperishable, undefiled and unfading** inheritance (1:3f.). As one writer has pointed out, however, "the right of co-inheritance supposes a particular affinity, a profound union between those who participate in this good." The unity of the Christian couple is likened by Paul to the unity between Christ and His church (Eph 5:22ff.), a unity so close that they are actually made one. "Even so," said Paul, "husbands should love their wives as their own bodies." The union is so close that "he who loves his wife loves himself" (Eph 5:28). Paul speaks of this as a "mystery," but a mystery made possible by the grace of Christ.

The grace of life means "the grace which is life," **life** being an explanation of what **grace** means here. Since this life is "eternal," and according to Jesus there will be no differentiation between the sexes in the life to come, for "when they rise from the dead, they neither marry nor are given in marriage, but are like angels in heaven" (Mk 12:25), Peter seems to be reminding his readers of the conclusion to which Paul came: for Christians *now*, who are already **joint heirs of the grace of life,** "there is neither male nor female; for you are all one in Christ Jesus" (Gal. 3:28). In other words, the *oneness of the couple* should illustrate their *oneness in Christ,* so that even if the social custom of the time demanded that the wife should defer to the husband, she was deferring to one who rendered her a like deference. Whatever the social custom, the reality of the couple in their life together involved no servility nor humiliation. The reality of the kingdom to come was already operative in the kingdom of this world. A genuine religious unity will guarantee finally a social unity.

The third motivation for Christian considerateness on the part of **husbands** is that their **prayers may not be hindered.** Prayer is the primary channel through which God's grace is bestowed on His children. It is the means by which God's strength is given to overcome our weaknesses and maintain our spiritual health. Jesus taught His disciples "that they ought always to pray and not lose heart" (Lk 18:1). Prayer is the conduit of spiritual strength and courage. The secret of maintaining the unity of the couple is common prayer. Jesus taught us that reconciliation to an alienated brother is a prerequisite to effective prayer (Matt 5:23f.). He indicated that our debts to God would be forgiven as we also forgive others (Matt 6:12, 14f.; 18:21ff.). Mutual forgiveness and accord, then, are essential to an effective prayer life, which in turn is essential to the unity of the couple. One writer has observed that prayer does not occupy a large place in this epistle; "nevertheless, here it is honored as the summit of the life of the couple and, at the same time, the test of the quality of its unity."

When Peter's whole picture of the relation of the couple is brought together, it makes of Christian marriage something sacramental, a twilight memory of the bliss of the Garden of Eden before the fall, and a foretaste of the Paradise to come. **Wives** are to show deference to their **husbands,** to maintain a **reverent and chaste behavior,** to adorn themselves with the inner beauty of a **gentle and quiet spirit,** to live with calmness, and to value what in **God's sight is very precious. Husbands are to live considerately with their wives, bestowing honor** on them, protecting them as members of **the weaker sex,** against danger, both from themselves and from without, valuing them as **joint heirs of the grace of life** and making them partners in their communion with God through their **prayers.** What could be grander than this! Granted that in our sinfulness, we are unable fully to embody this picture of what Christian marriage should be, and that in the blending of two lives into one, differences, tensions, disagreements, conflicts will arise, these can be surmounted by the **grace** of God and used as steppingstones toward an ever greater respect and love on the part of both members of a couple.

G. The Life of the Christian Community in the World
(3: 8-12) (Exhortation)

Having dealt with the relations of Christians as citizens, slaves, wives, and husbands, Peter now turns his attention to their group life within their own community as it relates to their influence in a pagan world,

Finally, or "lastly," or "to finish off the subject," binds the exhortations here to what he has been saying. He wants not only their individual responses as Christians to be a witness to the gospel among the pagans, but desires that their life together within the Christian community be a corporate witness to the unbelieving world of what life in loyalty to the Christian God should be. He deals first, in verse 8, with the spirit which should prevail within the group toward one another; and then, in verse 9, with what the attitude of the entire group should be toward those outside who, misunderstanding them, may revile and persecute them.

Verse 8, in the original, after addressing **all of you**, consists of just five words, all of them adjectives, each defining a quality of life within the community which should be directed toward the surrounding world. Although the translators have made a sentence out of verse 8, and ended it with a period, it is really a part of the larger sentence, with the period belonging at the end of verse 9. Two participles in verse 9 describe the behavior that Peter is suggesting for the group characterized by the adjectives of verse 8.

Unity of spirit is the first quality mentioned. It is difficult to find a one-word equivalent for this in English. "Like-minded" is used by some. This does not mean, however, "congealing all Christians into the same mold." It "does not mean 'be of the same opinion,' or 'agree to the same platform,' but 'have the same orientation,' 'aim at the same mark,' (here, to seek to please the Lord!)." It means that, springing from the same faith and the same love, "believers, with an origin humanly so disparate, should have identical purposes and inclinations and responses, even in the most chance spheres." It is the miracle of grace wrought at Pentecost, when, we are told: "Now the company of those who believed were of one heart and soul" (Acts 4:32). This is not to obliterate all distinctions of individuality, nor to homogenize the Christian group into one-dimensional folk who respond alike to a "monolithic or centralized" authority as automatons. It does mean, however, that there should be a generally "Christian" way of looking at things on the part of those whose responses are **mindful of God** (1 Pet 2:19), in contrast to those who are rooted in the natural man apart from God. Peter was saying to his readers: "You must all think about life in the same way."

Sympathy, too, should characterize Christians. The word literally means to "feel with," and describes the inner capacity to make one's own the experiences of others. Paul pretty well defined it when he said: "Rejoice with those who rejoice, weep with those who weep" (Rom 12:15). He said on another occasion, when he was admonishing the Christian group to "have the same care for one another": "If one member suffers, all suffer together; if one member is honored, all rejoice together" (1 Cor.12:25f.). The great example of true sympathy is seen in the coming of our Lord into human flesh, making our human experience His own; so that, as our High Priest, He could "sympathize with our weaknesses" and know our lot from within (Heb 4:15). No matter how abandoned one may feel, then, no one can rightfully say: "Nobody understands!" There is One who does, our great High Priest, who "ever lives to make intercession," at whose "throne of grace . . . we may receive mercy and find grace to help in time of need" (Heb. 7:25, 4:16). Peter is here proposing that some reflection of this profound **sympathy** should characterize Christians' feelings for one another, so that the spirit of Him who is head of the church should permeate His body.

Love of the brethren is another concept that is packed into one word in Greek. It literally means love for one's blood brother or sister, but in the New Testament is used figuratively for other Christian believers. This means that the early Christians thought of themselves as one family, each member of which had a kinship to all others as close as blood kinship. This feature was so characteristic of the early church that the pagans sensed it as one of the marks of their fellowship. One of the pagan writers in the first half of the second century, said: "Their Lawgiver has persuaded the Christians that they are brothers." It is interesting that this pagan critic not only was impressed by this aspect of the Christians' life, but that he caught from them the fact that it went back to their founder. Jesus Himself had told them, while here in the flesh: "you are all brethren" (Matt 23:8). And Paul referred to Jesus as "the first-born among many brethren" (Rom 8: 29).

A glance at a concordance under either the word "brethren" or "brother" indicates that this was the favorite title that Christians gave to one another in New Testament times. Peter himself referred to the church as "the brotherhood" (2:17). As a French commentator has remarked: "It is not so much because the Christians are members of the same religious community, as at Qumran and the societies of that epoch ... but in virtue of a spiritual kinship: They have God for their Father ... so that the adjective *philadelphian* puts them all on the same level and prescribes this true and reciprocal affection which is experienced between members of the same family." Human nature seems to have a need to "belong," to be connected, to be attached to others beyond the consanguinity of blood kinship. To fill this need, various societies or organizations are formed, where "like-minded people feel closer to one another than they do to humanity at large." Those of similar tastes, or interests, or needs, tend to associate with one another for mutual stimulation in their work, or satisfaction of their desires, or fulfillment of their impulses. Professional societies, service clubs, lodges and secret orders, country clubs, Alcoholics Anonymous, or Gamblers Anonymous, or families of alcoholics, or gamblers, or recovering cancer patients, or parents with problem children, or investor's clubs, or photographic groups, or a hundred other types of support groups, arise to fill this need. Most of these groups are necessarily exclusive, in that to belong, one must have a special type of interest or need or qualification. Some of them are voluntarily exclusive, designed to express pride or superiority to others, either of wealth, or status, or ability. The family of the church, however, differs from these others. In one sense, it is the most exclusive group in the world—it excludes all who do not take God and His will for individuals and society seriously. When the church is at her best, no others need apply! On the other hand, it is the most inclusive group in the world, in that the things which disqualify for entrance into other groups are totally irrelevant, and *anyone who seriously wants to know God and serve Him on terms that He has laid down in His Word* are welcome. The major qualification for entrance into the real church, the church as God sees it, is to know that one can never qualify, save by renouncing everything which runs counter to the will of Him who extends the invitation into His fellowship.

The fourth adjective Peter uses to describe the relation of

Christians to one another in the family of faith is translated **a tender heart**. Again, this is one word in the original, meaning "tenderhearted," "compassionate." It means literally, "with healthy intestines." Since the ancients thought of the intestines as "the seat of the emotions," probably because intense emotions were felt in one's mid-section, "healthy intestines" led to "healthy feelings," therefore to a tender or compassionate heart. This ancient connection between the body and the feelings came into our early English, and is reflected in the *King James Version* of the Bible where, for example, Job 30:27 was translated: "My bowels boiled, and rested not." Modern translators have changed this to: "My heart is in turmoil, and never still." In the *King James* translation, Colossians 3:12 exhorted: "Put on therefore . . . bowels of mercies," which in current translation reads: "Put on . . . compassion."

How does a **tender heart** differ from **sympathy**? Sympathy could exhaust itself in feeling, whereas tenderness of heart is associated in the New Testament with concrete action toward the one pitied. One has remarked that it carries the nuance of "maternally tender," the pity of a mother, which always leads to action. It is more, then, than having "a good heart," but involves the "authentic kindness" of the Good Samaritan who took costly action in favor of one in need (Lk 10:33ff.); or the pity of God who, like the king in Jesus' parable of the hopelessly indebted servant, "released him and forgave him the debt" (Matt 18: 27).

The final quality called for here is **a humble mind**. Humility was not extolled among the pagans in New Testament times. It seemed to them to smack of groveling, cowardice, lack of self-will, lack of achievement, weakness, pusillanimity, subjection. Jesus, on the other hand, both embodied humility in Himself, and made it "the cornerstone of character" for His followers. He was "gentle and lowly [humble] in heart" (Matt 11:29), and taught that "whoever humbles himself like this child, he is the greatest in the kingdom of heaven" (Matt 18:4). True humility is not a self-conscious manner affected to make an impression on others, nor a practiced asceticism designed to demonstrate one's self-effacement. Paul called this sort of humility "self-abasement," and cautioned against it (see Col 2:18, 23). True humility is based on "self-knowledge and consists in entire self-committal to God's grace. . . . It is to become a child again before God, i.e., to trust Him utterly, to expect everything from Him and nothing from self." True humility is an awareness of one's creaturehood in the light of God as Creator, and of one's sinfulness in the light of God's holiness, and of one's emptiness and inadequacy in the light of God's sufficiency and all-giving grace. One can be realistically aware of his gifts and achievements, but certain also that all such things are the tokens of God's favor and not the marks of his own self-achieved worth. In this knowledge, the man who is humble before God does not flaunt himself before men. "For every one who exalts himself will be humbled, and he who humbles himself will be exalted" (Lk 14:11).

By concluding his list of adjectives describing the ideal Christian fellowship with humility, Peter is indicating that if a Christlike community is to function with **unity of spirit, sympathy, love of the brethren.** and **tenderness of heart,** "then there is need of a disposition which is ready for service to others and which does not lift up itself above others."

Two participles embody the type of action toward others that the five adjectives, if achieved, would express. The first is negative. **Do not return evil for evil or reviling for reviling.** Here the Old Testament law of retaliation is surpassed. That law was an advance at the time it was promulgated. It said: "If any harm follows, then you shall give life for life, eye for eye, tooth for tooth, hand for hand, foot for foot, burn for burn, wound for wound, stripe for stripe" (Exod 21:23ff.). Retaliation was at least limited to the amount of damage done. Two eyes could not be taken for one eye lost, or a life be taken in repayment for the loss of an appendage. But here Peter, following his Lord (Matt 5:38ff.), transcends this, not by arithmetically weighing the amount of the payment in kind that is permissible, but by suggesting a wholly different sort of payment—a positive response: **on the contrary bless.** Paul indicated that "revilers" will not "inherit the kingdom of God" (1 Cor 6:10). Peter warns against excluding one's self from the kingdom by repayment in kind of one who is outside the kingdom. In fact, ultimately we shall all appear before the Judge whose **eyes are upon the righteous,** but whose **face . . . is against them that do evil.** So, remarks one: "If you return evil for evil, you fall under the blow of your own sentence, for who has not done evil to Jesus Christ?" Peter is here echoing words he had heard from his Master: "bless those who curse you, pray for those who abuse you" (Lk 6:28). Paul not only re-echoed these words (Rom 12:14), but put them into practice: "When reviled, we bless" (1 Cor 4:12).

What does it mean to **bless**? The root meaning goes back to the idea that there are forces of good or evil in the universe which affect human destiny, and of which men may be the channels. To curse, then, is to seek to be the instrument of an evil power whereby one may release destructive powers on one's enemies. To **bless** would be exactly the opposite, to seek to be the channel of a power for good whereby one may release constructive and healing powers on others. To bless, then, is not only to say kind words, but to invoke whatever beneficent powers there may be in behalf of the one blessed. It seeks to convey divine power through prayer. We experience what is intended here in the benediction with which worship services close. The minister, seeking to be a channel of God's grace, calls down on the departing congregation the power of God to be with them wherever they go and to do for them what only God can do. Jesus associated prayer with blessing. "Bless those who curse you," He said, "pray for those who abuse you" (Lk 6:28). We are told, too, that Jesus took little children "in his arms and blessed them, laying his hands upon them" (Mk.10:16). The hand gesture was designed to convey power to these children from God. Paul speaks of the "blessing of Abraham" coming on the Gentiles through the death of Christ (Gal 3:14), referring to the gift of the Holy Spirit to them. He also speaks of being "blessed . . . with every spiritual blessing" (Eph 1:3), including all that God has done for us in Christ.

To **bless**, then, is not merely to return kind words when one is reviled, but to respond with "an active kindness" in deeds wherever possible, and "to pray for the blessing of God" on one's enemies. One modern translator has caught this: "You must ask God to bless people who treat you badly." This would ultimately issue in a prayer for their eternal salvation. A commentator has remarked of this: "This is the retaliation of love substituting itself for that of justice."

For **to this you have been called, that you may obtain a blessing**. Here Peter returns to his thought expressed in 2:21, that the calling of the Christian is to share in the task of his Lord, and to suffer if need be to fulfill it. The suffering, however, is balanced either by the goal of the calling, **that you may obtain a blessing**, or the **fact** of the calling, "because you have been called to inherit the blessing."

The Greek here reads literally; "inherit a blessing." Peter has earlier referred to our salvation as an **inheritance** (1:4). Both there and here his word probably reflects a word he had heard Jesus use, when He described the Last Judgment: "Then the King will say to those at his right hand, 'Come, O blessed of my Father, *inherit* the kingdom prepared for you from the foundation of the world'" (Matt 25:34, emphasis added). The appeal to **bless** instead of **reviling** also reflects what he had heard Jesus say: "For if you forgive men their trespasses, your heavenly Father also will forgive you" (Matt 6:14). If Peter is here referring to the goal of our calling, he is saying: "you have been called to bless, in order that you might inherit the blessing." "Bless, for as we have done, so shall we be done by." This would not necessarily involve a "self-seeking and calculating piety." While we are in the flesh, we shall never get beyond the necessity of being warned about possible failure.

If, however, he was saying: "Bless, because you have been called to inherit the blessing," it would be more in line with customary New Testament teaching. "Since you have already inherited the blessing, bless others," Peter would then be saying. "The Christian is gracious because he is first himself the object of grace. In the Bible, the heritage is a gift before it is a law." Even so, the element of warning would still be in the background. Just because the Christian has been the object of grace, he is to be the source of grace to others. If he shirks the responsibility that grows out of privilege, he is under condemnation. As one writer has put it: "If you are not willing to share God's gifts, you show that you are not worthy to receive them yourself." Did not Jesus say of the servant whose great debt had been forgiven, but who in turn refused to forgive a small debt to a fellow servant: "You wicked servant! I forgave you all that debt . . . , should not you have had mercy on your fellow servant, as I had mercy on you?' And in anger his lord delivered him to the jailers" (Matt.18:32ff.).

Just as Peter had set before Christian women **Sarah** and **the holy women** who hoped in God as examples to be followed (3:5f.), he uses the 34th Psalm as an Old Testament example of what he is speaking of here. It is the example of a pious writer in ancient Israel who saw that those who would **obtain a blessing** from God must subject themselves to the moral requirements that accompany that blessing. Although the New Testament never teaches that we are set in right relations to God by our good works, still it constantly reminds us that works pleasing to God are to be the appropriate response to God's grace. A Scottish scholar has said of this: the promise of "divine blessing" appeals to "the universal longing for personal benefits," by commending righteousness as a way of life and warning against unrighteousness. "Our behavior matters." He adds: "Nothing that the Bible says elsewhere about undeserved grace can alter this fact. . . . Nothing suggests that divine grace and forgiveness have rendered righteousness unnecessary or irrelevant. The point of grace is that it forgives transgressions of the law; it does not state that the law does not matter." If one desires to **obtain a blessing** from God, it must be his desire also to live in a fashion commensurate with the wishes of the God whose blessing is sought.

What does it mean to **love life and see good days?** It goes beyond mere *joie de vivre*, ebullience, high spirits. A clue to its meaning here may be found in John 12:43, where we are told that some "loved the praise of men more than the praise of God." There **love** means to "set a high value on" something. In 2 Timothy 4:10, where Paul tells us that "Demas, in love with this present world, has deserted me," Demas preferred, or set a higher value on, this world than on the things which Paul was espousing. To **love life,** then, would be to set a high value on it, to live it to the full, to find its deepest meaning. This would be to value life as did the man who discovered the hidden treasure in the field (Matt.13:44), or the merchant who found the pearl of great value (Matt 13:45f.), and "in joy" to sell all that one has to purchase it. It would be exactly the opposite of the frustrated, disillusioned writer of Ecclesiastes, who "hated life" and found his days "grievous," for "all was vanity and a striving after wind" (2:17). To Peter, to **love life** would be to live it as a gift of God, to treasure it as such a gift, and return it to the Giver fully matured, having lived **mindful of God** (1 Pet. 2:19), as His heir, as His child. A French commentator has expressed it in an interesting way, when he speaks of this as "a beautiful instance of love . . . of one's self." The highest self-interest is to become what one is potentially in the love of God!

How is this valuing of life to be expressed? Negatively, by keeping one's **tongue from evil and his lips from speaking guile,** and turning away from evil. Few things are more harmful to the unity of a Christian fellowship than idle gossip and rumors. Outright falsehood should have no place whatever in the Christian community. In general, Christians should distance themselves from everything which is inferior, worthless, injurious, base, harmful, wrong, sinful; in other words,

Commentary 3:10-12

everything that is counter to the will of God and the interests of His kingdom. The Christian response is a healthy No to all that is degrading, or morally damaging. Positively, the Christian is to **do right, to seek peace and pursue it.** The Christian response is a healthy Yes to all that is fit, morally uplifting, spiritually edifying, kind, upright, of good intention, to all that is consonant with the character of a holy God, with special emphasis on trying to promote harmony and **peace** in the almost universally discordant relations among men.

Verse 12, however, keeps these ethical do's and don'ts from being mere principles that operate automatically as guides to human welfare. Christian ethical hehavior is prompted by an intimate personal relation to a redemptive God. It is the Christian's effort to live, not by rules, but by gratitude to his most intimate personal companion, **the God and Father of our Lord Jesus Christ** (1 Pet 1:3). This is the only motive strong enough to sustain ethical behavior when the promises it holds before us are grasped only by faith and not by sight. There is a brand of Christianity being pushed vigorously in our time which might be called "slot machine" Christianity. The idea seems to be that God exists for the sake of man's happiness, and that if one acknowledges this God, He will always arrange life to the believer's desire. One puts the required number of coins into the divine machine, and the appropriate product comes tumbling out! There was a widely broadcasted radio ministry of some years ago, whose theme was: "If you know what you want, you can have it!" God will give you anything you want if you make it crystal clear to Him what it is! A somewhat more sophisticated form of this is to be found in two forms of Christian teaching—"positive thinking" on the east coast, and "possibility thinking" on the west coast. The gospel seems to be that God gives us whatever we think about positively, or fulfills all possibilities for us if we set them high enough and concentrate on them sufficiently. God then becomes a tool of man, a cosmic power to overcome difficulties and achieve possibilities that would be otherwise unfulfilled.

What seems to be forgotten in these is that God's promises, at long last, belong to that kingdom which "is not of this world" (John 18:36). The King of that kingdom once faced the positive promise of ruling "all the kingdoms of the world and the glory of them" (Matt 4:8), but by maintaining His loyalty to His Father, ended up on a bloody wooden beam. He once sensed the possibility of finding an easier way when He prayed: "My Father, if it be possible, let this cup pass from me" (Matt 26:39). But, bending to the possibility of doing His Father's will (Matt 26:42), the outcome was suffering, unspeakable loneliness, abandonment by both man and God, and a despair which no human being has the capaciity to fathom.

God sometimes delivers us, and sometimes hides from us. The absence of God is as marked as His presence. It was the cry of a very good man: "O Lord, how long shall I cry for help, and thou wilt not hear?" (Hab 1:2). And this cry, "How long?" has echoed down the centuries to the latest victim of starvation, or war, or earthquake, or hurricane, or flood, or homelessness, or untreated disease, or the foulest treachery of trusted loved ones or friends. And, apparently, it will continue to echo and re-echo until the end of the world; for in the Book of Revelation, even those who have run their course, finding escape from the maelstrom of evil only through martyrdom, and are now in the other world, are still crying out: "O sovereign Lord, holy and true, how long . . . ? (6:10). Psalm 34, from which Peter is quoting here, abounds in promises: "This poor man cried, and the Lord heard him, and saved him out of all his troubles" (vs 6). But the poor man had to undergo his troubles! "Many are the afflictions of the righteous, but the Lord delivers him out of them all" (vs 19). He may be delivered, but he has the afflictions nonetheless! "The Lord is near to the brokenhearted, and saves the crushed in spirit" (vs 18). But hearts are broken, and spirits crushed!

Wonderful is it when God responds in deliverance. But what of the times He doesn't? Can you encourage one who is being ushered into one of Hitler's gas chambers that if he just turns away from evil and does right, God will deliver him? Yes, you can, if you know what *deliverance* means. Dietrich Bonhoeffer, one of Hitler's victims, when summoned to go to his death, could say: "It is the end. For me, it is but the beginning!" If one's response is not to a principle, or a theory, but to a Person, he can **obtain a blessing** in life's starkest tragedies, and can triumph in defeat. But he may have to go through death to do it. When, during the Second World War, a Scandinavian bishop was threatened by one of Hitler's henchmen: "Do this, or we will kill you"; he replied: "and *then*, what will you do?" One can neither frighten, nor coerce a man like that. Because he trusts in a Person, who Himself was defeated, but triumphed in defeat, and conquered death with life.

So, here, Peter is telling his readers that the sanctions against the evil and the rewards of the righteous are not drawn from cold ethical principles, but from a warm, personal relationship to a living God, whose vindication may have to await the final judgment. He depicts Him as a God who has **eyes, ears,** and a **face.** He "sees" human need. He "hears" human prayers. His face is turned in anger **against those that do evil.** Once, a little girl complained to her mother that she was afraid to go to sleep in the dark alone. Her mother encouraged her by telling her that God would be with her. "But," replied the little girl, "I want someone with a face!" When ethical demands are laid on us to be borne in the darkness of chaos and brutality and meaninglessness, we cannot meet them by adherence to principles and ideals. They need to be personalized. They need a face! And that is exactly what we have in Jesus Christ.

A recent writer has said that the "content of the law is God himself." In this, he was interpreting the Reformation's greatest theologian, who said that "the true and pure religion was so revealed in the law, that God's face in a manner shone forth therein." God's law does not operate like the law of gravity. It is rather an expression of what a personal, loving heavenly Father desires for us, and calls forth a response from us because we are persons and love Him. The law is "the content of the personal response of sonship to the fatherly love of God on the part of His children." The personal aspect of the soul's relation to God can hardly be better stated than it was by a great nineteenth century English poet:

> It is .... my flesh, that I seek
> In the Godhead! I seek and I find it. O Saul, it
>   shall be
> A face like my face that receives thee; a Man like
>   to me,
> Thou shalt love and be loved by, forever; a Hand
>   like this hand
> Shall throw open the gates of new life to thee!
>   See the Christ stand!

Trust in this living, loving, personal God, says Peter, is the final sanction for Christian ethical living. Loving Him demands righteous living as a testimony to the world, even if it does not work in this life. Peter's readers were suffering, or about to suffer. Hold steady, and trust, was Peter's word to them.

This leads naturally into the next section, which contains Peter's observations on a saying of His Lord: "Blessed are you when men revile you and persecute you . . . on my account" (Matt 5:11).

H. The Christian Community's Response to Persecution *(3:13-4:6)*

Peter has been speaking of "the pursuit and practice of goodness." Now his mind turns directly to a theme he has introduced before (1:6ff., 2:12, 18ff.), the likelihood that this pursuit will bring suffering because of persecution by their pagan neighbors. When his readers raise the question: "Why do we suffer for doing good and being loyal to God?" Peter counsels them to accept this suffering without fear or retaliation, and thus turn it into a blessing. Through it they will have opportunity, both by word and life, to witness to their faith and to demonstrate that by suffering **for doing right, if that should be God's will,** rather **than for doing wrong** (3:17), they have put themselves on the right side in the struggle for final victory in a moral universe. All doubt of this is dispelled by the example of their Lord, who suffered for doing right, **the righteous** taking the place of **the unrighteous** (3:18). Christ, therefore, "at once transmuted suffering and conquered sin." In so doing, He established Himself as the supreme Lord of the Universe, as He now sits in **heaven . . . at the right hand of God, with angels, authorities, and powers subject to him** (3:22). Peter counsels his readers, **arm yourselves with the same thought and live for the rest of the time in the flesh no longer by human passions,** as do those who persecute you, **but by the will of God,** the God who **is ready to judge the living and the dead** (4:1ff.).

1. *The Blessedness of Suffering for Righteousness' Sake* (3:13-17) (*Exhortation*)

Peter begins this discussion with a question: **Now who is there to harm you if you are zealous for what is right?** The latter expression literally describes "zealots," or "enthusiasts for goodness." A zealot is one who deeply desires something, is totally committed to it, strives with all his heart to achieve it. Modern translators have attempted to convey this by using expressions such as "devoted to," or "committed deeply to," or "have a passion for." The expression describes those who "are passionate for moral integrity, in that they take delight in it and are enthusiastic in making it triumph." A French commentator has defined **right** here by the context as "proper behavior in society (2:14-15), to give value to 'civil justice,' but also and especially to seek after justice in behavior approved by God." In other words, to be deeply concerned for the establishment of God's will in all human relationships. The command not to **return. . . reviling for reviling,** however, would seem to give the term an even broader application, including personal aspects of behavior as well as social.

The word for **harm** in the Greek is the verbal form of the noun used in verse 12 which speaks of **those that do evil.** It might, then, be translated, as one modern version has done: "who can do you evil?" It is a general term, designating any sort of injury, or harm, or mistreatment. The implied answer to Peter's rhetorical question, **who is there to harm you** if you are totally committed to doing good? is "No one." Does he really mean that? I suspect that his readers could have named several of their neighbors; or those with whom they worked; or, if slaves, those who were their masters; who were continuously poking fun at them, or railing at them, or perhaps even physically mistreating them. Peter himself goes on: **even if you do suffer for righteousness' sake,** and exhorts: **Have no fear** of those who do you evil, **nor be troubled** by their actions. Obviously, then, Peter was aware that the Christians would be mistreated for their faith. In fact, worthy moral behavior often irritates miscreants, and drives them to unseemly behavior toward those who embody it. Goodness, then, could spawn **harm.** In fact, this word is used elsewhere in the New Testament to describe both persecution and martyrdom. The Egyptians are described as ill-treating the Hebrews four hundred years (Acts 7:6), and Herod is said to have "laid violent hands upon some who belonged to the church," at which time he "killed James the brother of John with the sword" (Acts 12:1f.). In each of these passages, the word here translated **harm** is used. What, then, did Peter mean by **harm**?

He was not suggesting that no one would oppose them, nor disturb their peace of mind, nor cause them suffering and sadness. But, he was saying, if one is persecuted **for righteousness' sake,** and if **it should be God's will** that he **suffer for doing right,** the persecutor could not objectively, really hurt him, if he believed in the final victory of good over evil in the kingdom of God. As one has said: "To resolve the tension between this discourse and experience, . . . it is necessary to read this phrase in the light of Christ and in reference to the final victory announced by the New Testament." This is to confirm in experience what Peter says: **if you do suffer for righteousness' sake, you will be blessed.** Peter affirmed this on the authority of his Lord, who said: "Blessed are those who are persecuted for righteousness' sake, for theirs is the kingdom of heaven" (Matt 5:10). To **suffer for righteousness' sake** is to confirm one's membership in God's kingdom, that kingdom "that cannot be shaken" (Heb 12:28). What Peter meant was: unjust suffering cannot "touch the condition of the believer" in his relation to his Lord. As our commentator from Hitler's prison wrote; "Why should you be troubled by misfortune, when for you there is only one misfortune: that of being separated from your Lord?" And did not Paul write: "Who shall separate us from the love of Christ? Shall tribulation, or distress, or persecution, or famine, or nakedness, or peril, or sword? No, . . . For I am sure that neither death, nor life, nor angels, nor principalities, nor things present, nor things to come, nor powers, nor height, nor depth, nor anything else in all creation, will be able to separate us from the love of God in Christ Jesus our Lord" (Rom 8:35ff.). *This* is what Peter was thinking of when he said: **you will be blessed.** True blessing is "the distinctive religious joy which accrues to man from his share in the salvation of the kingdom of God."

If Peter's readers could find it in their heart to believe this, his next exhortation naturally followed: **Have no fear of them, nor be troubled.** "Serene confidence and sublime joy" could replace fear. An Old Testament word lies behind Peter's counsel here. The Assyrians had been threatening Israel in Isaiah's day. Isaiah had tried to get King Ahaz to trust in God for deliverance rather than to attempt clever political alliances, but the king refused to listen (Isa 7). The prophet then turned to the people, to try to persuade them to his view, but the people likewise refused (Isa 8). God then spoke to the prophet: "do not fear what they fear, nor be in dread. But the Lord of hosts, . . . let him be your fear, and let him be your dread" (8:12f.). Here, Peter is trying to get his readers to embody the spirit of the prophet in their dangerous circumstances, and to discard all fears prompted by the dread of what their persecutors could do to them.

But was this merely a call for human heroism, a sort of pre-battle effort of a general to stir up the adrenalin in his followers and whip them up to disregard danger as they make the charge? No, Peter had a higher motivation to which to appeal. It, too, was based on the Isaianic prophecy. Isaiah sought to replace one fear with another—the fear of men with the fear of God—"the Lord of hosts, . . . let him be your fear, and let him be your dread" (8:13). But on what was the "fear" and "dread" of God based? Him "you shall regard as *holy*" (vs 13, emphasis added). It was the dread which overcomes a sinful man in the presence of the absolutely Holy One that was greater than any fear that was merely human. Regarding Him as holy, then, was so to exalt His claim on their lives that they feared disobeying Him more than anything that man could do to them. Isaiah had seen the Lord "high and lifted up," with the heavenly beings calling to one another in his presence: "Holy, holy, holy is the Lord of hosts; the whole earth is full of his glory" (6:1ff.). When He spoke, the foundations of the temple shook as though there were an earthquake. The temple was filled with smoke because of His burning presence. Isaiah could only cry out in dread: "Woe is me! For I am lost; I am a man of unclean lips; for my eyes have seen the King, the Lord of hosts!" Then, a heavenly being took from God's altar a coal, too hot for him to handle, with tongs, and touched Isaiah's lips, taking away his guilt and forgiving his sin. It was *this* God whom Isaiah now feared.

So, said Peter to his readers: **in your hearts, reverence Christ as Lord**. Replace your fear of persecuting pagans with the dread of the holy God who has made Himself known to you in Christ. **Fear** Him, and Him alone. Make the first petition of the Lord's Prayer a reality in your life: "Hallowed be thy name." Capture the mood of the author of the Revelation: "Worthy is the Lamb who was slain, to receive power and wealth and wisdom and might and honor and glory and blessing!" Peter changes Isaiah's "Lord of hosts" to **Christ**, indicating that he held Him to be God Himself with us. **To reverence Christ as Lord**, this One who by His death and resurrection has ascended to the supreme place of authority in the universe, is the cure for **fear** of any lesser lords.

Would we dare to believe this, if we were actually facing persecution and perhaps even martyrdom for our faith? It all seems so theoretical and unreal to us who live in a world which, rather than opposing our faith, is merely indifferent to it, holding it in disdain, but not considering it of sufficient worth to persecute us for it. Suppose the fires of persecution were suddenly lighted, and we had to witness to the enthronement of **Christ as Lord** by imprisonment, torture, and even death. Would we stand? One can only hope that grace would be given equal to the demand in such an hour of trial. At least, we know that many in Peter's day did shift their **fear** from men to God, saying with the Psalmist (118:6) what was later repeated by the writer to the Hebrews (13:6):

> The Lord is my helper,
> I will not be afraid;
> what can man do to me?

One example is that of Ignatius of Antioch, who died a martyr's death early in the second century, who said: "he who is near to the sword is near to God; he that is among the wild beasts is in compamy with God; provided only he be so in the name of Jesus Christ." An Apocryphal Gospel lists as a saying of Jesus: "Who is near the fire is near to the kingdom."

The freedom from **fear**, of which Peter was speaking, would enable the Christians quietly to witness to their faith to the pagan world, both by word and deed, particularly the latter. Peter refers first to verbal testimony to the faith. **Always be prepared to make a defense to any one who calls you to account for the hope that is in you.** Some scholars hold that the word **defense** refers to a formal trial in a court of law. Undoubtedly, the word was so used on occasion. It does not carry that meaning in itself, however, and the context here suggests that Peter was referring to an unofficial personal **defense** of their beliefs. They are to be ready **always**, not just on court days; and the **defense** is to be made **to any one** who inquires, not to a judge (see pp. 38f.).

It is interesting that Peter uses the word **hope** rather than "faith," as the subject of the defense. It has been suggested that "where the church is under oppression or persecution, preaching tends, by a natural inclination, to put the accent on the dimension of hope." Akin to this is the suggestion that for Peter, **hope** is the central and characteristic description of the Christian faith. One scholar has proposed that 1:21 should be translated: "so that your faith may also be your hope in God." It is certain that Peter described the faith as **a living hope** at the outset of his epistle, the hope of an imperishable **inheritance** (1:3f.). And in a pagan world that was jaded and morally fatigued, the scintillating glow of hope which characterized the lives of many of the early Christians certainly must have made the pagans wonder what was the secret of it. The fact that **hope** was characteristic of the group is reflected by some translators who believe that the plural phrase **in you** does not reflect merely a number of individuals but is rather a group designation: "the hope all Christians share."

Peter cautions his readers against either over-boldness in their testimony, or a spirit of irritation with the questioners. The testimony is to be given **with gentleness**. The word means "humility," "courtesy," "considerateness." It is the avoidance of "arrogance or insolence." Although sure of one's faith, testimony to it ought not to manifest "the arrogance. . . which dogmatizes and condemns, nor the anger aroused by unjustified accusations." The apostle Paul's address to King Agrippa would be a good example of the mood advocated here (Acts 26:2ff.). He begins by congratulating Agrippa on his excellent knowledge of religious matters (vss 2f.). He reasons with him as an intelligent man (vs 8). He gives a frank and full account of his Christian conversion and his toils since (vss 9ff.). He interprets Christ in the light of the Old Testament, which was Agrippa's Bible (vss 22f.). Again, he congratulates Agrippa, both for his knowledge of current affairs and his understanding of the Old Testament (vss 26f.). And King Agrippa is captured by Paul's attempt to bring him to faith (vs 28). Paul handled the entire episode in a manner which permitted him to give a clear **defense** of the **hope** that was his, but in no way offended King Agrippa, who would have recommended his acquittal if the legal system had permitted it (vs 32).

Courteous and considerate testimony should also be accompanied by **reverence**. This is a translation of the word "fear." It could refer to men, involving "simple respect for the interlocutor," in which case it would mean "in a respectful fashion." Since, however, in verse 14, Peter has just warned them against having **fear** of men, it is more likely that "fear" here is rather directed towards God. One translator has phrased it: "with responsibility to God," suggesting the devout spirit in which Christian testimony should be undertaken.

This responsibility to God leads naturally to the next requirement for worthy Christian testimony: **keep your conscience clear**. It has been pointed out that a good **conscience** exists only where there is **good behavior in Christ**. As one has put it: "Authentic testimony is that which one's conscience approves when he speaks, because his life is in accord with his speech." This is not a call to a perfect life, but to the avoidance of anything which weakens one's own **conscience** or leads outsiders to discredit the faith. "The best response to slanderous denouncers is a transparent life." Peter's expression **in Christ** was a favorite with Paul, who used it 164 times, carrying the theological meaning that Christians are united with Christ and are actually "one with him." Peter uses the expression only three times, with perhaps less theological content than Paul, but nonetheless with the insight that Christ is the ground of good behavior and the criterion by whom it is to be judged. In 5:10 Peter says that we are **called to eternal glory in Christ**, and in 5:14 he describes the church as composed of all who are **in Christ**. These both come sufficiently close to Paul's meaning to avoid any deep difference.

In Peter's call for readiness in defense of the gospel and his commendation of a worthy life to accompany it, he was describing what was perhaps the most effective method of evangelism in the early church—that each individual Christian should be a messenger of the "good news," both by word and life. It is interesting that the worthy life preceded the verbal witness, for observing their manner of life would liikely be the stimulus that would make people call them **to account,** or ask them "to explain" the reason for such living. What was it about those early Christians which made people wonder as to the source of their life? It was hardly difference in clothing, or diet, or political views, or level of general knowledge. There were, of course, a few outward signs which impressed the pagans. One pagan remarked: "How these Christians love one another!" There was a mutual concern for others which marked them off as different. And their gentle response to those who persecuted them must have made men wonder why they were willing to suffer unjustly with such patience and forbearance. And, of course, their standards of sexual purity and their disinterest in the theatrical gladiatorial combats and the raucous indulgence in all sorts of gross forms of entertainment which the pagans had concocted to rid life of its boredom, must have piqued the interest of the pagans.

Beyond these, however, there must have been some subtle, indescribable quality or tone of life which marked them as different and made their neighbors wonder. A strange quality of childlike innocence, which could be felt but not accounted for; a lack of general raucousness; a gentle reverence about life; a strange sense of detachment from material things; the lack of a tendency to drive hard bargains for selfish gain; a dignity about life which bespoke a familiarity with the transcendent and the eternal; a transparent look in the eye which suggested that things had been seen which are not readily visible and things had been heard that do not normally fall on mortal ears; a demeanor that suggested that their sources of satisfaction came from unseen and intangible realities; a bearing which seemed to reflect a Presence, real to them but hidden from others; a mood of quiet joy in life; a hint that there were reserves of spiritual energy to be called upon in the crises of life; the reflected glow of a "light that never was on land or sea"; a spirit that seemed to be refreshed from divine aquifers too deep to be contaminated by the septic waters of the surrounding barnyard morality—such things as these must have impressed the pagans, and prompted some of them, at least, to ask for an explanation.

Thus the church grew, in spite of its numerical and social and material weakness, and despite ridicule, isolation and mistreatment. Does the behavior of Christians today suggest to outsiders that they march to a different drummer and have their sources of life in an unseen, higher world? And will not some such thing have to take place within the group before the churches again begin to grow and have some meaningful influence in society?

The desired result of the verbal **defense** of the faith, and its commendation by **good behavior in Christ,** was that those **who revile your good behavior in Christ may be put to shame.** We have already seen that well-doing often excites the wrath of men rather than their praise (p. 204). Either through people's reaction to those who are different, or through envy, or through misunderstanding, or through downright truculence or malevolence, **good behavior** often leads men to **abuse or revile.** Peter sees that ultimately, good behavior will **put to shame** those who **revile** it. At the final judgment, when they see that God honors those whom they **abused,** their shame will be self-condemning. However, as Peter expressed in connection with his instructions about the behavior of Christian **wives** toward pagan **husbands,** he must have hoped that through their shame, some of them would even now **be won** to the faith (3:1).

Verse 17, if taken out of the setting of the passage, sounds rather like a pointless moral observation, without much significance and with no teeth in it. **For it is better to suffer for doing right if that should be God's will, than for doing wrong.** Apart from the ultimate outcome of things at the last judgment, it would be difficult to convince many that it is better to suffer for doing right than for doing wrong. A recent television interview showed a young man who was cheating on the welfare system, claiming benefits from it as a homeless and unemployed person when he had a home and a job. He had not been caught, and intended to continue the practice. "I didn't tell them the truth," he admitted. "But," he added, "why should I tell them the truth. I'm interested in myself. I'm trying to get all I can out of the system." If he got caught, he might suffer for wrongdoing. If he told the truth, he would suffer a lessening of his income. He preferred, if he were going to suffer at all, to suffer for **doing wrong** rather than for **doing right**, even though, if caught, his suffering for **doing wrong** might conceivably be greater than his suffering for **doing right**.

Some have seen in this passage a warning against reacting to unjust sufferings with violence, mentioned in verse 16. It would mean, then: "You had better suffer than do that." Others have interpreted the passage in a moral or religious sense, comparable to what Socrates said: "To injure, as compared with being injured, is, according to the measure of its ugliness, in that proportion worse. . . doing me and my belongings any wrong whatever, is worse and more disgraceful to the doer than to me who suffer[s] it." Still others have interpreted **better** as bringing more satisfaction to the sufferer, in that by his suffering unjustly the believer "creates good" as Christ, by His innocent death, "has shown how . . . to bring a blessing on others." Yet others find the satisfaction in that they are "on the way to blessing opened by Christ" if their suffering is willed by God. The emphasis of the passage, however, seems not to be on the "feelings," or the "moral satisfaction" of "joy" on the part of the sufferer, but on the final outcome of things at the Last Judgment, when the verdict of **him who is ready to judge the living and the dead** is rendered (1 Pet 4:5).

The contextual terminology of the passage seems to favor this view. The expression **put to shame** is elsewhere used of those who are found wanting at the Last Judgment. For example, 1 John 2:28 reads: "abide in him, so that when he appears we may have confidence and not shrink from him in shame at his coming" (see also Rom 9:3, 10:11, 1 Pet. 2:5). Our passage is not contrasting suffering for **doing right** with escape from suffering, but with suffering for **doing wrong**. One must suffer either from one or the other. If one chooses to suffer **for doing wrong**, when will that be? Obviously, when he appears before the final Judge. So, says one: Peter is speaking of a "reversal of circumstances, a 'turning of the tables' on pagan despisers of Christianity." The verse, then, could be paraphrased: "If it should be God's will that we suffer, it is better to suffer now, as doers of good at the hands of evil men, than on the day of visitation, when these same evildoers shall receive their just punishment from the eternal Judge of all men."

The distinction, then, between **doing right** and **doing wrong**, ":is not between good and bad citizenship in the Roman state as two options for the Christian, but between two groups into which the whole race of man is divided—'doers of good,' who *may* have to suffer in this age, and 'doers of evil,' who certainly *will* suffer in the age to come. It is 'better' (i.e. more advantageous) by far to belong to the first group than to the second." Is this not just another way of saying what Jesus taught, when He said: "do not fear them who kill the body but cannot kill the soul; rather fear him who can destroy both soul and body in hell" (Matt 10:28).

One writer has commented: the conviction that **it is better to suffer for doing right ... than for doing wrong** "is not yet verifiable by experience; the oppressed Christian has sometimes great pain in persuading himself of it. . . .Consciousness of it can be reclaimed only in faith." I once had a colleague who, although badly crippled, had somehow gotten over a high compound wall and hidden in the bushes at night while serving as a missionary, when their compound had been attacked by marauding Chinese who had turned on all foreigners. He escaped with his life, but said that ever after that, he had some difficulty singing with any gusto Faber's hymn,

> Our fathers, chained in prison's dark,
> Were still in heart and conscience free;
> How blest would be their children's fate,
> If they, like them, could die for Thee.

Apparently, others share this hesitation, for that stanza is left out of a highly touted new denominational hymnal! Such truths are grasped only in faith, at least in the hour of testing.

2. *The Example of Christ Who Triumphed Through Unjust Suffering* (3:18-22) *(Proclamation)*

The next five verses are the most problematic in 1 Peter, perhaps in the entire New Testament. Whole books have been devoted to trying to solve the problems raised by them; countless monographs have wrestled with them; and all commentaries on 1 Peter necessarily have to face them. In spite of all efforts, however, these verses seem to raise unanswerable questions.

One leader of the Reformation said of them: "This is a strange text, and a more obscure passage, perhaps, than any other in the New Testament, for I do not certainly know what St. Peter means. . . . I cannot understand, I cannot even explain it. There has been no one hitherto who has explained it." A recent writer has cautioned: "It is possible that there is no satisfactory interpretation . . . available. It is too commonly a preoccupation of commentators to set down at all costs some interpretation for every difficult passage in the Bihle. But it surely does not insult Scripture humbly to admit that there may be contexts to which the key is lost or not yet found. The teacher of Scripture is under no obligation to explain everything, and to claim ability to do so would touch the edge of absurdity." These judgments caution us that we must move tentatively in presenting any conclusions on this passage.

Both 2 Peter (2:4ff.) and Jude (vss 6ff.) have similar passages, which may suggest that the thought background on which 1 Peter presumes was quite widespread at the time. And, of course, the churches had pastors—Peter calls them **elders** (5:1ff.)—whose task it was **to tend the flock of God**, which could include *teaching* the faith (see Gal 6:6; Col 3:16; 1 Tim. 4:11, 6:2). If Peter's readers did not understand what Peter meant, their **elders** might have been able to explain it to them. But 2 Peter and Jude are of a quite different character of writings from 1 Peter. They have elaborate details and include other materials about the issues under discussion in these verses of which 1 Peter makes nothing. The apocryphal Book of Enoch, too, seems to furnish a background for both 2 Peter and Jude, and may furnish the background of thought on which Peter was leaning in this passage. One writer has made the bold statement: "To try to understand II Peter 3:19-20 without a copy of the Book of Enoch at your elbow is to condemn yourself to failure." The question is raised, of course, whether the simple laymen to whom Peter was writing had a copy of the Book of Enoch at their elbows. And since Peter is not writing a systematic doctrinal treatise, but coming much closer to what we would think of as writing a sermon to suffering laymen in need of instruction and encouragement, to help them understand their lot and help them to hold steady in the faith under adverse circumstances, it is difficult to know how much he may have had the thought world of the Book of Enoch in mind. Since it embodies a world of thought which Peter seems to touch upon in this difficult passage, however, we shall, with caution, seek to follow what clues it may suggest to aid in unearthing Peter's message here.

It seems to me that we are justified, insofar as we are able, in allowing the context of the passage to control what we see here. Would not the simplest way to approach the difficulties of the passage be to set it in the sweep of Peter's thought, and ask ourselves why he may have used the materials here to further what he has already been saying; then to try to place ourselves in the situation of the first readers, and ask ourselves how it may have furthered for them what Peter has been saying? Any considerations which lie beyond the nexus of the intersection of Peter's mind and the minds of his readers at that time seem to me to be irrelevant to the meaning of this passage.

It seems quite clear that Peter has been writing to encourage his readers to endure whatever unjust suffering might come to them from the misunderstanding or malevolence of their pagan neighbors. He has just told them that it is preferable to suffer the unjust judgment of their fellowmen **for doing right**, than to endure the just judgment of God **for doing wrong**. Now, to illustrate what he means and to clinch his encouragement, he says: "Let me remind you of the unjust suffering of your Lord at the hands of evil men, and how that turned out for utmost good, both for men and with God." The connection between what Peter has been saying, and what he is about to say is made strong by the conjunction **for** and the word **also**. This section, then, "serves as the basis of his theme and to the exhortation already expressed." He follows the section with: **Since therefore Christ suffered in the flesh, arm yourselves with the same thought.** What, then, do verses 18-22 do to strengthen the faith of Christians under unjust suffering, and to encourage them to follow Christ's example? This, and this alone, is what should be sought for in these verses.

Again, it seems inconsequential whether Peter composed these verses as they lie, or whether he was making use of previously formulated materials. Some see in these verses "a pre-existent text, formed by the life and the traditions of the churches, a sort of an embryo Creed": others a "hymn"; still others "liturgical or catechetical components" taken from a "baptismal catechism," or something similar. These views are based on the rhythmical quality of the writing, and on "the existence of New Testament formularies comparable to certain elements of these verses" (for example, 1 Tim 3:16; Rom. 8:3f., 34). We certainly have here the makings of that which eventuated in the Apostles' Creed. A German scholar has listed the various elements: "Christ's death, his reinstatement into life, his descent into Hades, his ascension, his seating at the right hand of God, his lordship over angels and authorities and powers." How closely these accord with the later developed Apostles' Creed: "suffered, . . . crucified, dead, and buried, . . . descended into hell, . . . rose from the dead, . . . ascended into heaven, . . . sitteth at the right hand of God." It takes nothing away from Peter to have made use of these materials, whatever their source. It would be like a preacher today speaking of the power and example of Christ, saying: "This is the Christ whom we confess when we say: I believe in Jesus Christ His only Son, our Lord; who was conceived by the Holy Ghost, . . .'" If Peter has done this, he has worked it into the flow of his thought in such a way that we should try to see what use he has made of each element, rather than to deal with some of the material as though it were here "only by virtue of its belonging to a traditional totality, borrowed as a whole by the author."

The question any interpreter should put to this whole section is: What would the Christians of Asia Minor have gotten from it in searching for light on their situation of suffering unjustly for their faith? As one writer has insisted: "It is not good enough to accuse [Peter] of exercising his private theological hobby-horses in an irrelevant academic digression set in the middle of a serious piece of pastoral exhortation. . . . each point is relevant to the readers' situation. . . . [Peter] does not lose sight of his readers, and each point, however obscurely connected with what precedes, has a practical bearing on the situation of a persecuted church."

The **also** in verse 18 ties the unjust sufferings of Peter's readers to the sufferings of their Lord. They were suffering unjustly, a fate imposed on them by those who were **doing wrong** (vs 17). In this sense they were suffering for the **sins** of others (vs 18). In this way, Christ could be their **example**, they could **follow in his steps** (2:21). But because of who He was, what He accomplished in His **example** they could not do. They could only imitate Him because He had done for them, and for all men, what they could not do. **He died . . . once for all.** His act of death was unique, unrepeatable, final. In one deed He accomplished all that ever needs to be done. He died **for sins**, not His own but the sins of others. He was the **righteous,** dying **for the unrighteous.** In *themselves*, when His followers suffered, even if they died martyr's deaths, it was a matter of the *unrighteous* dying **for the unrighteous.** In this, there was no cure, no redemption, no setting of things right. His followers were only *relatively* righteous, not absolutely righteous. If they died, even because of the sins of others, they still deserved to die, for they too were sinners. They were *righteous* not in themselves, but only as they were united to Him, and shared His righteousness. Their righteousness was derivative, His was self-contained. Their righteousness was a gift, He was the Giver. Their righteousness was in progress, His was absolute. Their righteousness was mediated, His was self-generated. He died for the **sins** of all, the persecuted and the persecuting. It was His unique, once-for-all suffering that gave His followers strength to suffer, and gave to their suffering its significance. By their patient endurance of unjust suffering, they were proclaiming to the world by example the "good news" that God Himself had patiently endured unjust suffering to reconcile the world unto Himself. Christ's once-for-all act of unjust suffering was a redemptive deed; their continuing unjust suffering was a proclamation of the saving significance of that deed.

The prepositions in verse 18 are significant. **Christ . . . died for sins.** The preposition **for**, when used in the Bible with **sins**, means "to take away, to atone for." For example, Leviticus 5:6ff. speaks of a guilt offering "for the sin" which has been committed, by which "the priest shall make atonement . . . for his sin." In the New Testament, this theme is taken up by the writer to the Hebrews, when he speaks of the function of a high priest being that of offering "gifts and sacrifices for sins" (5:1; see also 10:18, 26). These sacrificial offerings were designed to "take away" sin. So, here, Christ died as a sacrifice "for sins," or "to take away" sins. This thought is greatly strengthened by the preposition in the phrase **the righteous for the unrighteous.** The preposition in itself means literally "over." It has, however, resultant meanings. The "over" may be "overly" or "excessive," as in the word "hypersensitive." It may also mean "over" another in the sense of standing over one who is in danger, to shield him from the danger by taking it on one's self. In this case, it means "in behalf of," or "instead of." Paul makes a vivid use of this meaning in Galatians 3:10ff., where he tells us that all who seek salvation through keeping the law are *under* "a curse." It is as though such were standing under a Damoclean sword, which could fall at any moment. But, says Paul, Christ "redeemed us from the curse of the law, having become a curse for us" (vs 13). The "for" here is the word used by Peter when he says **Christ . . . died for sins.** It is as though Christ stood over us, allowing the sword to fall on Him rather than on us. In this case, it would mean "in behalf of" us, or "in place of" us.

The ancient Greek papyri, which contain the same type of Greek as that of the New Testament, abound in cases where people act "in behalf of," or "in place of" others. The Fourth Gospel gives a graphic illustration of this use of the preposition when the High Priest, Caiaphas, says: "it is expedient that one man should die for the people" (John 11:50). He was speaking politically, not theologically, but it is clear that he meant that Jesus should die "instead of" the people, or "in place of" the people, who, in case the Romans sensed an insurrection on their hands, might be destroyed as they were later in A.D. 70.

The expression **the righteous for the unrighteous** likely came to Peter's mind out of the contemplation of Isaiah 53:11, where the prophet, speaking of the Suffering Servant, says that "the righteous one" shall make "many to be accounted righteous," and adds that He will do this by bearing "their iniquities."

The purpose of Christ's sacrificial death was **that he might bring us to God.** This expression is used in the Old Testament in connection with the sacrificial system, sometimes of the sacrificial animals being brought before God, and sometimes of the cleansed priests coming before God. In any case, it involves coming into God's presence, having *access* to God in worship. On occasion, the term is used in a legal setting, where legally qualified people bring others before magistrates. In other places, it refers to "those who make friends of others, . . . mediators or reconcilers," who bring separated people together. In the Old Testament, the term sometimes designates God's own action in bringing people to Himself, as in Exodus 19:4: "You have seen what I did to the Egyptians, and how I bore you on eagles' wings and brought you to myself."

All the richness of this term may be applied to the redemptive work of Christ. As one scholar has remarked, this is not the result of "the overloading of a simple term by exegetes who do not observe the limits of the lexicographer," but because of "the complexity which demands different images set alongside or superimposed on one another if it is to be properly grasped." **That he might bring us to God,** Christ has become the consecrated High Priest to present us to God. He is also qualified to bring us before the court of the heavenly Judge to plead our case, since He "always lives to make intercession" for us (Heb 7:25), and continually stands "at the right hand of God" as our advocate (Acts 7:55f.). He is also the great Reconciler, or Mediator, to make it possible for us to come into the very presence of the Eternal King. And, since "God was in Christ reconciling the world to himself" (2 Cor 5:19), His action in bringing us to God was God's own action in bringing us to Himself.

When all aspects of this rich verse (18) are brought together, it is plain that Peter thinks of the death of Jesus as a "sacrificial, atoning, reconciling act"; as the decisive, substitutional, vicarious atoning event in the moral universe, which has made it possible for sinful men actually to have access to a holy God. Now, slaves, and unappreciated wives, and ordinary husbands, and small shopkeepers, and shepherds, and tillers of the soil, and carpenters, and stone masons, and groomers of horses, and galley slaves, and sailors, and soldiers, and tax collectors have "obtained access" to "the King of ages, immortal, invisible, the only God" (1 Tim. 1:17); those who formerly were "strangers to the covenants of promise, having no hope and without God in the world, . . . have been brought near in the blood of Christ" and "have access in one Spirit to the Father" (Eph 2:12ff.). The curtain which for centuries had hung in the temple before the Holy of Holies, indicating that sinful men had no direct access to the presence of the holy God save through the mediation of the High Priest, but could not themselves appear there, was "torn in two, from top to bottom" (Mark 15:38). Christ had "entered once for all into the Holy Place, taking not the blood of goats and calves but his own blood, thus securing an eternal redemption (Heb. 9:12). He has "appeared once for all at the end of the age to put away sin by the sacrifice of himself" (Heb 9:26). He has opened "the new and living way . . . for us through the curtain" that hid God from us (Heb. 10:20), so that we, unworthy as we are, may "with confidence draw near to the throne of grace, that we may receive mercy and find grace to help in time of need" (Heb 4:16). God is no longer alien, nor far away. We, *whoever we are*, have "access" to Him.

The meaning of the latter part of verse 18 is debatable: **being put to death in the flesh but made alive in the spirit.** The prepositions placed in the translation as **in** are not in the text, but must be supplied from the meaning of the grammatical significance of the words **flesh** and **spirit**. They are forms which could be taken as instrumental, that is *"by* the flesh," and *"by* the spirit"; or they could be seen as forms of reference, meaning *"with the reference to,"* or "as to" the "flesh" and the "spirit." Since it would make no sense to speak of Jesus having been put to death by the flesh, and since both expressions are parallel and must grammatically be understood alike, the referential significance must be the correct one, which our translators have captured: Jesus was **put to death in the flesh but made alive in the spirit**

But what is meant by the antithetical terms **flesh** and **spirit**? At this point judgments diverge. Some make the antithesis an "anthropological" one, distinguishing "body" from "soul," or the "physical" from "spiritual" nature of Christ. His body died, His spirit kept on living. This is highly questionable, since it parallels the pagan thought of that day, when it was considered that at death, the soul escaped the prison of the body and entered some sort of disembodied existence. Peter, however, would have been thinking in terms of Old Testament and Jewish intertestamental literature, which would likely have had no conception of a disembodied spirit. To their way of thinking, in His death, the total Christ—**flesh** and **spirit**—died; and, in His resurrection, the total Christ was raised. This would seem, therefore, to disallow any use of this passage to posit an appearance of Jesus in a disembodied state in the world of the spirits between His death and His resurrection.

The contrast which Paul often drew between **flesh** and **spirit** would hardly make sense here either—that between the desires that arise out of the fleshly or carnal appetites of man's sinful nature and that which "God approves and inspires."

The judgment of a French commentator would seem right: "It is a matter of differentiating two modes of existence, the earthly, visible, mortal existence on the one hand (that of Christ up to the Cross), and the heavenly, invisible, exalted existence on the other hand, which was inaugurated by the resurrection." This understanding fits well with the context. It is a reminder to the suffering readers that their Lord was "done to death," but He lives. They are doubly "privileged." Not only do they have "access" to God, but the One who made that access possible "lives and is Conqueror!"

Verse 19, in which **he went and preached to the spirits in prison,** is the crucial assertion of the entire passage. Views about it are legion. In order to avoid confusion and to save space, we shall not attempt a history of interpretation nor an exhaustive survey of all the possible nuances of thought seen here by various scholars. We shall merely suggest some of the reasons for rejecting certain views, and try to set the meaning of the verse in its context, as we see it.

The salient question is: *Who* did the preaching? In the Greek text, the first five letters of the expression **in which . . . and,** which stand together there, spell the word "Enoch." Since the apocryphal Book of Enoch tells of a mission of Enoch to fallen angels who are imprisoned in the abode of the dead, some have suggested that the original text of 1 Peter read: "In which Enoch preached . . . ." The same five letters allegedly stood directly side by side in the text here, and a careless copyist, having put them down once, failed to put the second group of letters down. If this explanation were acceptable, it would make the passage merely a reference to the story in the Book of Enoch, and would relieve the necessity of answering any questions about Christ having preached to **the spirits in prison.** This view has found its way into two modern translations of 1 Peter, but has been largely discarded, simply because there is no textual evidence for it whatsoever. Many copies of the text were made, and one would expect that if one scribe made a mistake by omitting the name of Enoch, others would have copied the text correctly, and there would be some texts that fit the explanation. If there were *even one* ancient text which carried the name of Enoch, the view might be given some credence. But, since there is no such evidence, it must be discarded as pure conjecture. As the text now stands, Christ, not Enoch, is the one who did the preaching.

But *when* did Christ do this preaching? Saint Augustine came up with a view which seemed to solve many of the problems of the passage, by suggesting that Christ preached in His Spirit, through Noah, in

His preincarnate days. Earlier in his epistle, Peter spoke of **the Spirit of Christ within** the prophets (1:11), as though Christ were speaking through them. Why not, thought Augustine, give a like reading to this passage, and have Christ preach in the days of Noah through him. The **prison**, then, would be the prison of sin and unbelief.

The difficulty with this is that in speaking of the prophets, Peter clearly says that Christ was speaking through them. Here no such thing is said. Furthermore, this expression is part of a long sentence, which begins in verse 18, which seems to be tracing the activities of Christ in a time sequence. He **died** . . . **in the flesh,** He was **made alive in the spirit** (resurrected), then He **went and preached,** after which He went **into heaven** and is now **at the right hand of God** (the ascension). To interrupt this time sequence. and place His preaching **to the spirits in prison** hundreds of years prior to the other events mentioned, seems to be without merit. Again, the expression **in which** that begins verse 19 links the phrase in question to verse 18, either to the last antecedent, **spirit,** which would mean "in which spirit," or to the entire phrase **made alive in the spirit,** which would mean "in this resurrected, or spiritual mode of existence." In either case, the referent is not to something that took place in the days of Noah, but after the resurrection. Great as Augustine was, it does not seem wise in this instance to follow Him.

Where did Christ go when He **preached to the spirits in prison**? Much thought and writing have been dedicated to solving this problem. Did he "descend" into the lower parts, or "ascend" into some heavenly location?

The same word is used to speak of Christ's "going" to the **spirits in prison** and His "going" into heaven at the time of the ascension (Acts 1:10, 11). If there were a choice, therefore, between "up" or "down," the idea of "going" into heaven might well be preferable. But are such questions relevant, or important, or even intelligible, in trying to understand Peter's thought here? As a phenomenon of experience, the sun rises in the east and sets in the west. Astronomically, it does neither. It is the rotation of the earth that is involved. We still, however, speak of the sun "coming up" or "going down," but it makes no scientific difference; the terms have no relation to reality. So, if unseen spirits exist in the universe, "descending" or "ascending" to them is a manner of accommodating speech, with no relation to reality.

Who were the recipients of this preaching, **the spirits in prison**? Were they human **spirits**, or is this a reference to superhuman powers in the universe? If they were human **spirits**, were they "rebellious" **spirits,** or believers in God and the good, both in Judaism and in paganism, who now had the gospel of Christ preached to them, indicating to them by what means they were saved, which could not have been known by them before the saving events took place? Although the latter view has been held by many, it seems difficult to justify in the light of the context here. The text seems to refer explicitly to those who **formerly did not obey.** Why were the disobedient **in the days of Noah** singled out from all the other disobedients in the history of the race? A satisfactory answer to this could well be that those who resisted Noah's preaching, which eventuated in the flood, were typical of the most extreme advocates of wickedness, and are mentioned as an illustration of the totality of rebellious humanity. The **Noah** reference, therefore, makes sense, whatever conclusion one reaches about the recipients of the preaching, or its substance, according to this view.

The most satisfactory view of **the spirits in prison** is that they were "supernatural powers." There is only one use in the entire New Testament of the word **spirits** being used to refer to dead mortals. Hebrews 12:23 speaks of "the spirits of just men made perfect." Normally, the New Testament, in speaking of the dead, uses the word *psyche*, or "souls." This is well illustrated in the passage with which we are dealing, where, in verse 20, Peter speaks of **eight persons,** or "souls" being saved in the ark, whereas all the other "souls" died. And when, in late Judaism, the word "spirit" is used of the dead, it is never used by itself, absolutely, but "is always qualified by 'of the dead,' 'of the righteous,' etc." One would expect that if human spirits were meant here, it would hardly read that the **spirits ... did not obey** but that "the spirits of men did not obey," since those involved were still in the body when the disobedience took place.

The plural, **spirits,** referring to supernatural beings, usually evil, is common in the New Testmment and in extrabiblical Jewish writings. Matthew 8:16 tells us that Jesus "cast out the *spirits* with a word" (emphasis added). Mark tells us that Jesus, with authority, "commands even the unclean *spirits*" (1:27, emphasis added). Luke speaks of the "spirits" being subject to the authority of Jesus' disciples (10:20). Paul speaks of "deceitful spirits," referring to the nether world (1 Tim

4:1). One of the apocryphal books calls God "the Lord of Spirits." "Spirits," then, were supernatural beings, more than once referred to as "principalities," or "powers," or "thrones," or "dominions" (see Rom 8:38; Eph 1:21; Col 1:16, 2:10, 15). These unseen "powers" were thought of as using human beings in the historic process to resist the purposes of the Almighty. Supernatural powers accounted for human actions. When Paul spoke of "the rulers of this age" having "crucified the Lord of glory" (1 Cor. 2:8), he was not referring to the Jewish and Roman authorities, but to the cosmic demonic powers who were acting through them.

Sometimes these were thought of as fallen "angels," and were associated with the actions of men in the days of Noah and the flood. These were depicted as being held in some sort of detention, or "prison," to await the final judgment, all of which parallels closely the passage we are discussing. 2 Peter says that "God did not spare the angels when they sinned, but . . . committed them to pits of nether gloom to be kept until the judgment," then goes on to speak of God sparing Noah "when he brought a flood upon the world of the ungodly" (2:4f.). The Book of Jude also refers to "angels that did not keep their own position," who have been kept "in eternal chains in the nether gloom until the judgment of the great day" (vs 6). These are illustrative of the late Jewish tradition upon which Peter seems to have been drawing, when he wrote of **the spirits in prison, who formerly did not obey . . . in the days of Noah**. This tradition is stated most vividly in the apocryphal Book of Enoch, which refers to the fallen angels as "spirits," connects their disobedience with Noah and the flood, and tells of Enoch's going to preach judgment to them. Lacking any other, or better, parallel to Peter's strange passage about **the spirits in prison,** it seems reasonable to interpret Peter's words in the light of this. The **spirits in prison,** therefore, to whom Christ **preached,** were likely the spirits of these fallen angels who were representative of the cosmic powers Peter believed to be "the source of evil on earth."

But *what* was **preached** to them? Perhaps the most widespread view held today is that the "gospel" was **preached** to them. The passage, then, becomes a basis for what is sometimes called the "larger hope," that even the worst of sinners, the most resistant to the will of God in their lifetime, have an opportunity in the next life to repent and believe. If the "worst" of sinners, those who brought on themselves the judgment of the flood, had the "good news" of redemption **preached** to them, there is hope for all. This leads, therefore, to universalism—the view that ultimately *all men* will be saved; or, to a possible modification of that view, that at least only the *eternally impenitent* will be lost. This view was held by some of the early church fathers, and it is often argued that it has a basis in other Scripture in such passages as Ephesians 1:3, where God purposes "to unite [or bring to a head] all things in him, things in heaven and things on earth."

This is not the place to debate that issue in all its dimensions. It seems to me, however, that one would be hard put to it to utilize 1 Peter 3:19 to bolster that persuasion. In my judgment, the context simply will not allow it. Peter is writing to groups of Christians who are suffering for their faith at the hands of those who disbelieve their gospel and ridicule that faith. He is seeking to give them courage, to enable them to hold on to their faith, even if it should mean martyrdom. What would be the purpose, then, of his throwing in an aside, telling them that ultimately, eternally, it makes little difference whether they hold fast, because finally all will be saved anyway. It surpasses all logical and rational thought to demand such of this passage. The whole point of the passage is that, although Noah was ridiculed when he built the ark, he remained faithful to his task and message. By that faithfulness, he and seven others were saved, whereas the others perished in the flood. The driving force of Peter's exhortation to his readers is: Even though you be few, and despised, and without broad influence in your world, remain true to your task and message come what may, for thereby you will be saved, though all others perish!

If this be true, how did the view arise that **preached** involved "preaching the gospel"? Linguistically, it is based on the judgment that ordinarily the word translated **preached** means to "preach the gospel." This view seems to have been in the minds of the translators of the *Revised Standard Version*. The literal meaning of the word translated **preached**, however, is to "proclaim," "make known," "announce by a herald." In the Greek translation of the Old Testament, the expression "is used as often of bringing bad news as of good." The word in itself is "neutral." This "neutral" use is found in Revelation 5:2, where an angel issues a proclamation which has no bearing on the gospel: "proclaiming with a loud voice, 'Who is worthy to open the scroll and break its seals?'" If the word in itself does not demand a positive content, the context must determine that to which it refers in any particular passage. For that reason the *Revised English Bible* changes **preached** to "made his proclamation to the imprisoned spirits." In this way, the content of the "proclamation" is not limited to an offer of the gospel.

As we have already seen, the context here seems to forbid the announcement of the gospel. Enoch's mission, already referred to, was to proclaim judgment to the imprisoned spirits. The immediate context of Peter's use of this expression speaks of **angels, authorities**, and **powers** being **subject to him**, not *believing* on Him (vs 22). The larger context of the whole epistle, encouraging persecuted Christians to faithfulness, is "better served" by reminding the readers of Christ's victory over the spirits than by proposing an offer of the gospel to them. What was proclaimed, then, was "an announcement to the fallen angels of [Christ's] triumph over them and all evil through His death and resurrection, which have placed all spiritual powers under his control." Peter's concern, then, is not to speak of a possible purgatory, nor a "second chance" for the impenitent, but to bolster his readers' faith and courage, reminding them that their Lord is Lord of all evil powers, both in the realm of the seen and the unseen.

Verse 20 reminds us of the **patience** of God which **waited in the days of Noah, during the building of the ark**. We have already seen that the tradition on which Peter may have been drawing, associated the **spirits in prison** with Noah and the flood story of Genesis 6. Although the flood is a story of judgment, it is also a story of grace, in that God announced the judgment prior to its coming, and through the ark arranged a way of escape for all who were willing to take His warning seriously. The long period from the creation to the flood, including the time during the building of the ark—during which Noah, both by word and deed, was "a herald of righteousness"—was a warning of coming disaster to which others could have paid attention. God's judgment was not without warning. It fell on those who knew of its possibility. This indicates that God is "forbearing . . . , not wishing that any should perish, but that all should reach repentance" (2 Pet 3:9).

The Noah experience, says Peter, was an "antitype," a "pattern," or "model." The corresponding element between Noah and baptism is not the last word of the preceding expression, **water**. It is rather the entire phrase, **saved through water**. One creditable scholar puts it thus: What Peter means is, Noah was saved through water, "the counterpart to which now saves you also, I mean baptism. It is not the prefiguring baptism that saves us, nor the water used in Christian baptism. It is *baptism in the sense to be defined in the next clause that saves* and that answers to the salvation of Noah." It is not the water that binds the experience of Noah to that of Peter's readers, nor baptism, but the fact that both are saved—one through the ark, the other through the saving work of Christ that baptism represents. God's salvation of Noah is a sort of illustration, or picture, of His salvation of all.

The significance of **baptism** is defined first negatively—not a **removal of dirt from the body.** This rules out any conception of ceremonial or ritual cleansings, whether of Jewish or pagan origin. The outer act of baptism is a "sign and seal" of inner spiritual realities, and it is these realities which give baptism its efficacy, not the sign in itself, nor any special grace granted to the one who performs the ceremony. The qualifying concepts between the first and last clauses of verse 21 must be omitted to capture Peter's concept of baptism. If omitted, the sentence then would read: **Baptism . . . now saves you, . . . through the resurrection of Jesus Christ.** The preposition **through** is instrumental, suggesting the "means," the "instrument," or the "agency" by which something is accomplished. **The resurrection of Jesus Christ,** then, is the "means," or the "efficient cause" of baptism's efficacy. It is the regenerating power of which **baptism** is the outward sign.

The relationship to Christ and His resurrection is significant in capturing the full implications of the parallel between Noah's saving and ours. The major New Testament dimension of the meaning of **baptism** is not "washing" or "cleansing," but "burial" and "ressurrection." In Romans 6:4, Paul tells us that we were "buried therefore with him by baptism into death, so that as Christ was raised from the dead . . . we too might walk in newness of life." The waters of the flood were God's judgment on rebellious humanity. If we were left to bear our judgment, we, like the sinners in Noah's day, would go to our death in the water. But Christ has been engulfed by those waters of judgment in our stead. As one has said: "On the cross, Jesus was treated no better than the men of the flood. Thus whoever believes in him and accepts baptism, truly dies in the waters of baptism, but with a salutary death, a death to sin, a death which makes him live as a new man and to sail miraculously over the deeps where his old life had been cast, . . . he is saved by the death of his Lord from those waters which destroy his sin. Such an one need no longer fear the deluge of the last day, . . . since all that could be judged in him has been judged, since he will be in the eternal ark of mercy." Those words were written in prison by the French pastor who was awaiting at any moment Hitler's call to death. This bespeaks their reality!

Peter positively describes **baptism as an appeal to God for a clear conscience.** The essential contrast with the earlier negative expression is that between **body and clear conscience.** One is the *outer* man, the other the *inner* man, or the "heart," where "the decisions which direct behavior are made." This emphatically confirms that the external elements of **baptism** do not "constitute either its essence or its power." If the word **appeal** is correctly translated here, which may be correct as to its basic meaning, then the statement would mean that one should come to **baptism** with a "request" or a "prayer to God for a clear conscience." This would involve the fact that we are beggars, asking God to give us what we cannot give ourselves. Or it could mean "a prayer to God based on a good conscience," depending on whether we interpret the case in the original as *objective* (the first) or *subjective* (the latter). The latter would seem to be ruled out by the rest of the New Testament. We do not bring good consciences to God, but come to request them.

Another possible meaning of the word translated **appeal** however, and perhap a more likely one, is an "engagement," a "word given to a partner," a "pledge." This would mean that in accepting **baptism,** one is entering into an "engagement" with God, or making a "pledge" to Him to maintain **a clear conscience,** to respond affirmatively "to God's request for faith and obedience," to make the ethical response called for by the wondrous gift of God's forgiving grace. One definition of a sacrament is "an oath, a spiritual covenant between God and man." It has been aptly pointed out that the original meaning of *sacramentum* in Latin was a military oath, which then came to be applied to **baptism** and the eucharist. To be baptized was to take the oath of allegiance to God, who by His grace was willing to accept that oath and pledge Himself to carry through His end of the bargain.

The entire section is climaxed in verse 22, where the suffering Christian is encouraged to sustain his loyalty at any cost by the reminder that it was by enduring unjust **suffering** at a level deeper than was possible to them, their Lord was now triumphantly seated **at the right**

hand of God, sharing God's power, with angels, authorities, and powers subject to him. This was Peter's way of recalling and repeating what he had heard his Lord say years before: "Fear not, little flock, for it is your Father's good pleasure to give you the kingdom" (Lk 12:32). Or, perhaps he had another of his Lord's words in mind: "Blessed are you when men revile you and persecute you and utter all kinds of evil against you falsely on my account. Rejoice and be glad, for your reward is great in heaven" (Matt 5:11f.). Jesus' ascension had now confirmed those words in an unmistakable way. No matter how small were the Christian groups to which Peter was writing (the group was only eight in Noah's day!), no matter how poor, how lacking in social status; no matter how restricted their visible influence; no matter how despised they were by their neighbors; no matter how powerful was the worldwide empire who misunderstood them; no matter how unjustly they were treated; they were "blessed," they were "heirs" of an eternal inheritance, they were subjects of the King of kings and Lord of lords, whose kingdom is forever!

Does this have the ring of reality? Is it really true? Or was it merely the idle daydreaming of a pious first-century apostle? And does it have meaning for us today? If we should be caught in a situation similar to that of Peter's first readers, would these words quicken in us a high resolve, and steady our fears, and nerve us to face suffering, or even death, with courage? That cannot really be known until we are in such circumstances. We can say, however, that it does manifest its reality in the lives of some who have had to put it to the test. At the risk of too frequent reference to the French pastor who wrote a commentary on 1 Peter from Hitler's jail, I will venture to cite him once more as a living example of the truth of Peter's words. Imprisoned for his resistance, under conditions very similar to those endured by Peter's first readers; at the mercy of a man mad with power; risking his life if the small pencil and bits of wrapping paper he kept stuffed in his mattress were discovered—under *those circumstances* he put Peter's words to the test. And this is a part of what he scribbled out.

"It is essential" that the Christian "know that the Lord to whom he belongs by faith is not his personal Lord only, but is also King of kings, the Master of the world and the sole ruler of all things. And that is true now. If Jesus has not yet appeared in his glory and manifested his omnipotence, he nevertheless reigns already over his enemies, he is already the one to whom all power has been delivered by his Father, and without whose assent nothing happens on the earth, nor in the heavens. He reigns over every human institution (2:13). Nothing escapes the authority of the one whom the world never ceases putting on the cross. Whether they wish it or not, men do his will, in disobeying him for their ruin or obeying him for their salvation. . . . And that . . . reminds us that our life and our heritage are *in him* sovereignly protected against all possible celestial or terrestrial powers . . . ."

Peter's words apparently met the test for him.

3. *Worthy Living in Response to Christ as Example and Judge* (4:1-6) *(Exhortation)*

This paragraph is tightly connected with what precedes by the word **therefore**. It is not merely a connective or transitional word, but has an inferential use. What it introduces "is the result of an inference from what precedes," and means "consequently," or "accordingly." That which connects it to what precedes is the theme of **suffering unjustly** (2:19), which brings **God's approval** (2:20). It is raised to a high level of importance **because Christ also suffered for you, leaving you an example** (2:21) in that **when he suffered, he did not threaten** (2:23); and through having been **put to death in the flesh but made alive in the spirit** (3:18), He achieved His goal to **bring us to God** (3:18) and became Ruler of the universe (3:22). **Therefore**—because of all this—Peter's next exhortation naturally follows.

What is the exhortation? **Arm yourselves.** To accept unjust suffering means that there is a battle on! This cannot be done easily, nor without effort. It is a glorious thing that we now, through the death and resurrection of Christ, have access to God. But the task of daily living remains, and the meaning of this access to God must be worked out in "the common round, the daily task," in a world that is set against the kingdom of God and its members, and must be resisted continually. During the Huguenot persecutions in southern France, a young girl was imprisoned in the tower at Aigues Mortes. She could have been released any day, simply by renouncing her faith, which through many years she refused to do. It was discovered later that she had chiseled into the stone of her prison: *Resistez!* Her access to God had to be made from her prison tower. The access of all Christians to God must be made from the prison of a surrounding world which is at enmity with

God. It is therefore necessary constantly to be armed!

But armed with what? With **the same thought** as was Christ's when He suffered in the flesh. Here flesh means "the bodily, earthly existence capable of suffering," climaxed in His death on the cross, spoken of in 3:18. This means that Christ Himself endured assaults on His own faith while in the flesh. As the writer to the Hebrews tells us: "he had to be made like his brethren in every respect," and "in every respect has been tempted as we are" (2:17, 4:15). The assaults on His followers, therefore, are to be borne as sufferings with Him and according to His example.

But what was **the same thought** as that of Christ? The word **thought** means "the judgment, the insight, the perception, and the spiritual composure growing out of them." In Hebrews 4:12, the translators have rendered the same word "intentions"; or we might say, the "dispositions" of the heart, or one's "fundamental convictions." One writer has described it as "a disposition of spirit . . . that directs the whole of moral conduct . . . an intuitive power, . . . signifying that the Christian life is a progressive assimilation to the crucified and risen Savior, and that the 'sufferings in the flesh,' . . . envisaged by faith as a blessed conformation to Jesus Christ, ought to be accepted and borne with the same spirit as He."

In both 4:4 and 5:9, the word **same** refers to what has preceded it rather than to what follows. It is likely, then, that here it points to what Peter has been saying about Christ having **died for sins once for all, the righteous for the unrighteous** (3:18), **that we might die to sin and live to righteousness** (2:24); and the Christian's "pledge" to this dying, rising Lord to live, by His grace, a life that would issue in **a clear conscience** (3:21).

The **same thought** or outlook, or disposition of Christ, then, would be to view death to sin as the pathway to life—both moral and spiritual life— **for the rest of the time in the flesh**, and life eternal in the world to come. The Christians' suffering, like their Lord's, will purge them from evil and eventuate in eternal life. Therefore, accept it as He did! As one commentator has said: "Whoever arms himself with this persuasion, prepared for suffering, will through suffering neither become uncertain of his faith, nor will he flee suffering, nor through suffering fall into a crisis of faith. On the contrary, he will look on suffering for the faith which God permits as evidence of a genuine Christian existence and as a blessing."

To whom is reference made in the words **for whoever has suffered in the flesh has ceased from sin**, and what do these words mean? They could hardly refer to Christ, for He did not **cease from sin** through His suffering. It is the testimony of the entire New Testament, furthered by Peter, that **he committed no sin** (2:22). The expression translated **yourselves** is two words in the Greek—**you also**, which expression focuses the thought on the readers' suffering as the stimulus that would lead them to cease **from sin**. These words, then, must refer to Peter's readers rather than to Christ.

Perhaps the tense forms used can give us a clue to the meaning of this expression. The word **suffered** is in a tense form referring to a specific point in time, with no duration indicated. It involves something that happens, takes place at a particular time, an "event." The word **ceased**, on the other hand, imvolves something that has happened in the past, but has continuing results; it is "a present situation determined by a cessation which has taken place in the past." What single event of suffering in the past lives of Peter's readers could be related to the death of Christ, which had continuing results down to the time of writing, which would lead them to live **no longer by human passions but by the will of God**? Would it not be the event of their conversion to the Christian faith, witnessed by their baptism? The terminology here is so reminiscent of general Christian teaching that it is difficult to avoid this conclusion. Paul states that "all of us who have been baptized into Christ Jesus were baptized into his death" (Rom 6:3). He adds: "For he who has died is freed from sin" (Rom 6:7). Peter here, then, in line with this, seems to be saying to his readers: "Your costly decision to break with sin, made at your entrance into the faith, which took place here in your earthly existence, was the result of, and in a profound sense, likened to Christ's suffering in His human existence when He died, and enabled you to make a break with sin which should lead you **to live the rest of the time in the flesh no longer by human passions but by the will of God**." The antithetical expressions **the rest of the time** and **the time that is past** also strongly point to the time of his reader's conversion. That was the point that separated *past* from *future* for them, the decisive turning point in their existence, when they died to their old lives and were **born anew to a living hope through the resurrection of Jesus Christ from the dead** (1:3). The costly step of casting their lot with Christ was the point at which their suffering **in the flesh** began, which leads to a continuing life of avoiding sin.

Some have given a psychological interpretation to the fact that **whoever has suffered in the flesh has ceased from sin.** This would express a principle that if one is willing to expose himself to suffering, he is more likely to seek to do the will of God in all circumstances. Others have given it a theological interpretation: since sin's point of attack on fallen human nature is the flesh, suffering in the flesh drives men to see their need of a savior, in line with Paul's delivering a man "to Satan for the destruction of the flesh, that his spirit may be saved in the day of the Lord Jesus" (1 Cor 5:5). It would seem better to accept the above explanation as an experiential and realized statement of fact: "You made the break, you have been living a life free from sin; now don't let the pressures which come from misunderstanding neighbors drive you back into the slavery of your former life. You wasted enough years in that wretched condition. Live **the rest of the time** in freedom from it, until you are vindicated for so doing by the One who is **ready to judge the living and the dead**" (4:5).

To make vivid the contrast between life lived **by human passions** and life lived by the **will of God,** Peter reminds his readers of the excesses which were descriptive of the pagan life from which they had been called. Regrettably, these characterize much of life today, unrestrained by the controls on natural urges which the Jewish-Christian tradition has historically given to society. Peter indulges in a bit of sarcasm in saying, **let the time that is past suffice for doing what the Gentiles like to do. Gentiles** here means not non-Jewish, but pagan. "You have wasted enough time on this," says Peter; meaning, of course, "far too much.'" And in reminding them of the type of life they used to live, he is suggesting how illogical it would be to invest any more time in such slavery to appetites.

Peter divides his listing of pagan grossness into three types: 1) sexual sins; 2) intemperance; and 3) immoral religious practices. **Licentiousness** and **passions** are two expressions relating to unbridled sexual indulgence. **Passions** are simply "desires," neutral in themselves, but in the context here they relate to illicit sensual desires which express themselves in **licentiousness.** This is a strong word depicting unbridled "sensuality," license in the physical sphere, "voluptuousness," "debauchery," "sexual excess." Human beings are *spiritual animals*, a strange combination of the "spiritual" and the "animal." There is a constant war between the "spiritual" and the "animal" sides of our natures. History seems to confirm the fact that to the degree that men are cut off from God, or are under the control of false gods, the "animal" part of human nature masters the "spiritual." Paul says that when men are "alienated from the life of God" they become "darkened in their understanding"; they "become callous" and give themselves up "to licentiousness, greedy to practice every kind of uncleanness" (Eph 4:17ff.; see also Gal. 5:18ff.). Today's society confirms this.

Drunkenness, revels, carousing refer to habitual imbibing, orgies, and drinking parties, where participants drug themselves into insensibility, seek to outdo one another in debauchery and perverted "animal" behavior. **Lawless idolatry** is idol worship which is offensive to God, **lawless** in the sense of breaking His commandment to worship no other gods. It may be that Peter also had in mind the fact that some of the excesses of Eastern mystery cults drew the attention even of Roman law. There were, of course, many upstanding, virtuous pagans, some of whom protested the degradations of popular pagan life. The moral tone of the pagan world in Peter's time, however, was generally depraved, demonstrating "the incapacity of paganism to control the most unwholesome aspects of the human heart. What is more, immorality and religion often reciprocally encourage one another."

Today, in our Western world, we have largely eliminated the true God from our public life. Whatever be the explanation of it, we are rapidly losing control of the vicious forces of society, which are turning our "ordered lives" into chaos. It remains to be seen whether society can be tamed without a recovery of an acknowledged relationship between societal virtue and God. A recent responsible theologian has judged it impossible. He has described as "a major crisis of our day" the fact that two "visions of the American political experiment are struggling for supremacy." One is that "democratic rule depends on people recognizing God-given principles of justice and morals"; the other "that the nation is not bound to any fixed truths of morality . . . ." By eliminating religion from public life, we are "establishing secularism." Although "spirituality and politics are distinct," he said, they are "not separable. Political judgments are inevitably permeated with moral and religious assumptions . . . Morality cannot he firmly established in the absence of religious faith." Is it possible that "a new barbarism" is arising from our "secularism" which will ultimately be the death knell of democracy as we know it?

When Christian converts made their radical break with their old lives, beginning to live **no longer by human passions but by the will of God**, their unconverted pagan neighbors were **surprised** that they did not **join them in the same wild profligacy** in which they had formerly engaged. It is easy to see how they would be "astonished," or "think it very queer," when suddenly their "former companions" withdrew from their fellowship and abandoned their patterns of life. **Wild profligacy** it was, in many instances. Modern translators have tried to capture the flavor of this expression in various ways: "unbridled dissipation," "welter of debauch," "violent wasting of life." A "flood of profligacy" perhaps comes nearest to conveying the meaning of the phrase in modern English. It literally involves a "pouring out" of a "stream," which suggests a "flood of debauchery." The picture, therefore, is that of diving into a badly polluted stream or a cesspool—a fetid mass of **licentiousness, passions, drunkenness, revels, carousing, and lawless idolatry**. The word **join**—running together with others to do something—pictures a group running alongside a swimming hole to leap into the water together. The passage here, then, might be translated: "They think it queer when you do not plunge together with them into the same stream of debauchery," or "join in the mass dive into the cesspool of shameless lasciviousness."

Was Peter's description of the pagan behavior of that day overdone? Admittedly, it was biased in favor of a Christian understanding of the meaning of life. Peter was a Jew, and the Jews, even before the Christian era, had despised the moral grossness of paganism. As a *Jewish Christian*, Peter would have been even more morally cricical of pagan immoralities than were the Jews. Yet his picture is likely not highly overdrawn. Most of the Roman public festivals were "connected to offerings and cultic acts" to the supposed gods of household, family, and state. Drinking bouts and riotous behavior accompanied these festivals. The pagan theater, which had its rise "in the ceremonial worship of the god Dionysus," often contained highly "immoral scenes." Some pagan temples included intercourse with temple maidens as a part of their worship.

From all of this, the Christians withdrew. Their break with such pagan customs was decisive. The author of the novel *Quo Vadis*, in depicting a pagan young man who had infiltrated the Christian group, captured the nature of this break. As the young man listened to Peter preach, he "felt that if he wished . . . to follow that teaching, he would have to place on a burning pile all his thoughts, habits, and character, his whole nature up to that moment, burn them into ashes, and then fill himself with a life altogether different, and an entirely new soul."

The Christians' isolation from customary pagan social behavior led to much misunderstanding on the part of their pagan neighbors, to "suspicion, insinuations, ill-willed reproach and complete rejection." Christians were branded as "haters of humanity," as followers of "corruptible superstition," as purveyors of "perverse practices" such as cannibalism, in their claim to eat the body and drink the blood of Christ in the eucharist. The pagans were truly **surprised**, and thought it "very queer" when Christian converts suddenly broke with their former manner of life.

Little wonder that the pagan reaction was to **abuse** the Christians. The word thus translated means literally to "blaspheme," which, when applied to God, has the flavor of "irreverence" or "sacrilege," but when applied to men means to "injure the reputation of, revile, defame." It describes the response of some bold onlookers at the crucifixion, and one of the thieves who was then hanged, when they "derided" Jesus (Mark 15:29) and "railed at him" (Lk 23:39).

In our time, the line between Christians and pagans is so blurred that it is difficult to tell on which side of it one stands. "Tolerance" is the highly valued mood of the day in religious matters. Religious convictions are considered matters of personal taste or preference, and are no longer highly charged matters of life and death. What one believes is largely a matter of public indifference, akin to such things as whether one prefers to drive a Buick or an Oldsmobile. In the first century, however, religion played a major role in life for both pagan and Christian. It was not possible for one's faith to escape detection. Belief affected behavior, and outlook on life, and social customs, and final loyalties. Those who were captured, therefore, by **the things which have now been announced . . . by those who preached the good news; that they had been redeemed from the futile ways inherited from** [their] **fathers through the costly blood of Christ by God, who raised him from the dead and gave him glory;** and had thereby offered them **a living hope as an inheritance . . . kept in heaven** for them; which, while they waited for that, laid on them the obligation to purify their lives by **obedience to the truth,** living **no longer by human passions but by the will of God,** and submitting themselves continually to the judgment of Him **who is ready to judge the living and the dead;** together to become a new humanity, **God's own people,** set in the midst of those who were alienated from God **to declare the wonderful deeds of him who called** [them] **out of darkness into his marvelous light,** necessarily stood out from their neighbors, surprised them, "astonished" them, seemed "'queer" to them. The lines were so clearly drawn that their neighbors either accepted their message and joined them, or "abused" them, "defamed" them, "maligned" them, "vilified" them.

This state of things has been experienced by Christians in our time, either in countries which have been officially atheistic or who adhere officially to non-Christian faiths. Multitudes of Christians have known social ostracism, economic disadvantage, political harassment of the sort Peter's first readers were enduring. And strange though it may seem, given the widespread presence of Christians in the modern world, it is likely that more of them have died martyrs deaths for their faith during the last fifty years than in any half century since Peter wrote his letter. Who knows what the future holds for readers of his letter in time to come? It is well to remember, however, that whatever Christian suffering has been imposed by a hostile world "was made necessary" by the fact that **Christ suffered in the flesh** to enable Christians to cease **from sin.** This "deliverance from a life of enmity to God," then, was "worth any price."

In verse 5, Peter encourages his readers to endure whatever trials their faith may bring to them by reminding them that, in the long run, the only thing that really matters is the approval of God at the last judgment. Both persecuted and persecutors must finally **give account to him who is ready to judge the living and the dead.** A picturesque use of the phrase **give account** is found in Jesus' parable of the Dishonest Steward, who was charged by his wealthy employer with "wasting his goods." The employer summoned the steward, and said: "Turn in the account of your stewardship" (Lk 16:1ff.). Just so will each one of us be summoned finally to "turn in the account" of the stewardship of our lives: "each of us shall give account of himself to God" (Rom

14:12). Christians can endure the adverse judgment of men if they can have the vindication of God at the last judgment.

The fact that the judge is **ready** to pass judgment may reflect Peter's hope that the final end was near. On the other hand, it may mean that all is in readiness because the judgment will he made in the light of Christ's redeeming work which is now completed and will be the standard by which the judgment is to be made. It may best be understood in the light of Peter's word in 4:7 (see pp. 294ff.).

Some scholars interpret verse 6 in the light of 3:18-22, making the reference to the dead apply to the spirits in prison to whom Jesus allegedly preached the gospel (see pp. 276ff.). As we have seen, however, the word preached in 3:19 is a different word from that in 4:6, and thus likely involves a different message. Here the passage definitely affirms that **the gospel was preached.** And since a different word is used for **preached,** there seems to be no contextual connection with the statement here and that in 3:18-22. I agree, therefore, with those who hold that the preaching here is "the normal preaching of the gospel on earth" to men who have died since they heard it. The context fits well with what one has termed "the required contrast between the fate of persecutors and those whom they persecute. Those who judged others in their lifetime will one day he judged themselves, those who were judged and condemned in their lifetime will be upheld by God at the final judgment." Peter also is indicating that those who have died before the final judgment and those who are still living when it happens, all stand on the same footing and will be vindicated in the same way (see 1 Thess 4:13ff.). The *Revised English Bible* translators have captured the meaning of the verse: "although in the body they were condemned to die as everyone dies, yet in the spirit they might live as God lives."

I. The Church's Witness to the Glory of God in Its Own Life *(4:7-11)* (Exhortation)

This paragraph concludes the rather long section on the life of the Christian in society, beginning in 2:11, with a summons to the church to witness to the pagan society by embodying in her own life the sort of behavior which glorifies God. Important as their demeanor toward their pagan neighbors was, it was equally important to relate themselves properly to one another. This was particularly true in the setting of misunderstanding and persecution in which Peter's first readers were living. To endure the obloquy and ridicule of pagan neighbors demanded the mutual undergirding of one another in the Christian group. Corporate prayer, unity, mutual love and forbearance, hospitality, an effort to use one's gifts for the good of the group rather than for self-aggrandizement—all these would be mutually strengthening and would aid in enabling them to be an inextinguishable lighthouse in the raging sea of paganism described in verses 3 and 4. Paul developed a similar theme in writing to the Philippians when he counseled them to "stand firm in one spirit, with one mind striving side by side for the faith of the gospel, and not frightened in anything by your opponents" (1:27f.). Unity of purpose within the Christian group was essential in overcoming the fear kindled by opponents. Courage was kindled as they stood together, shoulder to shoulder.

This unity is the outgrowth of a continuing mood, or habit of mind. It is the predisposition to see all things in the light of eternity, to live with a continual awareness that **the end of all things is at hand.** Although this sentence, which begins a new paragraph, seems to be a rather abrupt intrusion into the sequence of thought, the original introduced it with a simple connective, indicating that in Peter's mind, it was closely related to what had gone before. Mention of the **end of all things** is a continuation of the thought of verse 5, which reminds his readers that their tormentors must **give account to him who is ready to judge the living and the dead.** In the light of this, says Peter, the certainty of the final judgment should be all the more decisive in the life of the Christian. Of all people, the Christian should live each day in the light of eternity. How strongly this was felt in the life of the early church may be seen from a word of the church father Ignatius, in his letter to the Ephesians, written early in the second century, as he journeyed from Antioch to Rome to be martyred: "The last times are come upon us. Let us therefore be of a reverent spirit, . . . and let our present and true joy be only this, to be found in Christ Jesus, . . . Do not at any time desire so much as even to breathe apart from Him. For He is my hope; He is my boast; He is my never-failing riches, on whose account I bear about with me these bonds from Syria to Rome, these spiritual jewels, . . ."

But the final judgment has a positive side to it. Not only will evil be judged, but righteousness will be vindicated. That was the **living** hope spoken of at the beginning of the letter (1:3). That final triumph of righteousness was what made their suffering worth while. In a proleptic sense, therefore, the Christians could even now participate in the final consummation of righteousness by embodying in their own community those graces which will be regnant when God finally "reconcile[s] to himself all things, whether on earth or in heaven" (Col 1:20). Together, they could create a small community patterned after **the will of God** (4:2) which would demonstrate in miniature what a society would be where the living **God was glorified through Jesus Christ** (4: 11). As one has phrased it: "that new time coming could already be enjoyed now in the Christian fellowship. The way Christians now acted and were to act toward one another was simply a foreshadowing of that time when all of society would be transformed by the visible rule of God." A hymn writer phrased it:

> .... what-e'er may come,
> We'll taste, e'en here, the hallowed bliss
> Of an eternal home.

What is **the end of all things**? The end sometimes means "cessation," "extinction," "dissolution," "annihilation," "nonbeing." One can say that the Hapsburg dynasty, which had ruled Austria in one form or another from 1282, ended in 1918. It went out of being. It no longer exists. There is a sense in which this applies to Peter's meaning here, inasmuch as the Bible indicates that the world as we now know it will one day be no more. "For," said Paul, "the form of this world is passing away" (1 Cor 7:31). This "age" must give way to "that which is to come" (Eph 1:21). The "present evil age" (Gal 1:4) must vanish when "the kingdom of God, and his righteousness" is finally established (Matt 6:33 KJV).

In a deeper sense, however, it is only the evil in the present world that will "cease." All else will be transformed into "new heavens and a new earth in which righteousness dwells" (2 Pet 3:13;, see also Rev. 21:1). This means that the **end** will not be so much a "cessation" as a "conclusion," a "consummation," a "completion," an "accomplishment," an "outcome," the "achievement of a goal." It is the culmination of the purpose for which creation was originally designed, the final outworking of the intention of God to restore all that had been distorted and ravaged by sin. In other words, it will be the final accomplishment of salvation.

It was the conviction of the New Testament writers that this **end** had been achieved in principle in the birth, life, death and resurrection of Jesus Christ. Paul writes that God "has made known to us his secret purpose, in accordance with the plan which he determined beforehand in Christ, to be put into effect when the time was ripe; namely, that the universe, everything in heaven and on earth, might be brought into a unity in Christ" (Eph 1:9f. REB). The early Christians believed that this had been accomplished in Christ and was known to those who believed. The preparatory stages in the history of salvation were consummated in the coming of Christ into the world and in His triumphant return to His Father, who "enthroned him at his right hand in the heavenly realms, far above all government and authority, all power and dominion, and any title or sovereignty that commands allegiance, not only in this age but also in the age to come" (Eph 1:30 ff. REB). The one crowning stage in this accomplishment was to manifest it to all men in His *final* coming, at which time "at the name of Jesus every knee should bow, in heaven and on earth and under the earth, and every tongue confess that Jesus Christ is Lord, to the glory of God the Father" (Phil 2:10f.). In the meantime, while waiting for this final manifestation, Christ "must be received into heaven until the time comes for the universal restoration of which God has spoken through his holy prophets from the beginning" (Acts 3:21 REB). The **end** was actually achieved, but was still hidden, seen only by the eyes of faith.

When the atomic bomb had been prepared, only a few knew of it. It was secret until it was dropped. So, redemption is now achieved by God, but only those know it who have faith. One day, however, it wll be openly displayed, and all will know of it. The church now lives, therefore, between the time of salvation's accomplishment and its open manifestation in Jesus' coming to final judgment—judgment to the unbelieving but deliverance to the believing. When the New Testament speaks of the "last days" (Heb 1:2), the "last time" (Jude 18), the "last hour" (1 John 2:18), it is referring to this period between the resurrection and ascension of Jesus and his final manifestation in glory. Ever since Jesus ascended to His Father, we have been living in the **end** time. A French scholar has said of this: "it designated the last period of the world according to the plan of salvation, inaugurated by the Incarnation and Calvary: the preparations are completed, the realization is present, . . . although it is not fully concluded." One might illustrate it by a baseball game. The starting time has come, the game begins and is under way, but it will not be complete until the third out in the second half of the ninth inning, which could be a long time away. The time of waiting for the game is ended. *It is here, but it isn't over.* When the umpire thunders "Play ball!" the "time has come,"' but the duration of the time until it is ended cannot be determined. Just as salvation has a threefold dimension, in that we "have been saved" by a past act of redemption; we "are being saved" in our present fellowship with Christ; but we "will be saved" at the final judgment; so the **end** of the world has three dimensions. Preparation for it was made "from the foundation of the world" until the Incarnation of our Lord; it arrived when He came and died, rose and ascended; it will be consummated at His final coming.

What does **at hand** mean? This is the same word used by John the Baptist and by Jesus when they announced that "the kingdom of heaven is at hand" (Matt 3:2, 4:17). It is the perfect tense of the verb meaning to "approach," or "come near," which means the **end** is near and will remain near. Nearness may relate either to space or time. If it relates to space here, it would involve not linear space so much as spiritual space, carrying the meaning which Paul probably had in mind when he said: "The Lord is at hand" (Phil 4:5). In other words, He is nearby, available for our help. This echoes what the Psalmist said: "The Lord is near to all who call upon him" (Ps 145:18). In this instance, however, inasmuch as Peter has been speaking of the last judgment in verses 5 and 6, and returns to the same theme in verse 17, it more likely refers to time, meaning "everything will soon come to its end."

If we take it to mean this, shall we say that Peter was mistaken? After all, it has been nearly 2,000 years since he said it, and he seems to have miscalculated pretty badly! Many scholars think that the early Christians expected the Second Coming of Christ to take place within a very short time span, and have been proved by history to be downright mistaken. It seems certain that at least some Christians held to this view, for Paul had to reassure them that those who had died before the end came would suffer no disadvantage by that fact (1 Thess 4:13ff.).

How mistaken Peter was we cannot know, for it is impossible to get inside his mind to read the time sequence there, if he had one.

We may, however, say some things with certainty. When he wrote that **the end of all things is at hand,** he was certainly not setting a date for the Second Coming. We cannot know what he thought about its closeness in time. In Mark's Gospel, which tradition tells us was the recording of the message preached by Peter himself, we are told that "of that day or that hour no one knows, not even the angels in heaven, nor the Son, but only the Father" (13:32). It is not likely, therefore, that Peter was here dabbling in chronological guesses. Furthermore, the church carried in its canonical Scriptures the truth that "with the Lord one day is as a thousand years, and a thousand years as one day" (2 Pet 3:8), suggesting that God's time is not our time; so that if one thinks something is about to happen within the year, it might be a thousand years away!

The Oriental mind differs from our western view of time. To us, who live by the clock, "right away" means "right away"—at least, within the next few minutes. This is not so with the Oriental. I was once with a Korean missionary who had conducted a Sunday morning service in a distant village. He had to be home for another meeting in late afternoon, so took along a picnic lunch to eat en route, so as to return in time. The hospitable Koreans would not hear of us leaving without eating lunch. "We do not have time to wait for lunch," said the missionary, "for I have another engagement this afternoon." The Koreans insisted, with a pressure that was irresistible, that they would serve lunch "right away," and there would be no wait. We stayed. After a half hour's visit in their home, tea was served. In another half hour, fruit was served. Sometime after that, the meal arrived. Some forty-five minutes after that, we got away! What the Koreans meant when they said "right away" was that preparing the meal was the next item to which they would give their attention! But "right away" could turn out to be an hour and a half away! So, Peter may have been suggesting that the next item in God's redemptive drama to which attention should be given was the **end of all things**, but he may not have been scheduling the time between now and when it happened.

But nearer yet to Peter's meaning is the reality that literally, in truth, we have arrived at the **end.** The French commentator, writing clandestinely while in prison, phrased it this way: the end "is at no moment far from us. This does not mean that we may not have to await it a long time, but we wait as a prisoner who, looking forward to his liberation for days or years, is never far from the door which will be opened. He strengthens himself in the dreadful depths during the time of his captivity, so that he surfaces *instantaneously* on the day when freedom comes, whatever be the depth to which he has descended." Or, as another has said: "When you awake in the night and hear a cock crow, you doubt not for one moment that midnight is past and the morning breaks. . . . If in March, or even earlier, you see a primrose beginning to bloom in a protected place behind a garden hedge, you are no longer in doubt that Spring is coming, though there may still be much frost. . . . The Apostles had seen . . . a shoot springing up . They had seen the risen One. And from that came the joyousness of the declaration, 'The end of all things is at hand!'"

We have already seen that the time before Christ came was a time of preparation for Him. It involved a long series of historic events —the call of Abraham; the formation of a family and a clan; a period of slavery in Egypt; an Exodus; a wilderness wandering; a conquest of a land; and judges, kings, priests, and prophets; another captivity in Babylon; a return to the Promised Land; a hectic rebuilding and continuing struggle under Persians, Greeks, Seleucids, and Romans; all designed "to introduce [Christ] into the world. . . . But when once the Christ had come, . . . and had suffered, and had risen again . . . nothing more was left to do. Earth had had its most solemn event, and seen its most august sight; and therefore it was the last time."

In the light of this, one of England's greatest nineteenth century preachers effectively illustrated how the situation changed when Christ came, and how the end has been near ever since, however much time elapses before it is consummated. He said: "up to Christ's coming in the flesh, the course of things ran straight towards that end, nearing it by every step; but now, under the gospel, the course has (if I may so speak) altered its direction, as regards his second coming, and *runs not towards the end, but along it,* and on the brink of it; and is at all times equally near that great event, which, did it run towards, it would at once run into. Christ, then, is ever at our doors; as near eighteen hundred years ago as now, and not nearer now than then; and not nearer when he comes than now. When he says that he will come soon, 'soon' is not a word of time, but of natural order. This present state of things . . . is ever *close upon* the next world . . . . As when a man is given over, he may die any moment, yet lingers; . . . as a crumbling arch hangs, we know not how, and is not safe to pass under; so creeps on this feeble weary world, and one day, before we know where we are, it will end" (first emphasis added). It is as though one were walking from Kansas to the Atlantic ocean. After a long journey, he arrives at the sea. From then on, he can move north to Maine or south to Florida, now moving not *toward* the ocean but *along* it, as near to it in Maine as in New Jersey or in Florida. The ocean is always there, near, at hand. So is it with the new age.

The fact that Peter was not interested in setting dates for the end, nor in using its nearness for stimulating curiosity or exciting hurried preparations for it through bizarre efforts to read the signs of the times, is to be seen in his accompanying admonitions: **keep sane and sober** (for **sober**, see comments on 1:13). The first of these involves "control of one's mental faculties"; the second refers more to the senses, or emotions. One translation of these words is: "keep your senses awake." "The two together," one has said, "denote complete control of oneself, resulting in calmness, sobriety, self-control, sensibleness, steadiness." Another translation is: "Be serious and connected." Still another: "Steady then, keep cool." This is the very opposite of excitement and breathless agitation. Peter is not suggesting that the nearness of the **end** should stimulate frenzied concentration on it which would detract energies from one's ordinary daily activities, but rather proposing that all of one's doings should be continually and seriously brought under the light of eternity. The nearness of the **end** is the reality in the light of which every activity should be undertaken.

I have read that a lady once excitedly said to Emerson: "The world is coming to an end." Emerson replied: "That's quite alright; we can get along very well without it!" And there is the famous story of Abraham Davenport, immortalized in Whittier's poem of that name. He was a member of the Connecticut legislature which was meeting in May of 1789 on "one of those queer days when the sky unaccountably and fearfully darkens at midday and a strange twilight falls." Some thought that it was a sign of the end of the world. They were discussing an "act to amend an act to regulate the shad and alewive fisheries." Someone proposed adjournment.

In Whittier's words, Davenport rose in "the intolerable hush," and said:

"This well may be
The Day of Judgment which the world awaits;

> But be it so or not, I only know
> My present duty, and my Lord's command
> To occupy till He come. So, at the post
> Where He hath set me in His providence,
> I choose, for one, to meet him face to face—
> No faithless servant frightened from my task,
> But ready when the Lord of the harvest calls;
> And therefore, with all reverence, I would say
> Let God do His work, we will see to ours.
> Bring in the candles." And they brought them in.

The poet concludes that Davenport's action was

> A witness to the ages as they pass
> That simple duty hath no place for fear.

Today men live in fear of atomic annihilation or extinction through ecological neglect. This is a far cry from the early Christians, who hoped that the world would not last this long and longed for the consummation of righteousness, when this flawed world would give way to God's redeemed world, constantly praying the prayer with which the Bible ends: "Come, Lord Jesus!" (Rev 22:20). They were secure in the knowledge that they belonged to "a kingdom that cannot be shaken," which, when what can be shaken is shaken "may remain" (Heb 12:27f.).

Not long after Hiroshima, when fear that the atomic bomb might cause the end of the world had become almost hysterical on the part of some, an "alarmist" group made a presentation at a theological seminary. The centerpiece of their emotional thrust was a report that someone who controlled the apparatus for unleashing a general atomic attack had misread an indicator, and that we had been within five minutes of his pushing the button which could have resulted in the destruction of our planet. In a chapel service shortly thereafter, one of the professors made reference to the presentation by using Peter's words: "The end of all things is at hand." He reminded his hearers that the apostles had faced the possibility of which the "alarmists" were speaking nearly two thousand years ago, and did not seem to be greatly disturbed. He went on to conjecture that if one could have gotten through to the Apostle Paul in the 5th century with the earth-shaking news of Rome's fall, he would probably have said: "I'm so sorry to hear it. I had hoped it would not last that long!" The apostles knew that however and whenever the world ended, that **end** would be good. They wished for its coming. They had already seen it in the risen Lord! The **end** had been **at hand** ever since the first Easter day! The **end** would be a "consummation," an "achievement," a "completion"; the final triumph of righteousness over evil; the accomplishment of "the eternal purpose which [God] has realized in Christ Jesus our Lord" (Eph 3:11), "that all human history shall be consummated in Christ," giving "history its fulfillment" by "restoring the whole creation to find its one Head in Christ" (Eph 1:10, translations by Phillips, Knox and Weymouth). They faced the **end** hopefully and calmly, knowing its triumphant outcome through Him who is now "enthroned . . . at [God's] right hand in the heavenly realms, far above all government and authority, all power and dominion, and any title of sovereignty that commands allegiance, not only in this age but also in the age to come" (Eph 1:20f., REB).

How does one acquire such calmness in the light of the nearness of the **end**. By one's **prayers**. The preposition **for** which goes with **prayers** could be interpreted *temporally*, suggesting, that one should **keep sane and sober** "while he prays." It is perhaps better, however, to understand it as *purposeful*, meaning to **keep sane and sober** "in order to be able to pray" as one should; or "in order to give one's self to prayer." This does not necessarily mean to make long prayers, or to spend an inordinate time in prayer, but "to live in a state of prayer" so that one's activities are undertaken in total dependence on God and as offerings to God. This can hardly be done unless one habitually takes certain periods of time during the day to make himself aware of the presence of God; to listen for God's voice in His Word; to readjust one's focus on eternal realities; to lay before God the planned activities of the day, that they may be in accord with His will; and to try to "bear one another's burdens" by speaking to God of the needs of loved ones and other companions of the journey of life, even of those who do not acknowledge God as their helper. Prayer is the best means of permitting the light of eternity to fall on the activities of time, of reminding one's self that the **end of all things is at hand**.

From a mood of continual awareness of the nearness of God's kingdom, generated and sustained by prayer, the other admonitions of the passage follow naturally.

First, **above all hold unfailing your love for one another.** As is characteristic of the New Testament as a whole, **love is above all**, or "the most important thing of all." It was the most highly prized characteristic of the Christian faith by the New Testament writers. It was one of the three graces which abide the eternities—*faith, hope, and love*—"but the greatest of these is love" (1 Cor 13:13). **Unfailing** is not the best translation of the adverb in this sentence. The word seems to refer less to *constancy* than to *intensity* (see comment on 1:22). Other translators use "fervent," "strong," "intense," "earnest," to describe the quality of love recommended. The word involves "the maximum of intensity and extension."

One writer points out that Peter is not here referring to "warmth of feelings or that of the words which accompany them, but to the strength and steadfastness of the resolve to place one's self at the disposal of his brothers." This is what distinguishes Christian love (*agape*) from the highly-touted erotic love, both of the ancient world and of today, whose aim is always "through the love of the other to enrich and advance one's own life." *Agape* love has been described as "pure love of one's brother, which does not waver nor cease according to the behavior of the other, which is not endangered by either party involved doing wrong, but endures even through such grievances, which even overcomes what again and again destroys human fellowship . . . ."

The motivation Peter gives for this fervent **love** is that it **covers a multitude of sins.** The source of this saying is in dispute. It sounds very much like Proverbs 10:12: "Hatred stirs up strife, but love covers all offenses," and many commentators list this as its origin. The difficulty with this is that the Greek translation of the Old Testament, which Peter habitually uses for the sake of his Gentile readers, has quite another reading in this passage. It says that "friendship covers all those who are not addicted to quarrels," or "not loving strife." Since the statement "has all the earmarks of a current maxim" or "a well-known Christian proverb," and gives no indication that it is introducing an Old Testament quotation, it is quite possible that it came to Peter's mind as a familiar popular saying which fit his purposes, and therefore needs no firm tracing to a particular source.

The meaning of the statement is also in dispute. There are three main lines of interpretation. First, some interpret it in the light of James' use of the same proverb wherein the sin involved is wandering from "the truth," and is "covered" by leading the sinner back to repentance (5:20). The context, however, makes this interpretation highly questionable here. James is clearly speaking of a former believer who has left the faith, whereas Peter's use of the expression **one another** three times (vss 8, 9 and 10), just as clearly indicates that he is speaking of the action of a believer toward believers, and has no reference to reclaiming "lapsed" brothers.

A second interpretation makes the love cover one's own sin, and becomes "a means of making amends for personal faults." Those who advocate this view refer to Jesus' counsel "to forgive . . . so that your Father also who is in heaven may forgive you" (Mk 11:25), and to parallels to this thought in rabbinic literature and in some of the church fathers. A competent French interpreter, however, has countered this on three grounds: 1) In Jesus' words there is a *correlation* between a disposition to forgive and being forgiven, but the latter is not based on the former; 2) this interpretation clearly contradicts the teaching elsewhere in the letter, where the forgiveness of sins in no way rests on anything that the believer does, but is uniquely and totally the result of what God has done for us in Christ (1:18ff., 2:24); and 3) the earliest recorded use of the idea by a church father, Clement, before the end of the first century, applies it clearly "to the relations between members of the community and confers on it no expiatory virtue."

The third, and in my judgment correct, interpretation is that **love covers a multitude of sins** by overlooking the sins committed by Christians toward one another in the group. This was Peter's way of saying what Paul said elsewhere: "if a man is overtaken in any trespass, you who are spiritual should restore him in a spirit of gentleness. Look to yourself, lest you too be tempted. Bear one another's burdens, and so fulfil the law of Christ" (Gal 6:1f.). It is only selfless love, based on the self-giving love of Christ to us, which can overlook the countless wrongs done by Christians to one another in the church, and thus enable the group to rise above pettiness and quarreling and disunity into a true fellowship of believers in Christ,

This love has two practical avenues of expression. The first is the practice of **hospitality**. This was a grace much valued among the early Christians (see Rom 12:13, 1 Tim 3:2, Titus 1:8, Heb 13:2). Frequently, converts were disowned by their families, and became homeless save as they were taken in by fellow Christians. Many Christians, too, were poor and, when traveling, could not afford public accommodations; thus were dependent on their brothers in the faith. Public inns were usually very uncomfortable, and sometimes guests were robbed. Christian travelers therefore welcomed the cordial hospitality of a Christian home. By staying in homes, missionaries and visitors from other churches became links of communication between the Christians in different places. Then, too, the Christian groups usually met in homes, when common meeting places were a vital necessity for maintaining group cohesion. Some translators have sought to convey this needed grace more vividly by using such expressions as "open your homes," "keep open house," "welcome one another as guests."

One writer has reminded us that love is always costly, in time, and money, and energy and work, and "presupposes unceasing victories over natural egoism." One can imagine the irritation, and weariness, and strain that might be incurred in a household, where a group customarily—at least weekly—arrived for an early morning worship service; or where a continual stream of traveling guests demanded extra energies at the wash tub and in the carrying of extra water pots and in providing provender for donkeys, and placed a strain on an already meager budget; and where a refugee or two interfered with customary family privacy and crowded to the limit a house already cramped for space. Peter counsels: **Practice hospitality ungrudgingly,** or "without grumbling," or "complaining" or "with a good heart." In spite of the fact that **hospitality** was to be refused to those who used it to spread false teaching (2 John 7ff.), and discrimination was necessary to weed out parasites and "spongers" who preferred receiving **hospitality** to honest work (2 Thess 3:10ff.; 1 Tim 5:5ff., 11ff.), the opening of Christian homes was commended as a privilege and an opportunity to express their unfailing ... love for one another.

The second means of expressing **love** was **service: As each has received a gift, employ it for one another, as good stewards of God's varied grace.** It has been observed that "the concept of serving others is virtually new in Christianity. ... Neither in the Old Testament nor in the Hellenistic world of the time was the concept of work as service to be found. It stems from Jesus. ..." He it was who said that He came "not to be served but to serve" (Mark 10:45). He also indicated that in other circles he "who sits at table" was "greater" than the "one who serves," but that in His kingdom this was all reversed: "I am among you as one who serves" (Lk 22:24ff.). This has prompted a commentator to write: "The deepest essence of authentic love is that it will

Commentary 4:10

serve. In the practice of service this essence becomes visible." Another interpreter finds in this section on service in the congregation "one of the most remarkable pillars of New Testament ecclesiology [the doctrine of the church]." The church is a household of love, of mutual nurture, and of service, all centered in the glory of God.

Two major antitheses are harmonized in this section. The first is that of *variety* and *unity*. **As each has received a gift, . . . whoever speaks, . . . whoever renders service**—these expressions include all the individuals in the congregation. Each has his own **gift**, and each is a steward of **God's varied grace**. The word **varied** means "diversified," "manifold," "many-colored,," "variegated"—a word which suggests the rich variety of gifts which God has distributed to individuals who make up the community of faith. And yet, **love** is to be **for one another**; **hospitality** is to be practiced **to one another**; the **gift** of **each** is to be employed **for one another**. Three times the group is mentioned. And, obviously, **whoever speaks** or **renders service** does these for others.

All individuality is to be coalesced into the unity of the group. Where there is only diversity, unity is destroyed; where there is only unity, the individual is "lost in the conglomeration of a uniform organization, in the mass. The Christian congregation, as a fellowship of serving love, manifests a unique union of unity and variety." An ideal congregation would be like a great choir, where each voice, melodious in itself, blends unnoticed into the concord of the whole to make "one swelling burst of harmony." A true Christian community is achieved when, without desire for credit or any self-serving, each serves all and all serve each.

The second antithesis harmonized here is that between the *horizontal* and the *vertical*. As one has said: "the use of gifts is always viewed in the realm of behavior toward others, but it is also considered in its relationship to God who bestows the capacities and entrusts the 'administration' of his grace." In this way, "the unique, decisive place of God in the life of the church" is emphasized. The word for **stewards** describes a "servant" or a "public official" to whom is entrusted the management of the resources or the interests of another. Jesus spoke of such twice, depicting a servant who was put in charge of the "possessions," or "goods," of his "master" (Lk 12:4ff., 16:1ff.). The steward owned nothing; he was responsible solely for the possessions of another. Paul uses the word to describe "Erastus, the City treasurer" (Rom

16:23). Erastus owned nothing that was put in his charge, but managed the funds of the public. Paul also speaks of "trustees"—the word translated **stewards** in our passage—who are charged with handling the estate of a minor until he is old enough to take charge of his own affairs (Gal 4:2). Again, the "trustees" own nothing, but have what belongs to another given into their charge. Peter stresses the fact that **each has received a gift**. Whatever the **gift**, it comes from the store of **God's varied grace**. If one **speaks**, he is to do it as **one who utters oracles of God**. If one **renders service**, he is to do it **by the strength which God supplies**. The *horizontal*, therefore, is always an expression of the *vertical*. All that one has to give to another is first given to him by God; and both giving and receiving are encompassed by the purpose that **God may be glorified through Jesus Christ**, Action and worship belong together. Works without faith are unavailing. Faith without works is dead.

Of God's varied graces, Peter singles out two for special attention: speaking and serving. These are two general types, one involving the enrichment of mind and spirit through words—preaching, teaching, exhorting, encouraging the fainthearted; the other involving concrete action in behalf of others—helping the poor, visiting the sick and imprisoned, binding up the hurts of the wounded, feeding the hungry, welcoming strangers, clothing the unclothed.

What Peter means when he counsels those who speak to do so **as one who utters oracles of God,** is difficult to determine. Some think that he is referring to the subject matter, insisting that it should be based on the apostolic interpretation of the word of God in the Old Testament. Others think that be refers rather to the manner, or mode, of speaking, as though he were saying: One must speak "as if he were uttering the very words of God himself." In this case, the stress would be on recognizing that any authentic word of God is given by Him, is a gift from Him, never to be claimed as our own independently of Him. It is difficult, if not impossible, to reach a firm conclusion as to which is preferable.

In my judgment, however, as others have pointed out, the epistle itself would seem to favor the first interpretation. In 1:10-12 Peter suggests a "practical equivalence" between the Old Testament message as the apostles understood it in the light of Christ, and the gospel which had been preached to his readers. In 1:22ff. Peter suggests that it was this gospel which had brought his readers new birth, and closely connects it with the Old Testament message. Also, in 1:22 and 2:8 Peter insists that it is this word which is the "truth" and claims their "obedience." It seems that Peter is suggesting that there is already a general agreement in the church as to what the true gospel is—an interpretation of the Old Testament revelation by the apostles, which could be found in Paul's early letters and in the tradition of the apostolic proclamation in the sermons later recorded in the Acts, but which, by the time Peter wrote, was likely available either in oral or fragmentary written form. Those who preached or exhorted or taught in the churches, therefore, should know that the Holy Spirit functions through *that word and no other*, and that all charismatic utterances of gifted speakers were to be measured thereby. One who dared to speak for God to others must be **as one who utters oracles of God** rather than his own ideas, thus giving the apostolic faith control of all future developing tradition. This profound insight should be the corrective for the curse of the "personality cult" in Christian pulpits and study groups, where both speakers and hearers should be measuring what goes on not by the quality of what is said as entertainment but by its power to blot out the human instruments and confront the hearer with the living truth of the living God.

Service is to be rendered by **the strength which God supplies, with the goal that in everything God may be glorified through Jesus Christ.** All virtues have their corresponding vices. Service may require the sacrifice of laziness, and comfort, and energy, and money for the good of our fellowmen and the glory of God. On the other hand, it may be the occasion of self-centeredness and self-aggrandizement, designed more to enhance one's reputation, or raise one's status, or enlarge one's power than to assist others or to glorify God. A clergyman who participated in the Selma, Alabama march for civil rights returned home complaining that he was assigned to the garbage detail and nobody knew he was there, while a fellow minister was asked to lead a public prayer and thus gained some notoriety! Did this say anything about his motivation in going? In the Sermon on the Mount, Jesus touched the tender nerve of this flaw in human nature when he cautioned against "'practicing your piety before men in order to be seen by them" (Matt 6:1). The outcome is "no reward from your Father who is in heaven."

When we serve others, we have nothing to give save what God

has first given us. And our service will be ineffective unless it is blessed by God. "It is God who inspires the generosity, supplies the resources, measures the results." To focus on the good of our brother and the glory of God will help to conquer our self-centeredness and make our service a genuine expression of **unfailing ... love for one another.** One has reminded us that the pathway to this service is to keep our minds set on Christ. Then, "the glory which he has rendered to God once for all on the cross fills our heart and our actions and thus produces the miracle" which enables us to serve our fellows and to glorify God. "God gives his power to those who cease to count on their own."

The section closes with the doxology: **To him belong glory and dominion for ever and ever, Amen.** There are those who believe that Peter intended to conclude his letter here; and, after an interruption, decided to add a few further words. Others look upon what follows as a second letter, bound in with the first (see pp. 21ff.). Such views, however, are unnecessary. Only three letters in the New Testament end with a doxology (Rom 16:25ff., 2 Pet 3:18, Jude 24f.). On the other hand, doxologies more than once appear with other materials following, indicating that a doxology is not a signal for the end of a letter (see Eph 3:20f., 1 Tim 1:17, 6:16). Furthermore, the character of 1 Peter as a letter does not require that the author should follow precisely an ordered outline, but was free to let his mind return to thoughts already mentioned in earlier places. I once knew a young man in love who wrote to his beloved once a week. During each week he kept notes on what he wanted to say, then incorporated those in logical sequence as he wrote his weekly letter. This is the only letter writer of this type I ever heard of, and I am sure that Peter was not a second one!

Since Peter was writing to suffering Christians, his pastoral concern for steadying them in the face of trials would naturally turn his thoughts more than once to their plight, and lead him to repeated interpretations of it and encouragements in it. Then, too, having twice before mentioned their suffering in its relation to the "end" time, **at the revelation of Jesus Christ** (1:7), **on the day when he comes in judgement** (2:12), it was natural that, having referred again to the **end of all things** (4:7), he should reinforce the connection of their sufferings to that final climax. Peter's doxological outburst of praise in verse 11, therefore, is simply a spontaneous expression of the sublime mood in which he ended this section, when he described the purpose of the church's total existence, both in worship and in deeds—that God may be glorified through Jesus Christ.

This is the God to whom belong glory and dominion for ever and ever, Amen. Peter worshiped as he worked!

VI

A CHRISTIAN INTERPRETATION OF SUFFERING (4:12-19)

In the light of the previous paragraph, where Peter has brought all of life under the white light of eternity, he returns to the central aim of his letter—to comfort and strengthen his readers in persecution. The term **Beloved**, with which he addresses them, both signals a new section of thought and introduces the mood in which he is addressing them. It is a term of endearment—"beloved ones," "dear ones," "you whom I love," "you, my cherished friends"—designed to kindle on the part of his readers the depth of feeling which Peter felt for them.

A. The Normalcy of Suffering *(4:12a)* (Exhortation)

A scholar of repute has pointed out that Peter's admonition **do not be surprised,** is not in a grammatical form to warn against a possible reaction, but one which "challenged a sentiment already felt." They were surprised, and Peter is telling them that they should not be, if they understood their situation properly. The pagans were perhaps justified in being **surprised** (4:4) at what seemed to be the "strange" behavior of the Christians in renouncing their pagan frolics; but the Christians should not have been **surprised** at the pagan reaction to them. The Christians were evaluating their situation in purely human terms, when they should have been using God's standard of measurement.

From the human standpoint, it *was* surprising that the pagan world accepted all sorts of new and strange religions from the East, yet maligned the Christians. It was natural to ask: Why the difference? Then, too, the Jewish converts to the Christian faith, who had accepted Jesus as their Messiah, had been reared on the hope that when Messiah came, all would be peace and tranquillity. How different from this was their suffering now **for the name of Christ**. Furthermore, as has been pointed out: "All believing generations find it similarly 'abnormal' to be faithful to God and nevertheless to be tried: 'What have I done to God that he should treat me thus?'"

Peter raises their eyes to a new level of looking at their plight. Why should you be **surprised,** "amazed," "staggered over your lot," he asks, **as though something strange were happening to you**? Difficult though it is for us to accept it, *not* to suffer **for the name of Christ** would be abnormal. Of this Jesus spoke several times. Mark's Gospel, which embodies Peter's own remembrance of his Lord's words, quotes Him thus: "they will deliver you up to councils; and you will he beaten in synagogues, and you will stand before governors and kings for my sake, . . . and you will be hated of all for my name's sake" (13:9ff.). The Fourth Gospel quotes Jesus: "Remember the word that I said to you, 'A servant is not greater than his master.' If they persecuted me, they will persecute you" (15:20). "In the world you have tribulation; but be of good cheer" (16:33). Paul and Barnabas encouraged some of the early converts to the faith in Asia Minor, some of whom may have been among Peter's readers, by telling them "that through many tribulations we must enter the kingdom of God" (Acts 14:22). To the early church, then, suffering **for the name of Christ** was *normal*, it was to be expected.

Peter's description of his readers' situation as a **fiery ordeal** has led some to see an immediacy of persecution here, in contrast to its mere potential earlier in the letter, and have imagined that this is part of a different letter. Others suppose that news has just come to Peter of a new outbreak of persecution, which gives to his writing here a tone of immediacy different from the earlier part of the letter. We have earlier dealt with these views, and are unpersuaded of their validity (see pp. 21ff.). The word translated **ordeal** is the word commonly used for "temptation" or "trial," and carries no special quality of abnormal severity beyond that implied earlier in the epistle. Furthermore, Ephesians speaks of "the shield of faith, with which you can quench all the flaming darts of the evil one" (6:16), indicating that the word translated **fiery** was in common use as a description of the *ordinary* sufferings of Christians in the ancient world. This most certainly means that the word *fiery* in itself does not imply that Christians were being "burned" at the stake. Although they may have been so treated by Nero in Rome, there is no evidence that such a fate was handed out to Christians in Asia Minor at that time. If there is any special reason for introducing the word *fiery* into Peter's writing here, it could well be that "fire" was associated with the end of the world (see 2 Pet 3:10; 1 Cor 3:13), and he was at this point viewing his readers' situation in the light of the final judgment. It is likely that the **fiery ordeal** to which Peter was here referring was merely the drudgery and service to which he had referred in verses 10ff., and "the dreadful retinue of questions which invaded their spirits" when they suffered the ostracism of their neighbors, and made them "prisoners of perplexity."

Peter now gives them a Christian interpretation of their sufferings.

B. Suffering As a Test of Faith *(4:12b)* (Exhortation)

The first element of his interpretation was one which he had mentioned before in 1:6f.—that the quality of their faith may be *tested*, or **prove**[d]. A "test" has the double function of *evaluating* and *strengthening* one's faith As an evaluation it "puts to the proof," or "tries the genuineness" of the quality of something. As a part of a runner's training, there are periodical "tests" with a stop watch, to determine the quality of the runner's performance. In addition to this, however, the "test run" also exercises his capacities in a way that is intended to improve or heighten his performance. So, says Peter, the trials through which his readers were passing were designed both to test the **genuineness** (1:7) of their faith, and to help to exercise that faith in a way that would strengthen, purify, and increase it, until finally it has "the approval of the Lord himself."

C. Suffering As Participation in Christ's Sufferings *(4: 13-16)* (Exhortation)

The second element of Peter's interpretation is that his readers' suffering was *a participation in Christ's suffering* which, rather than surprising them, ought to be a source of joy. What does it mean to **share Christ's sufferings**? Some see in this a reference to baptism, in which Christians are "baptized into his death" (Rom 6:3), and thus all "suffering after baptism is suffering shared with Christ" as a member of

His mystical body. This is largely dependent on interpreting the entire letter as a baptismal document, which we have already branded as highly questionable (see pp, 11ff.).

A more likely interpretation is to see in Christian suffering a participation in the "messianic woes" which the prophets and the early church foresaw as heightened just before the end of the age. Since this passage is related to the **end of all things** (4:7), and since the original uses the article with **Christ,** making it mean literally "the Christ," referring to the office rather than to His name, this interpretation is inviting.

A third interpretation, and one which is not in conflict with the second, but is less precise and more general, is to explain it in terms of the Christian's *recapitulating the experience of Christ* in his suffering.

Paul spoke of his desire to "share his sufferings, becoming like him in his death" (Phil. 3:10). This would mean that "you are sharing what Christ has suffered" and what He continues to suffer in His mystical body, the church. What the head of the church suffers, the body likewise suffers. Therefore, we are "heirs of God and fellow heirs with Christ, *provided we suffer with him* in order that we may also be glorified with him" (Rom 8:17, emphasis added). This does not mean that our suffering adds anything to the redemptive efficacy of Jesus' suffering. He **died for sins once for all. . . that he might bring us to God** (1 Pet 3:18), and no further action is necessary to achieve that end. It does mean, though, that in the struggle with evil in which He was, and is, engaged, we stand with Him against His enemies, and by so doing receive the world's wrath which necessitated His death, and thus **share**, in our measure, in His **sufferings.**

This understanding of Christian suffering is the foundation of genuine joy in the midst of it. With a strong imperative, in a tense form of continuing action, Peter commands his readers to **rejoice**—to "keep on rejoicing," to "rejoice continually." As one has phrased it: "Since you really participate in the sufferings of Christ, seize your privilege, joy!" The fact that the imperative *commands* joy suggests that the joy involved is not a mere emotion. One can hardly command his emotions. Something deeper than mere feeling is involved. It is rather the settled conviction that suffering for Christ's sake is eminently worth while; that it is a privilege to be identified with Him in what He went through. Strange as this may seem to us, who have had to suffer little for our Lord's sake, this mood was exemplified by the early Christians. We are told that they left the legal court in Jerusalem where they had been put on trial for their faith, "*rejoicing* that they were counted worthy to suffer dishonor for the name" (Acts 5:41, emphasis added). This was obviously the result of a reasoned conclusion about the meaning of their suffering rather than an exuberance of feeling.

There is a future aspect of joy, however, which grows out of this settled conviction. If, by faith, one can now rejoice in the costliness of his loyalty to Christ, this will eventuate in another joy of an even deeper sort, when he shall **reioice and be glad when his glory is revealed**. "This vibrant joy of anticipation" of Christ's final coming will be, when it is consummated, one of high emotional exaltation. The "gladness" here mentioned is the same word used by Jesus in the Sermon on the Mount when, telling His disciples that they would be persecuted and reviled on His account, He encouraged them to rejoice and "be glad" (Matt. 5:12). The word **glad** carries the intensity of transcendent joy—"overjoyed," which has led some to interpret Peter here: "that you might shout for joy." Peter's teaching here, then, is not that one suffers now and rejoices later, but that there is a present joy in suffering based on the past, on "the unique and historic sufferings of Christ," and a deeper joy based on the future, the "final seal" of unutterable joy when Christ's final glory is revealed. The coherence of that future anticipated joy with the present was caught by the hymn writer, when he wrote:

> And when the strife is fierce, the warfare long,
> Steals on the ear the distant triumph song,
> And hearts are brave again, and arms are strong. Alleluia!

Verse 14 once more takes us back to the words of Jesus in the Sermon on the Mount. **If you are reproached for the name of Christ, you are blessed**, is reminiscent of Jesus' words: "Blessed are you when men revile you and persecute you and utter all kinds of evil against you falsely on my account" (Matt 5:11). Only the first of the verbs used by Jesus is repeated by Peter ("revile" is the same word as **reproached** in Peter), and it is a milder term than "persecute;" suggesting that the sufferings of Peter's readers likely took the form of "outrage," "mockeries, insults, blows," rather than martyrdom. These sufferings likely had a deeper meaning for those **reproached** than for those who perpetrated the outrages. The name "Christian" was a nickname, first given to the followers of Jesus in Antioch of Syria (Acts 11:26). It was first a term of derision, then later became a title which it was illegal to bear. Many pagans, therefore, without understanding anything about Christianity, would malign the "Christians" merely because they bore that title. To the Christians, however, a name was more than a mere title. The name represented the person. "Christian," then, meant all that Christ had done in His redemptive deed on Calvary, all that He was continuing to do in His fellowship with His followers, and all that He would do finally in His cosmic triumph. To be a "Christian" was to belong to Him, to be identified with Him in His work, and to hope in Him for eternal life.

Those who were **reproached for the name of Christ** were **blessed**, because **the spirit of glory and of God** rested upon them. The word **blessed** is the same word used by Jesus in the Beatitudes. It is a word hard to define, and harder still to grasp. Many efforts have been made to give it a one-word equivalent, but none quite does it. "Happy," "joyous," "blithesome," "fortunate," "blissful," are some of them. These all fall short, for they suggest an emotion, a state of mind, a feeling, a subjective quality of well-being. But those of whom Jesus spoke as "blessed" were "the poor in spirit," "those who mourn," "the meek," "those who hunger and thirst for righteousness," "the merciful," "the pure in heart," "the peacemakers," "the persecuted for righteousness' sake" (Matt 5:3ff.). These could hardly be thought of as emotionally exhilarated! Nor does "blessedness" relate to fortunate outer circumstances, but to inner qualities. The Old Testament defines **blessed** quite apart from emotional states or circumstances. To be **blessed** is to be In right relation to God. "Blessed is the man to whom the Lord imputes no iniquity" (Ps 32:2). "Blessed is he whom Thou dost choose" (Ps 65:4). "Blessed is the man who makes the Lord his trust" (Ps 40:4). "Blessed is the man who fears the Lord, who greatly delights in his commandments" (Ps 112:1) In these, and countless other Old Testament passages, "blessedness" is an objective thing, quite apart from subjective human emotions. It is descriptive of how man stands "in the estimate of God." Therefore, although "blessedness" may not be totally detached from one's feelings, it is not dependent on them and embodies a reality that abides the tragedies of life, when feeling is at low ebb. **If you are reproached for the name of Christ, you are blessed.**

Peter then mentions the foundation on which this "blessedness" rests, in a statement rather difficult to interpret: because **the spirit** of glory and of God rests upon you. A problem immediately arises: Does the and in the sentence separate two different realities? Are there two subjects to the verb rests? If so, since in the Greek the word spirit is associated only with God, then the first part of the sentence would mean that "a glory," or "a glorious reality" rests upon you, in addition to the spirit of God. This is doubtful, for two reasons. First, a double subject would call for a plural verb, but the verb here is in the singular, indicating that it has only one subject. Second, since Peter would have no reason for separating glory from God, it seems best to see here a reference to the same reality in both cases. In other words, the "glorious reality" *is* the spirit of God! The spirit of glory and the spirit of God are one and the same thing. The and is not a connective between two realities, but is *explanatory*. Peter is saying: "the spirit of glory, namely, the spirit of God, rests upon you."

What does it mean that the spirit of God rests upon you? Some take this to mean that God's spirit is given as "an exceptional grace, a spiritual privilege reserved for those who are persecuted for the faith." This view is supported by such statements of Jesus as: "When they deliver you up, do not be anxious how you are to speak or what you are to say, for what you are to say will be given to you in that hour; for it is not you who speak, but the Spirit of your Father speaking through you" (Matt 10:19f.).

Although it is true that the Old Testament does contain instances of the Spirit being given on special occasions and for special tasks (Num 11:25, Isa 11:2, for example), and there are examples in the New Testament of a similar sort (Matt. 3:16, John 20:22f.), such an interpretation does not do justice to Peter's thought here. The current of thought here seems to flow from the fountainhead of grace at Pentecost. There the Holy Spirit did not function as an infusion of grace to empower that particular set of individuals for a special mission, or as a unique gift to some who were under unusual trial, but was rather the permanent arrival of the Spirit in the life of the whole church, whereby it was brought into being. That was the point at which God "breathed" into the nostrils of the church, so to speak, and that otherwise dead body "became a living being" (Gen 2:7). That was the event foreseen by the prophets, when the Messianic Age dawned and the church was born. The Spirit which brought the church into being came to remain permanently to nurture and sustain it. As John the Baptist witnessed of

Jesus, the Spirit not only descended on Him, but "it remained on him" (John 1:32). It can *still* be said of the church **that the spirit of glory and of God rests upon you.** Wherever the church is, **the spirit of glory and of God rests upon** it. This manner of speaking is undoubtedly based on the "glory of the Lord" which shone from "the cloud of the presence" during the wilderness wanderings of ancient Israel, which marked "the nearness of the holy God and his gracious protection; it was a sign of the covenant, a pledge of alliance." The continuing presence of the Spirit of God in the Church is the seal of God's covenant that wherever even "two or three are gathered in my name, there am I in the midst of them" (Matt 18:20).

A French scholar has well summed up the meaning of verse 14: "the outrages borne in the name of Christ delimit an objective privilege, to know what it means to belong to the people of God, to that nation which journeys toward the time of fulfillment, and to share the accompanying glory already in the ministry of the Spirit. Suffering for Christ becomes a seal which the Lord affixes on his own. What consolation for the harassed readers: this rugged and bruising way is indeed 'the true grace of God.'"

What does this mean for us today? In many parts of the world during the last half century, this has been for a multitude of Christian readers a blueprint of their own experience. Thousands have suffered greatly for no reason other than that they dared to identify themselves with **the name of Christ.** They need no explanation of Peter's words! They can read them, and say without hesitation: He is talking about us! At a biblical symposium held in this country just before the collapse of the Berlin wall, a New Testament scholar from East Germany told the group that we in the West did not really understand the New Testament as they did; for they were living exactly as the New Testament church did—under a hostile government, with no political freedom, and only their faith to sustain them. When Peter spoke of suffering, and the necessity of inward securities to endure the lack of outward securities, he was addressing them directly and personally.

But do Peter's words have any meaning for us who have never known physical, or even psychological, suffering because of our identification with Christ? Do Peter's words touch the nerve of our experience at any point? May we venture to suggest that if they do not, we should give careful scrutiny to the state of our commitment to Christ.

Suffering may be not only physical or psychological, but *spiritual*. Although we may not be physically or psychologically harassed for our loyalty to the **name of Christ**, if we are truly **aliens and exiles** on earth (1 Pet 2:11); if we are truly "seeking a homeland," "a better country," a "city which has foundations, whose builder and maker is God" (Heb 11:14, 16, 10); it would seem unavoidable that occasionally, if not often, we would have at least an inner spiritual clash with the customs, and standards, and ambitions, and values and sources of satisfaction of "the present evil age" (Gal 1:4). As Peter remarked earlier in his letter, there are aspects of this world which **wage war** against our souls (2:11). And neutrality is seldom possible in a war. And wars are seldom pleasant. And war means wounds. And Peter tells us that our Lord suffered **wounds** in the battle to redeem us (2:24). Is it possible that we shall totally escape **wounds** if we are on His side of the battle?

Such wounds may come in many forms. I once knew a quiet, but deeply committed, Christian who sat on a bank board. I was told by a fellow member of that group that every time the board had to approve a request for a loan, this man always asked, not how good a business deal it was, but whether the purpose for which the loan was to be used was wholesome and socially uplifting, or whether its use would be socially and morally damaging to the community. He paid a price for this. Among those whose sole goal was to make profit, he was **reproached for the name of Christ.**

I once knew a professor of law who could have lead a comfortable life in his profession, but whose ambition was to serve his Lord through his legal skills. He therefore gave up his teaching and became head of the Legal Aid Society in his city, thus spending his time and skills protecting the legal rights of the indigent. He served at a minimum salary, paid out of the Community Fund, a fraction of what he could have earned in his own practice, if money had been his goal. By those of worldly ambition, he was **reproached for the name of Christ.** I have known ministers who were able to transcend what even many in the church would call "rising to the level of their abilities," who sincerely sought to live **by the will of God** (1 Pet 4:2) in their ministry, eschewing financial and social gains and rejecting the "success" syndrome in terms of size of church and influence, for the sake of service. They have lived by the wisdom offered as the closing words of a Seminary commencement address: "God does not call you to be successful but to be faithful." Then, the speaker added: "In God's eyes *faithfulness is success. . . . up there the only sign of succsess is faithfulness.*" Such are **reproached for the name of Christ** by many.

I have known young people—seemingly all too few these days—who have gone through high school and college, holding to high standards of honesty and purity, refusing to bow to the campus gods of sex and pleasure and to take the short cut to so-called academic success by "cheating" on exams or paying others to write term papers for them. There are people, too, in the business world who insist on giving a full day's work for their pay, who refuse to misrepresent their products for gain, or to cut corners on contracts for profit. In the eyes of the conscienceless business world they are **reproached for the sake of Christ**

These, and countless other ways, involve "voluntary suffering that one could easily avoid but chooses not to because of the commitment of one's faith." There are many ways other than public mistreatment or outright persecution to **share Christ's sufferings**—voluntarily to identify with Him in costly ways by ethical behavior patterned after His holiness and undertaken for His sake. In all such instances, those who do so are **blessed**: they are possessed of a quiet sense of the Spirit of the covenant-keeping God abiding with them and owning them as His own.

Not all suffering, however, is **blessed**. It is only the suffering which is honestly and sincerely undergone **for the name of Christ**, and **according to God's will** (vs 19) and not brought on by one's own folly, that is blessing. Peter, therefore, inserts a word of caution, directed either to fanatics or imposters, or both, to protect his comments on suffering from being misunderstood. He writes: **let none of you suffer as a murderer, or a thief, or a wrongdoer, or a mischief-maker.** The original language lumps the first three together, and sets the fourth apart for special attention, which, without any explanation for it, raises some difficulties. The first two words of the first triad—**murderer, thief**—are specific, whereas the third is general—**wrongdoer.** It has been felt by some that this third word must have had some specific reference in Peter's mind, along with the first two, They have hazarded a guess as to what that may have been. The church father, Tertullian, at the end of the second or beginning of the third century, translated the term "magicians." It has been noted that magicians were often professional "poisoners." Is it possible that there were murderers, thieves, poisoners in the churches of Asia Minor in Peter's day to whom he had to issue warnings?

When it is remembered that some of the Christian converts had come out of raw heathenism, and were not yet maturely versed in the meaning of the Christian faith, it is just possible that they may have reacted to their persecutors with a rather unsophisticated brand of "liberation theology," thinking they were serving Christ by killing their enemies by force or by poison, or relieving them of their goods by robbery. On the other hand, it may be that since this triad is grammatically set off from the fourth, Peter was merely using them rhetorically as contrasts to "what life 'according to the will of God' should be." There is a possibility, too, that some imposters, or infiltrators, had entered the Christian congregations, either to "sponge" on their hospitality or to be informers for their enemies, and that Peter's warning was intended for them. Then, too, it is possible that some people, totally misunderstanding the Christian faith, may have sought to utilize its manifest powers for their own ends. Simon the Magician, for example, had been baptized into the Christian movement in Samaria, and "was captivated when he saw the powerful signs and miracles that were taking place." He offered the apostles money, saying, "Give me the same power, so that anyone I lay my hands on will receive the Holy Spirit." Peter said to him: "You thought God's gift was for sale? Your money can go with you to damnation! You have neither part nor share in this, for you are corrupt in the eyes of God" (Acts 8:18ff., REB). It may have been to such as he that Peter's words in verse 15 were directed.

The word mischief-maker is a word used here only in the New Testament, and is not found in nonbiblical Greek writings until the second century A.D. Comparative philology, therefore, is of no help, and we are left to try to define it from the two Greek words which are conjoined in it—one who "watches over" or "looks after" things which are "irrelevant" to him. Many guesses have been made as to its meaning here. "Revolutionaries," "spies," "informers," "interferers with other people's business," "political agitators," "adepts from some illuminist sect," "financial swindlers who resort to litigation to extort funds," "Christian zealots, preaching proletariat or the freeing of slaves," have all been put forward as those described by this term. We cannot know who they were. In any case, whatever their activities, they were not authentic involvements in **Christ's sufferings** and they were therefore excluded from the blessings promised to those who were **reproached for**

the name of Christ.

This warning of Peter's has contemporary relevance, for there are those in every age who are drawn to the church because of certain personal advantages which seem to be available thereby. They need to be reminded that any blessings promised to the adherents of the Christian faith are gifts of the overflowing love of God, which are to be received with humility and gratitude and not sought after for self-aggrandizement of any sort.

A scholar well versed in early Christian history has said: "We scarcely realize today the shame which an honest Christian felt at being suspected by the civil authorities, arrested, imprisoned, condemned as an evil-doer (2 Tim 1:12, 2:9), or at acknowledging his relationship and friendship with those who endured such evil treatment . . . . It is at this point that 'to blush, to be ashamed' of the gospel or of Christ is an expression of fear or cowardice . . . and even of denial and apostasy." So, Peter cousels his readers: **If one suffers as a Christian, let him not be ashamed.** The nickname **Christian** described what Jesus' followers looked like to those outside the faith. It spoke not of institutional or legal status, but of their "personal and immediate attachment" to Christ as their Lord. They were "partisans of Christ (as soldiers of an emperor), his disciples (faithful to his doctrine and imitators of his example), consecrated to him and living from him (as branches from the vine), in a fashion that to touch a Christian was to get at the very person of Christ." Rather than being **ashamed . . . under that name,** the Christian should remember his "identity with his Master, that he represents and suffers for his cause," and boldly, yet humbly, glory in this identification by "heroic fidelity."

The word **glorify** is a "striking antithetis" to the word **ashamed.** "Shame" means "embarrassment," and when one is embarrassed he usually "blushes" and gets "red in the face." The outer coloring of the countenance, then, expresses the inner state of feeling. By looking at an embarrassed person, one can tell that he is **ashamed.** To **glorify** is to reveal the inner essence of something, to let its reality become visibly apparent. The rays of the sun, for example, **glorify** the sun. The light and heat of the rays make manifest what the sun really is as fire. To **glorify God,** then, would be so to act that the glory of His essence would become visible, so that what is hidden may be opened up to others. When Stephen made his great defense before the council, which resulted in martyrdom, we are told that he "gazed into heaven and saw the glory of God" (Acts 7:55). His boldness in witnessing for his Lord was manifested on his countenance: "the council saw that his face was like the face of an angel" (Acts 6:15). But even more than by his countenance, he reflected "the glory of God" by his words, which embodied the spirit of his Master: "Lord, do not hold this sin against them" (Acts 7:60); by which he irradiated his Lord's plea: "Father, forgive them, for they know not what they do" (Lk 23:34). Thus, both by word and demeanor, Stephen "glorified God," by manifesting the divine nature of the One for whom he died. So, counsels Peter: "Don't be red-faced with shame, but let your radiant face and worthy action under persecution show forth the nature of your Lord."

D. Suffering in the Light of Final Judgment *(4:17-19)*
(Exhortation)

Peter's sudden introduction of the element of **judgment** must be understood in the light of his general sweep of thought here. He has been seeking to encourage his readers to fidelity and courage in the light of their suffering for their Lord. His word about **judgment**, therefore, must be an additional "motive for joy and thanksgiving in the midst of persecutions." The conjunction with which the subject is introduced, translated *for*, reinforces this connection. It could well be translated "because," introducing a further reason for joy in persecution. The word used for **time** is a special word, referring not so much to the hands of a clock or the pages on a calendar, but to *quality* of time—a "fitting time," or an "appropriate occasion," or "the critical moment." It also sometimes refers to a "period of time," or a "stage in the development of the history of salvation." It was the conviction of the New Testament writers that in the coming of Jesus into the world, and in what He accomplished in His life, death, resurrection and ascension, a new stage of history had been inaugurated—the coming kingdom of God had drawn near and entered time. The years went right on after that as before, lineal duration did not change, but a "new age" had dawned. Henceforth, there was one "favorable time," one "today," which would last until the end of lineal time—the day of salvation, when men were to hear the good news of the gospel, and respond. Paul spoke of this as "the present time," or literally, "the now time" (Rom 3:26). The **judg-**

ment here mentioned is hardly the "last judgment," referred to by the word **end** in verse 17, but an ongoing judgment to be undergone by those who continue to **do right**, while committing their future to a faithful creator (vs 19). It is quite likely, therefore, that the **time** of which Peter is speaking is the period "inaugurated by the sufferings of Christ."

In what does this **judgment** consist? It is that which shows what God thinks of things. When Jesus said, referring to His coming act of redemption on the cross, "Now is the judgment of this world" (John 12:31), He meant that His death would reveal both what God thought about evil—it must be done to death, and what He thought about how it was to be destroyed—by suffering love. God's holiness necessitated the destruction of evil. Holy God and evil could not forever coexist. One or the other must be destroyed. But how can evil be destroyed without destroying men in whom it dwells. The New Testament answer is that God became man, identified Himself with sinful humanity, and in His Son, so to speak, destroyed evil by destroying Himself, in place of man. This revealed both His holy wrath against sin, but also His holy love for the sinner. By rescuing His Son from death through the resurrection, He also demonstrated His victory over evil.

Those who believe in the merit of Jesus' death and resurrection to overcome evil, become identified with Him in the struggle with evil in the world. As He told His disciples, "'A servant is not greater than his master.' If they persecuted me, they will persecute you; if they kept my word, they will keep yours also. But all this they will do to you on my account, . . ." (John 15:20f.). Since the redemption of the world came through suffering, the church must perforce join Him in whatever suffering the gospel provokes from a hostile world.

But more than that, the church is identified with the sinful world, and shares its tragedies. As a German commentator has said: "Why should not the house of God, the congregation of God's people, not first know judgment? They know the holy God. They can be the least astonished if they first experience judgment. . . . They do not escape the shocks and catastrophes which the wrath of God allows to come on the world. They experience and endure in common with the world the storms of judgment." But they, of all people, knowing something of the costliness of God's suffering in overcoming evil, are aware of the justice of God's judgments.and of their purpose. When **judg-**

ment strikes them, they can only acknowledge its justice, and plead for forgiveness and mercy. No alleviating virtues can they plead, as did the Pherisee in Jesus' parable, but can only join the publican in saying: "God, be merciful to me a sinner" (Lk 18:9ff.).

There is a certain type of biblical interpretation widely promoted in our time which teaches that before the world ends, there will be a "great tribulation" when evil will be rampant on the earth. The church, however, according to the teaching, is to be snatched up to God's abode, and escape this. The appeal, then, is: "Come to Jesus, so that you will not suffer as do those outside the church." Peter seems to counter this by insisting that the church is under **judgment** the same as the world. God "sends rain on the just and the unjust" (Matt 5:45). He also sends His judgments on the justified and the unjustified.

In fact, there is a strain in the Bible which suggests that **judgment** may fall first, and even more severely, on the people of God than it does on the world. "You only," God said through Amos, "have I known of all the families of the earth; therefore I will punish you for all your iniquities" (3:2). Jeremiah spoke likewise: "I shall first punish the city which bears my name; do you think that you can be exempt? No, you will not be exempt, . . . " He then adds: "I am summoning a sword against all the inhabitants of the earth" (25:29, REB). As human heings, the members of the church are bound up in the convulsions which shake the earth through resistance to God's will, and therefore bear God's **judgment** in this way. And because the church is unable to live up to the demand of God in her own life, she is under **judgment** for her own failure. The fact of **judgment** is reason to acknowledge her failure, and to plead again for God's mercy.

But God's **judgment** not only reminds the church of its failure and need of repentance; it also has the positive value of testing the church's faith. If it is necessary for perishable **gold** to be **tested by fire**, how much more must **your faith** be tested, so that its **genuineness** may be both demonstrated and refined (1 Pet 1:6f.). The testing process separates the pure metal from the dross, sifting out of the group those who were a part of it for unworthy reasons, as well as removing the elements of alloy in genuine faith which needs to be refined. **Judgment** both tests and purifies.

Remembrance of God's **judgment** also enables one to live in **fear**, or reverence, knowing that He **judges each one impartially ac-**

cording to his deeds (1:17). God's **judgment**, therefore, encourages one to **do right** (4:19), seeking to perform works which may meet the approval of Him **who is ready to judge the living and the dead** (4:5). It is a stimulus to respond to the divine command: **You shall be holy, for I am holy** (1:16).

Finally, the remembrance of God's **judgment** is a source of courage and fidelity in the struggle with evil. The pattern of encouragement here is Jesus, who was **reviled, but did not revile in return,** who **suffered** but **did not threaten, but rather trusted to him who judges justly** (2:23). With Him as our pattern and indwelling life we, too, when we **suffer according to God's will,** may have the courage to continue to **do right** for His sake, entrusting ourselves to a **faithful creator.**

The last half of verse 17 and verse 18 raise a frightful question. If God's **judgment . . . begins with the household of God . . . what will he the end of those who do not obey the gospel of God?** And, **"If the righteous man is scarcely saved, where will the impious and sinner appear?"** We have seen that the Christian, in solidarity with the sinful world, must bear **judgment** along with the whole human race. But this **judgment** has a separating effect; it works different outcomes on those who **obey the gospel,** and those who refuse it. God's judgments in history are prelude to a final **judgment,** which will separate those who respond to God's judgments now from those who do not. For those who respond to God's gracious taking of human sin into Himself on the cross—where He has shown what the final **judgment** will be, separation from God which Jesus experienced when He cried out: "My God, my God, why hast thou forsaken me?" (Mk 15:34), as He went out into the moral abyss of the universe seemingly alone and without His Father's sustaining presence—this fearful separation will not have to take place. Jesus has undergone it for them, and their willingness to suffer for Him in history has shown how genuine their faith in Him is. But what of those who refuse to believe? They are called **those who do not obey the gospel of God;** but to the early Christians the worst form of disobedience to God was to refuse to believe what He had done for men in Jesus Christ. To **disobey,** then, was to disbelieve— to refuse to hear the **gospel,** the *good news* of God's intervention in their hehalf by taking His final holy judgment into Himself and setting them free. What will happen to them?

Peter sharpens this question by a quotation of the Greek translation of the Old Testament, which shows that for him the question is an old one. **If the righteous man is scarcely saved, where will the impious and sinner appear?** Obviously, Peter does not mean by righteous those who are morally faultless in themselves; but those who, in spite of their own unrighteousness, have heard and obeyed the **gospel of God** by believing it, and entrusting **their souls to a faithful creator.** The idea that they are **scarcely** saved does not infer that the redemption wrought for men by Christ is uncertain or inadequate. This refers rather "to the difficulty of the way that leads to it." Peter is saying that the sufferings and trials which believers undergo in their journey toward the eternal city are trivial in the light of what it would mean to miss that city and be eternally cut off from fellowship with the holy God. He is encouraging them, therefore, to hold steady, at whatever cost, in their loyalty to Christ, in the light of the alternative if they do not. There will be a *reversal,* he says. Those who suffer now will finally be honored, and those who impose the suffering will know a fate in comparison with which the Christian's present suffering is trivial.

Peter is not interested in describing the form of the fate of those who disbelieve. Who could know what it would be like to be banished from the presence of God? He is concerned only to face his readers with the alternative outcomes of believing and not believing, and encouraging them to hold fast to their faith. In so doing, he is joining the writer of 2 Thessalonians: "This is evidence of the righteous judgment of God, that you may be made worthy of the kingdom of God, for which you are suffering—since God deems it just to repay with affliction those who afflict you . . . when the Lord Jesus is revealed from heaven . . . . They shall suffer the punishment of eternal destruction and exclusion from the presence of the Lord . . . when he comes . . . to be marveled at in all who have believed (1:5ff.).

These are harsh words for our generation, from whose lives all sense of **judgment** has largely disappeared. And, unfortunately, there have been Christians who have reveled in such words with a vindictiveness and a self-righteousness and a spiritual pride in the contemplated destruction of others which is far from the spirit of the One on the cross who is the final Judge. And were the final judgment made on an arbitrary, vindictive basis, well might we all be shocked by it.

To understand the final judgment in the light of the whole

teaching of the Bible, however, is to give it a different tone. In our hymnody we sing of the "King of mercy and of grace":

> Thou hast the true and perfect gentleness,
> No harshness hast Thou and no bitterness.

God's judgments are never vindictive. They are made from a cross! And all men are judged equally by that cross! If we were given our just deserts, *all* of us would be eternally banished from the presence of the holy God. The only difference between men at the last judgment will be that believers have found in that judgment *salvation*, and have gladly accepted God's gracious forgiveness, while disbelievers have refused to do so. And in the light of Peter's use of the present tense in the word **obey**, a tense form describing prolonged and continuous action, the unbelievers have made it a life habit to refuse. Therefore, those who face "exclusion from the presence of the Lord" do so not because God has so determined it, but because they themselves have insisted on it. God does not wish "that any should perish, but that all should reach repentance" (2 Pet 3:9). No man's eternal state is finally settled until he has made a determined decision to refuse God's desire to save him. And, if any go to perdition, they will have to stumble over a rugged cross to get there!

The reason men find God's **judgment** of those who refuse His proffered love difficult to accept is that they seem unable to grasp the nature of the God of the Bible. To say that "God is love" is to utter a falsehood, unless "love" is understood in terms of the nature of God. God is *holy* love! It is His nature to be holy. If He ceased to be holy, He would cease to be God. And holiness is the very antithesis of evil. Evil cannot exist in the presence of God without being destroyed, any more than germs can exist in the white light of a tropical sun. For germs to be destroyed by sunlight is not the result of the choice of the sun. It is just the nature of reality. That is the way things are! The wrath of God, then, in the Bible does not describe a fit of anger on God's part, or a decision God makes to be wrathful. It is just a way of describing the nature of God's holiness. In the Bible, when men have direct dealings with the holy God, they are amazed when they live through it. Said Jacob: "I have seen God face to face yet my life is spared" (Gen 32:30 REB). Said the Revelator: "When I saw him, I fell at his feet as though dead" (Rev 1:17). And between these two experiences from the first and last books of the Bible there are many indications of the human recoil from the holiness of the deity in whose presence sinful existence seems to be impossible. God's wrath against sin, then, is not personal pique, but the reality of His nature as holiness. Were He not that way, He would not be God.

If we knew this we would know that our very coming into His presence, even in sincere penitence and pleading for forgiveness, would be our undoing were it not that God has taken into Himself the costly action of redemption, by which He can keep faith with His own nature as holiness, yet justify unjust men. Our coming to Him is so often in the vein of students who bring to their mentor work that is faulty and ask: "Well, professor, did I get by?" We bring our faulty moral achievements into His presence, asking Him to let us by on the basis of His good nature or His indulgence, not knowing that if He did, He would violate His own nature as holiness, and destroy the very foundation of the moral universe.

Instead of dealing with us as we deserve, or in a fit of anger taking it out on us, so to speak, the *personal* aspect of God's love is seen in His *will to save us*, in spite of our unworthiness. In so doing, to maintain His holiness, He had to take into Himself the holy judgment on our sin, place Himself under that judgment in the awful tragedy of the cross, contriving thereby, at a cost too infinite for human calculation, to destroy our evil without destroying us. When men refuse to accept God's merciful offer to die in our place; to deal graciously with us by dealing ungraciously with Himself; to offer us a way of escape by refusing to escape Himself the consequences of His own holy nature; there is nothing more He can do. The situation then is like that of a man on a tall building who wants to get to the ground but refuses to use the elevator provided, insisting rather on jumping. His fate is not the choice of the one who has planned and provided the elevator, but his own. Destruction becomes then self-destruction.

Let no man blame God for his destruction, or the destruction of anyone else. "For God so loved the world that he gave his only Son, that whoever believes in him should not perish but have eternal life. For God sent the Son into the world, not to condemn the world, but that the world might be saved through him. He who believes in him is not condemned; he who does not believe is condemned . . . . And this is the judgment, that the light has come into the world, and men loved darkness rather than light . . ." (John 3:16ff.).

Verse 19 is a fitting conclusion to Peter's rather long section on the sufferings of the church in a hostile society. If they **suffer according to God's will**, they should continue to **do right** at whatever cost, and **entrust their souls to a faithful creator**. To entrust is to "give over" something into the care or protection of another of whose fidelity we are certain. This is the same word used by the Psalmist (31:5) which Jesus quoted as He died: "Father, into thy hands I *commit* my spirit!" (Lk 23:46, emphasis added). How could we do better than to face the crises of life as Jesus faced the crisis of death!

And who is the one to whom Peter counsels us to **entrust** ourselves? Our **faithful creator**! "The Lord is the everlasting God, the Creator of the ends of the earth" (Isa 40:28). He has "measured the waters in the hollow of his hand and marked off the heavens with a span, enclosed the dust of the earth in a measure and weighed the mountains in scales and the hills in a balance. . . . Behold, the nations are like a drop from a bucket, and are accounted as the dust on the scales; behold, he takes up the isles like fine dust. . . . All the nations are as nothing before him, they are accounted by him as less than nothing and emptiness. . . . it is he who sits above the circle of the earth, and its inhabitants are like grashoppers; who stretches out the heavens like a curtain, . . . who brings princes to nought, and makes the rulers of the earth as nothing" (Isa 41:12ff.). *This* is our **faithful creator**.

But, granted that He is mighty, is He gracious and trustworthy? "He will feed his flock like a shepherd, he will gather the lambs in his arms, he will carry them in his bosom, and gently lead those that are with young" (Isa 40:11). Yes, He is mighty, and He is **faithful**. We may safely **entrust** ourselves to Him, for time and eternity! A nineteenth century hymn writer has well captured Peter's thought about the church's suffering in a hostile world:

If I find Him, if I follow,
    What His guerdon here?
"Many a sorrow, many a labor,
    Many a tear."

If I ask Him to receive me,
    Will He say me nay?
"Not till earth and not till heaven
    Pass away."

Finding, following, keeping, struggling,
    Is He sure to bless?
"Saints, apostles, prophets, martyrs,
    Answer, 'Yes.'"

VII

FINAL ADMONITIONS (5:1-11)

In this last chapter, Peter focuses his admonitions more on the corporate life of the congregation than on individuals. It is introduced by a conjunction which may merely "indicate a transition to something new," and could be translated "now," which some translators use. It could, however, be used inferentially, "denoting that what it introduces is the result of or an inference from what precedes," in which case it could be translated "so," "therefore," "consequently," "accordingly." (The conjunction is omitted in some texts, but those which are considered best include it). It is likely that it has an inferential use here, thus tying what Peter is about to say with what he has been saying in the previous paragraph. This judgment is strengthened by the fact that Peter customarily uses this conjunction to introduce a consequence of what he has just been saying (see e.g. 2:1, 7; 4:1, 7). Furthermore, there is a parallel in the movement of thought here with an earlier section of the epistle. The passage 3:13-4:6, a section dealing with persecution, is followed by 4:7-11, "which deals with the common life of the church"; here, likewise, a section that discusses persecution (4:12-19) is followed by 5:1-6, which is "concerned with mutual respect and leadership in the church." There would seem to be a connection between the two in the mind of Peter.

What is the connection? If individual Christians were to be able to summon the courage and fidelity necessary to endure persecution, they needed the strengthening which comes through a sense of comradeship in the community of faith. They needed the encouragement of leaders who were faithful **examples to the flock.** They needed the common bonds of unity which knit them to the group through the subordination of the inexperienced **younger** members to the experienced **elders,** and the **humility toward one another** which subordinated the interests of each to the welfare of all. They also needed the encouragement which came through the knowledge that they were a part of a larger fellowship than their own little congregations. The **experience of suffering** endured by the **brotherhood throughout the world** would stimulate them to faithfulness **for their sake,** as together they all sought to be faithful to their Lord. They were all in it together, and none should let the others down!

A. Admonitions on Congregational Life *(5:1-5)*
(Exhortation)

It is likely that no group will rise higher than its leadership. No matter how skilled or brave individual soldiers are, no army can be effective without qualified officers who can, by efficient strategy, adequate tactics, and personal inspiration, transform the scattered efforts of individuals into a unified concentration of power. Since the documents of the early church preserved by later generations, now known as the New Testament, were more concerned with the church's message than its organizational structure, it is difficult to draw a complete picture of the titles and functions of church leaders in those far off days.

The only title given in 1 Peter to officers in the local church is **elders**. The terms **apostle** (1:1), **those who preached the good news** (1:12), and the untitled **Silvanus and Mark** (5:12f.), appear to apply to itinerants rather than to members of local churches. **Elders** are mentioned in the Book of Acts and the pastoral epistles as those who, both in the Jerusalem church and the churches of pagan origin, along with the "apostles," were the leaders. We are told that Paul and Barnabas, on Paul's first missionary journey, "appointed *elders* for them in every church" (Acts 14:23, emphasis added). They were associated with the "apostles" in determining doctrinal questions (Acts 15:6, 22, 23; 16:4; 21:18); they were pastors, preachers and teachers of the faith (Acts 20:28, 1 Tim 5:17; Titus 1:9); they presided over the church's almsgiving (Acts 11:30, 20:35); they governed the churches (1 Tim 5:17, 1 Thess 5:12); and they were devout leaders and guides, charged with the spiritual welfare of the church members (Heb 13:7, 17). Both the office and the functions of elders were taken over into the Christian communities from Judaism. Eastern respect for age and experience likely led to the assignment of community responsibilities to the mature in years. Later, the term was broadened to include some who may have developed maturity of judgment and spiritual insight while still young in age.

Peter's description of himself as **a fellow elder** is an expression found nowhere else in the New Testament. The term "fellow servant" is found 10 times; "fellow worker" appears 13 times; "fellow prisoner" 3 times; and "fellow traveler" twice; but **fellow elder** is unique here. There are those who would deny Petrine authorship to this letter on the basis that Peter was an "apostle," not an "elder." We have already seen that this is a doubtful conclusion (see pp. 70f.). Obviously, if Peter did not write the letter, whoever published it under his name intended its readers to believe that he did. If there were any possibility that this self-description here would have raised a doubt about Petrine authorship, whoever issued the letter under his name could very easily have solved that problem by not using this title here. The fact that he used it indicates that in his mind and in that of his readers there was no conflict between the title **apostle** (1;1) and **fellow elder** (5:1).

Three major reasons could well account for Peter's self-description as a **fellow elder**. Some have suggested that Peter may actually have served alongside elders in local churches in Asia Minor when, as a visiting apostle, he appointed them to service. This lies within the realm of possibility, but seems to be a conjecture introduced to solve a problem which can be solved better on other grounds.

Others see Peter here raising the office of **elder** to the level of that of the **apostle**, paralleling Paul's "daily pressure" of "anxiety for all the churches" (2 Cor 11:28) with the elders' task: **Tend the flock of God that is your charge.** This gives the office of elder a quasi-flavor of "apostolic successionism," thus investing the ministry of the **elder** with an apostolic-like authority. This would seem to place more theological freight on this one expression than it should have to carry. Had this been in Peter's mind, one would have expected him to develop it more clearly than merely introducing it in such a subtle fashion. Furthermore, there seems to be no direct support for the view elsewhere in the New Testament. To enunciate a doctrine of this weight on such flimsy underpinning is risky at best.

Others have seen here a touching reflection of the humility Peter is commending to others in verses 5 and 6. Even though he is an apostle, he places himself on the same level as the leaders of the local churches. His apostleship was his by virtue of circumstance as a participant in the historic career of Jesus, and as a witness of the resurrection, and by the inscrutable will of God, but not because of any special virtue in himself. God had willed to give him a special function as an apostle, yet he stood alongside his fellow elders in their common task of tending **the flock of God** in a community where he who would be "first" must be "slave of all" (Mk 10:44 REB). Peter's apostleship was never doubted, and his willingness to be a **fellow elder** with the others increased his status as an apostle. Even Paul, who had to fight to establish his "apostleship," and did not hesitate to do so when the interests of truth demanded it, more than once referred to himself as a "fellow worker" with other leaders of the church who were not apostles (Rom 16:3, 9, 21; 2 Cor. 8:23; Phil 2:25; Col 4:11; Philemon 24). If Paul could be an "apostle" and a "fellow worker" at the same time, why could not Peter have been both an "apostle" and a **fellow elder**? This appeals to us as the best interpretation of Peter's use of the title **fellow elder** here.

In addition to being a **fellow elder**, Peter designates himself as **a witness of the sufferings of Christ**. Three interpretations of this phrase have been proposed. 1) An eyewitness of Jesus' sufferings who reports what he saw; 2) a preacher who proclaims the life and work of Christ, an example of those whom Luke calls "witnesses" whom the risen Lord commissioned "that repentance and forgiveness of sins should be preached in his name" (24:47f.); 3) one who suffered for his faith in Christ, as did Stephen who was called a "witness" when his blood was shed (Acts 22:20). Although, since many commentators deny Petrine authorship to the letter, the third of these fits best with that denial, it seems to me that the first interpretation is the most natural here. For one thing, it can include the other two. It was the original group of apostles who were commissioned to be "witnesses" in the sense of "preachers," in "Jerusalem and in all Judea and Samaria and to the end of the earth" (Acts 1:8), so that Peter could have been an apostolic eyewitness of Jesus' last hours and a preacher as well. The original apostles, too, were forewarned by their Lord that they would "be dragged before governors and kings for my sake, to bear testimony ["witness" in the Greek] before them and the Gentiles (Matt.10:18). Hence, Peter could have been an "apostle" and still a "witness" in the sense of suffering for his Lord. There is no reason why, then, Peter could not at one and the same time have been a proclaimer of Christ, and a "witness" in the sense that he suffered for his Lord, and a witness of the sufferings of Christ as an apostle who saw with his own eyes the sufferings of Christ on the cross.

Grammatical efforts to remove the "eyewitness" quality from the expression **witness of the sufferings of Christ** seem strained and desperate. One has been to place Peter in the same category as his readers, when he describes them as those who **share Christ's sufferings** (4:13). The word **share**, however, has a quite different connotation from the word **witness**. Had he meant that, he could easily have called himself "a sharer" **in the sufferings of Christ**. Again, to note that Peter uses the article with **fellow elder** but not with **witness**, and to make the deduction that they therefore have the same point of reference, would hardly have occurred to the reader unless he had a preconceived thesis to prove. Had Peter wanted to bind his function as **witness** in with the experience of his readers, as he did his function as **elder**, he could very easily have called himself a "fellow witness." But he did not.

The two expressions, therefore, **fellow elder** and **witness**, convey two different things. The first expresses Peter's "solidarity" with his readers in understanding their task; the second expresses his difference from them as an authoritative **witness** to the Lord of whom he writes. In this dual reference, he indicates "that he is perfectly capable of understanding those to whom he is appealing, but . . . he distinguishes himself from them in that which is unique in his apostleship." After all, why should his readers accept what he is writing to them as authoritative? His purpose is to declare **that this is the true grace of God**, and to summon them to **stand fast in it** (5:12). He authenticates his message at the very beginning of his letter by declaring himself **an apostle of Jesus Christ** (1:1). It is difficult not to believe that here, at the close of his letter in 5:1, he is declaring to them that he was an *eyewitness* of **the sufferings of Christ**, and therefore knew of what he was speaking.

A further description Peter gives of himself is that he is **a partaker in the glory that is to be revealed**. This is a difficult expression to translate from the original language. The expression **is to be revealed** involves two verbs in the present tense, which ordinarily describes something going on presently, now. On the other hand, the present tense of the verb *is to be* may describe something that is "about to," or is "on the point of" happening. Again, it may simply be a round about way of speaking of the future. So, is Peter speaking of a **glory** which is now in progress, or one that is about to happen, or one that will take place in the future? Grammatically, it seems impossible to decide. The editors of the *Revised Standard Version* have opted for the third alternative, and probably rightly, in the light of other passages in the letter. Peter earlier speaks of **a salvation ready to be revealed in the last time** (1:5). He has counseled his readers to live in the light of the fact that the **end of all things is at hand** (4:7). He speaks of his readers as, at a later time, being **glad when his glory is revealed** (4:13). Shortly after this passage, he tells them that they **will obtain the unfading crown of glory** later on, **when the chief Shepherd is manifested** (5:4), and that **after they have suffered a little while,** the One who has called them **to his eternal glory in Christ, will himself restore, establish and strengthen** them (5:10). When, therefore, Peter speaks of **the glory that is to be revealed,** he likely is referring to Christ's final glory at the end of time.

But again, this passage may involve the frequent paradox in the Scriptures between the "then," and the "now," and the "one day"; between the "already" and the "not yet" (see pp. 134f.). In one sense the end has already come, yet we still await it. In cross, resurrection, and ascension, Christ has already triumphed over evil; yet that triumph is hidden, seen only by the eyes of faith, and still awaits the time when "at the name of Jesus every knee should bow, in heaven and on earth and under the earth, and every tongue confess that Jesus Christ is Lord" (Phil. 2:10f.). Although Christ's glory is yet to be revealed, like the sun before sunrise, it is already casting its rays on the eastern horizon, and those who believe in Him can in some sense bask in its wonder while waiting for it to burst over the horizon in all its splendor. Peter and his readers both could rejoice in its light, while awaiting its full revelation. Proleptically they could **partake in the glory that is to be revealed.** As Peter has said but a few sentences before: **the spirit of glory and of God rests upon you** (4:14). One writer has phrased this: "Participation in the glory which is going to burst forth at the final unveiling . . . exists now, is lasting, and is tied to no point in time."

His glory was dramatically manifested on special occasions in the past. At the Transfiguration, by "the transformation of his appearance and the unearthly whiteness with which his garments shone Jesus appeared for a moment in the state appropriate to the heavenly mode of existence." This was an "unveiling" which foreshadowed the final unveiling of the glory that is to be revealed. Peter was one of three present on that occasion. Furthermore, the risen Lord made a special post-resurrection appearance to Peter (1 Cor 15:5). It is difficult to believe that, as **with the suffering of Christ,** he both identified himself with the experience of those to whom he wrote yet differentiated himself from them as a historic witness of that which they had not seen, he is not doing the same thing here. As a **fellow elder** he stands *with* them as **the spirit of glory** rests upon the Christian community, but at the same time stands *above* them as an apostle who had witnessed Christ's glory at the Transfiguration and in a post-resurrection appearance (see p. 66). After all, who would have known about the risen Christ if those to whom He had appeared after His death had not made it known to others? As Peter himself told the group assembled in Cornelius' home: "God raised him on the third day, and made him manifest; *not to all the people but to us who were chosen by God as witnesses*" (Acts 10:40f., emphasis added).

The function of **elders** was to **tend the flock of God that is your charge**. The image of shepherd and sheep in relation to God and His people has its roots in the Old Testament. "The Lord is my shepherd" is perhaps the most widely known verse in the entire Hebrew Bible (Ps 23:1). "He will feed his flock like a shepherd" would be a close second (Isa 40:11). Both Jeremiah (23:1-4) and Ezekiel (34) broadened the shepherd figure to include those whom God had given charge over the spiritual welfare of His people. "I will give you shepherds after my own heart," said God through Jeremiah,"who will feed you with knowledge and understanding" (3:15). The New Testament took over this figure, first thinking of Christ as "the good shepherd" who lays down his "life for the sheep" (John 10:14f.), or, as Peter calls Him, the **chief Shepherd** (5:4); then applying the figure to the **elders**, who were the spiritual leaders of the congregations. Said Paul to the **elders** of the church at Ephesus: "Keep guard over yourselves and over all the flock of which the Holy Spirit has given you charge [made you "guardians," "superintendents," "bishops"], as shepherds of the church of the Lord, which he won for himself by his own blood" (Acts 20:28, REB). Tending sheep covered the entire range of a shepherd's duty— feeding, guiding, protecting, sheltering, healing their hurts, searching for them when they strayed. Peter's counsel to the **elders** to **tend the flock of God** has unmistakable echoes of his own experience with the risen Christ who, after testing his love, gave him the threefold admonition—"Feed my lambs," "Tend my sheep," "Feed my sheep" (John 21:15ff.).

Peter's reference to **elders** gives us few clues as to the organizational life of the church in his time, or to the precise assignment of tasks to various types of ecclesiastical leaders. The picture of an **elder** as a shepherd, as one writer has remarked, "does not serve to explain the meaning of a function, but rather to clarify the spirit of it. The attitude of a shepherd, more than his task, is taken into consideration." Furthermore, it is possible that leadership tasks in specific congregations may, in some measure, have been determined by local conditions. The two expressions—**the flock of God that is your charge** in verse 2, and **those in your charge** [literally, "those who fall to your lot"] in verse 3, are "limiting as well as indicative, having a nuance of allotment and of delimitation. . . . The same flock is divided into local groups each having their own structures and accountabilities."

The New Testament counsel that everything in the church should be done "decently and in order" (1 Cor 14:40) required some sort of government. As a leader of the 16th century Reformation said: "in every society of men, we see the necessity of some polity in order to preserve the common peace, and to maintain concord." He insisted, too, that "our ignorance . . . , slothfulness, and . . . the vanity of our minds require external aids" to the proper ordering of the church's corporate life. Rather than fixing these in universal, unchangeable, statutory ways, however, the church seems, under the guidance of the Holy Spirit, to have developed its outward structures of order and discipline as necessity arose, such as the appointment of deacons in response to a dispute over charitable distributions (Acts 6:1ff.). It is difficult, therefore, to piece together a complete picture of the organization of the New Testament church, or to draw from 1 Peter much clear guidance as to church order and polity. We see only hints of what was going on, at the time he wrote, in the local churches of Asia Minor.

The first, and central concern of a worthy **elder** in assuming responsibility for those placed in his charge is to remember that they are the flock of God. As a German commentator has noted: "They will rightly tend the flock if they continually remember, it is God's flock; responsibility for them is entrusted to us, but they are his possession." The moment any church leader begins to think that those in his charge belong to him rather than to God, he has missed his calling, trying to become an owner rather than a servant of those who rightfully belong to another owner, for whose sake they have been put in his charge. This is reinforced by the fact that some manuscripts in the original add, after the word **willingly**, "as God would have you." Should these words reflect Peter's thought, it is a double reminder that the flock not only belongs to **God**, but the service of the flock is a task directly willed by God, and is to be discharged solely in responsibility to Him.

This means that "the ownership-relation of the flock to God corresponds to the servant-relationship of the shepherd to God." Commentators rightly point to Peter's own experience with the risen Lord as the root of his counsel here. Peter had had the bitter experience of thrice denying his Lord on the night of His betrayal. On Easter morning, the angel who met the three women at the empty tomb, told them to "go, tell his disciples *and Peter* that he is going before you to Galilee" (Mk 16:7, emphasis added). Then later, the risen Lord asked Peter three times: "Simon, son of John, do you love me?" Upon receiving an affirmative answer, Jesus said to him: "Tend my sheep" (John 21:16). The penitent Peter now knew that he belonged forever to His Lord, and that his life's task from now on was to **tend** his Master's flock. Peter was Christ's; the flock was Christ's; tending them was his service to Christ. I once knew a minister who spoke of his people as a rather motley and speckled flock, whom all the perfumes of Arabia would not sweeten; but he insisted likewise that they were *God's* **flock** and his **charge**, and nothing would dislodge him from carrying out his responsibilities to them. He understood what the true relation of an **elder** to his people should be.

A textual problem is worthy of attention at this point. Some manuscripts, as the *Revised Standard Version* marginal note indicates, insert a word which may help to define the meaning of **tend**. It is the word from which our word "bishop" comes, and means to "exercise oversight." This is not a technical term, suggesting that episcopacy was already established in the church at that time, but a word descriptive of the *function* of those whom Peter calls **elders**. It means to "take care of," "to accept the responsibility of looking after," "to bend every energy toward the welfare of." The leaders of the church were, therefore, summoned to bear heavy and often costly responsibilities for the welfare of others. The task of the ancient shepherd sometimes involved weeks or months away from home, carrying full responsibility for the safety and welfare of the sheep, guarding them from accident, or straying, or from wild animals, or from thieves, sometimes at great risk to his own safety. Especially when a shepherd was a "hireling" who tended sheep which were not his own, the temptation was great to shirk duty, and to look out for one's own welfare rather than that of the sheep. That such behavior frequently took place is confirmed by the prophets' denunciation of shepherds who "have not attended to" the sheep (Jer 23:1ff.), who were feeding themselves instead of the sheep (Ezek 34:2ff.); and by Jesus' description of the "hireling and not a shepherd, whose own the sheep are not," who protects himself "and cares nothing for the sheep" when danger arises (John 10:12ff.). True shepherding took courage, commitment, effort, the refusal to "traffic with the good of others." In the light of the dangers facing the Christian groups of Asia Minor at that time, it is easy to see why Peter called the leaders of the churches to a faithful discharge of their responsibilities. In a time of crisis, the leaders were "guardians" of the welfare of others whom Christ had "obtained with his own blood" (Acts 20:28).

Peter now introduces three antithetical adverbial phrases which describe the *manner* in which **elders** should **tend the flock of God**. Because of parallels of "vocabulary and related motifs," as well as "the triadic, parallel and antithetic structure" of verses 2 and 3, some scholars conclude that Peter was making use of a "primitive Christian instruction for office" which was patterned after the role of the "supervisor" in the Qumran community who had oversight of the group. This is a disputed point among scholars, but seems of little interpretative consequence in the present passage. Whether Peter was making use of a slowly gathering body of teaching about the duties of church leaders, or spontaneously writing out of his own mind here, the meaning of his admonitions is the same.

First, he encourages the **elders** to undertake their difficult responsibilities **not by constraint but willingly**. The word used to describe the negative side of this antithesis, **not by constraint**, or "compulsion," is used only here in the New Testament. It seems to denote something done by "force," by "necessity," by "sheer duty." A great man once said that "duty is the noblest word in the English language." There can hardly be anything wrong in doing one's duty, and there are times, when one's spirit is low and his energies flagging, that he is held to his task by little more than duty. But this should not be the continual nor characteristic mood of the Christian leader. And when it settles on one, says Peter in the strong imperative, strive to overcome it, "renew your fervor . . . , acquire a better understanding of your task," go at it **willingly**, "gladly," "wholeheartedly." It has been said that there is "no greater temptation for the shepherd of souls than growing weary of souls. One prays without fervor, one preaches without enthusiasm, one goes through his ministry as a burden which remains sacred, but which weighs us down." It is against this mood that Peter is cautioning when he counsels Christian leaders to go at their task **not by constraint but willingly.**

Another textual difficulty obtrudes here. *The Revised Standard Version* lists an additional clause to the text—"as God would have you." This is omitted from the best texts, but "it is hard to explain why it was added if it was not part of the original text." If it is authentic, it would be of assistance in stimulating the **elders** to do their work **willingly** rather than "grudgingly and reluctantly," by reminding them that they were servants of God, that their task was assigned by Him, and that they were followers of the "good shepherd" who laid down "his life for the sheep" (John 10:11).

The second antithesis is: **not for shameful gain but eagerly.** From the very beginning of the church's existence, the leadership of the church was supported financially by the other members of the congregations. This likely had its roots in the arrangements for sustaining the religious leadership of ancient Israel, where the priests were given holdings of land among the various tribes and were supported by their share in the various offerings over which they presided (Deut 18:1ff., Num 35:2ff.). The New Testament clearly indicates that the principle involved in this Old Testament arrangement was carried over into the early Christian churches. Paul plainly states this: "Do you not know that those who are employed in the temple service get their food from the temple, and those who serve at the altar share in the sacrificial offerings? In the same way, the Lord commanded that those who proclaim the gospel should get their living by the gospel" (1 Cor.9:13f.; see also 1 Tim 5:17f.).

The acquisitive instinct in human nature is strong, however, and there were those who took advantage of this arrangement by thinking more highly of their support than they did of their ministry. The early Christians tried to weed out those whose motivation was more monetary than ministerial. Jesus Himself had denounced religious leaders who made "long prayers" but took financial advantage of the helpless (Mk 12:40). One of the qualifications which the churches established for an elder and a deacon was that he should be "no lover of money . . . not greedy for gain" (1 Tim 3:3, 8; Titus 1:7). Peter himself had rebuked Simon, the sorcerer, for seeking to "obtain the gift of God with money" (Acts 8:18ff.). Paul favored silencing false teachers who were "teaching for base gain" (Tit 1:11), and warned against "lovers of money" (2 Tim 3:2). Peter, knowing the weakness of the human heart, and the power of the temptation to surrender to the base motivation of **shameful gain**, warns the **elders** to whom he was writing to avoid it. For, as one writer has commented: "Nothing is as shameful and indecent as the spirit of filthy lucre in the service of souls."

The antithesis to this is to serve **eagerly**. This adverb is used only here in the New Testament. Its adjectival form, however, may throw interesting light on it. Both Matthew and Mark use it in describing the state of the disciples' spirit in the Garden of Gethsemane, when they fell asleep rather than watching during Jesus' prayer struggle. Jesus said to them: "the spirit indeed is willing, but the flesh is weak" (Mk.14:38, Mt 26:41). Could it be that, in writing to his **elders**, Peter suddenly recalled those words, and sought to reverse them in the experience of his readers: "Let the willing spirit overcome the weakness of the flesh!" The adjective is also used in describing Paul's strong desire to spread Christian truth throughout the world: "I am *eager*," he said, "to preach the gospel to you also who are in Rome" (Rom 1:15, emphasis added). The word "evokes good will, promptitude, spontaneity, earnestness, ardor, devotion, and even enthusiasm." An enthusiastic sense of the eternal worth of the gospel is a good antidote to overvaluing **shameful gain**.

Nearly a century ago, a promising minister was recruited to teach religion at a small church college, whose finances were in a rather desperate condition. He went, and stayed until he died. There was no professor on the faculty who had such a profound spiritual influence on the students as he, and no one knew of his financial struggle—not even his children!—until it was laid bare in his diary made available at his death. His salary was $400 per year! But he was not always sure of getting it, because of the precarious condition of the college finances. Three years after he undertook his assignment, he wrote in his diary: "My every-day suit is threadbare and almost ragged. Life is no kindergarten affair. Work constant and hard, educating pupils . . . , and shouldering the standing of the college, and a constant gnawing on account of an income too small for our needs which must be pieced out by special unforeseen providences. What we shall do to get through this present strait I cannot tell." Six years later, he wrote: "I am in a horror of great darkness over our finances. . . . My God, my burdens are more than I can bear, and my wife and some of the children are worn and weak. I only ask a living wage, but do give me that, so that we may serve thee without distraction. I solemnly promise to use every cent for thee, but let us not be so crushed any longer. . . . As for luxuries, leisure, and recreation, we leave them to [others], or as Thou wilt, but save us from crushing, paralyzing, maddening poverty." Here was a servant of God who could have benefited himself financially by turning elsewhere, but continued his faithful service where he was, under the compulsion of a conviction that God had called him to his work. As did Jeremiah, he took his complaint to God, and nobody but his wife knew of his desperate plight. To students and to the public, he continued to labor **not for shameful gain but eagerly,** and to demonstrate how enthusiastic dedication to Christ can overcome the lust for lucre.

Peter's third antithesis is: **not as domineering over those in your charge but being examples to the flock.** This is another instance where Peter's memory of His Lord's teaching may have fashioned his choice of words. The word translated **domineering** means to "lord it over," "show one's authority over," "rule." Translators have sought to give it vividness by such expressions as: "never be a dictator"; "do not be constantly shouting orders"; "do not act like little kings"; "do not act like a strong-armed chief"; "aim not at being little tin gods." These are efforts to convey the flavor of what Jesus said in Peter's hearing: "You know that those who are supposed to rule over the Gentiles *lord it over* them, and their great men exercise authority over them. But it shall not be so among you; but whoever would be great among you must be your servant, and whoever would be first among you must be slave of all" (Mk 10:42ff., emphasis added). The italicized expression is the exact Greek word used here by Peter.

The kingdom of God must have rule and authority, but it is not the sort illustrated by the "politico-military" rule of the kingdoms of this world. Earthly kings often manifest their authority by "tyrannizing their people and make themselves masters by brutality." They frequently display "a relish for power in itself, and often by a . . . contempt for subordinates." The exercise of authority in the church, however, is not a matter of rank, or status as a leader, but involves a spiritual authority which comes from God and is exercised by those who are supposed to have developed a spiritual maturity which in itself is authoritative. Real spiritual authority is self-authenticating. Where such spiritual authority exists, arrogance and autocracy are out of place. Often, in Paul's writings, one sees what the attitude of a true shepherd should be. He writes to the Corinthians: "Not that we lord it over your faith; we work with you for your joy" (2 Cor 1:24). He reminded the Thessalonians of his visit with them: "you know how, like a father with his children, we exhorted each one of you and encouraged you and charged you to lead a life worthy of God" (1 Thess 2:11f.). Timothy was reminded that church leaders should be "not violent but gentle" (1 Tim 3:3); not "quarrelsome but kindly to every one, . . . correcting his opponents with gentleness" (2 Tim 2:24f.). Titus was urged not to "be arrogant or quick-tempered . . . but . . . master of himself, . . . and self-controlled" (Titus 1:7f.).

It is interesting that Peter does not use an antonym as the corrective of **domineering,** such as "relax," ""be lenient," "indulge," "give quarter," "tolerate," "be humble." Humility might be a cure for **domineering,** but that was expected of all of them (vs 5), and was not a characteristic reserved for the leadership only. Peter solves his problem positively by suggesting that the **elders be examples to the flock.** In so doing, he was recalling an aspect of shepherd behavior mentioned by Jesus: "he goes before them, and the sheep follow him" (John 10:4). Peter had already focused attention on the **chief Shepherd** who had left them **an example** that they **should follow in his steps** (2:21). Now he proposes that the **elders,** following the **chief Shepherd,** should keep out in front of their **flock,** so that their sheep might follow in their steps as they, in turn, followed in Christ's steps. In other words, the function of spiritual leadership is to lead spiritually.

The authority of one's moral leadership is based not on position, rank, privilege, status, but on the degree to which the leader identifies himself with those who follow him and his willingness to take costly action in their behalf by following the **chief Shepherd** Himself. The authority of the **chief Shepherd** lies not so much in the command "'Go!" as in the summons: "Come, follow me!" Or, if His command should be "Go!" it is never "Go alone." His imperative is always accompanied with a promise. One may obey the imperative in the strength that comes from the Commander's word: "lo, I am with you always, to the close of the age" (Mt 28:20). Hence, in the church, leaders and followers together move forward in the confidence that they are accompanied always by One who issues no commands to go where He is not willing to go with them. The leaders lead as they follow their Leader, praying:

> Lead on, O King Eternal:
> . . . .
> Thy cross is lifted o'er us;
> We journey in its light.

It is heartening to know that

> Christ leads us through no darker doors
> Than he went through before.

A former student of mine, a second lieutenant during the Second World War, had been ordered forty-two times to make incalculably costly patrols behind enemy lines at night, to gather information. He finally decided that his superior officers, who issued the orders, were making no use of the information, but were ordering the raids largely to make their records look good in the hope of advancement in rank. When a major ordered him to make the forty-third patrol, he sent word back: "Tell the major, if he will come and go with me on the raid, I will do it; but otherwise I won't!" When told of this, I remarked that I did not know that such insubordination was tolerated in military circles. He replied: "There was no discipline they could have inflicted on me at that time that was worse than I was going through every day in battle, and I simply did not care what they thought."

However military men would judge his action, in my opinion the lieutenant had much on his side. If the leaders were unwilling to assume the risks they were ordering their men to undergo, especially when the risks were to no purpose other than to advance their own personal military standing, they had lost the moral right to leadership. It was on some such ground as this that Peter was counseling his **elders**. Don't act as **domineering over those in your charge**! Don't exercize authority by rank! Don't issue orders from above! Lead your **flock**! Go before them into danger! As your Lord has led you, **arm yourselves with the same thought** (4:1), and lead your people! They will be more likely to respond when they see you ahead than when they hear orders from behind! As a French commentator has said: "The first duty of elders is to reproduce as exactly as possible the traits of the Savior, with the maximum of lucidity, so that the faithful may learn how they may conform to the Savior in their own behavior. . . . Thus, the authentic Shepherd identifies himself with the message that he transmits, or better with Christ himself."

After the triad of antitheses with which Peter has sought to characterize the *mood* in which the responsibility of **elders** should be carried out, he climaxes his appeal by highlighting the ultimate *motive* for fidelity in their task. It is that **when the chief Shepherd is manifested you will obtain the unfading crown of glory.** The final approval of Him **who is ready to judge the living and the dead** (4:5), who **judges each one impartially** (1:17), who **judges justly** (2:23), is the highest goal worth striving for.

Peter has earlier referred to Christ as **the Shepherd and Guardian** of their souls (2:25), and has referred to the **elders** as those who **tend the flock of God** (5:2). Here he differentiates between them and their Lord by referring to Him as the **chief Shepherd.** This reminds the **elders** once more that the sheep do not belong to them but to God, and that they, too, are a part of the flock of the one great **Shepherd.** They are only "vice-shepherds," "subsitutes," "surrogates," "representatives," "vicars," who exercise their ministry "in imitation of Christ and in union with him."

The word **manifested** is used by Peter earlier in connection with Jesus' being born into the world to be made visible in His earthly life (1:20; see also 1 Tim 3:16). Elsewhere, it is used to describe the future coming of Christ when He "appears . . . in glory" (Col. 3:4; see also 1 John 2:28). As once His eternally invisible existence had become visible to human eyes in the form of His earthly life, so finally His present invisible existence will again become visible, so that "every eye will see him" (Rev.1:7). That will be the moment when "God judges the secrets of men by Christ Jesus" (Rom.2:16); when we shall discover that everything has been "open and laid bare to the eyes of him with whom we have to do," even to the "thoughts and intentions of the heart" (Heb 4:12f.). Ultimately, at long last, when time is no more; when hidden realities become plain, and we stand before the final judge with no defense but His mercy; the only thing that really matters is His verdict. If, as Peter counseled his **elders,** we shall go about our daily tasks with that moment in mind, how different life would be!

The word **obtain**, or "receive," "get back," "recover," has two nuances which are significant. First, it is used several times in the New Testament to describe what takes place at the last judgment. "For we must all appear before the judgment seat of Christ, so that each one may *receive* good or evil, according to what he has done in the body" is typical (1 Cor 5:10, emphasis added; see also Eph 6:8, Col 3:25). Secondly, the word evokes the picture of a return on an investment. It is found in the parable of the talents, when Jesus said to the man with only one talent: "you ought to have invested my money with the bankers, and at my coming I should have *received* what was my own with interest" (Mt 25:27, emphasis added). Peter here is speaking of the investment of life, the laying up of "treasures in heaven" of which Jesus spoke (Mt 6:20), the final reckoning made when the heavenly banker closes the books on one's life account and reckons its eternal worth.

The true value of one's life will be determined not by the register of values used in calculating worldly success, but by the standards of currency which are recognized by Him who alone establishes eternal values. Just as Verdi, who at the end of one of his operas, heard "the mad houseful's plaudits near out bang his orchestra," looked "through all the roaring and the wreaths" where sat "Rossini patient in his stall," aware that the thundering of the crowd was meaningless unless the musical master approved; so, at long last, we will search for the final register of life's work in the face of Him who is the "Lord and Master of us all." "At the end of ends, in the inmost of withins, before the ultimate judge, . . . a man must answer for himself," and **obtain** whatever interest has accrued to his investment. Peter is counseling his elders so to invest their lives that at that moment they will **obtain the unfading crown of glory**—the prize which is **glory** itself—that expected **glory** in which, Peter has already reminded them, they are proleptically participating in the very moment of their current trials (5:1).

The unfading crown of glory as a picture of the earnings on the investment of life would have been more familiar to Peter's readers than to us. Grammatically, the expression is explanatory; it means "the crown *is* the glory." This grammatical device is used elsewhere in the sacred writings. We read of "the crown of righteousness" (2 Tim 4:8); "the crown of life" (James 1:12); the "crown of rejoicing" (Ecclesiasticus 1:11). In each case, the crown is the thing described—

"righteousness," "life," "joy." They are the reality which the "crown" symbolizes. Greek and Roman civilization placed great emphasis on the body, and the crowning of athletes at the games was well-known and widely admired. Some crowns, made of silver or gold, were of value in themselves, but most of the crowns with which athletes were honored were made of the foliage of laurel, or olive, or pine. Of little value in themselves, they were highly valued as symbols. The ancient Greek poet, Pindar, who wrote countless odes to be sung at the celebrations welcoming athletic victors to their home towns after the games, is quoted as saying that the foliage crowns placed on their brows were "as precious as gold." Athletes strove for perfection, training for years to achieve the coveted victor's crown. Peter is suggesting that if such self-discipline and exertion are invested in the effort "to receive a perishable wreath" (1 Cor 9:25), a crown that will fade and wither, how much more should be expended to obtain the **unfading crown of glory,** a crown of eternal freshness. For, although "bodily training is of some value, godliness is of value in every way, as it holds promise for the present life and also for the life to come" (1 Tim 4:8). If the body, which returns to dust in its time, no matter how rewarding its achievements may be, is worth the investment of time and energy and self-discipline and sometimes costly sacrifice, *how much more* does the total person, body and soul, with its hope of eternal life, justify such expenditures! This **unfading crown of glory,** this prize of dwelling in the presence of God's glory forever, is the motivation Peter sets before the **elders** to whom he wrote in summoning them to fidelity in their task.

There will be those who will question such motivation as "pie in the sky, bye and bye," as though any appeal to a reward in the after life is an appeal to unworthy self-interest. Is this necessarily so? It is true that some appeals to concern about eternal sanctions may be crudely presented, and may appeal to the lower levels of human nature. But the demand for no concern for one's eternal destiny would seem to place an unreal demand on human nature. Is a distinction between self-concern and no self-concern a worthy one? Or is the worthy distinction not that between concern for the higher and the lower self?

What happens when people have no self-esteem? Do they not usually end up in aberrant behavior which is destructive of both soul and body? And do we not have it on the highest authority that we should value the "self" as of infinite worth? "What will anyone gain by winning the whole world at the cost of his life? Or what can he give to buy his life back" (Mt 16:26, REB)? And this Jesus said in relation to the last judgment, when He returns "in the glory of his Father" to "give everyone his due reward"; which is exactly the moment Peter has in mind here. The word for "life" placed on Jesus' lips could well be translated "self." It involves both the animal and the supra-animal parts of human nature—"life on earth in its external, physical aspects," and "the seat and center of life that transcends the earthly." Any worthy person values and protects the animal side of his existence. Why, then, is it considered unworthy to value the higher dimension of human life? To value one's "self" highly, to place on one's life the eternal value God has placed upon it by entering human life in Christ's incarnation and by dying to redeem it, can hardly be considered an unworthy self-interest. It is rather the highest act of wise discrimination that it is possible for human beings to make.

Did not Jesus say that one should love his neighbor as *himself* (Lk 10:27)? He thereby gave sanction to the right kind of self-love—not the narcissistic, indulgent, egocentrism which places one's own interests above the interest of others; but an altruistic, generous, benevolent loftiness of purpose which places a high value on *all* human life, both that of one's self and of one's neighbor, as that which is "the image of God," and which, for the sake of the God who gave it, must be treasured. To devalue the sacredness of one's own life would be to devalue the God who created it. A right understanding, therefore, of the motivation to live so as to have the approval of God at the last judgment, can be the highest form of God-centeredness. It is the life lived for one's own approval, which puts the human self at the center of reality, which is the ultimate selfishness. If man's "chief end" is "to glorify God, and to enjoy him forever," then the life which invests itself in activities which merit God's final approval is the fullest possible realization of the purpose for which man was created.

This is vastly different from the self-centered motivation concerned solely with escaping hell; as though if there were no hell to avoid, one would be free to follow his own bent in life, allow his passions free rein, and place his own interests at the center of reality. I was once asked if I were a "born again" Christian. I replied that all true Christians are born again, but that I did not know whether I would qualify in her view. The quick question then came, as though the questioner had been coached to follow a pattern of questioning: "If you should die tonight, would you go to heaven?" I replied that I hoped so, but that my deeper concern at the moment was how to find and do the will of God today; at which the conversation ended. Sincere and well-motivated as my questioner was, she had missed entirely the meaning of the rewards of a godly life here and now. The poet's words would have had little meaning for her:

> My God, I love Thee; not because
> I hope for heaven thereby,
> Nor yet because who love Thee not
> Must die eternally.

After detailing the costliness of Christ's love for those who were His enemies, the poet continued:

> Then why, O blessed Christ,
> Should I not love Thee well?
> Not for the hope of winning heaven,
> Or of escaping hell;
>
> Not with the hope of gaining aught,
> Nor seeking a reward;
> But as Thyself hast loved me,
> O ever-loving Lord!
>
> E'en so I love Thee, and will love,
> And in Thy praise will sing;
> Solely because Thou art my God,
> And my eternal King.

The true motivation for living **no longer by human passions but by the will of God** (4:2) is to avoid paining the heart of Him who paid the costly price of our self-centeredness, and at the end of the race to know that we have pleased Him and have His approval.

Verse 5 confronts us with three problems. 1) Why is it introduced with the word **likewise**? 2) Who are meant by the **younger**? 3) Are the **elders** mentioned the same as those in verse 1?

The word **likewise** grammatically could have any one of several antecedents. It could refer to **I exhort** in verse 1, meaning "Similarly, I exhort you." Or it could refer to the virtues prescribed for the elders in verses 2 and 3, meaning that those addressed should **willingly, eagerly, as examples** to others, submit themselves to the **elders.** Or, it could refer to the motivation set forth in verse 4: be **subject to the elders** so that you, too, may **obtain the unfading crown of glory.** Or, it could be seen simply as a "literary suture, without any precise connection to what precedes, and introducing an exhortation." It is difficult to know with finality which of these was in Peter's mind.

However, since Peter has twice before used the same word, in 3:1 and 3:7, where in both cases it links the following thought with what he has been discussing, it is likely that a similar use is made of it here. Since he has been discussing the relationship of the **elders** to their **flock,** it is quite natural that he is continuing his thought by turning to the relationship of those in the **flock** to the **elders.** It seems, therefore, that the word **likewise** is not merely a "literary suture" to introduce abruptly a new thought, but a means of uniting his continuing thought to what he has been discussing. The "demands placed on the **elders** constituted a form of subordination" in their relation to their **flock;** so, says Peter, there should be a like subordination of those in the **flock** to the **elders.**

But who are meant by **you that are younger?** Five views have been advanced.

1) To interpret **younger** solely in terms of age. The **younger** would then be "adolescents full of initiative and fervor, . . . often audacious and disorderly." In this case, Peter's word to them constituted a plea for them to subordinate themselves to the judgment of those more mature. The word **elders** in verse 5 would have no "ecclesiastical connotation," but would refer only to seniority of age, and thus differ from the use of the word in verse 1.

2) To make the same purely chronological interpretation of **younger** but to interpret **elders** in verse 5 ecclesiastically as in verse 1, on the basis of the fact that the leaders who bore special ecclesiastical responsibility for the churches "belonged certainly, for the most part at least, to the age group of 'older people.'" This involves a sort of double sense for the term **elders**—a "widening or inclusiveness of meaning." By an intermingling of terms for age with those of office or rank," the **elders** were both church officials and older men.

3) To see in the term **younger** a "group of responsible subordinates, auxiliaries, acolytes, deacons." This leaves the meaning of **elders**

in verse 5 the same as in verse 1, and posits a more elaborate community organization where groups of youth—perhaps between the ages of 18 and 40—were officially organized as "junior subordinates in the ministry." This view is based on studies of the role of youth in the Greco-Roman world and in the Dead Sea Scroll community, where there were multiplied youth associations designed for special religious, civic, or military purposes, who had a certain "legal, financial and social autonomy." The conclusion, then, is drawn that the churches took over into their lives the organizational structures of the surrounding world. The **younger** ones, therefore, "constituted a distinct class" in the Christian communities. If this is what is meant by the *younger* in 1 Peter, Peter's plea would be for them not to go off on their own, advocating doctrines and liturgical practices and behavior patterns which were novel and innovative, but to subordinate themselves to the teaching and customs of the **elders** who were the responsible teachers of the true apostolic faith.

4) To see in the term **younger** little or no reference to age, but to interpret it rather as describing recent initiants, or "neophytes in the faith," "the recently baptized," "the young in faith." In a context where Peter is dealing with both the dangers to the church from internal disunity and external persecutions, he then would be exhorting the recently converted to help create inner harmony and maintain the cohesiveness of a beleagured group by following the teaching and example of those whom God had set over them as **elders**.

5) To see in the term **younger** a designation of the entire membership of the church in distinction from the **elders**, the leaders of the community. It would, then, be a synonym for the phrase **all of you** immediately thereafter. The admonition to be **subject to the elders** would not apply to a specific class within the congregations, but to the entire Christian community of the Asia Minor churches.

We have seen that the answer to the question whether the **elders** of verses 1 and 5 are the same group varies with the interpretations. Most interpreters currently make them identical.

One thing is clear. When such vastly different interpretations of a passage can be argued with the intelligence and ingenuity of creditable scholars that have been expended on this passage, the evidence is not sufficiently clear to reach an assured conclusion. Present available evidence is simply not adequate to give a clear picture of the structural organization of the early church. In this one paragraph in 1 Peter which deals with the relation of church leaders to the congregations, the sacerdotal terminology applied in 2:4-10 to the function of the total church in the life of the world is avoided. The picture of the function of leadership in the church is taken from the simple and familiar life of the ancient world, that of the shepherd tending the **flock of God**. It has been pointed out that the terms **employ** (from which our word "deacon" comes) and **stewards** applied to the individual members of the congregation in 4:10, are not taken up again to describe the work of church officials in this passage. Peter looks upon the ministry in terms of service, and we look in vain for clear clues to a doctrine of ministry beyond that of willing, eager commitment to the people placed in charge of the leaders, and the examplary conduct which should accompany this. Both leaders and followers are to place self in the background and labor together in mutual love and devotion to God.

This is gathered up in the last sentence of the paragraph in a clear and succinct way: **Clothe yourselves, all of you, with humility toward one another.** These words are addressed to all, whether old or young, leaders or simple members of the church. Regardless of status or rank or function, all are to be humble. One commentator has remarked: "There is no parish life possible without humility and modesty, disinterestedly practiced by each one of the members (3:8); it is vanity and self-centeredness which are the source of jealousies, rivalries, disagreements and disunity."

We have already pointed out that **humility** was not valued highly in the ancient world (see pp. 250f.). It was not a pagan, but distinctly a Christian virtue. It is significant that the word, and its cognates, are used more than thirty times in the New Testament, and are found in the Gospels and in eight of the epistles, suggesting that it was universally valued among the New Testament writers. When Augustine was asked: "What is the cardinal Christian virtue?" he replied: "Humility." "What is the second?" he was asked. "Humility," he replied. "And the third?" "Humility!"

True **humility** is not making a falsely low estimate of one's abilities in relation to others, nor a feigned evaluation of one's achievements as lower than they are. **Humility** has nothing to do with abilities nor achievements. It involves an "inner attitude" of considering the interests of others before those of one's self. When in Philippians 2:3 we are admonished: "in humility count others better than yourselves," it is sandwiched in between two other expressions which help us to understand what humility means. "Do nothing from selfishness or conceit" precedes it, and it is followed by: "Let each of you look not only to his own interests, but also to the interests of others." **Humility**—counting others "better" than one's self, then, does not involve evaluating "personal excellence," but rather placing the interests of others above one's own. And the very act of focusing on the interests of others takes the attention off one's self, and is the cure for a false modesty, or a feigned humility, which is a self-conscious attempt to advertise one's own virtue. True humility is unstudied, natural, spontaneous. The humblest man I ever knew was a Rhodes Scholar and a man of great achievements, but who, without thinking, always put the interests of others ahead of his own. If you had told him that he was the humblest man you had ever known, it would have surprised him. He never thought about that! He was thinking rather of others.

The expression **clothe yourselves . . . with humility** evokes a familiar biblical expression, although Peter uses a picturesque word for it which is used only here in the New Testament. The risen Lord told His disciples that they would be "*clothed* with power from on high" (Lk 24:49, emphasis added). The apostles admonished their readers to "put on" certain virtues (Col 3:12, 1 Thess 5:8); to "put on the armor of God" (Eph 6:11; see also Rom 13:12); to "put on the Lord Jesus Christ" (Rom.13:14; see also Gal 3:27). Peter makes the figure vivid by using a word which has at its heart the idea of "tying, buttoning, girding." It envisages the "coarse apron which workers or slaves . . . placed over their tunic to protect it."

This recalls an experience that Peter had with his Lord which was indelibly traced on his memory, when in an Upper Room many years before, Jesus "rose from supper, laid aside his garments, and girded himself with a towel," then "poured water into a basin, and began to wash the disciples' feet, and to wipe them with the towel with which he was girded" (John 13:4f.). It is as though Peter were saying: As Jesus girded Himself, tying a towel about Him as a symbol of a servant, and expressed His consciousness "that the Father had given all things into His hands," that He had an eternal origin and an eternal destiny, and manifested His lordship by the most menial task of humble service available to Him, so **clothe yourselves** with a similar humility by serving the interests of others rather than yourselves.

There is abundant scriptural warrant for Peter's admonition here. He quotes the Greek translation of the Old Testament from Proverbs 3:34: **God opposes the proud, but gives grace to the humble.** The principle here, however, is found over and over in the Old Testament. Said the Psalmist: "For thou dost deliver a humble people, but the haughty eyes thou dost bring down" (18:27). In symbolic language, Ezekiel said: "all the trees of the field shall know that I the Lord bring low the high tree, and make high the low tree" (17:24). Isaiah said that the Almighty would "punish the arrogant boasting of the king of Assyria and his haughty pride" (10:12). It was Jesus, however, who put the touch of finality on this truth, both by word and example: "everyone who exalts himself will be humbled, but he who humbles himself will be exalted" (Lk 18:14). To be self-assertive in advancing one's own interests instead of the interests of others is to run counter to the grain of the moral universe. For **God opposes the proud.** He "resists," "thwarts," "works against" **the proud.**

This is not the result of any wounded pride on God's part, but rather the inescapable reality of the divine-human relationship. Because God is the Creator and source of all life, and man is His creature and only the recipient of life, man can only become what he is intended to be to the extent that he realizes his place in the universe. For man to exalt himself is to rival God, not "enjoy him forever." And if man is to "enjoy" God, he must do so only in the acknowledgement of who God is—his Creator, Redeemer, Sustainer, and Friend. To offer man the **grace** of joyous fellowship with Him, it is necessary that man know who he himself is in order to be in a position to receive it. To give **grace,** then, it is necessary for God to break man's pride by resisting it, until man is thereby in a position to be receptive. But He **gives grace,** "favor," "kindness," "special blessing" **to the humble.** They are those who are so overwhelmed with the **greatness of God** that it would not occur to them to say, "I am great." It is they who are capable of receiving God's **grace.**

B. Admonitions On Spiritual Warfare *(5:6 -11)*
   (Exhortation)

Some interpreters feel that these verses are "a mosaic of diverse fragments" brought together in Peter's mind as he concludes the letter. Rightly understood, however, it seems to me better to see in them a thread of connection which not only ties them together, but makes them grow naturally out of the preceding materials. As a German commentator has said: "The idea of humility at the end of the foregoing passage furnishes the occasion for a conclusion to the letter, in which in a concise, clear, and to the reader, an unforgettable form, the fundamental thoughts of the entire letter are summed up in a mighty finale." The entire letter has dealt with the existence of the faithful under pressure from a hostile world. In full accord with this framework, this existence is here presented as "at heart a conflict, implying confident submission to God who arouses it and directs it to its end, and determines resistance to the adversary who wishes to bring it to a ruinous end."

The **humility** toward one another of verse 5 is now turned toward a wider and more vital relationship: **Humble yourselves therefore under the mighty hand of God**. The **therefore** connects this with what has just been said. If **humility** toward one's fellow man is necessary because **God opposes the proud**, how much more indispensable it is toward God Himself! The self-effacement of the **elders** toward their **flock**, and the subjection of the **younger** toward the **elders**, and the mutual humility of **all** toward one another set forth in the preceding paragraph, all flow from a disposition to "recognize the divine sovereignty" and to live under God's will as Creator and Lord. This is life lived under **the mighty hand of God**.

God's **hand** is a frequent figure used oy the biblical writers to express God in action, either in creation, or redemption, or judgment. "As the hand upholds or strikes, God is considered as using his hand to help his own or to chastise his enemies." The creation of the heavens and the earth in the beginning is described as "the work of thy hands" (Heb 1:10, quoting Ps 102:25). No one "is able to snatch them out of the Father's hand" describes God's protective care of His people (John 10:29). The work of the early apostles flourished because "the hand of the Lord was with them" (Acts 11:21). God's hand is "strong" (Ps 89:13); by it His people were "redeemed" (Neh 1:10). Deliverance from Egyptian bondage in the Exodus is the classic example, both of the might and mercy of the action of God's hand. In a sense, the very heart of the entire Old Testament is to be found in the simple affirmation: "the Lord brought us out of Egypt with a mighty hand and outstretched arm" (Deut 26:8). And the "good news" embodied in those words finds its fulfillment in the New Testament in a new and greater Exodus. At the Transfiguration, Moses and Elijah, representatives of the law and the prophets of the Old Testament, conferred with Jesus about "his departure [the Greek word is "exodus"] which he was to accomplish at Jerusalem" (Lk 9:31). What was begun at the Exodus from Egypt was completed in the Exodus from Jerusalem! The Cross is the summit of the action of God's hand, both in might and in mercy.

Peter's admonition to live in humility **under the mighty hand of God** is significant. The preposition **under** means to be under someone's "power, rule, sovereignty, command." A vivid example of its meaning is seen in the word of the Roman centurion to Jesus: "For I am a man set *under* authority" (Lk 7:8, emphasis added). He meant that his authority was not his own but that of the Roman government which he represented. To live **under** that authority was to live under its might and rule. To live humbly, then, **under the mighty hand of God** is to live under the might and rule of God. This means the surrender of all autonomy, and the commitment of one's self to the might and mercy of God, accepting the lot in life that He has given, placing ultimate outcomes in His care, in the confidence **that in due time he may exalt you.** This is to believe that "every deed of faith-obedience" is "taken up into the unconquerable purpose of the will of God."

To Peter's readers, this meant the acceptance of the hostility of the Roman empire, and the sufferings which that imposed upon them, without rebelling either against the empire or God, and leaving the outcome to His righteous will, knowing that they lived **under** an authority greater than that of the Roman empire. To us, it means accepting the station in life which God has given us, remembering His power and our own powerlessness, and humbly committing the rule of life to Him as commander, obeying His will insofar as it is possiole for sinful human beings, and leaving the outcome of our endeavors in His hands. In **due time**, either at the last day, or at some time fitting to Him, He will **exalt you**.

We see here again the paradox expressed by Jesus: "For every one who exalts himself will be humbled, and he who humbles himself will be exalted" (Lk 14:11). To seek the high estimation of men as a self-centered goal is to miss the approval of God; but to commit one's self to the power and mercy of God, leaving all to Him, is to gain God's approval. And this means to live in hope and calmness of spirit. "Christian living means hope, it signifies a secure expectation . . . a greater, brighter day lies before the Christians, toward which they journey. A strong, mighty hand is continually at work to lead up to it. Whoever can believe that need not fear any humiliation nor wandering in the darkest valley. To this strong hand one may yield himself serenely, entrust himself in humble confidence that it will lead out of the valley of the shadow of death to the summit, when God's day and hour come."

The calm certainty which this gives may be seen in an incident in the life of John Wesley. He had planned a preaching trip to Canterbury, and had told his niece, Sally, that he would take her with him. Theological enemies of his had arranged for the publication of some false charges maligning Wesley's character. Charles Wesley had discovered this, and sought to persuade John to postpone his preaching trip to stay in London to thwart the publication of the offending materials. Charles argued that the importance of the reputation of a minister and the whole cause of religion should overcome his indifference to these charges, and lead him to stop the publication. John answered: "Brother, when I devoted to God my ease, my time, my life, did I except my reputation? No. Tell Sally I will take her to Canterbury 'tomorrow.'" Wesley had learned to live calmly, to **humble** himself **under the mighty hand of God**, in the confidence that **in due time** He would exalt him.

Such certainty would enable one to accept Peter's next admonition: **Cast all your anxieties on him.** Without signalling it in any way, Peter is here referring to Psalm 55:22, where we are admonished: "Cast your burden on the Lord." The Greek translation of the Old Testament uses the same word for "burden" as Peter uses here for **anxieties.** If Old Testament believers had reason to do that, how much more do Christians who have the fuller revelation of God's trustworthiness in Jesus Christ! The word translated **anxieties,** along with its verbal form, is used frequently in the New Testament, almost always in a pejorative manner. Two or three times it relates to a worthy concern for others (see 2 Cor 11:28, 1 Cor 12:25, Phil 2:20), but usually it describes undue concern or apprehension about one's own worldly interests. Jesus straightforwardly cautioned against this, insisting that we should trust our Father in heaven for the necessities of life (Mt 6:25ff.), in contrast to the pagans (Mt 6:32); for aid under persecution (Mt 10:19); for deliverance from undue distraction because of household cares (Lk 10:41); for deliverance from worry over the future (Mt 6:34); for freedom from "the cares of the world" (Mt 13:22, Mk 4:19). The hurtful **anxieties** of which Jesus spoke stem from a preoccupation with the things of this age which tend to obscure the realities of the coming age (Mt 13:22).

All these **anxieties** are to be **cast** on God. The word **cast** is a picturesque word. It is used, for example, in connection with the Triumphal Entry, where we are told that Jesus' disciples, "*throwing* their garments on the colt . . . set Jesus upon it" (Lk 19:35, emphasis added). It is the picture of taking something which one has himself carried, and *throwing it on another* so that he carries it instead. Peter's counsel is, therefore: take all the **anxieties**, worries, cares, concerns, which weigh down your spirit and *throw them on to God*, so that He now carries them rather than you. It is of significance, too, that the verb here is in the participial form, which means that it is not the main verb in the sentence, but is an expansion of the thought which goes before. Casting **all your anxieties** on God is a manifestation of the **humility** recommended in the previous verses. True humility takes life out of one's own hands and turns it over to God. It is pride that insists on managing life alone. Heroic though the "unconquerable soul" may seem, it is consummate pride that says:

> I am the master of my fate,
> I am the captain of my soul.

This is proudly to proclaim a self-sufficiency with which we are not endowed, and which, at least at the instant of death—that inexorable "moment of truth"—becomes a pathetic mockery.

Either unconsciously or dishonestly, in our pride and self-sufficiency, we thrash around desperately in life like shipwrecked men at sea without life preservers who do not know how to swim. It is humbling to call for help, finally to admit that we can no longer make it on our own. But humbling or not, how blessed it is to have a life boat arrive, to cast all anxiety on the life guard, give up the struggle and be rescued!

Or, as another has pictured it: "It is necessary to know the extremity of human fatigue, as a soldier on the evening of a long day's march says to his comrade: 'Take my knapsack or I fall! I can't take one step more!' It is necessary, in such a moment of human exhaustion, to have said to the Lord himself: 'Take my knapsack or I fall' to know what it is to obey this commandment [of Jesus: 'Do not be anxious'] and to receive in the very moment of our obedience the unutterable lifting of care, the blissful relief, the release from dreadful bondage.... God himself has come in Jesus Christ to be the companion of your journey, to march beside you and to take on himself everything which crushes you, from the anxiety about tomorrow to the burden of illness, prison or slavery. With the companion of the road, of the prison cell, of the hospital, of the battle trench, or the factory by your side, from hour to hour, cast yourself on him; that is your only means to keep going. Do not let him accompany you for nothing, but let him take care of you and put you on his shoulders, as did the shepherd of the sheep which he had found. These are not images or mere good words, but the strictest and most miraculous of realities."

I have quoted this writer at some length to give the words credence. For one like myself, who has suffered little, it might seem that these were "mere images or mere good words," and thus to be passed by as rhetoric. But the quoted words were from the French pastor who wrote them surreptitiously in Hitler's prison under threat of death, with a bit of a crayon on scraps of wrapping paper which he had salvaged from packages sent to him in prison. One suspects that he believed them!

Peter gives the indestructible foundation of his admonition here in five simple but breath-taking words: **for he cares about you.** One writer has said of these words: "This contains in one concise sentence the first major theme of the letter: hope for the day of eternity is a living power in the midst of suffering and grief and struggle." As Peter's readers faced the ridicule and pestering of their pagan neighbors and the hostile authority of local magistrates who did not understand them, they could be buoyed up always by the simple fact that **God ... cares about you.** What stupendous words!

God! What **God?** The **God** who created the universe; who placed whole galaxies in the skies thousands of light years beyond us; who positioned stars so far away that they may perchance have burned out and ceased to exist by the time their light comes to earth; who thrust stars into the skies so far beyond us that we may never be able visibly to trace their presence with the mightiest telescopes we can devise; the God who also filled the universe with countless miniscule things which may be even smaller than our most powerful microscopes can ever capture—*this* **God ... cares about you!**

Yes, you, individually, personally. He "pays attention to **you**," He "bestows careful thought upon **you**," He is "earnest" in His regard for **you**! The word translated **cares** here is used by John in speaking of a "hireling" shepherd who flees when wolves invade the flock because he "*cares* nothing for the sheep" (John 10:13, emphasis added). By contrast, Jesus, the "good shepherd," knows His own, and His own know Him, and "he calls his own sheep by name" (John 10:3). No matter how large the flock, or how variegated, God knows the "name" of every sheep in His flock. In oriental culture, "name" means more than a tag of identification; it means in the deepest sense the person himself—his characteristics, his idiosyncracies, the very "thoughts and intents" of his heart. The one, true, living **God**, who made the universe in all its vastness and smallness, **cares about you**, knows *you* personally by name, is interested in *your* welfare, is deeply concerned about *your* development to moral and spiritual maturity. What difference does it make, then, when eternity will reveal reality, what the Roman emperor, or Hitler, or Stalin, or an amoral American society thinks? Can we not conclude with the writer to the Hebrews, who, quoting Psalm 118:6, wrote:

"we can confidently say,

The Lord is my helper,
I will not be afraid;
what can man do to me?' " (Heb 13:6)

A lay person once asked a great scientist, who was a believing Christian, how he could believe that a God who was great enough to create the universe could be interested in such small things as individual human beings. He replied: "Your view of God is not great enough. You must believe in a God great enough to create the universe, but also great enough to concern himself with little people at the same time."

Verse 8 involves the paradoxical nature of the Bible. After Peter has just insisted that we should abandon all care to God, snatch all **anxieties** from our own shoulders and fling them on to the shoulders of God and let Him carry them, the next thing he says is: **Be sober, be watchful.** It seems almost as though he had said: Let God do everything for you, but do something for yourself! How can this be?

One commentator has remarked: "This marvelous serenity of the elect is neither insouciance nor torpor. On the contrary, the two . . . imperatives: **Be sober . . . , be watchful** . . . resound like a military commandant alerting soldiers to the approach of the enemy." Another has remarked: "Such genuinely founded Christian hope does not make one drunk, such care-free certainty is not like an enthusiastic delirium, but on the contrary makes one **sober and watchful**. Again and again our letter has enjoined the sharpest conceivable moral motivation. Whoever believes and hopes to see the eternal consummation, who resolutely journeys toward it, over whose life lies the seriousness of a holy responsibility, knows what he has to lose. He knows the danger." In picturesque biblical imagery the danger is this: **Your adversary the devil prowls around like a roaring lion, seeking some one to devour.** Casting our **anxieties** on God, then, is intended "not to encourage the torpidity of the flesh, but to bring rest to faith." One perceptive commentator has said that the tension between casting ourselves on God and putting forth our own effort to be **sober** and **watchful** is "irresolvable." The extreme view that true belief "in the sovereign power of God" means "that the Christian life requires no effort" he brands as "quietism"—almost a "fatalism" similar to Muslim faith. The opposite extreme is to place such weight on human effort that God's power in furthering that effort is a "mirage." This he calls "activism." Both are false.

The "quietist" view seems to demand that our own human wills are obliterated rather than redirected by God, which is counter to reality. Faith does not make our human wills nonexistent.

> Our wills are ours, we know not how;
> Our wills are ours, to make them Thine.

As the front wheels of a car get jostled out of line and must be realigned from time to time, so our wills must be realigned again and again with the will of God. Although realigned, they are still ours. We still will. *And with God's help, when realigned, we will to do God's will.* The "activist" view throws us back on our own resources without divine aid to overcome our weaknesses, and "leaves us with a sense of defeat, faced as we are by an impossible ideal." *Without God's help to realign our wills, we will to do God's will, but cannot.* We must learn at one and the same time to **cast all our anxieties on him**; and yet to **be** sober, be watchful, and resist our adversary the devil.

To be **sober** and **watchful** involves two aspects of one reality. Sobriety is negative, the avoidance of all that would produce "sloth and sleep," all that would create "spiritual lethargy" (see pp. 150ff., pp. 299ff.). Anything that would dull our spiritual and moral sensitivities, or drug us into indifference and spiritual lassitude, is to be laid aside. Watchfulness is the positive, alert vigilance of a warrior who knows that the enemy lurks near and makes it necessary to be ready for action at every moment. The Christian life is a warfare which demands constant preparedness.

As Peter nears the end of his letter, he returns to this theme of sobriety which he had introduced earlier, but places it in a broader and more serious setting. Sobriety was formerly advised in the light of certain aspects of the thought world which Peter was addressing (see 1:13, 4:7). Now he "personalizes" it, and demands sobriety and watchfulness in the light of a personal enmity in a cosmic setting. **Your adversary the devil** is now the enemy against which one must be **watchful**. The description of him as one who **prowls around like a roaring lion, seeking some one to devour** focuses on his power of *intimidation*—what can be more paralyzing or productive of a sense of defencelessness than to confront a roaring lion in the wilderness? his cruelty—he aims to devour, "swallow up," make his victim "totally extinct"; his feverish activity and restlessness—perhaps a characteristic taken from the description of Satan in Job as "going to and fro on the earth, and . . . walking up and down on it" (1:7). In this vivid way, Peter pictures a struggle which is dangerous, has serious consequences, and cosmic dimensions.

Psalm 22, quoted by Jesus on the cross (Mk 15:34), pictures Jesus' enemies as opening "wide their mouths . . . like a ravening and roaring lion" (vs 13). It also contains the prayer; "Save me from the mouth of the lion" (vs 21). The early Christians saw in this a picture of the final conflict of Jesus with Satan, begun at the Temptation (Mk 1:13); continued in His healings (Lk 11:14ff., 13:16), and in His dealings with men (Mk 8:33; Lk. 22:3, 31ff.); in the work of His disciples (Lk 10:17ff.); and finally completed in the cross and resurrection (Col 2:15). But, although Satan was decisively defeated, he was not annihilated. As a wounded animal grows even more ferocious, so his onslaughts on those who align themselves against him on God's side are the more vicious, and thus to be taken with utmost seriousness. Paul counseled: "Put on the whole armor of God, that you may be able to stand against the wiles of the devil. For we are not contending against flesh and blood, but against the principalities, against the powers, against the world rulers of this present darkness, against the spiritual hosts of wickedness in the heavenly places" (Eph 6:11ff.).

To reduce these "principalities" and "powers" to mere "apocalyptic imaginings" devoid of all reality, runs counter to the tone of the New Testament. It does not picture the human situation as one where false ideologies are to be corrected; or where men are to be led from immature to mature behavior by rational persuasion and the power of logic; or one that is to be solved by freeing men from their inhibitions and repressions and hangups and complexes and compulsions by psychological therapy. It pictures the human situation as a struggle against powerful cosmic evil forces with which man must do battle, but against whom he will lose unless he is rescued by One greater than he—the Good Shepherd, who protects man from the **adversary** who **prowls around like a roaring lion** and robs him of his prey.

Our battle is not merely against our own moral lapses, or the evil elements inherent in modern corporations, or our technological woes or ecological hazards, or the "isms" embodied in political or military organizations or persons. "The real warfare," said one, "lies deeper in the invisible realm where sinister forces stand flaming and fanatic against the rule of Christ." Peter himself knew this, both from memory and experience. Did not his Lord say to him one day: "Simon, Simon, behold, Satan demanded to have you, that he might sift you like wheat" (Lk 22:31)? And did he not remember all too vividly his threefold denial of his Lord (John 18:17, 25ff.), much against his own will, after having sworn undying fealty to Him (John 13:36ff.)? Peter knew all too well that we must be **sober**, be **watchful** against our adversary the devil, who **prowls** continually, seeking to **devour** the followers of the Lord whom he sought to destroy but failed. We must be unceasingly poised against attack.

The immediate attacks of the devil on Peter's first readers were taking the form of pagan misunderstanding, social ostracism, economic deprivation, perhaps local police harassment, fear of mobs, or even physical bludgeoning. It would be easy for us to see no parallel between their circumstances and ours, and to pass over Peter's admonition here lightly. On the contrary, his insistence on sobriety and watchfulness might be even more needed by us than it was by them. At least, they knew who the enemy was, and where attacks were coming from; whereas a greater danger arises when one has not taken the measure of his enemy, does not know that he is in hostile surroundings, and is therefore more open to the weapons of deceit and flimflam. Our **adversary** is cunning, clever in luring us away from the protection of our Shepherd into unprotected fields where he can attack us at will. He attracts us to a "broad way to make us elude a trial and abandon our birthright for some immediate ease. In many ways, he prowls around us to persuade us to escape a trial by an infidelity, or to make us lose all hope in the trial itself." We are perhaps more in need of sobriety and watchfulness under such circumstances than when the **adversary** roars, bares his teeth, and threatens to spring on us. He is the more dangerous when he "disguises himself as an angel of light" (2 Cor.11:14).

But what is the word, when attacks are threatened, or we are tempted by subtle allurements to let down our guard, dream, and wander from the protection of our Shepherd? **Resist him, firm in your faith.** This is a strong expression. **Resist**, "stand your ground," "oppose," "withstand," "set yourself against." There can be no compromise, no irresolution, no half measures, no timeserving. As we are told by our Lord: "No one can serve two masters" (Mt 6:24). The decisiveness of the resistance demanded is strengthened by the counsel to be **firm in your faith**. The word translated **firm** pictures something "compact" like a fortress, so solidly and closely built that it "permits no access"; something "stable," like an immovable rock in the midst of shifting sand dunes; or a firm foundation strong enough to carry all the weight laid on it; or something strong, like the limbs of an athlete; or even "headstrong, stubborn" in mind. Evil, then is not only to be resisted, but stubbornly, strongly, unrelentingly resisted.

But how does one **resist**? Peter speaks of three truths which are calculated to strengthen resistance. First, use **faith** as an instrument of resistance. He is not issuing a call to arms to defend righteousness with external force. He is admonishing, rather, to "continue in the faith, stable and steadfast, not shifting from the hope of the gospel" (Col 1:23). This is an inner resistance of spirit against all that would destroy one's personal confidence in God. It is God's power, not ours, that is effective in resisting evil. Early in his letter, Peter has told us that it is **by**

God's power that we are guarded . . . for a salvation ready to be revealed in the last time. But how is this divine power made available to us, and how do we appropriate it? Through **faith**, answers Peter. Is this not a reflection of Peter's experience with his Lord who, when He warned Peter that "Satan demanded to have" him, continued: "but I have prayed for you that your *faith* may not fail" (Lk 22:31f., emphasis added).

Faith, Paul tells us, is the impenetrable shield "with which you can quench all the flaming darts of the evil one" (Eph 6:16). Faith, then, is not mere theological correctness, worthwhile as that may be; but rather a living reality which enables us to stand protected behind the Almightiness of God when we are attacked by evil. As one has said: "to resist in faith is to place the all-powerful Lord at the heart of the dreadful encounter with the enemy." It is casting our **anxieties on him**, and letting Him defend us. It is to live by what we believe. Or, as one has stated it; "What Peter is talking about is not putting strength into believing but drawing strength from what we believe." Another has said: "Faith overcomes evil not as a human attitude but thanks to its content. . . . This is why the exhortation about persecution in the letter does not conclude with this imperative but with the promise in verse 10." God's *imperatives* are always summonses to respond to *promises*. "He gives, what he demands."

Peter's second truth about resistance is the encouragement which comradeship in suffering provides. **Be sober, be watchful . . . Resist . . . knowing that the same experience of suffering is required of your brotherhood throughout the world.** In any conflict, to feel alone is devastating. Resoluteness is stimulated by knowing that one has comrades who are engaged in common cause with him; on whose understanding, affection and courage he can count; and who he knows are likewise depending on him. Every soldier finds strength through comradeship in battle. So Peter not only strengthens his readers by reminding them that they are joined in their suffering by others, but also hints that they should remain faithful for the sake of encouraging other Christians who suffer (see 1 John 3:16).

One perceptive commentator has suggested that "the vision of the tribulation of the whole 'fraternity' . . . this vast family, this household of God, offers other encouragements and advantages." It brought to mind the "mysterious reality" that "invisible bonds" unite scattered

Christians to one another, because they are all united to Christ. To be members of the "body of Christ," is to belong to every other member of that body. "The communion of saints" confessed in the Apostles' Creed is stark reality. The loneliest, most isolated Christian is not alone when he remembers that he belongs to every other Christian in the world, and that they belong to him. This knowledge, if taken seriously, brings courage. Also, it reminds us that "suffering is inherent in the faith," because of our involvement with a suffering Lord and the necessity of burning out the dross of our human frailty. But perhaps above all, it demonstrates that individual suffering is a participation in a larger divine plan of world-wide dimensions, suffering for the sake of a "gospel which . . . in the whole world is bearing fruit and growing" (Col 1:5f.), suffering that will finally eventuate "in a promised world of justice, peace and glory." The **world** in the New Testament often stands for the organized forces of evil which are set against God (see John 15:18ff., 16:33), and are considered to be under the rulership of Satan (see John 14:30, 1 John 2:15ff.). But **throughout the world** there is another organized group, which twice by Peter (2:17, 5:9), and nowhere else in the New Testament, is called a **brotherhood**. Although not organized in an outward sense in Peter's day, it was a "spiritual fraternity" bound together by the Spirit of God which constituted them into an organization of **God's own people** (1 Pet 2:9; see slso 2:5), to "confront the attacks of Satan" and against whom "the powers of death shall not prevail" (Mt 16:18).

The word translated **required** in verse 9 is difficult to interpret. It is a word which often means to "finish," "bring to an end," "complete," "accomplish," "perform," "fulfill." Many translators make the passage mean simply: your brothers "undergo the same troubles"; "are having the same experience of suffering"; or are "going through the same kinds of suffering." There seems, however, to be a deeper meaning here. What is the **brotherhood** "fulfilling," or "accomplishing" by their suffering? The word implies the "fulfillment" of something, "achieving" something. For example, in Hebrews the word is used to describe the priests "performing their ritual duties," making them a "reality," "bringing them into existence" (9:6). It would seem that Peter here is suggesting that the "disciples of Christ crucified 'bring into reality' their vocation best, by the wounds which they receive in the combat of faith." Hence, the **brotherhood** of sufferers for Christ are in process of bringing into reality the end for which they exist, witnessing by their suffering to "that one far-off divine event, toward which the whole creation moves," when "the kingdom of the world has become the kingdom of our Lord and of his Christ, and he shall reign for ever and ever" (Rev 11:15). The word **required**, then, might better be given the nuance of "lead to good, to fulfilment, to accomplish to perfection." It has been suggested that the passage might preferably be translated: "knowing that the same experience of suffering of your brotherhood throughout the world is leading to a good end," or "to the fulfillment of God's purpose."

Peter's third point here, and the one with which he brings his letter to a close, is climactic, decisive, and final. The suffering endured for the sake of Christ is temporary, and will finally result in **eternal glory**, at which time the One for whom they have suffered **will himself restore, establish, and strengthen you**. No matter how long the sufferings of Peter's readers should last, in the light of God's **eternal glory** they can be but **a little while**. Though they may seem long to those who must endure them in history, what is three score and ten years when compared with eternity? Eternity has been pictorially described as a cube of granite, one thousand miles long, wide, and high. Once every thousand years a tiny bird lands on this cube to sharpen its bill on it. When, by this process, the entire cube has been worn away, one year will have elapsed in eternity! This, of course, is a fanciful attempt to stimulate the imagination into "feeling" what the mind cannot comprehend—the vastness of eternity! Would not the sufferings even of a lifetime be but **a little while** in comparison?

But far more important than the comparative shortness of the sufferings is **the God of all grace** in whose providence suffering comes, and for whose sake it is endured. One has observed that the "saving work of God dominates the last lines of the letter as it had inaugurated it." The letter begins: **Blessed be . . . . God** [by whom] **we have been born anew to a living hope** (1:3). It ends with the promise that **the God of all grace who has called** us to the hope of **his eternal glory** will make good on that promise. He **will himself restore, establish, and strengthen you** (5:10). "God has pledged not to leave his undertaking unfinished." The **God of all grace** means "the God whose grace is sufficient for every type of situation," whose character is sheer love and concern for the welfare of his people, even in their sufferings.

We have seen before how Peter brings together the coming world and this world; how eternity casts its light back on time (see pp. 321ff., 344ff.; also pp. 139., 266, 291, 313). Here again he insists that the God who will finally complete what He set out to do will furnish adequate resources to those who believe in Him during the **little while** that intervenes between now and then. He began the letter by affirming that we are **guarded through faith** until **the last time** comes (1:5). He concludes it by reaffirming this. Until we reach the eternal glory to which we have been **called**, God will **restore, establish, and strengthen** us. Other texts add a fourth—"settle," or place you "on a firm foundation," or make you "'immovable." These God will do for those who **resist** the **devil** (vss 8, 9).

The nuances of the four verbs Peter uses here to describe God's protective care are difficult to delineate. They are closely related in meaning, and probably are designed as a literary device to give force to the one idea of the all-sufficiency of God for those who believe in Him rather than to distinguish precisely four different aspects of the divine activity.

The word **restore** means "to put in order," "restore to its former condition," "repair whatever is damaged." Peter probably means that even if any damage has been left on one's faith from encounters in the struggle with evil, God will repair the damage and make him adequate to face whatever difficulties lie ahead. Some have translated it "will make you whole," or "will see that all is well again."

The word **establish** is the word used by Luke to describe Jesus' decision to "set his face to go to Jerusalem" (9:51). It involved a fixed, unshakeable, irrevocable decision which nothing could alter. Here it means to be established in faith, to be immutable, solid, fixed, with no inconstancy, vacillation, or fluctuation possible.

The word **strengthen** is used here only in the New Testament, and means just what it says, to "make strong." It here refers, however, not to physical strength, but to spiritual strength. God will give "strength of heart" or "strength of spirit" to remain constant under persecution, or whatever other tests of faith come to us. It is Peter's way of saying what Paul expressed: "God is faithful, and he will not let you be tempted beyond your strength, but with the temptation will also provide the way of escape, that you may be able to endure it" (1 Cor 10:13).

The fourth word, omitted in some texts but included in others, and placed in the margin by the translators of the *Revised Standard Version*, is **settle**. Basically, it means "to found," or "to lay the foundation of." Its core meaning is expressed vividly in the contrast between the wise and foolish builders with which the Sermon on the Mount concludes. One built his house "upon the rock," so that when the rain and floods and windstorms came "it did not fall, because it had been *founded* on the rock." The other built "upon the sand, "and when the rain, and floods and windstorms came "it fell" (Mt 7:24ff., emphasis added). Another instance of its use is found in Hebrews 1:10: "Thou, Lord, didst *found* the earth in the beginning" (emphasis added). It means that God builds the believer's life on "a firm foundation"—as stable and indestructible as the bed rock on which the universe is founded. God will "cause you always to endure," or "not to be moved in your trust in Christ."

The central character in Peter's entire letter is **God**. The total sweep of thought is placed between two doxologies. The letter opens: **Blessed be... God**. It closes: **To him be the dominion for ever and ever, Amen**. The word **dominion** means "power," "might," "rule," "sovereignty." Some translate the doxology: "His is the power, for ever and ever!" This concluding sentence indicates that the contemplation of God's graciousness leads always to an outburst of praise. Focusing on **the God and Father of our Lord Jesus Christ** so uplifts the spirit that the only appropriate response is worship, adoration, praise—the acknowledgement of His transcendent greatness which can find no adequate expression in verbal form, only in **unutterable and exalted joy** (1:9).

The doxology suggests more than that, however. It is the confirmation of all the affirmations of the entire letter. As one has stated: "If the apostle has not spoken to us in the name of the *Father all-powerful* he has nothing to say at all. And the revelation of Easter would not be a revelation of mercy, if it were not that of a mercy sovereign and asbolutely triumphant over ourselves and over all imaginable resistance in the present or in the future." Peter has spoken to us of a **living hope** (1:3); of an **inheritance which is imperishable** (1:4); of a **faith, more precious than gold** (1:7); of the **salvation** of our **souls** (1:9); of **grace** and of **glory** (1:10f.); of **good news** (1:12); of **the kindness of the Lord** (2:3); of being **God's people** (2:9f.); of having **God's approval** (2:20); of **the strength which God supplies** (4:11); of being blessed in suffering for Christ (4:14); of obtaining an **unfading crown of glory** (5:4); of the stupendous fact that **God cares about** us (5:7); that we are **called** to God's **eternal glory in Christ** (5:10). Is there any truth in all this? Or are we being led toward a false utopia like the followers of the late Rev. Jim Jones or the late Rev. David Koresh, who found it all a "will o' the wisp," dying in despair in a foreign land by drinking the poison mixed for them, or being burned alive in a vain gesture of defiance? Is it all but "a sleep, a dream, a story"? What would be the worth of all the promises Peter holds out to us, even though sincerely offered, if the One who has made them lacks the power to keep them? They would be

> ... like the shadows
> On sunny hills that lie,
> Or grasses in the meadows
> That blossom but to die.

But, says Peter, His is **the dominion**, not only in this age but in that which is to come—for **ever and ever**.

Peter was not alone in this confidence. Paul joined him in speaking of the "vast . . . resources of his power open to us who have faith. His mighty strength was seen at work when he raised Christ from the dead, and enthroned him at his right hand in the heavenly realms, far above all government and authority, all power and dominion, and any title of sovereignty that commands allegiance, not only in this age but also in the age to come" (Eph 1:19ff., REB). The Bible reaches its climax on a similar note: "Hallelujah! For the Lord our God the Almighty reigns. Let us rejoice and exult and give him the glory" (Rev. 19:6f.). Thus Peter ends his letter with praise. The One who **cares about you, . . . after you have suffered a little while . . . will himself restore, establish, and strengthen you. To him be the dominion for ever and ever. Amen** (5:7, 10f.).

VIII

CLOSING GREETINGS (5:12-14)

The letter concludes with a brief paragraph of greetings. The first name mentioned is Silvanus, the Latin form of the Greek name Silas, the companion of Paul who helped him in the founding of some of the Asia Minor churches and would likely have been well-known to at least some of the congregations to whom Peter was writing (see Acts 15:40f., 17:4, 18:5; 2 Cor 1:19). Many think that he was Peter's amanuensis, who actually put Peter's thoughts into Greek, or even translated Peter's letter from Aramaic into Greek. We have opted, however, for the view that his role was the same he had following the Council of Jerusalem (Acts 15:27, 32), to deliver the letter and to enlarge on what was written, by word of mouth (see pp. 62ff.). In the Greek, the words **to you** are separated from the words **I have written**, and are connected with the expression **a faithful brother**. The meaning is not that "I have written to you," but that "to you Silvanus is **a faithful brother**." Their prior experience with him had made him such to them, in which judgment Peter concurs in the words **as I regard him**.

I have written briefly is a "form of politeness," as witnessed by extra-biblical literature of the time. It also likely suggests that there is much more that could be said about the subjects discussed, which can be filled in by word of mouth by Silvanus. Peter's accreditation of him suggests that his mind and heart are so at one with his own that the readers may safely accept his verbal elaboration in reply to their questions as though it were his.

Peter's method of approach is described as **exhorting and declaring**—the twofold design of admonishing and witnessing; of encouraging to attitudes and styles of behavior and instructing in the deeper meanings of the faith they had confessed (see pp. 85ff.). Declaring, or "witnessing," is a strong word, "denoting that his testimony is true." Peter is emphatically **declaring** what he knows to be true about the Christian faith as an eyewitness of the historic Jesus and the resurrection, and doing it "without the slightest doubt."

What he is **declaring** is **that this is the true grace of God**. There is a difference of judgment as to the antecedent of *this*. To what does it refer? Some would limit its reference to what has just been said in verse 10, meaning that it is a **grace**, a "benefaction," a "privilege" to suffer for **a little while** to attain the outcome of God's **eternal glory in Christ.** Since the words **exhorting** and **declaring** obviously refer to the entire letter, however, it is more likely that **this** would at least refer to all that has gone before. This would make it mean: "What I have written in the letter" is **the true grace of God.** In other words, "all that I have been telling you about God's gracious action in His Son, including your suffering occasioned by your believing in Him, is a manifestation of pure undeserved favor on God's part."

It is possible, however, to see an even wider reference in Peter's mind than his own letter. Earlier uses of **grace** in the epistle refer "to the universalism of the Messianic prophesies (1:10) and expectations (1:13), and to the grace promised to those who are humble (5:5) and endure persecutions." The reference here may therefore go "behind the Epistle to the whole dispensation of the divine blessing which is its theme." This enlarges the conception to include the totality of the gospel about which Peter was writing, and which had dimensions broader even than those about which he had space or time to write. Another has summed up this view thus: "The grace which they had experienced in conversion, and in the blessedness and progress of Christian life, was no delusion, as they were tempted to suppose by their troubles, but the genuine grace of God."

The letter closes with cordial greetings, and a prayer for peace. **She who is at Babylon, who is likewise chosen,** sends greetings. Some see in this a greeting from the church universal, including all Christians everywhere, with **Babylon** being understood in a metaphorical sense as the place of exile where the chosen people of God live out their destiny as exiles. Since **Mark,** who is named next, is a real and not a metaphorical person, however, and since elsewhere in the New Testament **Babylon** is a code name for Rome (see pp. 43ff.), it is likely that it is here a reference to the church at Rome from where Peter is writing. **Mark,** an earlier companion of Paul (Acts 12:25; 13:5, 13), but later transferred to Peter's circle (see pp. 62f.), was with Peter at the time of writing, and joined in sending greetings. Finally, Peter commends the early church custom to **greet one another with the kiss of love.** That this was a widespread custom among the churches is confirmed by its use in several of Paul's churches (Rom 16:16, 1 Cor 16:20, 2 Cor 13:12, 1 Thess 5:26). Customs appropriate in one culture are awkward or misunderstood in another. To try to revive New Testament customs in our time, as some propose, by washing one another's feet, as Jesus did the feet of His disciples, or reviving the habit of greeting **one another with the kiss of love,** is not necessary to fulfill their meaning and purpose today. The end in view is to indicate that in the fellowship of the church there should be a deeper concern and care for one another than is prevalent among those in society at large. One translator has made Peter's admonition current by putting it: "Give each other a handshake all around as a sign of love." Another has suggested: "Greet one another in a way that shows your love for one another as believers."

Paul characteristically ended his letters with a prayer that "grace" be with those to whom he wrote. All thirteen letters attributed to him end in this fashion (others than Paul may have had a hand in writing som371e of them). Peter, however, ends with the benediction: **Peace to all of you that are in Christ Jesus. Peace** was the customary parting word of the Jews to one another. One has remarked that here the word **peace** takes on "a marvelous sonorousness, when one hears the roarings of the lion (5:8), and knows that tomorrow perhaps the believers could be martyred." Peter could remember what had been said on the worst, most fearful night of his early life, the night of the betrayal and trial leading to the death of Him whom he loved: "*Peace* I leave with you; *my peace* I give to you; . . . Let not your hearts be troubled, neither let them be afraid" (John 14:27, emphasis added). Those words had later taken on meaning for Peter which he now hoped he could pass on to his readers, a **peace** which remained with him even to a martyr's death. The "peace of God" is a "peace . . . which passes all understanding" (Phil 4:7). It is a gift from God, and "cannot be effected by human ingenuity," but is a by-product of being in right relations with God. In the New Testament it is "very nearly synonymous with salvation," which is "peace with God through our Lord Jesus Christ" (Rom 5:1). This **peace** survives "the tyrant's brandished steel, the lion's gory mane."

> The peace of God, it is no peace,
> But strife closed in the sod.
> Yet brothers, pray for but one thing—
> The marvelous peace of God.

Addressing simple folk who were victimized by the rancor of

society and the might of empire—poor, humble folk "whose only crime was Christ"; suffering now and facing what might be an even worse future; folk who had no legal defense and no organized aid; who were dependent only on God; Peter's last word was: **Peace!** What assurance had they that this word was valid? Not because they were identified with an organized religious society; or were members of a dissident group; or practitioners of certain deviant religious rites; but solely because they were **in Christ**. And to be **in Christ** is to "be united by faith to the historic, crucified Christ, to the present risen Christ, and to the future Christ who is going to be revealed." To be in union with Him, by faith, is to know **peace** in a sorrowing, broken, confused, and tragic-stricken world.

BIBLIOGRAPHY

I. Commentaries, Expositions and Special Studies

Achtemeier, Paul J., *I Peter, Harper's Bible Commentary*, ed. James L. Mays (San Francisco: Harper & Row, 1988).

Alford, Henry, *The Greek Testament*, IV (Cambridge: Deighton, Bell, 1866).

Arichea, Daniel C., and Eugene A. Nida, *A Translator's Handbook of The First Letter from Peter* (New York: United Bible Societies, 1980).

Balch, David L., *Let Wives Be Submissive: The Domestic Code in I Peter* (Chico, CA.: Scholars Press, 1981).

Bauer, Johannes B., *Der Erste Petrusbrief* (Düsseldorf: Patmos, 1971).

Beare, F,W., *The First Epistle of Peter* (Oxford: Basil Blackwell, 1951).

Bénétreau, Samuel, *La Première Épître de Pierre* (Vaux-sur-Seine: Editions de la Faculté Libre de Théologie Evangelique, 1984).

Bengel, Johann A., *Gnomon of the New Testament* (Philadelphia: Smith, English, 1860).

Bennett, William H., *The General Epistles* (New York: Henry Frowde, 1910).

Best, Ernest, *I Peter* (Greenwood, S.C.: Attic, 1971).

Bigg, Charles, *A Critical and Exegetical Commentary on the Epistles of St. Peter and St. Jude* (New York: Scribner's Sons, 1905).

Blaiklock, E.M., *First Peter: A Translation and Devotional Commentary* (Waco, Texas: Word, 1977).

Blenkin, G. W., *The First Epistle General of Peter* (Cambridge: Cambridge University, 1914).

Boismard, M. E. *Quatre Hymnes Baptismales dans la Première Épître de Pierre* (Paris: Cerf, 1961).
Brown, R. E., K. P. Donfried and J. Reumann, *Peter in the New Testament* (Minneapolis: Augsburg, 1973).
Brox. Norbert, *Der Erste Petrusbrief* (Zürich: Benziger, 1979).

Calvin, John, *Commentaries on the Catholic Epistles*, trans. and ed. John Owen (Grand Rapids: Eerdmans, 1948).
Cranfield, C.E.B., *I Peter* (London: SCM, 1960).
Cross, F.L., *I Peter: A Paschal Liturgy* (London: Mowbray, 1954).
Cullmann, Oscar, *Peter: Disciple, Apostle, Martyr* (Philadelphia: Westminster, 1953).

Dalton, William J., *Christ's Proclamation to the Spirits: A Study of I Peter 3:18-4:16* (Rome: Pontifical Biblical Institute, 1989).
_____, *The First Epistle of Peter, The New Jerome Biblical Commentary*, eds. Raymond E. Brown, Joseph A. Fitzmyer, Roland E. Murphy (Englewood Cliffs, N.J.: Prentice Hall, 1990).

Elliott, John H., *The Elect and the Holy* (Leiden: Brill, 1966).
_____, *A Home for the Homeless* (Minneapolis: Fortress, 1990).

Foakes-Jackson, F.J., *Peter, Prince of Apostles* (New York: Doran, 1927).
Fronmuller, G.F.C. , *The Epistles General of Peter*, trans. J. Isidor Mombert (New York: Scribner's Sons, 1889).
Fuller, R.H., *Hebrews, James, 1 & 2 Peter, Jude, Revelation* (Philadelphia: Fortress, 1977).

Goppelt, Leonhard, *Der Erste Petrusbrief* (Göttingen: Vandenhoeck and Ruprecht, 1978; ET. Eerdmans).
Grudem, Wayne A., *The First Epistle of Peter* (Grand Rapids: Eerdmans, 1988).

Hart, J.H.A., *The First Epistle General of Peter* (New York: Dodd, Mead, 1910).
Hiebert, D. Edmond, *First Peter* (Chicago: Moody Press, 1984).

Homrighausen, Elmer G., *The First Epistle of Peter, The Interpreter's Bible* 12 (Nashville: Abingdon, 1957).
Hort, F.J.A., *The First Epistle of Peter 1:1-2:17* (New York: Macmillan, 1898.
Hunter. A.M.. *The First Epistle of Peter, The Interpreter's Bible* 12 (Nashville: Abingdon, 1957).

Jowett, J. H., *The Redeemed Family of God* (New York: Doran, n.d.).

Kelly, J.N.D., *A Commentary on the Epistles of Peter and Jude* (New York: Harper, 1969).
Knoch, Otto, *Der Erste und Zweite Petrusbrief, Der Judasbrief* (Regensburg: Friedrich Pustet, 1990).

Leaney, A.R.C., *The Letters of Peter and Jude* (Cambridge: Cambridge University, 1967).
Leighton, Robert, *Commentary on First Peter*. 1853; reprinted by Kregel Reprint Library (Grand Rapids: Kregel, 1972).
Lenski, R.C.H., *The Interpretation of the Epistles of St. Peter, St. John and St. Jude* (Columbus, Ohio: Lutheran Book Concern, 1938).
Lowe, John, *Saint Peter* (New York: Oxford, 1956).
Lumby, Joseph R., *The Epistles of St. Peter* (New York: Armstrong, 1893).
Luther, Martin, *The Epistles of St. Peter and St. Jude*, trans. E.H. Gillett (New York: Anson D.F. Randolph, 1859).

Marshall, I. Howard, *I Peter* (Downers Grove, Ill.: Intervarsity, 1991).
Metzger, Bruce, *A Textual Commentary on the Greek New Testament* (New York: United Bible Societies, 1971).
Meyer, F.B., *Tried by Fire* (London: Morgan Scott, n.d.).
Michaels, J.R., *First Peter* (Waco, Texas: Word, 1988).
Moffatt, James, *The General Epistles, James, Peter and Judas* (Garden City, N.Y.: Doubleday, Doran, 1928).
Mounce, Robert H., *A Living Hope* (Grand Rapids: Eerdmans, 1982).

Patterson, Paige, *A Pilgrim Priesthood* (New York: Thomas Nelson, 1982).

Percy, E., *Die Problem der Kolosser- und Epheserbrief* (Lund: Gleerup, 1946)
Perrot, Charles, ed., *Études sur la première lettre de Pierre* (Paris: Cerf, 1980).
Phillips, K., *Kirche in der Gesellschaft nach dem ersten Petrusbrief* (Gütersloh, Mohr, 1971).
Plumptre, Edw. H., *The General Epistles of St. Peter and St. Jude* (Cambridge: University Press, 1893).
Pury, Roland de, *Pierres Vivantes* (Neuchatel: Delachaux & Niestle, 1946).

Reicke, Bo, *The Disobedient Spirits and Christian Baptism: A Study of I Pet. iii.19 and its Context* (New York: AMS, 1946).
_____, "Die Gnosis der Männer nach I Pt. 3:7," *Neutestamentliche Studien für Rudolf Bultmann*, ed. S. Eltester (Berlin: Topelmann, 1954).
_____, *The Epistles of James, Peter, and Jude* (Garden City, N.Y.: Doubleday, 1964).
Rendtorff, D. Heinrich, *Getrostes Wandern: Eine Einführung in den ersten Brief des Petrus* (Hamburg: Furche, 1951).

Schlatter, Adolf, *Petrus und Paulus nach dem ersten Petrusbrief* (Stuttgart: Calwer, 1937).
Schwank, B., *La Première Lettre de L'Apôtre Pierre* (Paris: Desclee, 1967). English translation, *The First Epistle of Peter*, trans. Walter Kruppa (New York: Herder and Herder, 1969).
Selwyn, E.C., *The First Epistle of St. Peter* (London: Macmillan, 1946).
_____, "Eschatology in I Peter," *The Background of the New Testament and its Eschatology*, eds. W.D. Davies and D. Daube (Cambridge: Cambridge University Press, 1956).
Stibbs, A. M., and A. F. Walls, *The First Epistle General of Peter* (London: Tyndale, 1959).
Spicq, Ceslas, *Les Épître de Saint Pierre* (Paris: J. Gabalda, 1966).
Steiger, Wilhelm, *Exposition of the First Epistle of Peter* (Edinburgh: Clark, 1836).

Talbert, C.H., ed., *Perspectives on First Peter* (Macon, Ga.: Mercer, 1986).
Thiede, Carsten P., ed. *Das Petrusbild in der neuer Forschung* (Wuppertal: Brockhaus, 1987).
_____, *Simon Peter: From Galilee to Rome* (Grand Rapids: Academie Books, 1988).

Wand, J.W.C., *The General Epistles of St. Peter and St. Jude* (London: Methuen, 1934).
Windisch, Hans, *Die katholischen Briefe*, rev. H. Preisker (Tübingen: Mohr, 1956).
Wuest, Kenneth S., *First Peter in the Greek New Testament* (Grand Rapids: Eerdmans, 1942).

II. Reference Works

A Companion to the Bible, ed. Jean Jacques von Allmen, (New York: Oxford, 1958).
Alter, Robert, *The World of Biblical Literature* (New York, Harper Collins, 1992).
Ante-Nicene Fathers, eds. Alexander Roberts and James Donaldson, rev. A. Cleveland Coxe (Grand Rapids: Eerdmans, 1981).

Babylonian Talmud, ed. I. Epstein (London: Soncino, 1948).
Barclay, William, *New Testament Words* (Philadelphia: Westminster, 1976).
Beasley-Murray, G.R., *Baptism in the New Testament* (London: Macmillan, 1962).
Bony, P., et al., *Le Ministère et Les Ministères selon de Nouveau Testament*, ed. Jean Delorme (Paris: Editions du Seuil, 1974).
Bruce, F.F. *Men and Movements in the Primitive Church* (Exeter: Paternoster, 1979).
_____, *Biblical Exegesis in the Qumran Texts* (Grand Rapids: Eerdmans, 1959).

Catholic Encyclopedia, ed. Charles G. Herkermann, et al., (New York: Appleton, 1907-1912).

Cullmann, Oscar, *The New Testament* (Philadelphia: Westminster, 1968).

Davis, Ozora S., *Vocabulary of New Testament Words* (Hartford: Hartford Seminary, 1893).
Deissmann, Adolf, *Bible Studies* (Edinburgh: T. & T Clark, 1901).
_____, *Philology of the Greek Bible* (London: Hodder & Stoughton, 1908).
_____, *Light From the Ancient East* (New York: Doran, 1927).
Dictionary of the Bible, ed James Hastings (New York: Scribner's Sons, 1898-1904).
Dictionary of Christ and the Gospels, ed. James Hastings (New York: Scribner's Sons, 1908).
Dictionary of the Apostolic Church, ed. James Hastings (New York: Scribner's Sons, 1916-1922).

Edmundson, George, *The Church in Rome in the First Century* (New York: Longmans, Green, 1913).
Encyclopedia Britannica, Fourteenth Edition, (Chicago: Encyclopedia Britannica, 1940).
Encyclopedia of Biblical Theology, ed. J.B. Bauer, trans. Joseph Blenkinsopp, et al. (New York: Crossroad, 1981).
Encyclopedia of Religion, ed., Mercia Eliade (New York: Macmillan, 1987).
Exegetical Dictionary of the New Testament, eds. Horst Balz and Gerhard Schneider (Grand Rapids: Eerdmans, 1991).

Fox, Adam, *Meet the Greek Testament* (London: SCM, 1952).

Guthrie, Donald, "Epistolary Pseudepigrapha," *New Testament Introduction*. rev. (Downers Grove, Ill.: Intervarsity, 1990).

Harper's Bible Commentary, ed James L. Mays (San Francisco: Harper, 1988).
Hatch, Edwin, *Essays in Biblical Greek* (Oxford: Clarendon, 1889).
_____, *The Influence of Greek Ideas and Usages upon the Christian Church* (London: Williams and Norgate, 1890).

Head, E.D. *New Testament Life and Literature as Reflected in the Papyri* (Nashville: Broadman, 1952).

International Standard Bible Encyclopedia, ed. James Orr (Chicago: Howard-Severance, 1915); rev. ed. Geoffrey W. Bromiley (Grand Rapids: Eerdmans, 1979-1988).
Interpreter's Dictionary of the Bible, eds. George A. Buttrick and Keith R. Crim (Nashville: Abingdon, 1976).

James, Montague Rhodes, *The Apocryphal New Testament* (Oxford: Clarendon, 1924).
Jewish Encyclopedia (London: Funk & Wagnalls, 1907).

Leon-Dufour, Xavier, *Dictionary of the New Testament*, trans. Terrence Prendergast (San Francisco: Harper & Row, 1980).

McKenzie, John L., *Dictionary of the Bible* (New York: Macmillan, 1965).
Moule, C.F.D. *The Birth of the New Testament* (London: A. & C. Black, 1962).

New Jerome Biblical Commentary, eds. Raymond E. Brown, Joseph A. Fitzmyer, Roland E. Murphy (Englewood Cliffs, N.J.: Prentice Hall, 1990).
Nicene and Post-Nicene Fathers of the Christian Church, ed. Philip Schaff (Grand Rapids: Eerdmans, 1987-1993).

Oxford Dictionary of the Christian Church, second edition, eds. F.L. Cross and E.A. Livingstone (Oxford: Oxford University Press, 1983).

Ramsay, William M., *The Church in the Roman Empire* (New York: Putnam's, 1893).
Richardson, Alan, *A Theological Word Book of the Bible* (New York: Macmillan, 1960).
Robertson, A.T. *The Minister and His Greek Testament* (London: Hodder & Stoughton, 1923).

_____, *Word Pictures in the New Testament* (New York: R.R. Smith, 1930).

Robinson, J.A.T., *Redating the New Testament* (Philadelphia: Westminster, 1976).

Schaff, Philip, *History of the Apostolic Church* (New York: Scribner, 1869).

Theological Dictionary of the New Testament, ed. Gerhard Kittel and Gerhard Friedrich, trans. Geoffrey W. Bromiley (Grand Rapids: Eerdmans, 1964-1976).

Trench, R.C., *Synonyms of the New Testament* (London: Kegan Paul, 1906).

Vincent, Marvin R., *Word Studies in the New Testament* (New York: Scribner's Sons, 1887-1900).

III. Periodical Articles

Achtemeier, Paul, J., a review of John H. Elliott, *A Home for the Homeless, Journal of Biblical Literature* 130 (1984) 130-133.

Agnew, Frances H., "I Peter 1:2—An Alternative Translation," *Catholic Biblical Quarterly* 45 (1983) 68-73.

Argyle, A. W., "Greek Among the Jews of Palestine in New Testament Times, " *New Testament Studies* 20 (1974) 87-89.

Arichea, Daniel C., "God or Christ? A Study of Implicit Information," *The Bible Translator* 28 (1977) 412-418.

Balch, David L., "Early Christian Criticism of Patriarchal Authority: I Peter 2:11-3:12," *Union Seminary Quarterly Review* 39 (1984) 161-173.

Bammal, E., The Commands in I Peter II:17," *New Testament Studies* 11 (1955) 279-281.

Best, E., "I Peter ii:4-10: A Reconsideration," *Novum Testamentum* 11 (1969) 270-293.

_____, "First Peter and the Gospel Tradition," *New Testament Studies* 16 (1970) 95-113.

——————, review of David L. Balch, *Let Wives Be Submissive: The Domestic Code in I Peter, Irish Biblical Studies* 4 (1982) 226-228

Blendinger, C., "Kirche als Fremdlingschaft: I Petrus 1: 22-25, " *Communio Viatorum* 10 (1967) 123-134.

Blevins, James L., "Introduction to 1 Peter," *The Review and Expositor* 79 (1982) 401-413.

Boismard, M.E. "Une liturgie baptismal dans la Prima Petri," *Revue Biblique* 63 (1956) 182-208; 64 (1957) 161-183.

Bovon, F., "Foi chrétienne et religion populaire dans le première épître de Pierre," *Études Théologiques et Religieuses* 53 (1978) 25-41.

Brooks, Oscar S., "I Peter 3:21—The Clue to the Literary Structure of the Epistle," *Novum Testamentum* 16 (1974) 290-305.

Brox, Norbert, "Zur pseudepigraphisch Rahmung des ersten Petrusbriefes," *Biblische Zeitschrift* 19 (1975) 78-96.

——————, "Situation und Sprache der Minderheit im ersten Petrusbrief," *Kairos,* neue Folge 19 (1977) 1-13.

——————, "Die erste Petrusbrief in der literarischen Tradition des Urchristentums," *Kairos* 20 (1978) 182-192.

Bruce, F.F., a review of *The First Epistle of Peter*, by F.W. Beare, *Evangelical Quarterly* 31 (1959) 118-118.

Burtness, James H., "Sharing the Suffering of God in the Life of the World," *Interpretation* 23 (1969) 277-288.

Chevallier, M.A. "1 Pierre 1/1 a 2/10: structure littéraire et conséquences exégétiques," *Revue d'Histoire et de Philosophie religieuses* 51 (1971) 129-142.

——————, "Condition et vocation des chrétiens en diaspora: remarques exégétique sur la 1re épître de Pierre," *Recherches de Science religieuse* 48 (1974) 387-400.

Cothenet, E., "Le realisme de l'esperance chrétienne selon 1 Pierre," *New Testament Studies* 27 (1981) 564-572.

Cranfield, C.E.B., "The Interpretation of I Peter iii.19 and iv.5," *Expository Times* 62 (1958) 369-372.

Dalton, W.J., "So That Your Faith May Also Be Your Hope in God," *Reconciliation and Hope*, ed. Robert Banks (Grand Rapids: Eerdmans, 1974).

_____, "The Interpretation of I Peter 3.19 and 4.6: Light from 2 Peter," *Biblica* 60 (1979) 547-555.

Danker, F.W., "I Peter 1:24-2:17—A Consolatory Pericope," *Zeitschrift für die Neutestamentliche Wissenschaft* 58 (1967) 93-102.

_____, "First Peter in Sociological Perspective," a review of *A Home for the Homeless*, by John H. Elliott, *Interpretation* 37 (1983) 84-88.

Davies, P.E., "Primitive Christology in I Peter," *Festschrift to Honor F. W. Gingrich*, ed. E.H. Barth (Leiden: Brill, 1972), 115-122.

Dijkman, J.H.L. "I Peter: A Later Pastoral Stratum?" *New Testament Studies* 33 (1987) 265-271.

Downing, F.G., "Pliny Persecutions of Christians: Revelation and I Peter," *Journal for the Study of the New Testament* 34 (1988) 105-123.

Easton, Burton Scott, "New Testament Ethical Lists," *Journal of Biblical Literature* 51 (1932) 1-12.

Elliott, J.H., "Death of a Slogan: From Royal Priests to Celebrating Community," *Una Sancta* 25 (1968) 18-31.

_____, "Ministry and Church Order in the New Testament: A Traditio-Historical Analysis," *Catholic Biblical Quarterly* 32 (1970) 367-391.

_____, "The Rehabilitation of an Exegetical Step-child: I Peter in Recent Research," *Journal of Biblical Literature* 95 (1976) 243-254.

_____, "Salutation and Exhortation to Christian Behavior on the Basis of God's Blessings (I Peter 2:11-3:12)," *The Review and Expositor* 79 (1982) 415-425.

Ellul, Danielle, "Un exemple de cheminement rhétorique: I Pierre," *Revue d'Histoire et de Philosophie Religieuses* 70 ((1990) 17-34.

Fackre, Gabriel, "I Believe in the Resurrection of the Body, " *Interpretation* 46 (1982) 42-52.

Feinberg, John S., "I Peter 3:18-20, Ancient Mythology, and the Intermediate State," *Westminster Theological Journal* 48 (1986) 303-336.
Filson, Floyd V., "Partakers With Christ: Suffering in First Peter," *Interpretation* 9 (1955) 400-412.
Fitzmyer, Joseph, "The Languages of Palestine in the First Century A. D.," *Catholic Biblical Quarterly*, 32 (1970) 501-531.
_____, "Crucifixion in Ancient Palestine, Qumran Literature, and the New Testament," *Catholic Biblical Quarterly* 40 (1978) 493-513.
France, R.T., "Exegesis in Practice: Two Samples," *New Testament Interpretation*, ed. I. Howard Marshall (Exeter: Paternoster, 1979).
Francis J., "Like Newborn Babes," *Studia Biblica* 3 (1980) 111-117.

Gaddy, Walton, "Preaching from I Peter," *The Review and Expositor* 79 (1982) 473-485.
Goodspeed, Edgar J., "Enoch in I Peter 3:19," *Journal of Biblical Literature* 73 (1954) 91-92.
Goppelt, Leonhard, "Prinzipien neutestamentlicher Sozialethik nach dem I. Petrusbrief," *Neues Testament und Geschichte*, eds. Heinrich Baltensweiler und Bo Reicke (Tübingen: Mohr, 1972) 385-396.
Gross, C.D., "Are the wives of I Peter 3.7 Christians?" *Journal for the Study of the New Testament* 34 (1988) 89-96.
Gundry, R.H., "The Language Milieu of First-Century Palestine," *Journal of Biblical Literature* 83 (1964) 404-408.
_____, "'Verba Christi' in I Peter: Their Implications Concerning the Authorship of I Peter and the Authenticity of the Gospel Tradition," *New Testament Studies* 13 (1967) 336-350.
_____, "Further *Verba* on *Verba Christi* in First Peter," *Biblica* 55 (1974) 211-232.

Halas, Stanislas, "Sens dynamique de l'expression *laòs eis peripoíēsin* en I P 2,9." *Biblica* 64 (1984) 254-258.
Hamer, J.C., "The Address of 1 Peter," *Expository Times* 89 (1978) 239-243.

Hanson, Anthony, "Salvation Proclaimed: I Peter 3:18-22," *Expository Times* 93 (1982) 100-105.
Hiebert, D. Edmond, "Designation of the Readers in I Peter 1:1-2," *Bibliotheca Sacra* 137 (1980) 64-75.
_____, "The Suffering and Triumphant Christ: An Exposition of I Peter 3:18-22," *Bibliotheca Sacra* 139 (1982) 146-158.
Hill, D., "On Suffering and Baptism in I Peter," *Novum Testamentum* 18 (1976) 181-189.
_____,"'To Offer Spiritual Sacrifices . . . ' (I Peter 2:5): Liturgical Formulations and Christian Paraenesis in I Peter," *Journal for the Study of the New Testament* 16 (1982) 45-63.
Hillyer, Norman, "First Peter and the Feast of Tabernacles," *Tyndale Bulletin* 21 (1970) 39-70.
Hughes, Philip Edgecombe, "The Languages Spoken by Jesus," *New Dimensions in New Testament Study*, ed. Richard Longenecker and Merrill Tenney (Grand Rapids: Zondervan, 1974) 127-143.

Jones, Peter Rhea, "Teaching First Peter," *The Review and Expositor* 79 (1982) 453-472.
Jonsen, Albert R., "The Moral Theology of the First Epistle of St. Peter," *Sciences Ecclésiastiques* 16 (1964) 93-105.

Kiley, Mark, "Like Sara: The Tale of Terror Behind I Peter 3:6," *Journal of Biblical Literature* 106 (1987) 689-692.
Kirk. Gordon E., "Endurance in Suffering in I Peter," *Bibliotheca Sacra* 138 (1981) 46-56.
Kirkpatrick, G.D. "I Peter 1:11 τινα ἤ ποιον καιπον," *Novum Testamentum* 28 (1986) 91-92.
Kirkpatrick, William David, "The Theology of First Peter," *Southwestern Journal of Theology* 25 (1982) 58-81.
Kline, Leslie, "Ethics for the End Time: an Exegesis of I Peter 4:7-11," *Restoration Quarterly* 7 (1963) 113-123.
Koester, Helmut, "Jesus the Victim," *Journal of Biblical Literature* 111 (1992) 3-15.
Kohler, Marc E., "La communauté des chrétiens selon la première épître de Pierre," *Revue de Théologie et de Philosophie* 114 (1982) 1-21.

Lamau, Marie-Louise, "Exhortation aux esclaves et hymne au Christ souffrant dans la première épître de Pierre," *Melanges de Science Religieuse* 43 (1986) 121-143.

Lash, C.J.A., "Fashionable Sports: Hymn-Hunting in I Peter," *Studia Evangelica* 7 (1982) 293-297.

La Verdiere, E.A., "A Grammatical Ambiguity in I Pet 1:23," *Catholic Biblical Quarterly* 36 (1974) 89-94.

Lecomte, Pierre, "Aimer la vie. I Pierre 3:10 (Psaume 34:13)," *Études Théologique et Religieuse* 55 (1981) 288-293.

Legasse, S., "La soumission aux autorités apres 1 Pierre 2:13-17: Version spécifique d'une paránèse traditionelle," *New Testament Studies* 34 (1988) 378-396.

Lohse, Eduard, "Paránèse und Kerygma im I Petrusbrief," *Zeitschrift für die Neutestamentliche Wissenschaft* 45 (1954) 68-89; tr. John Steely and republished as "Paranesis and Kerygma in I Peter," *Perspectives on First Peter*, ed. Charles H. Talbert (Macon, Georgia: Mercer, 1986) 37-59.

Love, Julian Price, "The First Epistle of Peter," *Interpretation* 8 (1954) 63-87.

Martin, Troy W., "The Present Indicative in the Eschatological Statements of I Peter 1:6, 8," *Journal of Biblical Literature* 111 (1992) 307-312.

McCaughey, J. Davis, "On Re-reading I Peter," *Australian Biblical Review* 31 (1983) 33-44.

Metzger, Bruce M., "Literary Forgeries and Canonical Pseudepigrapha," *Journal of Biblical Literature* 91 (1972) 25-32.

Michaels, J. Ramsey, "Eschatology in I Peter iii.17," *New Testament Studies* 13 (1967) 394-401.

Miller, Donald G., "Owner or Steward?" *Interpretation* 8 (1954) 163-169.

_____,"Salvation in First Peter," *Interpretation* 9 (1955) 413-425.

Moule, C.F.D., "The Nature and Purpose of I Peter," *New Testament Studies* 3 (1956) 1-11.

_____, "Once More, Who were the Hellenists?" *Expository Times* 70 (1958-59) 100-102.

_____, a review of *The Elect and the Holy*, by J.H. Elliott, *Journal of Theological Studies*, n.s. 18 (1967) 471-474.

Murphy, Larry, "African American Perspectives on Christology and Incarnation," *Ex Auditu* 7 (1991) 73-82.

Nauck, Wolfgang, "Freude im Leiden: Zum Problem einer urchristlichen Verfolgungstradition," *Zeitschrift für die Neutestamentliche Wissenschaft* 46 (1955) 68-80.

Nixon, R. E., "The Meaning of 'Baptism' in 1 Peter 3:21," *Studia Evangelium* 4 (1968) 437-441.

Omanson, Roger, "Suffering for Righteousness' Sake (I Peter 3:13-4:11)," *The Review and Expositor* 79 (1982) 439-450.

Osborne, Thomas P., "L'utilization des citations de L'Ancien Testament dans le première épître de Pierre," *Revue Théologique de Louvain* 12 (1981) 64-77.

_____, "Guide Lines for Christian Suffering: A Source-Critical and Theological Study of I Peter 2,21-25," *Biblica* 64 (1983) 381-408.

Oss, D.J., "The Interpretation of the 'Stone' Passages by Peter and Paul: A Comparative Study," *Journal of the Evangelical Theological Society* 32 (1989) 181-200.

Patsch, H., "Zum Alttestamentlichen Hintergrund von Röm. 4: 25 und 1 Petrus 2:24," *Zeitschrift für die Neutestamentliche Wissenschaft* 60 (1969) 273-279.

Pfeiffer, R.H., "The Fear of God," *Israel Exploration Journal* V (1955) 41-48.

Piper, John, "Hope as the Motivation of Love," *New Testament Studies* 26 (1979) 212-231.

Piper, Otto A., a review of *The First Epistle of Peter*, by F.W. Beare, *Journal of Religion* 29 (1949) 62-63.

Pryor, J.W., "First Peter and the New Covenant," *Reformed Theological Review* 45 (1986) 1-4.

Rodgers, Peter, R., "The Longer Reading of 1 Peter 4:14," *Catholic Biblical Quarterly* 43 (1981) 93-95.

Schlosser, J., "I Pierre 3.5b-6," *Biblica* 64 (1983) 408-410.
Senior, Donald, "The Conduct of Christians in the World: An Interpretation of I Peter 1:1-2:10," *The Review and Expositor* 79 (1982) 427-438.
Sleeper, C. Freeman, "Political Responsibility according to I Peter," *Novum Testamentum* 10 (1968) 270-286.
Snodgrass, Klyne, "I Peter 2:1-10: Its Formation and Literary Affinities," *New Testament Studies* 24 (1977) 97-106.
Spicq, Ceslas, "La 1ª Petri et le temoinage evangelique de saint Pierre," *Studia Theologica* 20 (1966) 37-61.
_____,"La place ou le rôle des jeunes dans certaines communautés néotestamentaires," *Revue Biblique* 76 (1969) 508-527.
Sylva, Dennis, "I Peter Studies: The State of the Discipline," *Biblical Theology Bulletin* 10 (1980) 155-163.
_____, "A I Peter Bibliography," *Journal of the Evangelical Theological Society* 25 (1982) 75-89.
_____, "Translating and Interpreting I Peter 3.2," *The Bible Translator* 34 (1983) 144-147.
Synge, F.C., "I Peter 3:18-21," *Expository Times* 82 (1971) 311.

Taylor, Vincent, "The First Epistle of Peter," a review of *The First Epistle of Peter*, by F.W. Beare, *Expository Times* 59 (1948) 90-91.
Teichert, Horst, "1. Petr. 3,13—eine crux interpretum?" *Theologische Literaturzeitung* 74 (1949) 303.
Thomas, J., "Anfechtung und Vorfreude: ein biblische Thema nach Jacobus 1:2-18, in zusammenhang mit Psalm 126, Röm. 5:3-5 und 1 Petr. 1:5-7, formkritisch untersucht und parakletisch ausgelegt," *Kerygma und Dogma* 14 (1968) 183-206.
Thompson, James, "Be Submissive to Your Masters: A Study of I Peter 2:18-25," *Restoration Quarterly* 9 (1966) 66-78.
Thornton, T.C.G., "First Peter, a Paschal Liturgy," *The Journal of Theological Studies*, n.s. 12 (1961) 14-26.
Thurneysen, Eduard, "The End of All Things," trans. Donald G. Miller, *Interpretation* 12 (1959) 407-411.
Thurston, R.W., "Interpreting First Peter," *Journal of the Evangelical Theological Society* 17 (1974) 171-182.

Tripp, David H., "Epērōtema (I Peter 3:21): A Liturgist's Note," *Expository Times* 92 (1981) 267-270.
Tuni, José Oriol, "Jesus of Nazareth in the Christology of I Peter," *Heythorp Journal* 28 (1987) 292-304.

Van Unnik, W.C., "The Teaching of Good Works in I Peter," *New Testament Studies* 1 (1954) 92-110.
_____, "Christianity According to 1 Peter," *Expository Times* 68 (1956) 79-83.
_____, "Peter, First Letter Of," *The Interpreter's Dictionary of the Bible* Vol. 3, 758-766.
Vorchert, Gerald L., "The Conduct of Christians in the Face of the 'Fiery Order' (I Peter 4:12-5:1)," *The Review and Expositor* 79 (1982) 451-462.

Wainwright, Geoffrey, "Praying for Kings: The Place of Human Rulers in the Divine Plan of Salvation," *Ex Auditu* 2 (1986) 117-127.
Wand, J.W.C., "The Lessons of First Peter," *Interpretation* 9 (1955) 387-389.
Winbery, Carlton L., "Introduction to the First Letter of Peter," *Southwestern Journal of Theology* 25 (1982) 3-16.
Winter, Bruce W., "The Public Honouring of Christian Benefactors: Romans 13.3-4 and I Peter 2.14-15," *Journal for the Study of the New Testament* 34 (1988) 87-103.
Wire, Antoinette, reviews of *A Home for the Homeless*, by John H. Elliott, and *Let Wives Be Submissive*, by David L. Balch, *Religious Studies Review* 10 (1984) 209-216.
Wolf, V.C., "Christ und Welt in I Petrusbrief," *Theologisches Literaturzeitung* 100 (1975) 334-342.

www.ingramcontent.com/pod-product-compliance
Lightning Source LLC
Chambersburg PA
CBHW071230290426
44108CB00013B/1360